Political culture in later medieval England

MANCHESTER 1824

Manchester University Press

Simon Walker with Richard III at Middleham Castle
© Andrea Walker

Political culture in later medieval England

essays by
Simon Walker

edited by
Michael J. Braddick

with an introduction by
G. L. Harriss

Manchester University Press

Manchester and New York

distributed exclusively in the USA by Palgrave

Published by Manchester University Press
Oxford Road, Manchester M13 9NR, UK
and Room 400, 175 Fifth Avenue, New York, NY 10010, USA
www.manchesteruniversitypress.co.uk

Distributed exclusively in the USA by
Palgrave, 175 Fifth Avenue, New York,
NY 10010, USA

Distributed exclusively in Canada by
UBC Press, University of British Columbia, 2029 West Mall,
Vancouver, BC, Canada V6T 1Z2

British Library Cataloguing-in-Publication Data
A catalogue record for this book is available from the British Library

Library of Congress Cataloging-in-Publication Data applied for

ISBN 0 7190 6826 6 *hardback*
EAN 978 0 7190 6826 3

First published 2006

15 14 13 12 11 10 09 08 07 06 10 9 8 7 6 5 4 3 2 1

Typeset in Photina
by Mudra Typesetters, Pondicherry, India
Printed in Great Britain
by Biddles Ltd, King's Lynn

For *Andrea, Dannish, Miriam* and *Adam*

Contents

Editorial note and acknowledgements

Simon Walker studied modern history at Magdelen College, Oxford, graduating with first-class honours in 1979. The same year he won a Prize Fellowship at All Souls College, Oxford, where he undertook doctoral research into the affinity of John of Gaunt. He was appointed to a Lectureship in History at the University of Sheffield in 1984 and was promoted to a Readership in 1995. In 1999 he was appointed to an Extraordinary Research Fellowship at All Souls, where he was working on a history of the college down to the seventeenth century. He died on 26 February 2004, shortly after his forty-sixth birthday, already a distinguished historian of later medieval England.

At the time of his death Simon was preparing this collection of essays for publication. As far as possible, I have followed his intentions in seeing the collection into press. Sadly, there was no publishable version of the projected introduction, but Gerald Harriss, who supervised his research into John of Gaunt's affinity, very kindly agreed to write an introduction in its place. No attempt has been made to reconstruct what Simon would have said but it has been possible for Dr Harriss to make use of Simon's proposal in writing his own introduction to this body of work. Chapter 3, 'Communities of the county in later medieval England', is the text of a paper delivered at a conference which Simon was revising for publication. The text has not been edited, but footnotes have been added, with the help of John Watts and Anthony Musson. Chapter 8, 'Remembering Richard: history and memory in Lancastrian England', survived as a complete text, intended for publication, but without footnotes. The text has since been published in Christine Carpenter and Linda Clark (eds), *Political Culture in Late Medieval England* (The Fifteenth Century, IV), Woodbridge, 2004. I am very grateful to the editors for their help in securing the inclusion of the essay in this collection, and to Linda Clark for providing footnotes to the text. Sadly, it has not been possible to recover the text of another unpublished essay intended for this volume: 'Soldiers of Fortune: poverty and prosperity in the fourteenth-century military community'. Edmund King, a close colleague of Simon's in Sheffield for nearly twenty years, kindly compiled the bibliography. In all other respects, this is the volume as Simon intended it.

Chapter one, 'Lordship and lawlessness in the palatinate of Lancaster, 1370–1400', was first published in the *Journal of British Studies*, 28 (1989), 325–48 (© 1989 by The North American Conference on British Studies, reprinted by permission of the University of Chicago Press); chapter two, 'Sir Richard Abberbury (*c.* 1330–1399) and his Kinsmen: the rise and fall of a gentry family', was first published in *Nottingham Medieval Studies*, 34 (1990), 113–40 (reprinted by permission of the editors); chapter four, 'Yorkshire justices of the peace, 1389–1413', first published in the *English Historical Review*, 108 (1993), 281–313 (reproduced by permission of Oxford University Press); chapter five, 'Janico Dartasso: chivalry, nobility and the man-at-arms', first published in *History*, 74 (1999), 31–51 (reproduced by permission of Blackwell Publishing); chapter six, 'Richard II's views on kingship', first published in *Rulers and Ruled in Late Medieval England*, ed. R. E. Archer and S. Walker (Hambledon, 1995), 49–63 (reproduced by permission of Hambledon and London Ltd); chapter seven, 'Rumour, sedition and popular protest in the reign of Henry IV', first published in *Past and Present*, 166 (Feb. 2000), 31–65 (reprinted by permission of the Past and Present Society); chapter nine, 'Political saints in later medieval England', first published in *The McFarlane Legacy: Studies in Later Medieval Politics and Society*, ed. R. Britnell and A. J. Pollard (Alan Sutton, 1995), 77–106 (reproduced by permission of Sutton Publishing); chapter ten, 'The Yorkshire risings of 1405: texts and contexts', first published in *Henry IV: The Establishment of the Regime*, ed. G. Dodd and D. Biggs (Woodbridge: York Medieval Press, 2003), 161–84 (reproduced by permission of Boydell & Brewer Ltd); chapter eleven, 'Civil war and rebellion, 1200–1500', first published in *An Illustrated History of Later Medieval England*, ed. C. Given-Wilson (Manchester University Press, 1996), 229–47 (reprinted with the permission of Manchester University Press). The styles used within individual chapters have been retained rather than standardised throughout this book, in order to reflect the different origins of the chapters.

Michael Braddick
University of Sheffield

Introduction

G. L. Harriss

When Simon Walker began researching the retinue of John of Gaunt in 1980, 'bastard feudalism' had been the subject of debate for thirty-five years. Beginning with the printing and analysis of indentures of retainer by N. B. Lewis, K. B. McFarlane and W. H. Dunham, controversy had centred on whether its mercenary character loosened feudal loyalties, encouraged lawlessness and corruption, and destabilised the polity to the point of civil war. As studies of individual retinues and the political structures of different counties began to appear in the 1970s, bastard feudalism came to be viewed in more neutral terms. It could be seen as a restatement of the traditional equation between a lord's protection and patronage and a vassal's service and fidelity, adapted to a more commercialised and multi-layered society. As emphasis shifted away from the military towards the peacetime function of the lord's retinue and wider affinity, so the question arose of its role in political society both at local and national level. How pervasive was the network of clientage and patronage exercised through the magnate affinity? Did the magnate affinity encompass all the gentry families of a region, or did the gentry families of the shire form an autonomous community? Such issues became increasingly significant in the fourteenth century as the gentry asserted their role as local magistrates, justices and members of parliament. Were they, in these capacities, servants of the crown or instruments of their lord? Was their allegiance given primarily to the affinity or to their local community? Such questions reflected a fundamental disagreement among historians over the relative social and political importance of magnates and gentry in this period.[1]

A study of John of Gaunt's retinue could be expected to throw important, if not decisive, light on these problems. For not only was his the largest retinue in late medieval England, but for thirty years the duke himself had a dominant role in the domestic, military and diplomatic policy of England. Further, the records for his household and estates, his military campaigns, and his political and diplomatic activity were voluminous. In these respects the project was of central importance, but dauntingly ambitious.

Simon Walker marked out his distinctive approach in the Introduction to his book, *The Lancastrian Affinity, 1361–1399*.[2] Where retinues had hitherto been studied as instruments of the lord's will, he reversed the perspective to ask 'how the *retainer* viewed the affinity he belonged to'. He sought 'to view the Lancastrian retinue from within' and 'to penetrate the real world of relationships which lies behind the lists of liveries and annuities'.[3] His starting point was the retainer's own concerns and ambitions rather than his membership of a retinue. But first he had to describe Gaunt's affinity, its size, cost, and composition. Growing from over 100 per cent in 1381 to 150 per cent by the early 1390s, it represented a larger element in his expenditure than the 10 per cent of their income which most of the nobility spent on their retinue. This reflected the duke's wider ambitions, which in the early part of his career while he was campaigning in France and Spain were primarily military. In his last decade the affinity was expanded to bolster Lancastrian fortunes at home during the volatile politics of Richard II's personal rule. But in all periods it attracted both soldiers of renown and the leading gentry among his tenants. If it served the mutual advantage of duke and retainer, what service did the former demand and what rewards could the latter expect?[4] With respect to service in war, Walker reached the paradoxical conclusion that for neither party was war necessarily profitable. Gaunt mainly, though not consistently, recouped his expenditure for the campaigns he undertook in the crown's service (his profitable bid for the Spanish crown in 1386–9 was a private venture). For his captains, war was a more risky business, the rewards in the shape of plunder, ransoms and wages being offset by the risk to life and liberty. Instead, Walker suggested that the greatest benefit to the retainer from war overseas was his access to Gaunt's lordship and patronage when he returned home.[5] This came not only in the shape of leases, offices and fees from the duke's lands, and the marriages of his wards, but also from his protection and support for the retainer's personal interests and ambitions. Beyond these material benefits was the honour and prestige of being in the duke's affinity, symbolised by the proud wearing of his livery collar of esses. But though membership of Gaunt's affinity was prized, and few left his service other than for that of the king, it is doubtful whether ultimately this was uppermost in the concerns of its members. For it was their kin and neighbours whom they remembered in their wills, and chose as their executors, and to their local parish churches that they looked for burial and perpetual commemoration.[6]

When, in the second part of the book, Walker turned to the operation of the affinity in the localities, he set himself to answer some of the questions currently in debate. Was the affinity an instrument for lawlessness and corruption, and did Gaunt use it in struggles with other magnates? Did his affinity monopolise the shire offices and administration and serve as the instrument for Gaunt's control of the shire? Did he discipline his followers, or did he connive at their own lawlessness and injustice? Walker selected four counties with differing political structures to examine the extent and nature of John of Gaunt's lordship: Sussex, Lancashire, Norfolk and the North Midlands.

In Sussex, Lancastrian lordship was novel and intrusive, arousing antagonism among a tightly knit gentry community whose traditional ties were with the earls of Arundel. In a high-profile contest over customary manorial rights with Sir Edward Dallingridge, Gaunt vindicated his lordship by procuring a legal victory, but Dallingridge had the backing of the Sussex gentry and Gaunt found it prudent to conciliate his enemy and accept the status quo.[7] While Sussex was an outlier of Lancastrian power, Lancashire was its heartland. Here the duke's lands were extensive, his palatine rights embraced offices and justice, and he enjoyed an unchallenged monopoly of favour and patronage, for there was no alternative lordship. Yet, as Walker argued, there were inherent limitations to his power. Although dominant, it could never directly encompass all the gentry of the county; no more than a third of them were his retainers. Moreover, because there was no alternative lordship, those outside the affinity could easily become dissidents, seeking attachment to the rival power of Robert de Vere and, later, Richard II in Cheshire. Some major Lancashire gentry like Sir Thomas Molyneux, Sir Ralph Radcliffe and Sir Robert Clifton thus became determined opponents of Gaunt's affinity. There was a further sense in which Gaunt's monopoly in Lancashire limited his active control. As supreme lord and justiciar he had obligations to the whole community to uphold law and order; yet he was often too dependent on the officials of his own retinue – as stewards and farmers of his estates – to check their oppressions and misdeeds. There was widespread complaint that those who wore his livery saw themselves as 'petty kings', immune from rebuke. Disorder thus more often sprang from a failure of ducal control than the exercise of ducal power. The more favour he showed to his retainers, the more disaffected would the rest of the community become. Thus the exercise of lordship had its own inner contradictions, which were magnified by the monopoly Gaunt enjoyed within the palatinate.[8]

Norfolk, again, lay at the periphery of Lancastrian influence; Gaunt rarely visited it and exploited his lands there more for their financial than political value. The county gentry were independent and prosperous, there were numerous lords to whom they could attach themselves, and few had an exclusive loyalty to Lancaster. Here his affinity had less cohesion and much less influence, but correspondingly aroused less opposition. By contrast, the Staffordshire-Derbyshire estates, centred on Tutbury and the Peak, were part of the historic core of the duchy, and one of the most important recruiting grounds for the military retinue. The duke's frequent presence at Tutbury enhanced the identity and power of the affinity whose activities provoked local opposition. To the west Gaunt's lands lay juxtaposed with those of the earls of Stafford, whose affinity had traditional ties with their family. But the death of Earl Hugh in 1386 and the ensuing minorities of his heirs created a vacuum of lordship which the Lancastrian affinity sought to exploit. Gaunt's retainers, who had returned from Spain enriched and fortified by the duke's protection, seized the opportunity to acquire lands and offices in Staffordshire, arousing antagonism among local families. Escalating disorders opened the door to royal intervention, particularly as Richard II built up a rival lordship in Cheshire.[9]

From these regional studies, Walker felt able to develop some general observations on the nature and operation of bastard feudalism.[10] They showed that the Lancastrian affinity, for all its size and prestige, was not a monolithic structure, obedient to the duke's will, and it could not easily be used to control the political society of a county. On the basis of the social grades and wealth of landowners figured in the tax returns of 1412 and 1436, Walker argued that even at its most extensive the affinity embraced only a minority of the fifty or so politically significant gentry in any county. That left a body of 'independent' gentry, either unattached to any retinue or enjoying a freedom of action by virtue of the multiplicity of their magnate connections. Set within the context of gentry society, the magnate affinity had limited influence. Even where the Lancastrian affinity was able, in three or four counties, to dominate the shire magistracy – i.e. the offices of sheriff, justice of the peace and member of parliament – it did not enjoy a monopoly. Nor could even such a monopoly deliver control of the shire to a lord, for Walker argued that retainers sought these offices to further their own interests and standing, rather than their lord's. Indeed, the other inherent limitation to a magnate's power was his inability to prevent his retainers from appropriating and exploiting his authority. This Walker saw as the key to interpreting the complaints of the parliamentary Commons against the lawlessness of magnates' retinues. Their prime target was not the lords themselves, but their retainers who, safe under magnate protection, acted as 'second kings', oppressing and intimidating their neighbours. But neither were the 'independent' gentry themselves blameless, being as ready to resort to law breaking in their own interests. Indeed, Walker could conclude that 'the position of the magnates and their dependants at the local level seems at times beleaguered – one which was defended against the lawless depredations of the gentry only with difficulty'.[11] In this verdict he was at odds with other scholars, both those like R. L. Storey who directly attributed lawlessness to the bastard feudal magnates, and with the more recent study by Christine Carpenter of how Richard Beauchamp, earl of Warwick, stabilised and controlled the West Midlands through an affinity which embraced most of the leading families and controlled the local administrative offices.[12]

It could be argued that Walker drew these challenging, and at times provocative, conclusions from the study of a wholly exceptional lordship: that Gaunt's retinue was primarily military in character; that it was too widely and thinly spread to be effectively disciplined and directed; that the duke's interests were primarily court, rather than county-centred; and that his overbearing personality invited opposition. There is truth in all of this, and Walker acknowledged that 'if there is a distinction to be made in the types of late medieval lordship – one type consisting of links between lords and gentry who resided locally, the other a looser network of connections between the great magnates of the realm and gentlemen residing in nearly every county of England – then Gaunt's lordship was clearly of the second sort.'[13] In this sense the Lancastrian affinity was perhaps less typical than those of the earls of Devon, Stafford and Warwick. But what Walker was primarily exploring was the balance between lords and gentry in the local polity, and his conclusion was that 'on examination the relationship between lord and man . . . turns out to be as much one of equality as of dependence. For all their wealth and influence, the magnates of later medieval England maintained only a limited control over their men, for . . . the gentry possessed other resources, other patrons, other refuge.'[14]

The Lancastrian Affinity was a tour de force of the subject. It addressed the central issues of bastard feudalism with penetrating originality, approaching the central relationship of lord and man from the latter's perspective and viewing it in the context of the local polity. It did not shun paradox in presenting new insights or qualifying an accepted viewpoint, and this reflected Walker's questioning and radical approach, though the work as a whole rested on detailed research as extensive as it was sure-footed. In its structure and exposition, as much as in its scholarship and judgements, this was a mature work, one which quickly became authoritative in its field. Yet Walker was not quite ready to leave the subject, feeling that there were issues he had raised but not wholly resolved. Foremost of these was that of the enforcement of law within a hierarchically structured society. Did this reflect, and was it conditioned by, the balance of power between political classes?

A long tradition of scholarship had seen the emergence of gentry justices of the peace with increasing judicial powers as a surrender by the crown to local interests, and a contribution to the disorder of late medieval England. This was already being questioned from different standpoints. Edward Powell had argued that the assize justices exercised professional surveillance over the peace commissions, and individual local studies showed that it was often lesser gentry with legal experience who most regularly held the sessions. Yet in broader terms both the crown and the magnates demonstrably influenced the commissions through their retainers. Walker decided that only a systematic examination of the operation of the commissions could resolve these questions, choosing Yorkshire under Richard II and Henry IV as an area and society with which he was already largely familiar.[15] He examined the role of the four elements in the commissions: magnates, assize judges, justices of the quorum (local legal practitioners) and local gentry. Despite the distrust of the magnates shown by the parliamentary Commons in 1388–9, their presence was normal and essential. Though mostly remaining in the background (no more than a third attended in person), their local power and royal backing gave weight to the commission. The king named only those he trusted, and could vet any justices who were their retainers and officers. Justices of assize (judges and sergeants at law) often attended quarter sessions and both there, and at the assizes, exercised supervision and direction over local justice from the centre. As ipso facto members of the quorum they could assess and select the professional lawyers (both local men and Westminster practitioners) who formed its core and did most of the active work. For the leading local gentry the evidence was mixed: a few were assiduous, but many were not. In Yorkshire, the crown's Lancastrian retainers were prominent, and in general the crown nominated those of proven diligence and loyalty. Through a detailed study of both the personnel and work of the peace commissions, Walker challenged the belief that they undermined the crown's control of local government. Rather, they 'considerably increased the ability of the royal administration to enforce its will in the localities'. More broadly, Walker took issue with the notion of 'opposition between central government and local autonomy, royal authority and gentry independence', asserting rather the integral character of political society, with its strong personal links and common assumptions at both centre and locality.[16]

In 1992 the publication of Christine Carpenter's massive study of political society in Warwickshire in the fifteenth century faced historians not only with two models of lordship, but with divergent views on the organisation of gentry society.[17] Did the gentry – a numerous, if steeply graded, class – enjoy autonomous status and power, or were they enmeshed by lordship? If the former, did they constitute a community, what form did this take, and, what conscious identity did it have? These were difficult questions to answer and, in an article in 1994, Carpenter pressed them against those who adhered to the notion of a county community. What evidence was there for such? Neither the meetings of the county court nor the quarter sessions showed the county acting as a corporate entity. The elite gentry families may have led and identified with the county, but their interests generally ranged far wider. In any case a true county community should embrace the numerous lesser families, whose solidarities were with their neighbours at a more local level. Carpenter argued that cohesion among the gentry could only come through noble lordship, subsuming the family and neighbourhood networks of the gentry and creating a sense of shire identity. She called for the term 'community' to be banned from academic discourse, as incapable of meaningful definition.[18]

Walker felt bound to make a riposte, but when he did so, and why he did not publish it, is uncertain. It is now printed in this volume for the first time, as he intended.[19] He observed that the concepts of a 'county community' and of 'independent gentry' were separable, and not identical. Similarly he asserted that a county community was compatible with magnate lordship, for horizontal and vertical ties could be complementary rather than antagonistic. Further, accepting that the county community was only one of a number of solidarities in local society (parish, kindred, affinity) was no reason to deny it a sense of social identity, of collective awareness and shared assumptions. Was it 'an imagined community' in men's consciousness? Walker adduced some evidence of contemporary personification of the shire, seen as 'a community of sentiment, endowed with a certain moral authority', notably on occasions when its elite acted to resolve disputes which threatened the social peace. Then the shire was perceived as a social entity whose repute was at stake and in which local status could be confirmed. It was, he concluded, not only a familiar administrative unit, but an imagined social body. Finally, Walker sketched out, schematically, the stages of its development from an administrative instrument of the crown (1300–50), to a hierarchically ordered community (1350–*c.* 1430), and subsequently to its independence from magnate influence.

In 1994, Michael Jones and Simon Walker published for the Camden Society an edition of all the surviving private life indentures for peace and war apart from those of John of Gaunt and William, Lord Hastings.[20] This provided a meticulous and definitive analysis of these important instruments of social relationships. Walker's introduction to the volume reviewed the evolution of life indentures, the range of services they embraced, the regulation of obligations for service and reward, and the changing role of such indentures over the period 1278–1476. The heyday of retaining for war was the fourteenth century, and by 1400, Walker suggested, the increasingly advantageous terms of indentures of retinue indicated a shortage of knights and men at arms willing to serve. Over the next three quarters of a century the indenture of service in war was in slow decline, occasioned partly by restrictive legislation, but mainly by the shift in social values from a chivalric to a civilian culture. The growing wealth and influence of the leading gentry made menial service to the nobility an anachronism, and noble affinities came to be increasingly composed of lesser gentry and yeomen.

From these broad investigations into the balance of power between magnates and gentry, Walker returned to examine how, in individual cases, two men from different backgrounds built their careers on noble and royal patronage. Starting as a minor Oxfordshire landowner, Sir Richard Abberbury had first taken service with the Black Prince in Gascony and Spain, passing naturally into that of the young Richard II and Queen Anne as her chamberlain. Though never among the central clique of Richard's favourites, his career was briefly checked by the Appellants in 1387, before resuming in the 1390s as a leading diplomat and financial administrator of the king. From the profits of favour he enlarged his Oxfordshire estates and built Donnington castle (1386). Not merely had his family joined the shire establishment, but his son Richard was set to replicate his career in the service of John of Gaunt and Henry of Derby, particularly when the latter usurped the crown. Yet at this point the mould broke. Having crusaded in Lithuania, joined Philip de Mézières' Order of the Passion, and been sent as a diplomatic envoy to the Middle East, Richard junior abandoned England for a prolonged pilgrimage in the Holy Land. Being childless, he liquidated his English estates, depriving his collateral family, who eventually subsided into the obscurity from which they had sprung. Whether from political miscalculation or idiosyncratic choice, the characteristic rise of a gentry family was thus frustrated.[21]

The interplay of professional careerism and personal insufficiency frustrated the ambitions of Janico Dartasso in a different way. Dartasso was a Navarese adventurer whose long and versatile military career under English captains such as John of Gaunt and Henry Hotspur brought minor renown and some profit (notably from the capture of Olivier du Guesclin in 1379). But if he hoped to emulate Guichard d'Angle under Edward III, or Jean Robessart under Henry V, he was disappointed. Though in much demand as a soldier in many theatres of war, Dartasso was never at the centre of political patronage. He was never knighted, nor rewarded with English lands, and ultimately had to be content with estates and offices in Ireland. Walker argued that this reflected the different ethos of chivalry after 1400, which became less international, more closely aligned to royal policy, and heavily imbued with chauvinism. Both studies show that the world of international chivalry, of which John of Gaunt was the supreme symbol, still offered a pathway to social status and landed wealth, but that miscalculation and insular prejudice could frustrate access to the political establishment.[22]

These were vignettes of those whom Fortune deserted, reminders that below the leaders and the achievers were their followers who, sharing the same aspirations and ideals, formed a supporting cast which underpinned the larger strategies and ambitions of those above. It was to an understanding of political society at this level that Walker's work gravitated after 1994. His interest focussed on the revolution of 1399, not so much as a political coup, but as how it was viewed by those who lived through it, starting with the king himself.

In the absence of any explicit statement by Richard II of his views on kingship, Walker sought to deconstruct Sir William Bagot's report of a conversation with the king at Lichfield in 1398. In this Richard insisted that the obedience rendered to a king by subjects was similar to that owed to God, a theme already expounded by Bishop Stafford in the 1397 parliament. Richard then set this in the context of history, claiming that his mission was to recover the ancient prerogatives of the Crown. Thirdly, he saw the Crown not as public property in which subjects had a legitimate concern, but as the expression of the dignity and will of the king. Finally, Church and Crown were mutually reinforcing and indissolubly linked in resisting rebellion. Richard's concept of kingship thus possessed coherence and was rooted in tradition. Yet his attempt to articulate and apply this in the final two years of his reign overreached the normal boundaries of royal action and was seen as novel and threatening. Richard was perhaps too much an ideologue, too little a politician.[23]

How subjects looked back to Richard's reign after his deposition was a subject to which Walker returned in different ways. The popular belief that Richard was still alive and would return to rid the realm of his supplanter was fostered by the friars and by a group in the Westminster sanctuary for whom Richard remained the legitimate king. But this phase soon passed, and it was the broader discontent with Henry IV's misgovernment – the issues of taxation and order – rather than doubts over the legitimacy of his title, that generated popular dissent. Richard's rule was recalled not as a golden age, but as an authority against which Henry's could be measured, thus enabling dissent to be expressed as an appeal to the ideal of true monarchy. As a rhetoric of protest rather than of political intent, this avoided sedition. Two principal conclusions thus emerged about political culture below the level of the literate political class: first, its ambivalence revealed a measure of sophistication and subtlety; and secondly, it nonetheless broadly connected with the issues of high politics.[24]

Walker then turned to examine the retrospective view of the 1399 revolution in literate culture. The construction of the 'social memory' of a recent event was bound to be more artificial than the popular reaction, and was repeatedly remodelled to meet changing political needs and circumstances. He traced this through the chronicles and political writings of the fifteenth century. Richard's deposition had at first been justified in terms of the tyranny of his acts and his insufficiency as a ruler. With very few exceptions the chroniclers had followed the parliamentary 'Record and Process', which explained and justified the deposition in these terms, drawing confirmation from their own hostile memory of the reign and the conventional scriptural parallels of young and wilful rulers like Rehoboam who had met a similar fate. As Lancastrian rule consolidated, its legitimacy no longer needed to be defended, and the fading memory of Richard's personal inadequacies allowed his fall to be schematised within the cycle of Fortune and even seen as predictable in the light of prophetic utterances. Even the Yorkist revolution of 1461, which denounced Henry IV's usurpation as the destruction of the rightful line, heralded no vindication of Richard's rule or rehabilitation of his reputation by the chroniclers. What political society looked for in these turbulent years was an affirmation of political continuity and national solidarity, and this was provided in the new genre of genealogical rolls of the kings of England, which presented a bland, but comforting, picture of historical succession from the time of Adam.[25]

Within this extended conspectus of contemporary reactions to the 1399 revolution, Walker made a more detailed investigation of the interests and attitudes of those who challenged Lancastrian rule in the major rebellion of the north in 1405. Historians had mainly treated this rebellion as the last serious attempt by the Percys to raise the north against Henry IV. Henry Percy, earl of Northumberland, was seen as the prime mover, inciting and manipulating Archbishop Scrope to raise a popular protest in Yorkshire to which the Percys could lend backing. Essentially this was seen as high politics and dynastic ambition exploiting the unpopularity of royal policies. Walker set out to show that this interpretation, which reflected the official account given in parliament and with some variations reproduced in the chronicles, gave insufficient weight to the complex of local grievances and personal convictions that could be extrapolated from the manifestos and hagiography produced by the rising. Several strands of protest could be distinguished. The archbishop himself was voicing clerical complaints of royal taxation of the Church, encroachments on its liberties, and the hostility to it of the king's entourage, all of which were well documented. The citizens of York had similar complaints of royal demands for loans and were enmeshed in discords over the city's governance. The Yorkshire gentry who joined the rising were partly Percy followers, but included others who resented and feared the expansion of Neville-Lancastrian influence that had followed the Percy debacle in 1403. There was some sympathy for Thomas Mowbray, the young earl marshal, who had been displaced by Neville ascendancy. For all these the archbishop's rising provided support and cover. It was a genuine local protest prompted by local, if disparate, grievances, and echoed the earlier warning to the king and appeal for good government by Philip Repingdon. Yet the role of Scrope remains ambivalent. Was he merely a misguided figurehead, ingenuous enough to believe that, at the head of an armed protest in the context of the Percy revolt, his claim to be mediating between the Crown and the local community would be seen as other than rebellion? Why, as an influential and devout churchman, did he ally himself with the unstable and devious young earl marshal?[26]

Walker was thus using these manifestations of dissent from Lancastrian kingship to explore the nature of political society in England. Both popular protest and literate reconstruction had shown anxiety to reaffirm monarchical rule as the headstone of the social order and to identify it with the continuity and identity of the state. Even Scrope's rising was intended to recall the king to the first principle of just rule, that subjects should be treated with equity and not oppressed. The function of royal government in the eyes of the ruled had been the theme of Walker's earlier study in this field, on the role of political saints. He began this by observing, on the one hand, that in the late middle ages sanctity was no longer automatically accorded to those who, like Becket, were martyred in defending the Church against the secular power and, on the other, that England was unique in the number of laymen who were popularly venerated for their opposition to the Crown. What was it in the English polity that encouraged the emergence of such cults? What was their place and purpose in English political life? After briefly reviewing the cults of Simon de Montfort, Thomas of Lancaster, Edward II, Archbishop Scrope and Henry VI, Walker noted that these did not simply represent the canonisation of opposition to the Crown, for in almost every case the cult had been fostered by royal protection and encouragement. How, therefore, did the political martyr provide common ground for veneration by both Crown and people? The link, Walker suggested, lay through the function of royal sacrality in uniting the political community with God. 'A king was as crucial to the political salvation of his subjects as a priest to the spiritual salvation of his flock.' When this unity was fractured by discord, it was the martyred saint who, through forgiveness, reconciled king and subjects and restored charity in the Christian commonwealth. 'Though fissile and disordered, later medieval English society was also rich in the resources of compromise and conciliation, not the least of which was this power of the saints.'[27]

Each of these later articles addressed the larger problem which Walker, along with other late medieval historians, found himself questioning in the decade that followed the publication of *The Lancastrian Affinity* – that is, how to interpret the apparent instability of late medieval society and the state, manifested in popular revolt, dynastic revolutions, financial demands and shortages, and the growing articulation of political complaint. In a short survey at the popular level published in 1996, Walker had asked whether these should be seen as reflecting structural weaknesses in the state or as short-lived episodes in a generally peaceful and effective political system. He was planning to return to the question in an Introduction to the present collection of essays, of which he prepared a short synopsis.[28] In this he cited for the latter view the work of Christine Carpenter and John Watts which *emphasises the common framework of assumptions – the 'constitution' – within which all the actors of late medieval England operated, and consequently concludes that the task of government was an essentially unproblematic one; there were no structural flaws in the English polity but only individual failures of political capacity*. However, other historians had *identified a series of deeper seated failings: the long standing Plantagenet commitment to war in France; the abiding moral and political uncertainties created by Henry IV's original act of perjured usurpation; a gradual attrition of the fiscal and military resources of the English state, either from strategic over-extension or fatal administrative inflexibility*. In 1996, Walker had argued that the widespread and instinctive fear of anarchy was sufficient to inhibit rebellion and underpin the rule of any king who 'did justice, had a disposition to act equitably, and was readily accessible to his greater subjects'. He doubted whether either disputes over dynastic legitimacy or the strains imposed by the war state were root causes of rebellion against the Crown. Flaws in the practice of kingship (the denial of justice, prodigality with royal resources, the addiction to favourites, and the failure to take counsel) were most likely to precipitate political revolt, but he went on to observe that what gave these resonance beyond the political elite or point of local impact was the nature of the English state. First there was its geographical coherence, the product both of its well-defined size and its long history of centralised government. Secondly, the Crown's reliance on 'a relatively extensive ruling class, with a vested interest in the political health and fiscal credit of the Crown and the political leverage to make their views effective', bred a responsive political culture. The later middle ages saw a *slow but appreciable expansion in the scope of the political nation*, with political awareness more widely disseminated, and *'infrapolitical' engagement taking the form of bill-casting, seditious speech and rumour*. Together these meant that even local and popular risings spoke the language of political justice and affirmed the mutual obligations of ruler and ruled. Among the political class, Walker noted *the gradual relaxation of the reliable bonds of deference and obligation that had previously allowed the landed aristocracies to assure themselves of their local hegemonies*. From this perspective *the volatility of contemporary politics appears . . . as neither the regrettable result of individual incompetence nor the unavoidable consequence of severe structural flaws*. Indeed, it attested *the sophistication and complexity of English political culture* in which a burgeoning political consciousness at all levels offered opportunities for compromise and negotiation, which underlined the identity of interest between kings and subjects. Walker concluded that *the disturbed political condition of late medieval England should not be seen as evidence for a serious deterioration in the quality of government, but as a price to be paid for the development of a cohesive and generally successful political order*.

Most of Walker's work thus dealt with relationships within the military and political structures of bastard feudalism. For the study of Richard Andrew, the first Warden of All Souls College, he had to adjust to a different ethos and familiarise himself with new sources. He met the challenge with characteristic insight and enthusiasm, rescuing Andrew from anonymity as a person, and using his conventional career to illuminate the character of Lancastrian rule in the middle years of the century. In his formative years at Winchester and New College, and in his early career as an ecclesiastical lawyer in Archbishop Henry Chichele's court of audience, Andrew enjoyed the patronage of a circle of churchmen of piety and learning who sought to promote order and devotion in public worship and knit together church and state as a reformed Christian commonwealth. Archbishop Chichele exemplified this ideal, founding All Souls College both to commemorate those who had fallen in war and to train the 'unarmed soldiers', the clergy who fought for men's souls. It was intended to be a nursery of public service, in government or in the Church, not unlike the humanist academies established in Italy. The appointment of Andrew as the college's first warden in 1439 probably owed much to another of this circle, Thomas Bekynton, under whose influence the young Henry VI founded Eton and King's with a similar purpose. In 1443 Andrew succeeded Bekynton as King Henry's secretary, but hopes that the young king's rule would promote this vision disappeared in the internecine struggles of the following decade. Andrew retained the favour of Henry VI, but not of his political controllers; he failed to become Keeper of the Privy Seal, his career stagnated, and in 1455 he moved to the deanery at York. There, for the next twenty-two years he maintained the liturgical tradition, reordered the chapter finances and finished the construction of the towers of the minster.[29]

For Walker, Andrew's uneventful life was not only a reflection of his integrity in an increasingly unprincipled society, but an example of those whose service underpinned the 'high politics' of Church and state. He believed that the detailed examination of such individual lives, and their social and political context, would afford an understanding of how political language and ideas informed the operation of power at all levels.

Though tragically shortened, Simon Walker's scholarly career was remarkably fruitful. To the still fluid interpretation of the English later middle ages he brought an alert and inquiring mind, feeling his way into problems by testing hypotheses and exploring paradoxes. From extensive reading and through his eirenic approach he acquired a deeply sympathetic understanding of the period. He had an instinctive sense for the intention behind a chronicler's anecdote or the message embedded in a popular prophecy. He subjected texts to meticulous scrutiny, not only to test the veracity of what they said, but the significance of what they did not. It was this sensitivity to what lay beneath the historical record that made him attend to the lives and voices of those below political society, those who served and suffered rather than those who ruled. He tried to read history from below because he wanted to see it whole. He used case studies to build up a picture of collective mentalities among different social grades and vocational worlds, hoping ultimately to construct a new approach to the tensions and strength of the late medieval polity. It was a challenging approach, for it meant working against the grain of the central sources, displaying a sensitivity to other incidental evidence, and using conjecture and imagination with the utmost discipline. But he believed that this was the only way to understand a political culture which he saw as increasingly encompassing all levels of society. One can only speculate how his work would have developed, but what he accomplished has permanently enriched out understanding of the period.

Notes

1 The literature on the subject up to 1980 is reviewed in the Introduction to K. B. McFarlane, *England in the Fifteenth Century: Collected Essays*, ed. G. L. Harriss, (London, 1981), ix–xxvii.
2 Simon Walker, *The Lancastrian Affinity, 1361–1399* (Oxford, 1990).
3 Ibid., p. 2.
4 Ibid., ch. 4.
5 Ibid., p. 77.
6 Ibid., pp. 94–116.
7 Ibid., pp. 117–41.
8 Ibid., pp. 141–81. Much of the material in this section was reused in the essay reprinted here as chapter 1.
9 *Lancastrian Affinity*, pp. 182–234.
10 Ibid., pp. 235–61.
11 Ibid., p. 260.
12 R. L. Storey, *The End of the House of Lancaster* (London, 1966, 1986); C. Carpenter, 'The Beauchamp affinity; a study of bastard feudalism at work', *English Historical Review*, 95 (1980), 514–32.
13 *Lancastrian Affinity*, p. 248.
14 Ibid., p. 261.
15 See ch. 4 of this volume, reviewing the preceding literature on pp. 81–2.
16 Ibid., pp. 99, 103.
17 Christine Carpenter, *Locality and Polity: A Study of Warwickshire Landed Society, 1401–1499* (Cambridge, 1992).
18 Christine Carpenter had criticised Walker's arguments for the limitation of magnate rule in the shires in 'Gentry and community in medieval England', *Journal of British Studies*, 33 (1994), 356–65.
19 See ch. 3.
20 M. Jones and S. K. Walker (eds), 'Private indentures for life service in peace and war, 1278–1476', *Camden Miscellany, XXXII*, Camden Society, 5th series, 3 (1994), 1–190.
21 See ch. 2.
22 See ch. 5.
23 See ch. 6.
24 See ch. 7.
25 See ch. 8. This was a reworking of 'Richard II's reputation', in Gwilym Dodd (ed.), *The Reign of Richard II* (Stroud, 2000), pp. 119–28, 152–4.
26 See ch. 10.
27 See ch. 9 (quotations at pp. 208, 214).
28 See ch. 11. The following paragraph incorporates passages from the draft synopsis, which are printed in italics.

29 'Between Church and Crown: Master Richard Andrew, King's Clerk', *Speculum*, 74 (1999), 956–90. A shorter version was delivered as a lecture in 1993: 'The college and the late medieval Church: the career of Richard Andrew', in *Unarmed Soldiery* (All Souls College, 1996), 14–32.

I

Lordship and service

1

Lordship and lawlessness in the palatinate of Lancaster, 1370–1400

The precise connection between 'bastard feudalism,' the characteristic form of aristocratic social organization in later medieval England, and the disordered condition of English politics in the later Middle Ages has long been a subject for debate among historians. While earlier writers had no doubt that the emergence of magnate affinities – bands of men bound to a lord by an indenture of retainer and a money fee rather than by a heritable fief in land – in the early fourteenth century had destructive consequences for the quality of public order, their unfavorable judgments have now been largely replaced by a more sympathetic account of the workings of magnate lordship, which portrays the late medieval affinity as neither an aberration nor a degeneration from the arrangements of an earlier age, but, rather, the logical successor to them.[1] The creation of this consensus represents, however, only the first stage in the effort to reach a proper understanding of the mechanics of lordship in later medieval England, for it raises a number of secondary questions that have yet to be resolved. How pervasive, for instance, was the network of clientage and patronage represented by the magnate affinity?[2]

One view holds that this network 'formed the fabric of contemporary life': a magnate could effectively control a county or counties by using his indentured retainers 'to diffuse the lord's influence through the areas where his estates lay, into the wider affinity, and even among landowners outside the affinity, using above all the power they could wield as local administrators.'[3] The natural corollary of this belief is to emphasize the crucial importance of the nobility in the politics of later medieval England, for 'where the magnates marched, the gentry followed . . . because [they] could hardly ignore the causes of their patrons.'[4] Yet others find it possible to speak of a body of independent county gentry 'who lived outside the embrace of bastard feudalism,' more concerned with the preservation of their patrimony and lineage than with any notion of allegiance to a noble household, and capable of responding to the summons to arms from their social superiors by a 'masterly inactivity' that left the magnates powerless.[5] Regional particularities clearly have much to do with these widely divergent conclusions but behind them lies a fundamental disagreement over the relative social and political importance of magnates and gentry in later medieval England.

To find the necessary evidence to resolve that disagreement means, however, setting the affinity within the context of county society. In the relationship created between lord and man by the indenture of retainer, money provided the material nexus between the two contracting parties, but it was the exercise of 'good lordship' that provided the real cement, and it was within the retainer's own social world, the county, that a magnate was usually called on to exercise this lordship by providing a variety of social services, ranging from charter witnessing to marriage brokering, by securing positions of power and worship in the county administration for his own followers, and preeminently by providing aid and comfort, both legal and extralegal, in the prosecution of his retainers' lawsuits. Without such a local context, there is a danger of disproportion distorting the analysis. The central problem in the study of 'bastard feudalism' since the first modern discussion of the subject has been to strike an adequate balance between the political and economic resources of the magnates and the stubborn independence of the county gentry, whose prejudices had to be respected and their loyalty won.[6] A growing number of local studies reiterate the same point: policy was made at Westminster but it was implemented, or thwarted, in the provinces.[7] In each shire, the crown, the aristocracy – both absentee magnates and resident local lords – and the body of the shire gentry all possessed legitimate claims to consideration and authority: power lay between them and was never the monopoly of a single group.

On the resolution of the first question turns, to a great extent, the answer to a second: how far was the magnate affinity responsible for the endemic violence and perversion of justice that appears to be so characteristic of later medieval England? Contemporary complaints about the quality of law and order singled out the great lords and their followers as the chief culprits and were never more vehement in doing so than during Richard II's reign. In 1381, the speaker of the Commons identified the oppression of the common people by magnate dependents as one of the principal causes of the Peasants' Revolt; in 1384, the Commons demanded a statute against certain local potentates, who were protected from justice by their magnate patrons; in the Merciless Parliament, they returned to the attack on the 'second kings' of the shires, identified this time as royal officials and magnate stewards.[8] In the succeeding parliaments at Cambridge and Westminster, their complaints became more narrowly focused on the lords' livery badges and their wearers, who acted like provincial tyrants in oppressing the common people.[9] If 'the affinity . . . was part of the normal fabric of society' in fourteenth-century England, contemporaries were nevertheless dissatisfied with the state of that society and blamed the magnate affinity for many of its evils.[10]

Recent historians have, however, been skeptical of these petitions, seeing in them, at the least, a serious oversimplification.[11] Intense competition and pressure for land, the ever-growing complexity of the law relating to landed property, the opportunities for manipulation and collusion this complexity created, all now seem more important causes of disorder than the deliberate lawlessness of the nobility.[12] When it did break out, violence was as much a means of seeking justice as a refusal to accept it, often a last, not a first, resort; its aim was to achieve a settlement acceptable to all parties in dispute, for this was the only way in which a lasting peace could be guaranteed.[13] Far from promoting disorder, the nobility had an important part to play by acting as extralegal umpires and arbitrators in promoting the hoped-for reconciliation and reestablishing the social peace.[14] Yet while admitting all this, it still remains possible to see violence as an essential ingredient of late medieval lordship, a necessary sign of its strength, for it was the permanent threat of physical harm and material destruction that, by making any form of protection that enhanced a man's security perennially attractive, provided a favorable context for the growth of clientage and dependence.

This article will examine the state of law and order in the palatinate of Lancaster under John of Gaunt, duke of Lancaster, in the light of the Commons' complaints, seek to assess the extent to which they were justified, and then use the conclusions derived from this local evidence to attempt a more general estimate of the nature and effects of 'bastard feudalism' in later medieval England.

* * *

The palatinate of Lancaster provides a unique case in the study of 'bastard feudalism,' an opportunity to observe the operation of a lord's favor almost unrestrained by the exercise of royal power. John of Gaunt's territorial preeminence in the county was unquestioned; his own estates there were valued at some £1,800 per annum, while the only other peers with lands in the shire – the Dacres of Gilsland, the Ferrers of Groby, the de la Warrs of Swineshead – were of minor baronial rank.[15] His legal predominance was even more pronounced for after he was granted palatinate rights within the shire in 1377, the jurisdiction of the duke of Lancaster over the men of Lancashire was limited only by the royal prerogative of pardon and the crown's right to correct errors of justice.[16] Even during the period between 1361 and 1377, when the county was theoretically under the jurisdiction of the crown, the justices at Lancaster continued to exercise a modified form of the palatinate crown pleas, and the duke enjoyed the right to appoint his own sheriff.[17] As a consequence, the duke retained a personal responsibility for the whole shire and its inhabitants, quite distinct from his role as a good lord to his own followers. There remained in his grants of favor and patronage a quality of personal grace that kept John of Gaunt constantly before the minds of his subjects. One suppliant obtained a pardon for his forest offences from the duke by thrusting a draft into his hands 'as he walked in the cloisters between the chamber and the hall after breakfast'; another received his pardon by the duke's word of mouth alone.[18] Inevitably, therefore, it was to John of Gaunt that the gentry of the county looked for advancement, and it was on his lordship that the shire ultimately depended for good government and justice.

Keeping the peace in Lancashire, a notoriously disordered part of the country, was, however, a difficult task. The enmities created by Adam Banaster's revolt in 1315 and the subsequent suppression of the Contrariants lasted well into Edward II's reign. Continued violence rendered necessary a rapid expansion of the peace commission until, by 1350, it was over sixty strong.[19] Neither this, nor the attempts of the county community at collective peace keeping did much good, for the coercive powers of the palatinate's law officers consistently proved too weak for their task.[20] Cattle rustling, inevitably frequent in an upland county, remained rife and often led to serious affrays.[21] There were attacks and trespasses on the duke's own lands, usually minor, but sometimes serious enough to necessitate a special commission of oyer and terminer.[22] Delegates of the duke's authority were particularly vulnerable to attack. When the palatinate justices came to hold their first sessions at Lancaster in 1377, proclamations had to be made against armed bands congregating to impede them. In the same year, one of the duke's coroners, William Bredkirk, was killed in the course of his duties, while in 1394 a justice of oyer and terminer in the palatinate was ambushed and killed on the highroad.[23]

How far can John of Gaunt and his servants be held responsible, as the contemporary Commons claimed, for this violence? Inevitably, members of the Lancastrian affinity played some part in the disorders of the shire. The duke's sheriff, Sir John Botiller, was accused of extortion and oppression; two of his officials, Sir Thomas Southworth and Sir Thomas Molyneux, maintained a long-running and disruptive feud; Southworth was later indicted for murder, as were at least two more Lancastrian retainers, Sir Hugh Dacre and John Sotheron.[24] Such incidents were, in themselves, unremarkable – the misdemeanors of the duke's followers could be matched by the crimes of gentlemen all over the North – though their disruptive effect on the peace of the shire is not in doubt. The question is, rather, the extent to which membership of Gaunt's affinity protected, even encouraged, his retainers in their crimes and so undermined the good order that the duke had a duty to maintain.

To the complaints of the parliamentary Commons that this was, indeed, the case, Gaunt once answered that every lord was competent to correct and punish his servants for their crimes.[25] Yet there is enough evidence to suggest that on occasion the duke of Lancaster displayed a leniency toward the misdeeds of his retainers sufficient to impede the machinery of justice within his own palatinate. The killer of William Bredkirk, the duke's coroner, for instance, was Nicholas Atherton, who had been a Lancastrian retainer since 1370.[26] He came to Gaunt's service with a reputation for violence already well established and continued to disrupt the peace of the shire over the next twenty years, but this did not prevent him rising in the administrative hierarchy of the palatinate to be bailiff of West Derbyshire, where his oppressions understandably aroused widespread complaint.[27] Sir Thomas Southworth, hardly less turbulent a figure than Atherton in the palatinate, similarly suffered no eclipse in the duke's favor; in August 1377, he was appointed Gaunt's deputy as constable and steward of Chester.[28] At the end of a year in which he had been convicted of participating in a serious confederacy of maintenance within the palatinate and then involved in a major breach of the truce on the Scottish March, a third retainer, William Tunstall, managed to escape all the consequences of his crimes by his faithful service to the duke during the Peasants' Revolt.[29] Each time, the point that John of Gaunt's favor put its recipients beyond the reach of the law was forcefully made to their less fortunate contemporaries, as it was again in 1396 when another retainer, Sir John Dalton, was pardoned a charge of conspiracy and murder within the palatinate at the duke's request.[30]

This was the crux of the problem John of Gaunt faced in ruling his palatinate. The influence of lordship on the course of justice was widely recognized and resented in fourteenth-century England, and in Lancashire this influence was formalized, legitimate, and openly acknowledged. When the abbot and convent of Whalley wished to pursue a claim against the duke at the common law, they took the precaution of first asking his permission to proceed 'without any damage or grievance being done them or their cause'; the duke sometimes instructed his justices to proceed with a case but to come to no judgment without his assent.[31] It was by the exercise of such powers that the duke was expected, as a good lord, to show favor to his servants in the county, yet it was no less his duty to mete out justice and reward to the whole shire. Success in either one of these tasks implied a dangerous failure in the other. The more favor he showed his own followers, the more disaffected the rest of the county community would grow; the less partial he was toward his retainers, the less he could rely on their loyalty. Yet the rest of the shire was too powerful to be ignored, even by the duke of Lancaster, for collectively it could call on enormous territorial resources. In all, about three-quarters of the identifiable manors in Lancashire were held by resident members of the gentry, leaving less than a quarter under aristocratic or ecclesiastical control.[32]

An assessment of the relative size and influence of John of Gaunt's affinity within the wider community of the county is, therefore, an essential part of any judgment on the quality of the duke's lordship in Lancashire. If 'one would scarcely expect the gentlemen of . . . the county of Lancaster . . . to refuse the chance of participation in so successful a joint-stock enterprise' as the duke's affinity, how many were given the opportunity in the first place?[33] There are a number of possible approaches to this problem and while each has its drawbacks, the evidence they collectively provide adds up to a reasonably coherent whole. To begin with the question that would have meant most to contemporaries: how many of those in the county entitled to bear arms were members of the Lancastrian affinity? Calveley's Book, an early fifteenth-century roll of arms that contains a large proportion of coats from the time of Edward III, gives 116 achievements for the Lancashire nobility and gentry.[34] In all, the arms of seventy families are displayed, twenty-five of whom appeared in the Lancastrian affinity at some stage during John of Gaunt's lifetime. While many of those featured most prominently in the roll – Sir John Botiller of Warrington, Sir Robert Urswick, Sir John Dalton – were also members of the duke's retinue, there remained a number of well-established county families for whom the duke could find no place – the Lathums, Boldes, Keighleys, Singletons, and Farringtons among them.

Administrative evidence refines this picture somewhat. Between 1361 and 1399, a total of fifty-two gentlemen were appointed or elected as sheriff, escheator, M.P., or justice of the peace in Lancashire; twenty-nine of these men, generally occupying the most prestigious offices, were in the duke's service at the time of their appointment.[35] But below this group of upper gentry was a larger pool of lesser men who were occasionally called on to perform administrative tasks and among them, the hold of the Lancastrian affinity was much less tight; sixty-two of the eighty-three men named as collectors of subsidies within the county held no other office and among all eighty-three in this group, only five ever possessed a discernible Lancastrian connection.[36] An examination of the fragmentary economic evidence available further demonstrates how large and important a section of the county community it was that remained permanently outside the Lancastrian affinity.[37] The surviving returns of the graded poll tax of 1379 show ten landowners assessed at the knightly rate of 20*s.*, one at 13*s.* 4*d.*, and eighteen at 6*s.* 8*d.*, the amount fixed for a landed esquire. Only three of those assessed at 20*s.* were Lancastrians (Robert Eccleston, Sir John Botiller, and Sir Nicholas Harrington) while four of the eighteen men assessed as esquires were connected with the Lancastrian affinity and administration. These proportions do not seem untypical; in 1392, when the sheriff of Lancashire was required to distrain all those who held lands worth more than £40 per annum, only three of the seventeen names he returned were Lancastrian.[38] Thus, while Calveley's Book suggests that approximately a third of the country gentry could find a place in the duke's affinity, the administrative and economic evidence suggests that Gaunt maintained links with a slightly higher proportion of the genuinely influential men in the shire but was much more eclectic in his recruitment from the mass of lesser esquires in which a county as poor as Lancashire abounded, picking and choosing as they recommended themselves.

In consequence, John of Gaunt was not as free to extend or withhold his favor as the critics of magnate lordship in the Commons liked to make out. To refuse a pardon to a retainer was to run the risk of losing his loyalty; to do that was to invite the intervention of other magnates, anxious to grant the good lordship that Lancaster would not. The prerogative of pardon was one of the few regalian rights the crown retained within the palatinate of Lancaster and, if the duke refused to solicit the king for a pardon, there were always others who would. When Richard Croft was pardoned in 1394 for the murder of Robert Blakeburn, the duke's justice of oyer and terminer, the pardon was issued at the request of Thomas Mowbray, earl of Nottingham, newly appointed justice of Chester for life by Richard II and anxious to demonstrate the quality of his lordship to the men of the North West.[39] Croft was the son of John Croft of Dalton, a servant of Gaunt's, and the pardon, significantly, proved an effective means of detaching the Croft family from their Lancastrian allegiance.[40] The fact that there were other influential royalists from Chester, such as Peter de Legh of Lyme and John Macclesfield, keeper of the great wardrobe, who could also make use of this loophole in the legal autonomy of the palatinate,[41] was, consequently, a matter of some concern to the duke, who could ill afford to be too sparing in his use of the prerogative of pardon or too unforgiving in his attitude toward breakers of the peace.[42] The disturbance that could arise from his liberality in this respect was not the result of a simple, unthinking abuse of personal lordship to the detriment of a system of public justice; rather, it arose from the ability of several patrons to exercise the same kind of lordship.

Nor was it only his fellow magnates who challenged Gaunt's authority within his palatinate. On their home territory, the local gentry were more capable of defending their own interests than the special pleading of their representatives in the Commons might suggest. The Holland family chased the duke's sheriff from the manor of Prestwich in 1374, for instance, and despite a ducal judgment against their claims, successfully resisted all attempts to oust them over the next fifteen years.[43] In a long struggle over the inheritance of the Lathum family, Sir John Stanley eventually expelled the Lancastrian farmers from the disputed lands by force, and it was only by a petition in Parliament – a voluntary but still humiliating surrender of his palatinate independence – that John of Gaunt was able to obtain an adequate compromise.[44] Faced with these deficiencies in the coercive power of public justice, it was natural that the duke's retainers, like the rest of the shire, could resort to a degree of self-help; their violent exploits may, in this respect, be taken as an indication of the limitations of Gaunt's lordship rather than as a sign of its overwhelming strength.

Realistically, the best the duke could do was to participate in the informal system of peacekeeping his followers pursued and do his best to turn it into official channels.[45] Arbitration and composition were as popular a means of dispute resolution in the palatinate of Lancaster as they were in later medieval England as a whole and though not an exclusively Lancastrian activity,[46] John of Gaunt and his affinity had an important part to play in bringing such agreements about. Lancastrian officials sometimes acted as the final court of appeal, in the event that the umpires chosen by either side could not agree, while the duke's chief steward in the palatinate might be asked to act as arbitrator in the first instance.[47] Occasionally, cases already initiated in King's Bench would be referred to Gaunt himself for a decision after due consultation with 'doctors and men wise in the law of Holy Church, as well as justices, serjeants and others skilled in the law of this land.'[48] The pardons the duke sought on his servants' behalf were, on occasion, the product of just such a process of conciliation and compromise, resulting in the imposition of a stringent set of conditions on his delinquent retainer.[49]

Seen in this light, John of Gaunt's influence on the course of justice within his palatinate, while appreciable, appears neither excessive in its extent nor baleful in its consequences. His servants and retainers might enjoy some advantage in the courts, but the dangers inherent in this display of favor were offset by the practical limitations on the duke's authority. If Gaunt's retainers were sometimes disturbers of the peace in the palatinate, his affinity also provided a means of resolving disputes by agreement without resort to the common law or to arms. If the duke was sometimes too lenient toward the misdeeds of his followers, he was often constrained to be so. Even in Lancashire there were other patrons who would offer their protection to wrongdoers if John of Gaunt refused his. 'Bastard feudalism,' in the sense of the duke's conscious exercise of lordship on behalf of his dependents, never constituted a very real threat to the peace of the shire, even a shire so dominated by a single great lord.

* * *

More serious, in the long run, was the second major element in the parliamentary Commons' complaints: the constant oppression and petty extortion practiced by royal and ducal officials in Lancashire in the name of their master. Lancashire was certainly not unique in this. As early as 1275, Edward I had legislated against the corruption of his sheriffs and bailiffs and, throughout the fourteenth century, the misdeeds of the unpaid officials on whom English local government depended, especially of those at the lower levels of authority, continued to be the subject of criticism and complaint.[50] Nevertheless, the incidence of official corruption in the county seems particularly high at this time; by 1376 it was so notorious that a general inquiry was instituted into all extortions and falsities,[51] and the prosecutions that arose from this inquiry give a vivid impression of the wide range of abuses committed. Both the county's coroners were called into King's Bench to answer the allegations laid against them; Henry de Chaderton, the duke's bailiff in West Derbyshire, was accused of extortions stretching over twenty years;[52] a whole series of complaints against William de Chorlegh, both in his capacity as escheator and as steward of Gaunt's court in Penwortham, testify to his notoriety.[53] These were the most conspicuous offenders but there were complaints against many lesser officials as well, and although the inquiry of 1376 brought a temporary halt to their depredations, it did little to effect a permanent improvement in the conduct of the duke's servants.[54] The abbot of Cockersand complained, for example, that whenever he appeared before the duke's swainmote court to plead his exemption from its jurisdiction, he was prevented from returning home by the men of the duke's master forester. William de Nessfield, the duke's chief steward, was found to have enclosed common land at Urmston to his own advantage; another steward of the duchy, Sir Robert Plessington, was removed from office for his embezzlements and erasures.[55] Even after Henry de Chaderton's removal from office, the duke's tenants in West Derbyshire continued to petition the duchy council for an investigation into the unjust practices of officials there while, as bailiff in the 1390s, Sir Nicholas Atherton pursued his work with a vehemence that makes it almost impossible to distinguish legitimate distraint from private vengeance.[56]

Such oppressions aroused complaint from the Commons on the grounds that they were a major cause of the lawlessness that characterized the age. But in seeking to assess the truth of this claim and the effectiveness of their suggested remedies, it is important to be clear what the Commons were complaining about. Men like Chaderton and Chorlegh were the 'second kings' of the shires, whose maintenance and oppressions were the target of attacks on more than one occasion. They commanded little inherited wealth – Chaderton had lands worth twenty-three marks a year, Chorlegh's were said to be worth only fifteen marks, though it was well known that he had acquired so much wealth by virtue of his office that the annual expenses of his household exceeded 300 marks – but their official position gave them an influence quite incommensurate with their social status. Randolph, lord Dacre, the prior of Penwortham, and the abbots of Whalley and Furness were all among Chorlegh's victims.[57] It was to this disruption of the social hierarchy that the Commons particularly objected; men of low birth were corruptly exercising power to which they were not entitled. In their eyes, the corruption of such men was the direct result of the protection they received from their magnate masters, symbolized in the gift of livery; remove this protection and much of the violence and disorder in the counties, which sprang from an inability to obtain adequate redress at law, would be removed as well. Yet there is little sign in the evidence presented above that the depredations of the duke's officials were in any way condoned or approved by Gaunt himself.[58] It was, however, particularly hard for the duke to appear blameless in Lancashire, for unauthorized oppression by a ducal official was scarcely distinguishable from the license allowed a favored servant by his lord. It was from such unauthorized corruption, rather than Gaunt's conscious exercise of his own lordship, that resentment at the duke of Lancaster's role within his palatinate most readily sprang.

The genesis and consequences of such resentment can be most clearly illuminated by an examination of Thomas Molyneux of Cuerdale's feud with Henry Chaderton, the duke's delinquent bailiff. It began with the murder of Richard Molyneux in 1369, allegedly committed at the instigation of Chaderton. He vigorously denied the charge,[59] but though the precise facts of the case are characteristically hard to disentangle, there is no doubt that the Molyneux clan continued to hold him responsible for the death of their kinsman. Chaderton procured a royal pardon in April 1377, but in a petition to the duke in May 1378, he complained that Molyneux had already attacked and wounded him once and now, accompanied by a large band of followers, continued to ride around the county in search of him.[60] The progression from the covert denial of justice to open violence seems clear. Unable to gain redress at the common law, the Molyneux chose self-help as the best way to avenge their dead kinsman. The real importance of the case lies in the fact that, having formed his confederacy to obtain what he saw as justice against a corrupt official, Thomas Molyneux then diversified into maintaining other people's quarrels as well as his own.[61] When he and his accomplices were finally brought to justice in 1380, the names and social standing of those involved indicate that it had grown well beyond its original purpose.[62] None of the culprits, with the exception of Molyneux himself, had any connection with the duke's affinity; the confederacy was an attempt by those outside the Lancastrian establishment to fend for themselves against those, like Chaderton, who had the advantage of swift access to the duke and his officers. It was an expression of discontent with the abuses endemic in the ducal administration, rather than of opposition to the duke himself, yet in seeking a remedy for their grievances, Molyneux and his supporters were obliged to undermine the whole basis of the duke's authority since Chaderton and his colleagues sought refuge behind it. The mayor of Liverpool, for example, had freed Molyneux from his imprisonment in Liverpool castle on his own authority and now refused to act on the duke's mandate for his rearrest.[63]

The Commons' analysis of the reason for local disorder thus fits the facts of the Chaderton case quite closely, but their preferred remedies hardly seem applicable to it at all. This was because they concentrated on the outward evidence of lordship, on the badges and liveries by which the magnates distinguished their followers. But the position of men like Chaderton and Chorlegh was too firmly attached to the administrative power they wielded by virtue of their offices ever to be disturbed by such external measures. Corrupt officials undoubtedly both valued and abused the protection of the magnates they served. William de Chorlegh, for instance, enhanced his social status by leasing quite extensive estates from Gaunt, took advantage of his office to oust potential rivals from their lands, and used his farm of the ducal fishery in the Ribble as the pretext for an attack on the prior of Penwortham and his servants.[64] Against the Commons' demands for specific legislation against this sort of abuse, the magnates maintained that they were capable of disciplining their own men and within the confines of the household and the indentured retinue, this was largely true. On their estates, however, they were heavily dependent on the efficiency and honesty of their officials, and their officials were precisely the class of men whom the Commons identified as the worst offenders against the law. Local violence was the inevitable reaction to this abuse of lordship, but the abuse was not practiced by the lords themselves, nor was it in their power to control it.

* * *

Nevertheless, in the febrile atmosphere of Richard II's minority, such local grievances could soon acquire a wider political significance and prove, in the long run, as damaging to the magnates as to the oppressed poor. The crises of 1387/8 and 1398/9 were certainly no simple consequence of an 'escalation of private feuds,' but in each case, the disturbed state of the palatinate of Lancaster and the grievances aroused by the exercise of John of Gaunt's lordship within it played their part in precipitating the national struggle.[65] As on other occasions in later medieval England, the growth of disorder encouraged the transition from private to public violence, and local quarrels became absorbed and intensified within a broader framework of magnate rivalries and political dissent.[66] Thomas Molyneux, disgraced by the duke of Lancaster in 1380, had reemerged by 1387 as the *precipuum consiliarium* of the duke of Ireland, 'of great power, at that time, in the counties of Lancashire and Cheshire.'[67] His newfound lordship quickly enabled him to defy the duke of Lancaster when, acting as Robert de Vere's deputy as justice of Chester, he refused to accept Gaunt's legitimate claim, as lord of the honor of Halton, to the manor of Barrow.[68] When Robert de Vere called on Molyneux to raise an army from the region in December 1387, the lines of division were as clear-cut at the local level as they were in national politics. De Vere was the current broker of royal patronage in the neighboring county of Cheshire; it is hardly necessary to invoke the harsh coercion alleged against Molyneux by the chroniclers to explain the ease with which he gathered an army;[69] his recruits, in Lancashire at least, were the casualties of bastard feudalism who had suffered from the Lancastrian administration of the shire and now saw, in service with the duke of Ireland, a chance of breaking its hold.[70]

Some, like Molyneux's principal ally in Lancashire, Sir Ralph Radcliffe of Blackburn, and the duke's retainer, Richard Massy of Rixton, had once enjoyed Gaunt's favor and now sought by force of arms to regain the place in the sun they had lost. Retained as an esquire by John of Gaunt in 1380 and employed on a number of commissions in the duchy, Radcliffe was appointed sheriff by the duke in March 1384 and so became ex officio one of the most powerful men in Lancashire. In order to gain the office, however, Radcliffe had proffered £80 per annum, twice the accustomed farm of the shire, and he evidently found an increment of this size impossible to sustain, for within two years, he was heavily in debt to the duke's officials. By July 1387, he had been removed from office altogether.[71] Massy refused to serve in Spain with the Lancastrian army in 1386 and although he sent an adequate substitute, had his annuity stopped in consequence.[72] Others, like Sir Gilbert Halsall and Sir Robert Clifton, came from well-established local families, but had been prevented, by their exclusion from John of Gaunt's affinity, from attaining the position in county society for which their birth had apparently fitted them. Halsall succeeded his father, himself a knight of the shire, in the manors of Halsall and Downholland by 1378, but the lack of opportunity for advancement in Lancashire meant that he had to make a career in the unglamorous business of soldiering in Ireland. Friendship and self-interest alike disposed him to look favorably on de Vere's call to arms, for by 1387, he was already a trusted associate of Sir Thomas Molyneux. Clifton's experience was similar, though the consequences of his exclusion from the Lancastrian affinity were harsher. In 1373 he had entered into a statute merchant of nearly £600 to one of the duke's retainers, Sir Robert Knolles, and, in order to meet his obligation, he was forced to mortgage his patrimony to a series of Lancastrian lessees. Unable to find the employment and patronage that could have eased his difficulties in the palatinate, Clifton turned to service in Ireland with Sir John Stanley, where he served in the same company as Halsall.[73]

A third group, including John de Aynesworth and John Radcliffe of Chaderton, had long been at violent loggerheads with the duke and his servants. Aynesworth was ejected from his manor of Middleton in 1366, when he was outlawed for a murder, and spent the rest of his life trying to recover the lost manor; this claim brought him into direct conflict with Gaunt and his clients since on Aynesworth's forfeiture the manor had been immediately seized by the duke and then granted out to a series of his servants. He attracted a large but loosely organized group of confederates, based on Manchester, whose activities were already causing the duke's servants anxiety in 1372.[74] Radcliffe was an illegitimate scion of the powerful Radcliffe clan, and his feud with Gaunt's retainer, William Barton of Rydale, brought him into alliance with John Aynesworth, giving him reason enough to wish for the overthrow of Lancastrian domination in the country.[75] For them, it was worth risking your head for the duke of Ireland. Radcot Bridge was only one more battle in a war they had long been fighting.

Precisely because the grievances that animated de Vere's supporters were largely local ones, they remained incapable of resolution as long as John of Gaunt and his servants continued to dominate the administrative and political structure of the palatinate. As a result, Lancashire did not share in the uneasy calm that descended on national politics once Richard II attained his majority in May 1389, for the North West was soon disturbed again by Sir Thomas Talbot's uprising. Although the roots of this insurrection have usually been sought in Cheshire, two of the three known ringleaders, Talbot and Sir Nicholas Clifton, were actually Lancashire knights, and it is in the context of John of Gaunt's control of the palatinate that this episode can best be understood.[76] Talbot's own career closely resembles those of his Lancashire contemporaries who were already hostile to the duke; he was a knight of some standing in the county who could find no place in the Lancastrian administration. In consequence, he made a name for himself by campaigning abroad and, while captain of Guines, attracted many Lancashire gentry to his company, including known dissidents like Sir Gilbert Halsall, Sir Robert Clifton, Sir Ralph Radcliffe, and John Radcliffe of Chaderton.[77] His command at Guines also gave him a specific grievance against the former Appellants and their government to add to an existing dispute with the duke of Lancaster over the manor of Rishton.[78] His confederate, Sir Nicholas Clifton, had been in trouble with the palatinate authorities as well and was currently pursuing a long vendetta against Thomas Foljambe, Gaunt's steward in the neighboring honor of the High Peak.[79] Both Talbot and Clifton thus nursed personal grievances against the Lancastrian affinity, which added vehemence to their opposition to Gaunt's support for a permanent peace with the French. Both were precisely the sort of professional soldiers and garrison captains who would find their occupation gone if a treaty were concluded with the French. The duke of Lancaster appeared responsible for denying them domestic advancement and now he seemed bent on removing their overseas employment as well. Their protest found an enthusiastic response in Cheshire, for there, too, Gaunt's lordship was felt to be damaging and intrusive. His most prominent retainer in the county, Sir Richard Aston, was currently locked in a dispute with Sir John Massy of Puddington, a former partisan of de Vere's, and in March 1392, the escheator of the palatinate, Adam Kingsley, was removed after a sharp struggle and replaced by Thomas Maistreson, another long-serving retainer of the duke of Lancaster.[80] When Richard II dispatched his envoys to pacify the North West, they were specifically instructed to assure the men of Cheshire that the duke would reform the abuses of his servants.[81]

The North Western rebellion of 1393 serves, therefore, to illustrate the tensions created by Lancastrian lordship in both its legitimate and illegitimate forms. Illegitimate lordship, in the sense of unauthorized oppression by the duke's officials, inevitably caused trouble. Yet the violence that broke out was not only the consequence of this abuse of lordship but, as in 1387, the inevitable result of its effective and legitimate use, which could not but lead to an increasing estrangement between the more and less favored within the palatinate. Consequently, it was only at the expense of his own followers that John of Gaunt could bring peace to the area; the chronicler's comment that, against the advice of many, the duke admitted the more important insurgents to familiar terms with him suggests that they were men of standing with some claim, hitherto unsatisfied, on his time and favor.[82]

In the short term, the discontents of the North West could be pacified by such concessions. But the problems that lay at the root of the region's characteristic violence remained unresolved, for the Lancastrian affinity continued to be the sole broker of power and patronage in the county palatine. Early in 1394, a statute was passed against the restiveness of Lancashire and Cheshire – the duke himself commented on 'the great malice at present reigning in our duchy' – but this did predictably little to calm the area; the appointment of a strong commission to apprehend outlaws in 1397 suggests that the palatinate remained chronically disturbed.[83] Far from condoning or encouraging this violence, no one suffered from it more than John of Gaunt himself. 'A magnate who tolerated . . . misrule in his country was damaging his own worship and inviting royal intervention,'[84] and from his power base in the palatinate of Chester, Richard II showed himself ready and willing to intervene.

However conspicuous their public concord, signs of tension in Gaunt's relationship with the king were visible in the North West as early as 1393. Both Talbot and Sir John Massy, leaders of the rising against the duke, were royal servants, and Nicholas Clifton was a client of the Holland family who stood high in Richard's favor.[85] The king had shown himself distressingly slow on that occasion to come to the aid of his uncle and he remained reluctant to bring Talbot, in particular, to justice.[86] If this was the freedom Richard allowed his followers, the duke could not fail to view the king's recruitment of an ever-growing band of royal retainers, principally from his own palatinate of Chester, with some concern.[87] Nor did Richard neglect to seek support from Lancashire as well; some members of the 'Cheshire guard' were certainly drawn from his uncle's palatinate and on a single day in March 1398, he took five knights and twenty-two esquires from Lancashire into his service.[88] Some of these men had seen service with Sir John Stanley in Ireland, the standard recourse for those unable to gain advancement in Lancashire itself, and others possessed a long history of opposition to the duke and his administration.[89] Six of the eight Lancashire gentlemen summoned before the Council to answer for their support of Robert de Vere were in Richard's service by the end of 1398.[90] Those who had most cause to resent Lancastrian control of the shire now held a position from which they could voice their grievances.

Gaunt's concern can be gauged by his reaction. Between September 1397 and his death in February 1399, nine of the fifteen surviving indentures of retainer the duke concluded were with Lancashire and Cheshire men;[91] a further seven undated grants of annuities assigned on the honor of Lancaster can be ascribed to the same period.[92] It is this program of defensive retaining, as much as Henry Bolingbroke's prudent generosity in 1399, that explains the steep increase in the cost of annuities charged to the palatinate, from £424 14*s.* 4*d.* in 1394/5 to £1,231 13*s.* 9*d.* by September 1400.[93] Yet despite the duke's heavy outlay on annuities, the pressure of royal government on Lancashire continued to mount for although Richard was content to allow his uncle an honorific position in his new principality of Chester, he was also concerned to sap Gaunt's independence with the palatinate of Lancaster by the exercise of his judicial prerogatives.[94] Cases before the palatinate justices were called into King's Bench with increasing frequency; the number of royal pardons for offenses committed within the duke's jurisdiction transmitted from Westminster escalated rapidly: from one in 1396, to four in 1397, to eighteen in 1398.[95] Richard II's growing influence on the affairs of the palatinate was soon signaled by the political renaissance of Sir Ralph Radcliffe. After his dismissal from the shrievalty in 1387 and his arrest in 1388, Radcliffe continued to trouble the ducal administration during the 1390s, but in September 1397, now a king's knight, he was returned as one of Lancashire's knights of the shire and at the Michaelmas immediately following, regained the shrievalty of the county at the old render of £40 per annum.[96] As sheriff, he was able to throw the considerable influence of his office behind the nascent royalist party within the palatinate, with the result that some of John of Gaunt's retainers ceased to enjoy the protection the duke's lordship had previously offered. The opponents of one Lancastrian, Robert Workesley, sought to win their suit against him by an overtly political appeal to the newfound strength of the crown, alleging that Workesley had ridden against the king at Radcot Bridge and claiming, further, that he had no fear for his illegally held lands while his lord of Lancaster lived.[97]

The political lineup was once again clear and the case a test of strength; the petitioner, Nicholas Workesley, was an archer of the crown in the Cheshire guard, while his principal maintainer, Sir John Massy of Tatton, had been one of the ringleaders of the 1393 uprising.[98] Predictably, the king took the part of his servants and ordered the sheriff of Lancashire to arrest Robert Workesley on sight; the man sent to transfer him to the Tower was Thomas Holford of Plumley, once a Lancastrian loyalist but now one of the seven esquire-commanders of Richard's praetorian guard, the Cheshire watch.[99] John of Gaunt's failure to do justice to all his subjects thus provided the king with a pretext to breach the privileges of the palatinate; Richard's lavish expenditure on annuities gave him the means to exploit that breach. Even in the heartland of his power, John of Gaunt was now threatened by the growth of the king's ambitions. Despite his heavy outlay on new annuities, the duke's affinity could not, by 1398, maintain the predominance that had been the condition of political life in Lancashire for the last thirty years. Viewed from the palatinate of Lancaster, Richard II's 'obsession' with Cheshire looks a good deal more rational and aggressive than a desperate search for security, while the accepted picture of close and amicable cooperation between the royal and Lancastrian affinities, lasting until Gaunt's death, needs to be heavily revised.[100]

* * *

What conclusions can be drawn from this study of John of Gaunt's lordship at work in the palatinate of Lancaster? The first relates to the duke of Lancaster himself. He was undoubtedly the richest and most powerful English magnate of his day, exercising an influence that aroused the envy, and sometimes the suspicion, of his contemporaries. Yet his local authority in Lancashire, as in some other parts of the country, seems less than effective.[101] He had difficulty enforcing the decisions of his own palatinate courts, he was unable to resolve the long-standing antagonisms that jeopardized the peace of the shire, and despite his best efforts, he alienated a sizable proportion of the county's gentry. The reasons for this appear to be structural rather than personal, inherent in the nature of the duke's authority rather than the result of any negligence on his part. There were magnates, such as John Holland, duke of Exeter, or George, duke of Clarence, who, by their own weakness or ineptitude, forfeited their inherited local authority.[102] But it is unlikely that John of Gaunt was one of their number; whatever else contemporaries thought of him, they remained impressed, even intimidated by his powerful and exigent personality.[103] Equally, while it may be argued that the courtly and chivalric principles on which the duke sometimes recruited his retainers reduced the effectiveness of his affinity as an instrument of local political dominance, the argument can hardly be applied to the palatinate of Lancaster, where Gaunt's landed preeminence and institutional privileges rendered him the inevitable ruler of the shire.[104] The uprisings and disturbances that characterized Lancashire during Richard II's reign make it clear that, whatever the limitations on his authority, the exercise of the duke's lordship still aroused powerful antagonisms. Yet this was less the consequence of an excess of Lancastrian lordship than of an absence of alternative lords capable of providing employment and reward for those who could not find a place in the duke's service. Active opposition to Lancastrian rule in the county from those who felt themselves denied their legal rights by the predominance of the duke's men was sparse and, save in the case of Sir Thomas Molyneux, inconsequential. Passive dissatisfaction on the part of those who felt themselves denied their rightful consequence was widespread. In his double role as lord of the whole palatinate of Lancaster and as a good lord to his own followers, John of Gaunt's lapses into partiality were few and relatively venial, but their consequences, in both regional and national terms, were serious. By their service with Robert de Vere in 1387, by their support for Sir Thomas Talbot in 1393, by their willing acquiescence in the royalist revanche of 1398, the dissatisfied within the palatinate took advantage of every crisis in national politics to undermine the local position of the duke and his affinity.

There is a sense, therefore, in which *more* lordship, not less, was the only answer to the palatinate's problems. A society more purely 'bastard feudal,' in the accepted sense of a number of lords each offering their patronage and protection to the gentlemen of the county, might have remedied many of the discontents so violently expressed in Lancashire. Yet it would not have removed the second great cause of offense highlighted by this study: the maintenance and oppression practiced by some palatinate officials. These were men who acted in the name of the duke but apparently without his authority or approval; within the confines of a single wapentake they could offer a form of lordship no less effective than the duke's. As the 'second kings' of the shire they were the object of attack by the parliamentary Commons, but the remedies suggested by the Commons, principally that the protection of the great should be removed, were hardly applicable to the realities of the situation in Lancashire. It is not to an excess of lordship that the disorders of the palatinate should be ascribed but to an older and less tractable problem, the endemic failure of medieval rulers to control their local agents. Far from encouraging the depredations of his officials, John of Gaunt suffered from them both financially, in terms of lost revenue, and politically, as the discontents created by the corruption of officialdom encouraged some of the Lancashire gentry to look outside the county for the lordship that would right their wrongs. In this sense the duke of Lancaster was himself as much a casualty of 'bastard feudalism,' a victim of his officials' oppressions, as any of the parliamentary Commons who petitioned him so vehemently for redress of their grievances.

Notes

1 Sir John Fortescue, *The Governance of England*, ed. C. Plummer (Oxford, 1885), pp. xv–xvi; J. E. A. Joliffe, *The Constitutional History of Medieval England* (London, 1937), pp. 424–30; H. M. Cam, 'The Quality of English Feudalism,' in *Law-Finders and Law-Makers* (London, 1962), pp. 53–8; J. G. Bellamy, *Crime and Public Order in the Later Middle Ages* (London, 1973), pp. 22–4.

2 C. Carpenter, 'The Beauchamp Affinity: A Study of Bastard Feudalism at Work,' *English Historical Review* 95 (1980): 514; G. L. Harriss, introduction to *England in the Fifteenth Century*, by K. B. MacFarlane (London, 1981), pp. ix–x.

3 J. R. Maddicott, 'Thomas of Lancaster and Sir Robert Holland,' *English Historical*

Review 86 (1971): 449; C. Carpenter, 'Fifteenth-Century Biographies,' *Historical Journal* 25 (1982): 732.

4 R. A. Griffiths, *The Reign of King Henry VI* (London, 1981), p. 570.

5 Nigel Saul, *Knights and Esquires: The Gloucestershire Gentry in the Fourteenth Century* (Oxford, 1981), p. 261; S. M. Wright, *The Derbyshire Gentry in the Fifteenth Century*, Derbyshire Record Society, no. 8 (1983), p. 147; I. Rowney, 'Government and Patronage in the Fifteenth Century: Staffordshire, 1439–1459,' *Midland History* 8 (1983): 49–69.

6 K. B. MacFarlane, 'Parliament and "Bastard Feudalism,"' *Transactions of the Royal Historical Society*, 4th ser., 26 (1944): 73.

7 For example, J. R. Maddicott, 'The County Community and the Making of Public Opinion in Fourteenth-Century England,' *Transactions of the Royal Historical Society*, 5th ser., 28 (1978): 27–43; R. R. Davies, *Lordship and Society in the March of Wales, 1282–1400* (Oxford, 1978), pp. 249–73; R. Virgoe, 'The Crown and Local Government: East Anglia under Richard II,' in *The Reign of Richard II*, ed. F. R. H. du Boulay and C. M. Barron (London, 1971), pp. 218–41; Wright, pp. 93–118; I. Rowney, 'Resources and Retaining in Yorkist England: William, Lord Hastings and the Honour of Tutbury,' in *Property and Politics: Essays in Later Medieval English History*, ed. A. J. Pollard (Gloucester, 1984), pp. 139–55.

8 *Rotuli Parliamentorum* (London, 1783), 3:100; L. C. Hector and B. F. Harvey, eds., *The Westminster Chronicle, 1381–1394* (Oxford, 1982), pp. 80–2; J. R. Lumby, ed., *Chronicon Henrici Knighton*, Rolls Ser. (1895), 2:266–70.

9 Hector and Harvey, eds., pp. 354–8; *Rotuli Parliamentorum*, 3:265.

10 G. Holmes, *The Later Middle Ages* (Edinburgh, 1962), p. 167.

11 C. Carpenter, 'Law, Justice and Landowners in Later Medieval England,' *Law and History Review* 1 (1983): 226–31.

12 P. R. Cross, *The Langley Family and Its Cartulary: A Study in Late Medieval 'Gentry,'* Dugdale Society Occasional Papers, no. 22 (1974), p. 14; J. M. W. Bean, *The Decline of English Feudalism, 1215–1540* (Manchester, 1968), pp. 148–97.

13 A. Smith, 'Litigation and Politics: Sir John Fastolf's Defence of His English Property,' in Pollard, ed., p. 73; S. J. Payling, 'Inheritance and Local Politics in the Later Middle Ages: The Case of Ralph, Lord Cromwell, and the Heriz Inheritance,' *Nottingham Medieval Studies* 30 (1986): 94–5.

14 E. Powell, 'Arbitration and Law in the Late Middle Ages,' *Transactions of the Royal Historical Society*, 5th ser., 33 (1983): 49–67; Carole Rawcliffe, 'The Great Lord as Peacemaker,' in *Law and Social Change in British History*, ed. J. A. Guy and H. G. Beale (London, 1984), pp. 34–53.

15 Public Record Office (PRO), Duchy of Lancaster (DL) 29/728/11976 m. 1, 11978 m. 1, 11980 m. 1, 11984 m. 1; M. J. Bennett, *Community, Class and Careerism: Cheshire and Lancashire Society in the Age of Sir Gawain and the Green Knight* (Cambridge, 1983), pp. 74–5.

16 W. Hardy, ed., *The Charters of the Duchy of Lancaster* (London, 1845), no. 11.

17 PRO, Justices Itinerant (JUST) 1/442/A mm. 15–22, 442/C; Exchequer (E) 199/21/9.

18 PRO, Palatinate of Lancaster (PL) 14/154/2/7, PL 3/1/171.

19 G. H. Tupling, ed., *South Lancashire in the Reign of Edward II*, Chetham Society, 3d ser., 1, (1949): xliii–xlix; *Calendar of Patent Rolls (CPR) 1348–50*, p. 533.

20 G. O. Sayles, ed., *Select Cases in the Court of King's Bench*, Selden Society, 82 (1965) 6:89–91; PRO, E 175/2/27.

21 PRO, King's Bench (KB) 27/453 m. 72, 463 m. 55, 458 m. 64.
22 PRO, Common Pleas (CP) 40/418 m. 258[d], 440 m. 403; PL 1/1 m. 7[d].
23 PRO, DL 37/3 m. 2; KB 27/463/Rex m. 28[d]; *CPR 1391–96*, p. 388.
24 W. Beamont, *Annals of the Lords of Warrington*, Chetham Society, o.s., 86 (1872), 1:201; PRO, PL 14/154/5/7; *Victoria History of the Counties of England: Lancashire* (London, 1907–14), 6:205 (hereafter cited as *VCH Lancs.*); PRO, KB 27/469/Rex m. 4[d], 460/Rex m. 14; Chancery (C) 260/89/64.
25 Hector and Harvey, eds. (n. 8 above), p. 82.
26 PRO, KB 27/463/Rex m. 28[d], 464/Rex m. 5[d]; N. B. Lewis, ed., 'Indentures of Retinue with John of Gaunt, duke of Lancaster, Enrolled in Chancery, 1367–1399,' *Camden Miscellany* 22, Camden Society, 4th ser., vol. 1 (1964), no. 2.
27 *Calendar of Close Rolls (CCR) 1364–68*, p. 179; PRO, JUST 3/165/A m. 11; PL 16/1/1 m. 2; DL 37/3/m. 1[d]; J. Parker, ed., *Lancashire Palatine Plea Rolls*, Chetham Society, n.s., 87 (1928): 45–6, 57–60.
28 PRO, Palatine of Chester (CHES) 29/80 m. 21.
29 E. C. Lodge and R. Somerville eds., *John of Gaunt's Register 1379–1383*, Camden Society, 3d ser., vol. 56 (1937), nos. 302, 388, 565, 37; J. Bain ed., *Calendar of Documents Relating to Scotland, 1357–1500* (Edinburgh, 1888), no. 299; see Lancashire Record Office (LRO), Crumblehome MS Dd/Cm/1/12–15, 18–19, for the difficulties a litigant faced in bringing Tunstall to answer an assize.
30 PRO, PL 14/154/3/82; *CPR 1396–99*, p. 177.
31 PRO, DL 42/1/76v; 37/3 m. 21; PL 14/154/6/121.
32 Bennett (n. 15 above), pp. 68–9.
33 MacFarlane (n. 6 above), p. 169.
34 J. P. Rylands, 'Two Lancashire Rolls of Arms,' *Transactions of the Historic Society of Lancashire and Cheshire* 37 (1888): 149–60; A. R. Wagner, *A Catalogue of English Medieval Rolls of Arms* (Oxford, 1950), pp. 63–5.
35 *List of Sheriffs for England and Wales*, PRO, Lists and Indexes 9 (1898), p. 72; *List of Escheators for England*, PRO, Lists and Indexes 72 (1932), p. 72; *Return of Members of Parliament* (London, 1878), 1:16–257; *CPR 1360–64*, p. 366, *1367–70*, p. 418; pp. 59–63; Duchy of Lancaster Records, *CPR, Reports of the Deputy Keeper of the Public Records* 40 (1879): 523 (hereafter cited as *DKR*); Bodleian Library (Bodl.), Dodsworth MS 87, fol. 78v.
36 *CPR 1369–77*, pp. 112, 127, 192, 229, 269, 388; PRO, Special Collections (SC) 1/58/43; *DKR* 40, pp. 521–4; Bodl., Dodsworth MS 87, fols. 75, 76v, 79. A similar division of responsibilities within the county community of Lincolnshire is indicated in B. W. McLane, 'A Case Study of Violence and Litigation in the Early Fourteenth Century: The Disputes of Robert Godsfield of Sutton-le-Marsh.' *Nottingham Medieval Studies* 28 (1984): 25.
37 PRO, E 179/130/24, 27, 28; 340/308(5).
38 PRO, PL 14/154/2(45).
39 PRO, PL 14/154/3/16; *CPR 1391–96*, p. 388; *DKR* 36 (1875), app. 2, p. 366.
40 Robert Somerville, *History of the Duchy of Lancaster* (London, 1953), p. 374; *CPR 1396–99*, pp. 310, 324, 434, 508.
41 PRO, PL 14/154/2/50, 60.
42 For example, one of Croft's accomplices, William Singleton, who also obtained his pardon at the request of Thomas Mowbray, was later granted an annuity by Gaunt. *CPR 1391–96*, p. 388; PRO, DL 42/16 f. 171.
43 W. Langton, ed., *Abstracts of Inquisitions Post-Mortem*, Chetham Society, o.s., vol.

95, no. 1 (1875), pp. 50–3; S. Armitage-Smith, ed., *John of Gaunt's Register, 1372–1376*, Camden Society, 3d ser., vols. 20–21 (1911), no. 1010; PRO, PL 14/154/5/26.

44 For the dispute, see PRO, PL 3/1/74; PL 16/1/1 m. 2; Bodl., Dodsworth MS 87, fol. 77v; PRO, PL 14/154/3/82; *Rotuli Parliamentorum* (n. 8 above), 3: 204. The duke eventually regained possession of the disputed lands and granted them to Katherine Swynford who, in her turn, sold them to Sir John Stanley. As a mark of favor he was forgiven 50 marks of the price. PRO, DL 28/3/2/18; LRO, Finch of Mawdesley MS Dd/Fi/8/5.

45 I. Rowney, 'Arbitration in Gentry Disputes of the Later Middle Ages,' *History* 69 (1982): 367–76; E. Powell, 'Arbitration and Law in England in the Late Middle Ages,' *Transactions of the Royal Historical Society*, 5th ser., 33 (1983): 49–68.

46 For example, the prominence of Sir Gilbert Halsall in negotiating such settlements: LRO, Molyneaux of Sefton MS Dd/M/34/19; LRO, Scarisbrick MS Dd/Sc/28/4, 37/10; J. C. Atkinson, ed., *The Councher Book of Furness Abbey*, Chetham Society, 3d ser., vol. 18 (1970), nos. 106, 221. For Halsall, see below, p. 27.

47 PRO, DL 37/3 mm. 17^{d}, 22.

48 Armitage-Smith, ed., *Register, 1372–1376*, no. 53; PRO, DL 42/15/45.

49 *CPR 1377–81*, p. 505; Lodge and Somerville, eds., *John of Gaunt's Register, 1379–1383* (n. 29 above), nos. 302, 565.

50 *Statutes of the Realm*, Record Commission (1810–28), 1:33–35; D. Hughes, *A Study of Social and Constitutional Tendencies in the Early Years of Edward III* (London, 1915), pp. 194–201, 213–15; W. R. Jones, '*Rex et Ministri*: English Local Government and the Crisis of 1341,' *Journal of British Studies* 13, no. 1 (1973): 1–20; cf. Saul (n. 5 above), pp. 149–50, 183, for comparable instances in Gloucestershire.

51 *CPR 1374–77*, p. 320.

52 PRO, KB 27/462/Rex m. 13, 454/Rex m. 13.

53 PRO, KB 27/442/Rex mm. 1^{d}, 4, 24^{d}, 444/Rex mm. 10, 10^{d}, 455/Rex m. 2; PRO, E 199/21/7, 8.

54 For example, PRO, JUST 1/442/B m. 5, 451/B m. 1; JUST 3/155 m. 9; PL 1/1 m. 9.

55 PRO, PL 3/1/174, 155, 83.

56 PRO, PL 3/1/39; *Lancashire Palatine Plea Rolls* (n. 27 above), pp. 46–7, 57–60.

57 Lodge and Somerville, eds., *Register, 1379–1383* (n. 29 above), no. 295; PRO, KB 27/455/Rex m. 2; PRO, E 199/21/7, 8.

58 Contrast J. R. Maddicott, *Thomas of Lancaster* (Oxford, 1970), p. 36.

59 In 1376, Chaderton alleged that the findings of the original inquest on the body had been maliciously fabricated by the coroners, William Bredkirk and Gilbert Norreys. Despite his previous record, the council seemed disposed to believe Chaderton's story and swiftly removed Bredkirk from his office. PRO, KB 27/454/m. 2; PRO, SC 8/39/1914, 1915, 99/4930, 166/8288; *CCR 1374–77*, p. 312.

60 *CCR 1377–81*, p. 125; PRO, PL 3/1/165, 180.

61 LRO, Blundell of Ince Blundell MS, Dd/In/53/48–50; see also LRO, Dd/M/34/19 for an example of Molyneux's maintenance, this time on his own behalf.

62 Although three members of the Molyneux family still formed the nucleus of the gang, the other members were esquires like William Tunstall, Geoffrey de Osbaldeston, and John Botiller of Marton. Lodge and Somerville, eds., *John of Gaunt's Register, 1379–1383*, no. 302; *CPR 1377–81*, p. 505.

63 PRO, PL 3/1/180.

64 PRO, DL 25/2096, 42/1/94; 15/38: LRO, Farington of Worden MS, Dd/F/1455[A]; Armitage-Smith, ed., *John of Gaunt's Register, 1372–76* (n. 43 above), no. 1116.

65 R. L. Storey, *The End of the House of Lancaster* (London, 1966), p. 27.

66 Hector and Harvey, eds. (n. 8 above), p. 222; Lumby, ed. (n. 8 above), 2: 251. See J. L. Gillespie, 'Thomas Mortimer and Thomas Molyneux: Radcot Bridge and the Appeal of 1397,' *Albion* 7 (1975): 164, for Molyneux's career.

67 Scott L. Waugh, 'The Profits of Violence: The Minor Gentry in the Rebellion of 1321–1322 in Gloucestershire and Herefordshire,' *Speculum* 52 (1977): 843–69; E. Powell, 'Proceedings before the Justices of the Peace at Shrewsbury in 1414: A Supplement to the Shropshire Peace Roll,' *English Historical Review* 49 (1984): 535–50; R. Jeffs, 'The Poynings-Percy Dispute,' *Bulletin of the Institute of Historical Research* 34 (1961): 148–164; R. Virgoe, 'William Tailboys and Lord Cromwell: Crime and Politics in Lancastrian England,' *Bulletin of the John Rylands Library* 55 (1973): 459–82.

68 P. Morgan, *War and Society in Medieval Cheshire, 1272–1403*, Chetham Society, 3d ser., 34 (1987): 192. The Lancastrian administration began proceedings to recover the manor in 1388 and eventually regained seisin in October 1390. PRO, DL 29/16/202 m. 2; PRO, SC 6/773/6 m. 3[d].

69 T. Favent, 'Historia Mirabilis Parliamenti,' M. Mcisack ed., *Camden Miscellany* 9 Camden Society, 3d ser., 27 (1926): 4–5.

70 *CCR 1385–89*, p. 393 and PRO, DL 37/3/m. 24[d] give a good indication of who supported de Vere in Lancashire.

71 J. S. Roskell, *The Knights of the Shire of the County Palatine of Lancaster, 1377–1460*, Chetham Society, n.s., 96 (1937): 83–7; PRO, PL 3/1/50, 51; DL 43/15/6 m. 3, 37/3 m. 3; Lodge and Somerville, eds. *John of Gaunt's Register, 1379–83* (n. 29 above). no. 1237.

72 W. Beamont, *An Account of the Rolls of the Honour of Halton* (Warrington, 1879), p. 22; LRO, Massy of Rixton MS, Dd/X/293/34; PRO, DL 29/16/202 m. 2.

73 LRO, Clifton of Lytham MS, Dd/C1/150; *CPR 1381–85*, p. 290, *1385–89*, p. 114, 232; PRO, E 101/247/1/m. 9, 41/18 mm. 1, 4. 12; *CPR 1391–96*, p. 549; LRO, Dd/M/17/39–43, 49/39–40; Dd/C1/174/1253–59; *CCR 1374–77*, p. 197, 365; *CPR 1385–88*, p. 214.

74 PRO, SC 8/44/2173; PRO, DL 42/1/142v; PRO, PL 16/1/1 m. 3; PRO, KB 9/55C m. 2; 27/449/Rex m. 1, 453 m. 72, 460 m. 41.

75 *VCH* (n. 24 above), 5: 116, n. 20; Bodl., Dodsworth MS 87, fol. 76; PRO, PL 14/154/1/28; W. Farrer ed., *Lancashire Final Concords*, Lancashire and Cheshire Record Society, no. 50. (1905), pt. 3, p. 37; PRO, KB 27/455/m. 31; 457/Rex m. 63; *CPR 1370–74*, p. 401.

76 J. G. Bellamy, 'The Northern Rebellions in the Later Years of Richard II,' *Bulletin of the John Rylands Library* 47 (1965): 254–74, gives the best account, now supplemented by Morgan (n. 68 above), pp. 193–6.

77 PRO, C 76/72/mm. 5, 16, 81/1048–55.

78 On appointment to his command at Guines in 1388, he was prevented from taking up the post for six months by the former captain, John Drayton, and was unable to obtain decisive support from the council. He was eventually compensated for the financial loss he incurred by Richard II in 1391. PRO, E 404/14/96 (July 22, 1391); *CPR 1385–89*, p. 416, 427; PRO, E 403/533 m. 14. *VCH Lanc.*, 6: 345; PRO, PL 3/1/146; Bodl., Dodsworth MS 87, fol. 79.

79 PRO, PL 3/1/31; KB 9/989 m. 15, 27/529/Rex m. 14^{d}; Bodl, Gough MS, Yorkshire 5, fol. 26; Nottinghamshire Record Office, Foljambe of Obserton MS, Dd/Fj/4/2/1; *CCR 1392–96*, p. 109; *CPR 1391–96*, p. 237.

80 'Recognizance Rolls of Chester,' *DKR* 36 (1875), app. 2, p. 13; *CPR 1391–96*, p. 40; *Calendar of Fine Rolls, 1383–91*, p. 342; ibid., *1391–99*, pp. 8, 18. For Maistreson in the duke's service, see Armitage-Smith, ed., *John of Gaunt's Register, 1372–76* (n. 43 above), no. 779; PRO, DL 29/738/12096 m. 3.

81 PRO, C 47/14/6/44.

82 J. de Trokelowe and Anon., 'Annales Ricardi Secondi et Henrici Quarti,' in *Chronica et Annales*, ed. H. T. Riley, Rolls Ser. (1886), p. 161; PRO, DL 43/15/6 m. 3 shows that many of the rebels were pardoned the fines imposed on them by the justices at Lancaster.

83 *Statutes of the Realm* (n. 50 above), 2:89; PRO, PL 3/1/19; Bodl., Dodsworth MS 87, fol. 80v; LRO, Towneley of Towneley MS, Dd/To/K/9/6.

84 Hariss (n. 2 above), p. xxi.

85 *CPR 1391–96*, p. 182; 'Recognizance Rolls of Chester,' *DKR* 36 (1875), app. 2, p. 330; PRO, SC 8/223/11128–30; KB 27/531/m. 52^{d}.

86 John of Gaunt issued a mandate for a commission to arrest Talbot within his palatinate on August 22, 1393; a similar order within the royal palatinate of Chester was not issued until October 22. See Bodl., Dodsworth MS 87, fol. 77v; 'Recognizance Rolls of Chester,' *DKR* 36 (1875) app. 2, p. 330; *Rotuli Parliamentorum* (n. 8 above), 3: 316–17; PRO, KB 27/532/Rex m. 16.

87 C. Given-Wilson, *The Royal Household and the King's Affinity: Service, Politics, and Finance in England, 1360–1413* (New Haven, Conn., 1986), pp. 219–23.

88 PRO, KB 27/550/Rex m. 18^{d}; *CPR 1396–99*, pp. 521, 524.

89 For example, John Aldelm, Sir Gilbert Halsall, Nicholas Orrell, PRO, E 101/42/18 mm. 12. 18; 10 m. 1; 'Recognizance Rolls of Chester,' *DKR* 36 (1875), app. 2, p. 215.

90 Sir Robert Clifton; Sir Gilbert Halsall; Richard Massy of Rixton; John Radcliffe of Chaderton; Sir Ralph Radcliffe; William Rixton. See PRO, E 101/42/10 m. 1; *CPR 1396–99*, pp. 521, 524; 'Recognizance Rolls of Chester,' *DKR* 36 (1875), app. 2, p. 407.

91 PRO, DL 42/15/46, 56, 56v; 16/42; Nottingham University Library, Middleton MS, Mi/F/10; Lewis, ed. (n. 26 above), nos. 32–42.

92 PRO, DL 42/15/6, 12, 21, 25v; 16/231.

93 PRO, DL 29/728/11984 m. 1; 738/12096 m. 1.

94 PRO, DL 42/1, f. 49; R. R. Davies, 'Richard II and the Principality of Chester,' in du Boulay and Barron, eds. (n. 7 above), p. 266.

95 PRO, KB 27/549/Rex m. 17; 552 m. 18; PL 14/154/3/84–94, 96, 99, 101–5; 6/4, 14, 71–3.

96 PRO, PL 3/1/34; DL 42/15, f. 114; Roskell (n. 71 above), p. 84.

97 *Rotuli Parliamentorum*, 3:445; PRO, CHES 2/69 m. 11.

98 *DKR* 36 (1875), app. 2, p. 540.

99 *CCR 1396–99*, p. 348; PRO, E 403/559 m. 14; J. L. Gillespie, 'Richard II's Cheshire Archers,' *Transactions of the Historic Society of Lancashire and Cheshire* 125 (1975): 19. When the Lancastrian inheritance was confiscated in February 1399, the late duke's seneschal and constable at Halton (Ches.) was removed from his office on the warrant of the duke of Surrey and replaced by Holford, PRO, DL 30/41/3 m. 2.

100 Given-Wilson (n. 87 above), p. 223; A. Tuck, *Richard II and the English Nobility* (London, 1973), pp. 209–10; Bennett (n. 15 above), p. 169.
101 S. K. Walker, 'Lancaster v. Dallingridge: A Franchisal Dispute in Fourteenth-Century Sussex,' *Sussex Archaeological Collections* 112 (1983): 87–94.
102 R. A. Griffiths, 'Local Rivalries and National Politics: The Percies, the Nevilles and the duke of Exeter, 1452–1455,' *Speculum* 43 (1968): 589–632; C. Carpenter, 'The Duke of Clarence and the Midlands: A Study in the Interplay of Local and National Politics,' *Midland History* 11 (1986): 23–48.
103 Hector and Harvey, eds. (n. 8 above), p. 112; *Rotuli Parliamentorum*, 3:313.
104 A. Goodman, 'John of Gaunt: Paradigm of the Late Fourteenth-Century Crisis,' *Transactions of the Royal Historical Society*, 5th ser., 36 (1987): 146–7.

2

Sir Richard Abberbury (*c.* 1330–1399) and his kinsmen: the rise and fall of a gentry family*

Sir Richard Abberbury of Donnington (Berks.) and his son, also Sir Richard, play a minor but instructive part in the history of Richard II's reign. Sir Richard *le pere* was, successively, a retainer of Edward prince of Wales, 'first master' to the prince's son and heir, Richard of Bordeaux, a knight of Richard's chamber and chamberlain to the King's first wife, Anne of Bohemia. Sir Richard *le filz* was a retainer, chamber-knight and, finally, chamberlain to Richard's uncle, John of Gaunt, duke of Lancaster. If 'the courtier civil servant is the important man, and the growth of this class the key to the history of the later middle ages',[1] then the Abberburys, father and son, were two such important men. A study of their respective careers, hitherto confused by historians,[2] if it cannot unlock the whole of later medieval history, can at least cast some light on the complicated politics of Richard II's reign, for Sir Richard *le pere* was intimately involved in the Appellancy crisis and the fortunes of Sir Richard *le filz* appear to have been deeply affected by the Lancastrian usurpation. Such a study may also be used to examine the social structure of medieval England. Members of an international chivalric class, by virtue of their extensive military and diplomatic experience, the Abberburys nevertheless retained strong links with the county society from which they sprang and sought, by their employment at court, to consolidate and advance their local standing. If, as it has recently been argued, both Richard II and Henry IV deliberately pursued a 'gentry retaining policy', born of 'a recognition of the crucial rôle played by the upper gentry, and . . . a hope that their local prominence could be harnessed, if necessary, to the cause of the crown'[3] then the means by which families like the Abberburys attained and exercised that local prominence bear more careful investigation than they have hitherto received. By setting the careers of father and son within the longer perspective of the rise and subsequent decline of the whole family, the Abberburys' position within county society can be fairly exactly defined and their efforts to improve it, by marriage and the purchase of land, by religious benefactions and ambitious building projects, examined in some detail. The results can be used to answer some of the questions historians are currently asking about the importance, the independence and the motivation of the late medieval gentry.[4] 'The compilation of biographies of the gentry is slow and tedious work'[5] but the task has a value beyond the antiquarian if, by examining English society in the later middle ages from the point of view of the retainer rather than the patron, it can illuminate the nature and workings of that network of clientage and patronage known as 'bastard feudalism'.

From the first, lordship had an important part to play in the fortunes of the Abberbury family. Established as early as 1208 as one of the leading peasant families in the north Oxfordshire village of Adderbury,[6] they owed their subsequent rise from the ranks of the free tenantry largely to the talents of Master Thomas Abberbury. An Oxford graduate, Master Thomas gained his first benefice through the patronage of a local monastic house, the abbey of Abingdon,[7] but it was in the service of successive Archbishops of York that he made his way and the fortunes of his kinsmen. One of Archbishop Wickwane's clerks by 1280, Master Thomas was appointed official of York in 1288 and continued to preside over the consistory court of the diocese until 1300.[8] As early as 1296, however, he had begun to form an association with a second patron, Walter Langton, Master of St. Leonard's Hospital in York, bishop elect of Coventry and Lichfield and, most important, Treasurer of England.[9] He was successively Langton's precentor, chancellor and vicar-general at Lichfield and when, in 1301, Langton was summoned to the Curia to answer the charges of corruption and immorality laid against him, Abberbury was appointed by the Pope to administer the diocese in the bishop's absence.[10] This association with Langton was the crucial advance in Master Thomas's career. As Treasurer, enjoying the full confidence of the ageing Edward I, Langton had a claim to be the most powerful man in England; none but the King could stand against him, he once boasted to an opponent. As his principal lieutenant and *abrokur*, Master Thomas had plenty of opportunity to share in, and profit from, his master's power.[11]

Abberbury's time at York had earned him the rewards appropriate to a successful ecclesiastical career, a prebend and a canon's seat in the Minster.[12] Langton's patronage brought him further benefits,[13] while Master Thomas's close association with the Treasurer in his financial dealings earned him some profitable opportunities in the land-market. Though Abberbury had been picking up scattered parcels of land, in several areas of the country, for some years past,[14] the start of his association with Langton in 1295 marks a new intensity and concentration in his purchasing. During the next ten years he acquired, in Oxfordshire, the manor and advowson of Steeple Aston, the manors of Souldern and Sibford Gower and quite extensive lands in Glympton, Clifton and Kidlington, thus creating a reasonably compact group of estates in the north-west of the county, lying largely between the valleys of the Cherwell and the Evenlode.[15] In Berkshire, his purchase of the manor of Bradley 'Gimmings' and two carucates of land at Eastbury began the consolidation of a second group of properties to the north of Donnington.[16] Between them these estates, which were to remain the core of the Abberbury family's holdings, cost Master Thomas a good £600, though since not all the lands were bought on the open market, this was probably some way below their true value. His manor of Old Shoreham, for instance, was acquired from the knightly family of St. Valery, who were heavily in debt to Abberbury's patron, Walter Langton; at Preston Bisset, acting as the Treasurer's agent, Master Thomas intruded himself into the sub-manor of Cowley by force; at Souldern, Langton maintained one of the litigants in a plea over possession of the manor and then, as the price of his support, ordered him to enfeoff Master Thomas in the property.[17] At his death in May 1307,[18] therefore, a convenient four months before the arrest of his patron, Abberbury left his family a sizeable estate in Oxfordshire and Berkshire, but one to which the title was, in some cases, debateable or defective.[19] The task of defending this uncertain inheritance fell to Master Thomas's brother, Walter, and Walter's eldest son, Richard.[20]

Already middle-aged by the time of his brother's death, Walter Abberbury pursued a policy of consolidating the family holdings in northern Oxfordshire at the expense of the Berkshire estates. Further purchases at Adderbury itself were followed by new acquisitions at Barford, Kidlington and Steeple Aston while, at considerable cost, Walter finally secured the contentious manor of Souldern.[21] In Berkshire, the family pursued a more selective strategy, purchasing a manor in East Hendred but selling off lands at Eastbury and Peasmore, as well as granting an estate at Bradley to the abbot and convent of Abingdon.[22] This apparent concentration of the Abberburys' interests in their native county of Oxfordshire was taken a step further by the increasing administrative prominence of Walter's son, Richard Abberbury. Richard had followed family tradition by seeking advancement in the service of an ecclesiastical lord, John of Pontoise, bishop of Winchester, during the 1290s,[23] but it was not until the end of Edward II's reign that he was able to establish himself securely amongst the county élite. As Edward II and the Despensers sought to bring the rapidly deteriorating crisis of disorder in the localities under some sort of control, Richard Abberbury, previously only a lowly 'constable of the King's peace', was one of the small group of gentry to whom they turned, as a 'potential force of county royalists',[24] in Oxfordshire.

Appointed a commissioner of array in April 1325, Abberbury became one of the three keepers of the peace in the county, with wide powers of inquiry and arrest, in the following October. Isabella and Mortimer, in their turn, found him as willing a local administrator as the Despensers had done; his appointment to a commission to supervize the keepers of the peace in November 1328, a task more usually reserved to magnates than confided to the local gentry, indicates Richard Abberbury's growing importance in Oxfordshire.[25] If his omission from the next two peace commissions suggests that Abberbury had proved, as knight of the shire for Oxfordshire in the parliament of October 1328, less staunch an ally of the régime than Mortimer had hoped, this did him no harm in the eyes of the young Edward III. Abberbury returned to the Oxfordshire peace-commission in 1331, transferred to the Berkshire commission in the following year and, in 1333, was appointed sheriff of Oxfordshire and

Berkshire, still the key position in local administration.[26] The importance of such commissions should not be exaggerated. Abberbury's attraction for successive régimes was that he was 'conspicuously inconspicuous',[27] a man of solid local consequence whose horizons and ambitions did not extend dangerously beyond his own shire. Nevertheless, the advancement he brought his family was an important one, confirmed by his knighthood (the first of his family to be so dignified) in 1333.[28] The Abberburys were now firmly established among the *buzones* of Oxfordshire and Berkshire, a position they maintained for the rest of the fourteenth century.

On Richard Abberbury's death in 1334, however, the local standing of the family underwent something of an eclipse for the next thirty years, until Sir Richard *le pere* himself began to establish his reputation. This was largely the result of a series of minorities and early deaths. John, Richard Abberbury's son and heir, was only sixteen when his father died and, although allowed early seisin of his inheritance,[29] had not had time to establish himself in county society before his death at the siege of Calais, where he was serving in the retinue of Richard, lord Talbot 'sleyn and dront on the sey . . . with many a man mo of worschippe'.[30] As a consequence, the family lands were divided between Richard Abberbury's younger son, Thomas, and his brother, John, who was settled on part of the north Oxfordshire estates,[31] neither of whom were to play much part in county society. In part, this was the result of a deliberate re-organization of the Abberbury inheritance, engineered by Richard in 1332 and marked by his transfer to the Berkshire peace-commission, which permanently endowed the cadet branch of the family with some of the Oxfordshire estates.[32] Although this solved one of the problems besetting all gentry families – how to make adequate provision for junior branches of the lineage without disinheriting the senior line – it meant that neither Thomas Abberbury, in Berkshire, nor John Abberbury, in Oxfordshire, could command the same income or exercise the same consequence as their elder brother had done. Indeed, between 1332 and 1364, no member of the family received a public commission or appointment; between 1331 and 1377, no lands were added to the Abberburys' existing holdings. This retrenchment was further encouraged by the difficult economic conditions of the period, which attenuated the estate income on which the Abberburys so largely depended. At East Hendred, for instance, the family lands, leased out for £7 6s 8d p.a. in 1332, were only producing £6 3s 4d by 1346.[33]

It was thus an ambivalent legacy that Sir Richard *le pere* finally inherited from his father, Thomas.[34] The considerable landed estate built up, under the protection of Walter Langton, by Master Thomas Abberbury remained largely intact, the sometimes shady circumstances of its acquisition now obscured by half a century of uncontested tenure. Yet only for a brief period, between 1325 and 1333, had these lands ever invested the Abberburys with anything but the most localized political or social consequence. In 1360, they were well-off but obscure; without discernible links at court or with a great magnate; rarely called upon to participate in the government of their county.

All this was soon to change, but Sir Richard Abberbury's own career got off to a start more in keeping with the recent obscurity of his family than its' earlier prominence. Born, on his own testimony, around 1330, Sir Richard did not succeed to the family lands until the early 1360s.[35] Like many another late medieval gentleman, his first claim to public attention was a crime for, in October 1366, Sir Richard, with a number of other Berkshire and Oxfordshire gentry, including his future colleagues Sir John Golafre and Sir Amauri St. Amand, made fine with the King for their part in the abduction of Joan, the wife of Walter Catewy.[36] This incident, though nothing out of the ordinary, was enough to earn Sir Richard his removal from the Berkshire commission of the peace, to which he had been appointed two years earlier, and he was to hold no other public appointment in England until his election as knight of the shire for Oxfordshire to the parliament of November 1373.[37] By that time, however, he was no longer an obscure county gentleman, but a figure of national, even international, repute. The transformation had been worked by two of the most characteristic ways to wealth in later medieval England, for it was by his service, in both peace and war, of Edward, prince of Wales, that Sir Richard restored and advanced the fortunes of the Abberbury family. Sir Richard's military career had begun in 1356 when he served with Henry of Grosmont, duke of Lancaster, in Brittany and Lower Normandy.[38] The Abberburys were tenants of the prince of Wales' honour of Wallingford, however, and it was to the service of his feudal overlord that Sir Richard transferred after the treaty of Brétigny. In 1366, he went with the prince to Aquitaine and served with him throughout the subsequent Najerá campaign. When he returned once more to Aquitaine in November 1368, with reinforcements for the beleagured principality, Sir Richard was already fifth on the list of knights of the prince's retinue and brought with him a small company of four esquires and ten archers.[39] His tour of duty in the principality was a long one, for he acted as the prince's seneschal in the Limousin between 1368 and 1371.[40] Once back in England, he was given further military responsibilities. Between March and July 1374, in command of a company of 40 men-at-arms and 40 archers, Abberbury served with the naval squadron that patrolled the Channel while, between June 1378 and May 1379, he and his Berkshire neighbour, Sir John Golafre, were joint-captains of Brest.[41]

This was, by the standards of the day, a highly respectable military career. Najerá was a famous victory at which to have been present, and Abberbury's appointments as seneschal of the Limousin, then under considerable (and successful) French pressure, and captain of the important fortress of Brest, at a particularly delicate time,[42] testify to the high regard he enjoyed among his contemporaries. Besides prestige, military service also brought him considerable rewards. After some hard bargaining with the Crown, for instance, Abberbury and Golafre succeeded in obtaining an indenture for the custody of Brest that left them with over £470 profit by land and sea at the end of their contract.[43] More important still, in terms of Sir Richard's own career, was the *entrée* his service abroad brought him to the retinue of the prince of Wales. On his triumphant return to England after Najerá, the prince retained Abberbury to serve him for life in peace and (with two esquires) in war at the substantial fee of £40 p.a., assigned on the lordship of Chester.[44] His esteem was more personally expressed by Sir Richard's appointment as the first 'master' of Richard of Bordeaux, the prince's son and heir, charged with a general oversight of the boy's education.[45] While Abberbury was not among the inner circle of the prince's administrators after his return to England, his subsequently close relations with Joan of Kent, the prince's widow, suggest that it was to the young Richard's service that he was, from the first, attached.[46] Certainly, for the brief time Richard was prince of Wales, Abberbury acted as the steward of his lands, thus enjoying a position second only to Sir Simon Burley's in the young prince's service.[47]

Naturally, on Richard II's accession to the throne in June 1377, Sir Richard acquired a new prominence. His first task in the new reign was to act, with William lord Latimer, Sir Simon Burley and Sir Nicholas Bonde, as an emissary of the court to the City of London, charged with persuading the citizens to reconcile themselves to John of Gaunt.[48] Appointed a knight of the King's chamber at the start of the reign, Abberbury remained one until 1387 and, in that capacity, served the young King in a variety of ways.[49] Besides his captaincy of Brest, he began to develop a diplomatic career. Between July and September 1380, he went with Master Walter Skirlaw to Brittany to advise the newly-reinstated duke, John de Montfort, on his rule in the duchy.[50] In December, he was sent to the Low Countries to negotiate for Richard's marriage to Anne of Bohemia and, in the following May, he and Sir Simon Burley were sent on a mission to John, duke of Luxemburg and Brabant.[51] Once Richard's new queen arrived, Abberbury was, from the first, closely associated with her service. He acted as her attorney as early as July 1382 and, by April 1383, is described as her chamberlain, a post he continued to occupy until, at least, 1386.[52] At the same time, although never formally designated a member of the Council, Sir Richard was often employed on a wide variety of Council business.[53] It was in the area of financial management that his particular talents seem to have lain. Besides acting as Queen Anne's chamberlain, Sir Richard was often in demand to wind up the tangled affairs of others. In 1377, he was one of those appointed to compile an inventory of the dead King's movable goods; in 1382, he was appointed a commissioner to extend and lease out the escheated Ufford estates at farm and, in 1389, he was ordered to sell off the lands forfeited to the Crown in the Merciless Parliament.[54]

These varied duties and responsibilities, typical of the versatility required of Richard II's chamber knights,[55] brought with them considerable rewards. Since 1367, Abberbury had enjoyed an annuity of £40 from Edward, prince of Wales, and this continued to be paid regularly after the prince's death.[56] But it was 1377, and his appointment as the young prince Richard's chief steward, that marked the real beginnings of prosperity. In that year he was granted duchy of Cornwall lands and offices worth nearly £120 p.a., which were followed in 1383 by a grant of the manors of Iffley (Oxon.) and Carswell

(Berks.), to the value of £40 p.a., in recognition of his service to Anne of Bohemia.[57] These two manors were conveyed to him in fee simple in 1385, in compensation for the loss Sir Richard had sustained by selling off his Sussex manors of Shoreham and Todham 'to support the King's estate in his youth'.[58] All in all, taking into account the fees and robes he received as a knight of the chamber, Abberbury must have enjoyed an income of at least £210 p.a. from Crown grants by 1385, quite apart from the unquantifiable windfalls of royal favour – such as the king's ship, *la Alice*, given him during his custody of Brest – that occasionally came his way.[59] It seems a safe assumption that this was rather more than the annual income Sir Richard derived from his own estates, which might be put in the region of £150 p.a.[60]

Abberbury's career was thus developing solidly, if a trifle unspectacularly, during the early 1380s. Dignified and responsible though his duties were, they were not ones that brought him into close contact with the young King, nor did they touch on politically sensitive ground. It may be significant that Sir Richard's most influential appointment, as receiver of the King's chamber, was one that he held for only four months, and that it was not until his removal from the office, in November 1382, that the chamber began to assume real political or financial importance as an instrument of the royal will.[61] Granted that he had occupied a position in Richard's administration, when he was prince of Wales, second only to Sir Simon Burley himself, there is a sense in which Abberbury failed to exploit his opportunities to the full. His rewards, though substantial, were paltry by the standards of the wealth Simon Burley had accumulated by 1387,[62] and, amongst the chamber knights, Sir James Berners, Sir John Salisbury and Sir John Beauchamp all enjoyed a greater degree of intimacy with the King and were more lavishly rewarded by him. Even a figure of the second rank, like Sir Nicholas Sarnesfield, was in receipt of over £300 a year in royal annuities.[63] Yet the degree of distance that existed, whether by design or default, between Sir Richard and the inner circle of the King's advisers was to prove invaluable to him during the prolonged political crisis of 1386–8.

Abberbury continued to be busily employed throughout 1386. In April, for instance, he was named as one of the three English negotiators entrusted with the task of drawing up a treaty of alliance with Portugal, prior to the duke of Lancaster's invasion of Castile, and negotiating with the duke, as titular King of Castile, a treaty of perpetual alliance between the two countries. In October, he was returned as knight of the shire for Oxfordshire to the 'Wonderful' Parliament.[64] However, the impeachment of Michael de la Pole and the appointment of a commission Council mark the beginning of a period of official obscurity for Abberbury, who did not receive another public appointment until May 1388 and was omitted from the peace-commissions issued in both July 1389 and June 1390.[65] Sir Richard carefully avoided too close an identification with the court during this difficult time by staying out of the way. Much of 1387 seems to have been spent in Oxfordshire, diligently discharging the duties of a justice of the peace.[66] Nevertheless, this did not save him entirely from the reckoning that followed Radcot Bridge, for he was one of twelve named persons required to abjure the court by the Appellants in January 1388 and to appear before them in the next Parliament.[67] Abberbury's position was not, however, as precarious as that of some of his colleagues for, just as he had been careful to avoid too close an association with the high-flying royalism of the chamber, so Sir Richard had also maintained good relations with at least one of the Appellant lords. During the year October 1387–8 Henry of Derby had been entertained at Abberbury's London house and had, on one occasion, sent an esquire into Oxfordshire with a letter for him. Together with Sir Thomas Trivet, Sir Richard received a red cloak from the earl and, at another time, Abberbury had been included by Derby in a gift of furs made to the other Appellant lords – Arundel, Warwick, Gloucester and Nottingham.[68] How this evidence is to be interpreted remains, in the absence of precise dates for these gifts, uncertain; the best guess may be that the Appellants made overtures to Sir Richard in the winter of 1387, failed to win his unqualified support and therefore dismissed him from the court, although they remained, despite his loyalty to the King, on relatively good terms with him. Abberbury evidently regarded his actions as capable of more than one interpretation, since he prudently took out letters of pardon for any offences committed against the King's majesty during this period in 1398.[69] Certainly, the Appellants found that they could not do without his administrative and diplomatic talents entirely, for in October 1388 Sir Richard was despatched to Aquitaine, to consult with the duke of Lancaster over the terms of the peace he proposed to conclude with Castile.[70]

All the same, Abberbury was quick to take advantage of Richard II's resumption of personal power in May 1389. Before the end of that month he had submitted a petition to the King asking for a variety of favours – free warren in all his lands; the release of certain rents due to him from the forfeited lands of Sir Robert Tresilian; exemption from holding any office against his will; the grant of a wardship. The first two of these were quickly granted, as a recognition of Sir Richard's 'sufferings' on the King's behalf, while the others followed piecemeal over the next few years.[71] His career soon resumed the even tenor of the early 1380s although, as befitted a man new in his sixties, the pace of his activities began to slow down. Abberbury remained chief of Queen Anne's Council and continued to act on her behalf until her death in 1394;[72] he continued to attend Council meetings, usually when diplomatic issues were to be discussed, and in 1390 he was one of a group of middle-ranking ambassadors appointed to open peace negotiations with the French.[73] Sir Richard's last major task was to organize and oversee the embarkation of the King's expedition to Ireland in the autumn of 1394. He must have accompanied Richard to Dublin as well for, in January 1395, he was sent back with the duke of Gloucester and Sir Philip la Vache to report on the King's progress to Parliament.[74] But while the burden of Abberbury's administrative duties was generally lighter during the 1390s, the volume of his judicial activities increased noticeably on its earlier levels. Besides continuing to act as principal justice on the Oxfordshire peace-commission Sir Richard sat, on several occasions, as a justice of assize and, on one, as a justice of gaol delivery, while being frequently appointed to hear appeals from the courts of the constable and the admiral.[75]

Sir Richard's standing in the 1390s was thus as something of an elder statesman around the court. His involvement in the business of government was less intense than it had been during Richard II's minority and the rewards he derived from that involvement, though useful, were consequently less substantial.[76] More of his energies were now devoted to his private concerns – in particular to the creation and consolidation of a landed estate in Oxfordshire and Berkshire that would adequately reflect the new status of the Abberbury family. This process had begun as early as 1377, when Sir Richard bought back the manor and advowson of Peasmore (Berks.) alienated by his uncle in 1321. In the same year, he bought himself a London town-house, in the parish of St. Nicholas, Coldabbey.[77] Thereafter, most of Abberbury's acquisitions were in Oxfordshire. Land at Wendlebury and Merton was purchased in 1378 for 100 marks; the reversion of the manors of Hanwell and Kidlington, the latter at a cost of £200, were added over the next five years and, in 1385, Sir Richard took out a lease on the manor of Drayton at 20 marks a year.[78] These purchases, together with the manor of Barton Odis, brought to Sir Richard by his wife Agnes and quitclaimed to the Abberburys in 1384, the acquisition of Iffley from Queen Anne, his life-interest in the manor of Langley and his purchase, at some unknown date, of manors in Bletchingdon and Thrupp, made Abberbury, by the 1390s, one of the largest landowners in a county notably lacking in resident magnates.[79] His increasingly dominant position in the middle Thames valley was acknowledged in 1394, when he headed the commissions of the peace issued for both Oxfordshire and Berkshire.[80]

Only in the last decade of his life did Sir Richard seek to expand the Berkshire lands of his family again, acquiring the manor of Winterbourne Mayne in 1393 and paying 100 marks for lands in Whittenham three years later.[81] The attraction of both these estates was that they lay conveniently close to his manor of Donnington, which Abberbury had chosen to make his principal residence and on which he lavished his greatest expenditure. Like Sir Edward Dallingridge at Bodiam and Sir Thomas Hungerford at Farleigh Hungerford, it was by building a castle that Sir Richard sought principally to advertise his new prosperity to the world. Donnington, strategically placed on a spur of high ground that dominated both the East-West route from London to Bath and the North-South road from Oxford to Southampton, was the ideal place to do so. Although it was as late as June 1386 that Sir Richard petitioned for, and was granted, a licence to crenellate,[82] the original buildings on the site are a little earlier in date; the general trajectory of his career suggests that they might be dated to the late 1370s.[83] The licence granted in 1386 was for the addition of an imposing gatehouse, which places Donnington within a group of late fourteenth century castles, such as Nunney, Bolton and Saltwood, that combined comfortable living-quarters with a prudent attention to the continuing need of defence. How much this 'whole of real architectural pretensions'[84] cost the Abberburys is impossible to say, but for Sir Richard it was money well spent. His castle at Donnington was effectively his *caput honoris*, a building which raised him above the ruck of the county gentry and announced his equality of status with long-established baronial families. Though Richard II 'had no desire to transform his chamber knights into territorial magnates',[85] this did not prevent some of those knights from making shrewd use of the profits of office to create for themselves a dominating position in local society.

Buying land and building a suitably imposing residence were two obvious ways in which such a local dominance could be created. Closely connected with the same endeavour were Abberbury's ecclesiastical benefactions. In these, he showed himself more orthodox than those chamber knights who are known to have been attracted by the ascetic teachings of the Lollards,[86] though there is perhaps enough evidence to suggest that some of the concerns that animated the Lollard Knights animated Sir Richard as well. Both conventional piety and family *pietas* lay behind his first benefaction, when he alienated the advowson of Steeple Aston, worth 16 marks p.a., to the Augustinian priory of Cold Norton, on condition that the prior and convent pray for the soul of Master Thomas Abberbury, clerk.[87] The same mixture of motives can be seen behind Sir Richard's projected re-endowment, in 1365, of a chantry chapel at Donnington that had originally been founded by his grandfather, Walter Abberbury.[88] By 1376, however, nothing further had been done about it and, in that year, Sir Richard was granted licence to convert the proposed chantry into a small dependent priory of Crutched Friars, who would then provide two chaplains to celebrate mass for his good estate and for the souls of his ancestors.[89] Abberbury's choice of the Crutched Friars was an odd one, since the order was small and struggling, while its London house had recently been involved in a scandal.[90] Nevertheless, it is characteristic of his ecclesiastical benefactions, of a piece with his patronage of Cold Norton and the Cistercian abbey of Bruern.[91] Both were local Oxfordshire houses, small and needy, and it was to these, rather than richer or more fashionable orders, that Sir Richard chose to devote his charity.

Abberbury's concern for the deserving poor found further, and striking, expression in his foundation of a poor house at Donnington in 1393. Twelve poor men and a *minister* were to be maintained from the revenues of the manor of Iffley and a yearly rent-charge of 13 marks, which Sir Richard alienated to his hospital.[92] The almsmen were to be drawn, for preference, from among the Abberbury family's poor tenants and servants; they were to have a chamber each and a penny a day and, in return, to hear mass daily at the adjacent priory of Crutched Friars and pray for the souls of Sir Richard, his eldest son, and their respective wives.[93] The intention behind the foundation was thus the highly orthodox one of securing a safe passage through Purgatory, but in the means Abberbury chose to effect this – by the prayers of poor men rather than chantry priests – he was giving expression to a current of practical piety particularly strong among the careerist soldiers of Richard II's court. His hospital bears comparison with the more lavish foundations of Sir Michael de la Pole at Hull and Sir Robert Knolles at Pontefract and, in his concern for the poor, Sir Richard's religion touches common ground with the Lollard sympathies of his colleagues among the chamber-knights.[94] At the same time, the friary and poor house he founded added materially to the imposing concentration of buildings his wealth had brought into being at Donnington and further attested to the new eminence of his family name.

Essential to Abberbury's ambitions in this respect was, of course, the progress of his own children, chiefly his two sons – the elder, also called Richard, and the younger, Thomas. They were the product of his marriage to Agnes, a younger daughter of Sir William Shareshull, CJKB.[95] This had been a shrewd match with a local Oxfordshire family which brought to the Abberburys a life-interest in Barton Odis, close to their own lands at Steeple Aston, and, while the Chief Justice himself lived, a potentially powerful protector.[96] The marriages Sir Richard sought for his own children were of the same kind – solid, county affairs with definite territorial gains in prospect rather than the socially more elevated, but more expensive, marriages that his contacts at court might have provided. His eldest son, Richard, married Alice, the widow of Edmund Danvers of Winterbourne and so brought to the family a useful accession of property around Donnington.[97] Thomas, his second son, was married to another propertied widow, Alice, formerly the wife of John Baldington of Albury, an Oxfordshire J.P.,[98] while his two daughters married into the ranks of the lesser gentry – Lucy to Richard Arches, member of a Buckinghamshire knightly family who eventually served as escheator in Berkshire and Oxfordshire,[99] and Elizabeth to John Beaufoy of Barford, a local esquire who enjoyed some favour from Richard II during the 1390s.[100] By such alliances, Sir Richard sought to consolidate the estates and extend the connections of his family at county level. They did little, however, to advance the social standing of his children. Further gains in that area, if they were to happen at all, had to come through royal and seigneurial service. Accordingly, it was in such service that Sir Richard placed his two sons.

His eldest son's career followed a pattern very similar to his own. Like his father, the young Richard Abberbury saw a respectable, though not unusual, amount of campaigning at home and abroad: in Aquitaine in 1370; as part of the Calais garrison in 1379; in Ireland in 1380; in Portugal, with Edmund earl of Cambridge in 1381, and in Scotland in 1385.[101] Like his father, he rose high in the service of a royal prince and reaped the considerable rewards of his success. The younger Abberbury's patron was John of Gaunt, duke of Lancaster. Richard was already an esquire in his household by 1370 and, although his connection with Gaunt over the next ten years is difficult to document, the prominent position he had attained in the duke's service by the early 1380s argues that most of the intervening period had been spent there as well. By 1381, for instance, he was already a fairly senior retainer of the duke's and, more important, one of the dozen knights of his chamber – a post which could give him considerable influence in the duke's counsels at a time when his father occupied an analogous position in the service of Richard II.[102] Further promotion came in the course of Gaunt's expedition to Castile, since the heavy mortality among the duke's followers wrought by the harsh Spanish winter left the young Abberbury as one of the duke's most senior advisers by the summer of 1387. On the death of Sir John Marmion, Sir Richard *le filz* succeeded him as chamberlain of the Lancastrian household and, in this capacity, was sent back from Bayonne to England with the delicate task of explaining why, contrary to his previous undertakings, the duke now proposed to make peace with the Castilians.[103] His promotion was marked by an increase in his annuity, to £50, which Abberbury then exchanged for a life-grant of the Lancastrian manor of East Garston, thereby adding further to his family's stake in Berkshire.[104]

To be chamberlain to John of Gaunt, the second senior position in the administration of the most powerful magnate in England, was considerable and rapid advancement for a man who can hardly have been older than forty. There seemed every chance that, after his return to England with Lancaster in November 1389, Sir Richard *le filz* would soon cut as influential a figure in domestic politics as his father. At this point, however, the careers of father and son began to diverge. By 1390 the younger Abberbury had given up his post as Gaunt's chamberlain in order to go on crusade in Prussia with Henry of Derby.[105] On his return to England, he remained one of the bachelors of Gaunt's chamber but appeared only infrequently at the Lancastrian court.[106] Instead, he began to be employed on royal business, developing rapidly into a diplomatic specialist. As Gaunt's chamberlain, he had already displayed some talent for delicate negotiations. In 1388, the duke had made Sir Richard his proctor to conclude a local truce with the French; in the summer of 1389, sent by Gaunt on an (ultimately unsuccessful) mission to obtain from the French court safe-conducts for the duke's passage through France, he had stayed in Paris long enough to have a conversation with the Constable, Olivier de Clisson, who boasted of freeing the young Charles VI from the control of his uncles.[107] The domestic implications of this brave talk can hardly have been lost on the younger Abberbury; it may even be that he acted upon the implicit advice since, on his return from Prussia, Richard II began to find work for Sir Richard *le filz*. In December 1393, when rumours that Charles VI was recovering from his attack of madness reached the English court, he was sent to discover and report upon 'the state and sanity of the King of France'. Between October 1394 and January 1395 he went, with the Bohemian chamber-knight Sir Nicholas Rebjnitz, to negotiate an alliance between Richard II and Rupert of Bavaria, count palatine of the Rhine; a task which was successfully concluded after a second mission, again with Rebjnitz, in the autumn of 1395.[108] Early in 1398 he set off again on the King's business, this time on an embassy, by way of Paris and Venice, to the eastern Mediterranean.[109] His diplomatic talents were in demand in England as well. When John of Gaunt got wind of a rumour against him circulating the royal court in August 1394, it was the younger Abberbury he dispatched from Pontefract to London to declare his innocence.[110] It would have been difficult to find a more appropriate go-between, for Sir Richard's double standing as a Lancastrian retainer and royal employee, quite apart from his father's long and faithful service to the King, lent the letter he carried added credence.

Sir Richard *le filz* was thus a well-established figure in English political life by the 1390s, known as an acute diplomat and a trusted servant of the duke of Lancaster. His younger brother, Thomas, found it harder to establish himself at court but, by the end of Richard II's reign, he too seemed assured of a profitable career there. Thomas first appears in 1374, in the company of the duke of Brittany, but he was later to serve as an esquire of the chamber knight Sir Nicholas Sarnesfield, a neighbour and colleague of his father's.[111] By 1383, when he was granted a wardship by the King, Thomas had moved to Richard II's service; three years later, his father transferred to him all his right in the valuable Cornish manor of Helston and the King enlarged the grant to last for the term of Thomas's life.[112] The intention behind this generous endowment was probably to enable him to support the order of knighthood, for it was as Sir Thomas Abberbury that he contracted to serve, with three men-at-arms and three archers, in the garrison of Calais in April 1386.[113] In the same year the new knight took the first steps towards building up a landed estate of his own by purchasing some land in East Anglia.[114] This rapid rise in status was undoubtedly facilitated by his father's position in the chamber for, once Sir Richard *le pere* was forbidden the court by the Appellants, his younger son's career went into temporary eclipse. The projected transfer of Helston did not, in the end, go through and, deprived of this financial support, Thomas was unable to maintain his pretensions to knighthood. When he appears again, accompanying the King to Ireland in 1394, he was still only an esquire of the royal household.[115] There he remained until 1397, when he was granted an annuity of £20 a year, until the King should ordain otherwise for his estate, and transferred to the nascent household establishment of Richard's new queen, Isabella, as master of her horse, discharging his duties under the direction of his father's old friend, Sir Philip la Vache, the queen's chamberlain.[116]

Thus, when Sir Richard *le pere*, choosing his moment with the discretion he had displayed throughout his life, died early in 1399,[117] he could be well satisfied with the provision he had made for the continued success of the Abberbury family. Besides the lands he had bought, the castle he had built, the hospital he had founded, his eldest son was a favoured Lancastrian retainer and his younger son seemed safely re-established in royal service; his two daughters had made sound, if unspectacular, marriages to local gentlemen. The political upheaval created by Richard II's counter-Appellancy in 1397 had been negotiated without mishap; both Thomas Abberbury and Sir Richard *le filz* appeared well-placed to draw advantage from the King's now unchallenged authority. Even the cadet branch of the family living in north Oxfordshire were sharing in the consequence of their more glamorous cousins.[118] John Abberbury of Cotesford, whose only previous experience of local administration was a brief and ineffective spell as a J.P., was re-appointed to the Oxfordshire peace-commission in 1394 and continued to play an active part on the bench until the end of Richard II's reign.[119] In the same year, he obtained the office of King's alnager in Oxfordshire and, soon afterwards, began expanding his estates in the north of the county, leasing the manor of Deddington from the canons of St. George's, Windsor.[120] When his cousin, Sir Richard *le filz*, was returned as knight of the shire for Berkshire to the Parliaments of January 1394 and 1397, John Abberbury's simultaneous return for Oxfordshire only served to emphasize the growing dominance of the family throughout the middle Thames valley.[121]

Within twelve months of old Sir Richard's death, of course, much was to change. By the spring of 1400, Richard II was deposed and dead; John of Gaunt was dead; his son, Henry of Derby, was King of England. Clearly, such upheavals posed problems of conscience and action for families like the Abberburys, who were dependent upon royal service and patronage for much of their prosperity. Even so, the Abberburys would have appeared adequately reinsured against the more drastic consequences of Richard II's deposition by Sir Richard *le filz*'s position at the Lancastrian court. He was on good terms with Henry of Derby; in John of Gaunt's will he had been left a bequest of 50 marks, one of only four men outside the duke's immediate family to be so honoured.[122] That distinction alone should have been enough to ensure Sir Richard *le filz* consideration and employment under the new régime. For many Lancastrian retainers, the change of dynasty in 1399 brought a new and lucrative prominence; those who had been on crusade to Prussia with the new King, as Abberbury had, seem to have been especially favoured.[123]

Yet the usurpation of Henry IV marks the beginning of a swift decline in the fortunes of the Abberbury family. Sir Richard *le filz* was appointed to the Berkshire commission of array in December 1399 but then received no further public appointments at all. Late in 1400 he settled a rent of £13 1s 6d from the manor of Thrupp on his father's house of Crutched Friars at Donnington and, in October, took out letters of protection while he was in parts beyond the sea.[124] The frequent reissue of letters of protection and general attorney to him suggest that he must have stayed abroad, apart from a brief visit to England in January 1402, for the rest of Henry IV's reign.[125] Although he still enjoyed the revenue from John of Gaunt's grant of East Garston in 1403, by 1406 he had lost possession of the manor.[126] In 1415, he began to sell up his entire inheritance. In Berkshire, the manors of Donnington, Peasmore, Pentlowe, Winterbourne Mayne and Winterbourne Danvers were all sold to Thomas Chaucer and a group of his feoffees for 1000 marks; Chaucer subsequently used them to endow his daughter Alice, then the wife of Sir John Phelip. The rest of the Abberbury lands in the county, at South Denchworth and Chipping Lambourne, went to local buyers for another 120 marks.[127] In Oxfordshire, the bulk of the family lands – chiefly the manors of Souldern, Steeple Aston, Sibford, Ludwell and Glympton – were sold to

Sir Richard's nephew, Sir Richard Arches, for a further 800 marks, while Thomas Chaucer paid 300 marks for the reversions of Kidlington and Hanwell. At a price of 2200 marks, Sir Richard and his wife had thus liquidated the family estate painstakingly built up over the previous 130 years, leaving themselves only a life-interest in Souldern, Hanwell and the adjacent lands at Barford St. Martin.[128]

Various possibilities can be canvassed in explanation, though none can command certainty. One, outwardly attractive, explanation would emphasize the political consequences of Henry IV's usurpation. It is certainly strange that Sir Richard *le filz* did not turn the high position he had held in John of Gaunt's esteem to greater advantage after 1399, especially in view of the importance of old Lancastrian servants in Henry IV's establishment. It is tempting, in consequence, to see this failure as stemming either from some distrust of Abberbury entertained by the King or from Sir Richard's scrupulous reluctance to serve a usurper. For, while most of Richard II's knightly servants experienced little difficulty in coming to terms with a new master,[129] there were those, like Sir Richard Waldegrave, who chose to dissociate themselves from Henry's court, and others, like the former King's standard-bearer, Sir Simon Felbrigg, who had that choice forced upon them.[130] What evidence there is, however, seems to be against the idea. Sir Richard's first reaction to the usurpation of 1399 was to bring a suit in Common Pleas for the recovery of his manor of Stainswick, in the well-founded hope that he could count on royal favour in the prosecution of his plea.[131] He was considered reliable enough to be appointed a commissioner of array in December 1399 and, two months later, he was on sufficiently good terms with Henry IV to obtain from him a writ under the privy seal, discharging him from several debts owed at the Exchequer.[132] His relations with committed Lancastrians, such as John Elvet and Sir Thomas Erpingham, remained close; Thomas Chaucer was to act for many years as Sir Richard's general attorney in England, which suggests that the growth of Chaucer's dominating influence in the Middle Thames valley, though largely at the Abberburys' expense, was accompanied by no great rancour on Sir Richard's part.[133] It seems, therefore, that his swift disappearance from political life after the accession of Henry IV cannot be explained on political grounds alone; Abberbury's renunciation was a voluntary one, which did not spring from any distaste for the new Lancastrian régime.[134]

The only real clue to the nature of this renunciation lies in a petition made by Sir Richard Arches in September 1408 on his uncle's behalf, asking that he be granted letters of protection for a further year. In that petition, Abberbury is described as '*en pilrynage outre le grant meer*'.[135] Sir Richard *le filz* had been on Crusade to Prussia; by 1395, he had been enrolled in Philippe de Mézières' Order of the Passion, which was dedicated to the recovery of the Holy Places; early in 1398, he had been sent on an embassy to the eastern Mediterranean, most probably to discuss the chances of a future Crusade with the Eastern Empire.[136] Abberbury was clearly interested and involved in the fashionable Anglo-French efforts to revive Crusading enthusiasm and it may well be that it was to this cause that he dedicated most of his time after 1399. Pilgrimage and Crusade were expensive pastimes, however – Sir Richard drew substantial bills of exchange, while he was abroad, on the Florentine banking house of Alberti[137] – and he may, in the end, have been forced to sell his estates in order to meet the high level of expenditure that his father's ambitious projects and his own chosen style of life imposed upon him. His father had, like most of his contemporaries, occasional crises of liquidity that necessitated a loan from London merchants[138] but, by the 1390s, there is a little evidence that the financial position of the family was growing more serious. In 1390, John of Gaunt had had to lend Sir Richard *le filz* £200 in order to enable him to follow Henry of Derby to Prussia and, after two years, the family fell behind on repayments of this loan. At Michaelmas 1394 the King lent Sir Richard *le pere* a further 200 marks and, in the course of the next two years, Sir Richard *le filz* twice had recourse to Gilbert Maghfield for small loans of £15 apiece; in 1399, he owed the earl of Salisbury another 20 marks.[139] In the father's case, this probably amounts to no more than the inevitable fluctuations of liquidity in an economy short of ready money. In the son's case, the evidence is more telling. Sir Richard *le filz* had sold a small parcel of his own lands as early as 1388 and was to sell off another portion to the Hyde family in 1408, before the final liquidation of his estates.[140] Before 1399, Sir Richard *le filz* appears not to have enjoyed any source of income beyond his Lancastrian annuity and this, too, was lost to him after 1406. Even after his inheritance of the family estates, the loss of his father's considerable income in pensions and annuities would necessarily have reduced the rate at which the Abberbury family could afford to spend, although the implementation of his father's wishes for the priory and hospital of Donnington certainly involved Sir Richard *le filz* in continuing expenditure.[141] Sir William Stonor was once advised 'that ye wolle not over wissh yow, ner owyr purchas yow, ner owr bild you; for these iii thynges wolle plucke a yongman ryth lowe'.[142] The Abberburys held their hands from none of these things and they may well have paid the price of their ambition.

Whatever the reason, Sir Richard *le filz*'s withdrawal from public life proved disastrous for the aspirations of the whole Abberbury clan. His younger brother, Thomas, was too closely identified with Richard II's service to survive the usurpation of 1399 unscathed. He continued to act as master of Queen Isabella's stables while she remained in England but her return to France in July 1401 effectively ended all Thomas's contact with the court.[143] Although his £20 annuity was quickly confirmed by Henry IV and continued to be paid with as much regularity as could be expected in the straitened circumstances of Henry's reign,[144] Thomas was eventually induced to surrender it in November 1409 in favour of William Bradwardyn, an esquire of Henry, prince of Wales.[145] On Thomas Abberbury's death in 1416, what remained of the family estates in Berkshire, now concentrated around Newbury, passed to Katherine, his second wife, and their son Richard.[146] This Richard Abberbury still retained enough of a toe-hold at court to be able to obtain a minor royal wardship in 1432 but the decline in the social standing of his family, which inevitably followed upon the sale of their estates, was marked by his designation as merely a 'gentleman', below the 23 esquires of the county, when he and many others were called upon to swear not to maintain disturbers of the peace in 1434.[147] What was left of the family lands continued to disappear. In 1440 Richard and his mother granted away all their right in the manor of Walford while, by 1456, the substantial Abberbury holdings in the Newbury suburb of Speenhamland, still intact in 1428, had been broken up.[148]

A more significant transaction took place in 1448, when Richard re-entered and took possession of all the lands in Oxfordshire and Berkshire that Sir Richard, his grandfather, had granted to the Friars of the Holy Cross, on the grounds that the order was no longer providing two chaplains to sing mass in the family chantry at Donnington priory. Once in possession, he immediately granted his estate in the lands to William de la Pole, duke of Suffolk.[149] Suffolk already possessed a considerable estate in Berkshire, in the right of his wife Alice, daughter of Thomas Chaucer, and throughout the 1440s he had been busily consolidating his holdings. Already most of the former Abberbury lands in the county were in Suffolk's possession and the lands of the Danvers family, previously enjoyed by Sir Richard *le filz* in the right of his wife, were now passing into his hands as well.[150] Richard Abberbury's re-entry into the lands of Donnington priory, together with his subsequent grant of seisin to Suffolk, consequently offered the de la Poles a convenient means of rounding-off and consolidating their possession of the former Abberbury estates. A petition from the prior and brethren of the Crutched Friars, datable to 1452/3, reveals how the re-entry was managed. They claimed that the duke of Suffolk disseised them of the lands of the priory, worth £20 p.a., by collusion with Thomas Wythwood, then governor of the Abberbury hospital at Donnington, who had abstracted all the deeds of title belonging to the priory and delivered them to de la Pole, in return for the promise of collation to a benefice worth 40 marks a year.[151] Since Suffolk, then the most powerful magnate in England, was in the habit of granting a suit of his livery to those with whom he did satisfactory business, Abberbury was probably happy enough to acquiesce in this scheme, even at the expense of his family chantry, for it offered him the chance of attaching himself to a powerful patron.[152] He can have derived little advantage from his complaisance, for Suffolk was impeached and murdered within two years, but even this disaster did not diminish his widow's avid acquisition of Berkshire lands. In 1465, Richard Abberbury once again granted a portion of his exiguous liflode to Alice, duchess of Suffolk; in the same year, he quitclaimed two of his remaining tenements in Newbury, which left him only one.[153]

Reduced though his circumstances were, they were at least no worse than those of his cousin Thomas, head of the Oxfordshire branch of the family, who then occupied a tenement outside the East Gate of Oxford.[154] For the Oxfordshire Abberburys, who had never risen so high, the experience of social decline was less dramatic, though no less inexorable. Although he lost both his position on the county bench and his post as king's alnager in 1399, John Abberbury of Cotesford remained prosperous enough to continue the expansion of his estates in the early fifteenth-century, taking up the lease on the Winchester demesne at Adderbury and purchasing the manor of Walton by King's Sutton in 1405.[155] By the time of his death in 1420 he had established his eldest son, also called John, securely on the ladder of ecclesiastical preferment.[156] But deprived of the influence and patronage of their grander cousins, the Oxfordshire Abberburys were never again to command the position they had enjoyed in county society in the later years of Richard II's reign. Thomas Abberbury, who inherited the family lands on his brother's death in 1438, sought his fortune in the French wars but could do little to reverse the process of decline. Walton was sold in 1447 and, within a decade, even the Abberburys' original tenement at Adderbury was gone.[157]

At first glance, the history of the rise and decline of the Abberbury family may seem amply to bear out Thomas Fuller's comments on the fluidity of the land market in their adopted shire:-'Sure I am that ancient Gentry in this county sown thick in former, come up thin in our Age . . . the lands in Berkshire are very skittish, and often cast their Owners, which yet I impute not so much to the unruliness of the Beasts, as to the unskillfulness of the Riders'.[158] Certainly, when Master Thomas Abberbury was creating the basis of the family estate in the 1290s, he was able to take advantage of the insolvency and incompetence of knightly families like the Romillies of Steeple Aston. Equally, when the Abberburys failed in the male line in the early fifteenth century, there were local families like the Hydes of South Denchworth, ready and eager to rise on their backs.[159] Yet the Abberburys' decline has, in the end, less to do with 'unskillfulness' than with the scale of priorities by which the later medieval gentry conducted their lives. It was the decision of Sir Richard *le filz*, apparently unprompted by outside pressure, first to turn his back on a promising career in England, then to sell off his family lands in order to finance his pilgrimages in the East, that reduced the Abberburys from one of the leading families of Oxfordshire and Berkshire to modest burgesses of Newbury within a single generation. One conclusion to emerge from this family history is, then, the considerable ambivalence of attitude towards the institutions of the family evinced by the actions of the Abberburys. On the one hand, a strong strain of family pride and piety runs through their benefactions. Master Thomas found a chaplain to sing for the souls of his ancestors in York Minster; Walter Abberbury was a benefactor of Abingdon abbey, the first patron of his brother and benefactor, Master Thomas; Sir Richard *le pere* re-endowed the chantry chapel established at Donnington by his grandfather, Walter; Sir Richard *le filz* took care to fulfil his father's intentions towards the priory and hospital of Donnington before he went abroad.[160] Great care was taken to provide adequately for as many members of the family as possible even if, as in the 1330s, it meant a considerable reorganization of interests within the family. Yet 'such sentiments often served to dignify, even to endow with an air of altruism, what might otherwise have looked like a rapaciously selfish struggle' in the cause of self-aggrandisement.[161] Was it for his family, or for himself, that Sir Richard *le pere* undertook his expensive building projects at Donnington? All that can be said with certainty is that he had little use for his kindred in his business transactions. Only once does any other member of his family witness any of his surviving charters; only rarely does he appear on the same witness-list as one of his kin.[162] The same independence of the family and its claims may be seen in the actions of his descendants. Sir Richard *le filz* preferred the pursuit of his own inclinations to the future prospects of his brother's children. His great-niece, Joan Dynham, was later to claim that 'having no issue and being of great age' he had sold his Oxfordshire estates to his heir-apparent, Sir Richard Arches.[163] This was not the whole story, however, for Sir Richard's younger brother, Thomas, was still alive at the time of the sale and Thomas's son, also called Richard, was to survive them both for many years.[164] The prospects of this branch of the family were entirely ignored by Sir Richard *le filz*. No two families were the same, of course, but if in some cases 'it is impossible to exaggerate the earnestness with which a gentry family looked to the maintenance of its inheritance',[165] it must be recognized that, in others, this anxiety was not extended beyond the bounds of the nuclear family to include the collateral kindred.

A second conclusion concerns the nature of political society. It has recently been remarked of 'the men who managed things' in later medieval England that 'if power is to be located in one place then it should be with these gentlemen'.[166] For thirty years the Abberburys, father and son, were two such men but, when set against their careers, this view seems a little exaggerated. Power remained firmly where it had always been, at the court of the King and his magnates; individual gentlemen might share in that power, but only as servants and subordinates of the great. The patronage of a great ecclesiastical magnate, Walter Langton, first established the fortunes of the family; in the middle years of the fourteenth century, while they remained out of seignurial service, the Abberburys languished in obscurity; the favour of a King and two royal princes revived their fortunes and brought them to a new eminence; once severed from this fount of honour, the family quickly vanished. Yet, if the Abberburys' case seems to bear out the contention that 'for all who had pretensions to gentility the network of clientage and patronage formed the fabric of contemporary life',[167] it remains important to emphasize that the service of the great was not the only thread in that fabric. This can be illustrated by an examination of Sir Richard *le pere*'s charters and the charters of those who used him as a witness. Their evidence serves to put the undoubted importance of royal and seignurial service to the Abberburys in a wider perspective for, in general, they show that Sir Richard *le pere*'s contacts among the magnates were not, for a longstanding courtier, particularly extensive, and his dependence upon them far from exclusive.

Among the lay peers, John lord Lovell of Titchmarsh and his kinsman, Sir John Holland, created earl of Huntingdon in 1388, were his closest associates.[168] William of Wykeham, for whom Abberbury did business over many years, and Thomas Arundel, successively bishop of Ely and archbishop of York, were his principal ecclesiastical contacts.[169] Even at this level, local associations were important, for both Lovell and Wykeham were landowners of some standing within the Abberburys' own area of influence. Equally, the chamber knight with whom Sir Richard was most closely associated, Sir Philip la Vache, possessed, as farmer of the royal forest and manor of Woodstock, an Oxfordshire interest that coincided closely with his own.[170] This is not to say that Sir Richard shared the 'narrow horizons' that have been imputed to the county gentry in general,[171] nor that he had little interest in what happened beyond the county boundaries. His dealings with the goldsmiths, Nicholas Twyford and Dru Barentyn, gave him valuable contacts in the City of London,[172] while the series of transactions he oversaw on behalf of the king's Secretary, Roger Walden, show that he was careful to maintain an ally close to the king's person.[173] More frequently, however, Sir Richard is to be found in the company of the heads of other knightly families from Oxfordshire and Berkshire – Sir Amauri St. Amand of Bloxham;[174] Sir Thomas Paynel of Ufton Robert;[175] Sir Gilbert Wace of Ewelme;[176] Sir Thomas Poure of Black Bourton.[177] His chief man of business, William atte Wode, for whom he procured a stewardship on one of Queen Anne's estates, came from Newbury,[178] and it was from such middling gentry families as the Willicotes of Great Tew and the Barentyns of Little Haseley that he sought witnesses, mainpernors and executors most frequently.[179] If Sir Richard's closest associates were men like Sir Philip la Vache and Sir John Golafre,[180] whose interests coincided with his both at court and in the county, it nevertheless seems clear that it was to his local friendships and alliances, not to the network of magnate patronage, that he turned to secure and convey the lands that his service at court had won.

A third conclusion, about contemporary politics, may be suggested. Although the kings of later medieval England were prepared to pay out quite large sums to the upper gentry in the 'hope that their local prominence could be harnessed, if necessary, to the cause of the Crown',[181] the case of the Abberbury family suggests that that hope must often have been a forlorn one. There was certainly a sense in which Sir Richard *le pere*'s patiently-acquired local standing worked, incidentally, to the advantage of his royal patron. From March 1382 until his death, Sir Richard *le pere* served as a justice of the peace in either Berkshire or Oxfordshire, sometimes simultaneously in both counties. He was appointed, in addition, to eleven commissions of *oyer et terminer*, three commissions of array and three miscellaneous commissions of inquiry in his native counties.[182] His co-operation in undertaking these tasks was clearly important for the smooth and peaceable running of local government, and his conscientiousness in discharging them was sharpened by an appreciation that such appointments conferred upon him an additional consequence in local society that he owed directly to the favour of the Crown. Equally, by recruiting kinsmen and neighbours to serve abroad in his retinue of war, Sir Richard was effectively harnessing local networks of alliance and support to the service of the Crown.[183] Yet when called upon by their patrons to make a commitment of a more positive and risky kind, neither father nor son would oblige. Sir Richard *le pere* steered so careful a course through the Appellancy crisis that neither the king nor the Appellants could unequivocally count him among their supporters or their opponents. Sir Richard *le filz* had received some £700 in retaining fees from John of Gaunt, but he chose to disengage himself from Lancastrian service at precisely the moment, early in 1400, that the new king's régime was most in need of his support. Their pusillanimity is understandable, for the penalties of miscalculation were high; Thomas Abberbury's career, blighted by the events of 1387/8, prematurely terminated by those of 1399, was a dismal reminder of how easily the winds of fortune could shift. Some protection might be sought by cultivating as wide and non-partisan an acquaintanceship as possible – the Abberburys' ranged from former Appellants like Derby and Arundel to royalist partisans like Holland and Walden – but, in general, the factions and feuds of the magnates must have seemed to the courtier-gentry a dangerous inconvenience, to be avoided as far as possible. With so many members of the political nation possessing a vested interest in political inertia, the hope of mobilizing the upper gentry on their own behalf was one fraught with danger for the kings of later medieval England. Edward IV's desire to make things 'sit stil and be quiet'[184] seems, on the evidence of the Abberbury family, to have been a more realistic ambition.

Notes

* I would like to thank Edmund King and Gerald Harriss for their comments on an earlier draft of this article.

1 E. F. Jacob, *Essays in Later Medieval History* (Manchester, 1968), p. 150.

2 T. F. Tout, *Chapters in the Administrative History of Medieval England* (Manchester, 1923–35) iv. 341, v. 261; R. H. Jones, *The Royal Policy of Richard II: Absolutism in the Later Middle Ages* (Oxford, 1968), p. 134; K. B. McFarlane, *Lancastrian Kings and Lollard Knights* (Oxford, 1972), p. 25.

3 C. Given-Wilson, *The Royal Household and the King's Affinity: Service, Politics and Finance in England, 1360–1413* (New Haven, 1986), pp. 262–7.

4 K. B. McFarlane, 'Parliament and "Bastard Feudalism" ', *T.R.H.S.*, 4th Series, xxvi (1944), 53–79 marks the origin of this interest; J. S. Roskell, *Parliament and Politics in Late Medieval England*, vols. ii–iii (London, 1981) collects some pioneering case studies. For current thinking, P. R. Coss, *The Langley Family and its Cartulary: a study in late medieval 'gentry'* (Dugdale Soc., Occasional Papers, xxii, 1974); A. J. Pollard, 'The Richmondshire community of gentry during the Wars of the Roses', *Patronage, Pedigree and Power in Later Medieval England*, ed. C. Ross (Gloucester, 1979), pp. 37–59; M. J. Bennett, 'A county community: social cohesion among the Cheshire gentry, 1400–1425', *Northern History*, viii (1973), 24–44; N. Saul, *Knights and Esquires: The Gloucestershire Gentry in the Fourteenth Century* (Oxford, 1980); idem, *Scenes from Provincial Life: Knightly Families in Sussex 1280–1400* (Oxford, 1986); C. Richmond, *John Hopton, A Fifteenth Century Suffolk Gentleman* (Cambridge, 1981); S. M. Wright, *The Derbyshire Gentry in the Fifteenth Century* (Derbyshire Record Soc., viii, 1983); *Gentry and Lesser Nobility in Late Medieval Europe*, ed. M. Jones (Gloucester, 1986).

5 G. L. Harriss, 'Introduction', in K. B. McFarlane, *England in the Fifteenth Century: Collected Essays* (London, 1981), p. xxvii.

6 P. Hyde, 'The Winchester Manors at Witney and Adderbury (Oxon.) in the Later Middle Ages' (unpub. Oxford B. Litt. thesis, 1954), pp. 105, 115.

7 A. B. Emden, *A biographical register of the University of Oxford* (Oxford, 1957–59), i. 2; *Episcopal Registers, diocese of Worcester. Register of Bishop Godfrey Giffard*, ed. J. W. Willis-Bund (Worcestershire Historical Soc., xv, 1902), i. 28.

8 *The register of William Wickwane, lord Archbishop of York, 1279–1285*, ed. W. Brown (Surtees Soc., cxiv, 1907), pp. 67, 78, 259; *The register of John le Romeyn, lord Archbishop of York, 1286–1296*, ed. W. Brown (Surtees Soc., cxxiii–cxxviii, 1913–17); i. 27, ii. 329.

9 B[ritish] L[ibrary], Stowe Charter 647; *C[alendar of] P[atent] R[olls], 1292–1301*, 224, 236.

10 *Liber epistolaris of Richard de Bury*, ed. N. Denholm-Young (Roxburghe Club, 1950), p. 301; *C.P.R. 1301–7*, 392; P[ublic] R[ecord] O[ffice], SC 8/236/11754; *C[alendar of] . . . P[apal] R[egisters]. Letters, 1198–1304*, 601.

11 Tout, *Chapters*, ii. 87–93, 175–7; *Records of the Trial of Walter Langton, bishop of Coventry and Lichfield, 1307–12*, ed. A. Beardwood (Camden Soc., 4th series, vi, 1969), pp. 276–8.

12 *York Minster Fasti*, ed. Sir C. T. Clay (Yorkshire Archaeological Soc., cxxiv, 1959), ii. 44–5, 85–6.

13 *John le Neve: Fasti Ecclesiae Anglicanae 1300–1541 X: Coventry and Lichfield*, ed. B. Jones (London, 1964), p. 66; *C.P.R. 1292–1301*, 345; *C[alendar of] C[lose] R[olls], 1297–1302*, 245, 311.

14 *Rotuli Hundredorum* (Record Commission, 1812–18), ii. 866–7; PRO, CP 25 (1)/9/33/17; *The three earliest subsidies for the county of Sussex in the years 1296, 1327, 1332*, ed. W. Hudson (Sussex Record Soc., x, 1910), p. 58; *C[alendar of] I[nquisitions] M[iscellaneous], 1307–49*, no. 504; PRO, C 143/29/11. All documents cited are, unless otherwise indicated, in the Public Record Office, London.

15 CP 25 (1)/188/12/29, 39, 49, 70; 13/35, 64; Leicestershire Record Office, 26 D 53/90: H. Barrett, *Glympton. The history of an Oxfordshire manor* (Oxfordshire Record Soc., v, 1923), p. 32.

16 CP 25 (1)/9/36/23, 37/7, 20.

17 CP 40/215, deeds, m. 1; *Records of the Trial of Walter Langton*, pp. 262–70; *C.I.M., 1307–49*, nos. 504, 566; A Beardwood, *The Trial of Walter Langton, Bishop of Coventry and Lichfield, 1307–12* (Transactions of the American Philosophical Society, new series, liv, 1964), p. 17.

18 *C[alendar of] I[nquisitions] P[ost] M[ortem], 1300–1307*, no. 432.

19 Souldern, in particular, was to prove a thorn in the Abberbury's side. By 1316 they had been violently ejected from the manor by the aggrieved Lewknor family, one of the original litigants for seisin. In 1318 the family were further threatened by a demand for £1000, on the strength of a forged statute merchant which Master Thomas had allegedly given to bishop Langton as security for the manor, and it was not until 1323 that the Abberburys' right to Souldern was finally vindicated. *C.I.P.M., 1307–1316*, no. 619; *Feudal Aids, 1284–1431*, iv. 169; *C.C.R. 1313–18*, 297; *Select Cases concerning the Law Merchant*, ed. H. Hall (Selden Soc., xlix, 1932), iii. 21–2, 43–47; E 199/36/4/6; *C.I.M., 1307–49*, no. 838.

20 *C.I.P.M., 1300–1307*, no. 432; CP 25 (1)/188/12/39.

21 CP 25 (1)/188/13/18, 189/14/20, 46, 133; *Registrum Henrici Woodlock, diocesis Wintonensis, 1305–16*, ed. A. W. Goodman (Canterbury and York Soc., xliii, 1940), pp. 689–91; *C.C.R., 1323–7*, 4; *Records of the Trial of Walter Langton*, pp. 276–8.

22 N[ew] C[ollege] M[uniments], 10370–2; *C.I.P.M., 1316–27*, no. 527; CP 25 (1)/10/49/14; 50/19; C 143/73/23.

23 *C.P.R. 1292–1301*, 180.

24 *C.I.M. 1307–49*, no. 2107; Coss, *The Langley Family and its Cartulary*, p. 6.

25 *Parliamentary Writs* ed. F. Palgrave (Record Commission, 1827–32), II. i. 712, 719, 724, 732; *C.P.R. 1324–7*, 231, 286–7; *ibid., 1327–30*, 89, 355; *C[alendar of] F[ine] R[olls], 1327–37*, 40.

26 *Rotuli Parliamentorum* (London, 1783), ii. 441; *C.P.R. 1327–30*, 429, 481; *ibid., 1330–4*, 137, 288, 295, 296, 349; *C.F.R., 1327–37*, 377.

27 B. H. Putnam, 'Shire Officials: Keepers of the Peace and Justices of the Peace', *The English Government at Work, 1327–36*, ed. J. F. Willard and W. H. Dunham (Cambridge, Mass., 1950), iii. 188.

28 W[estminster] A[bbey] M[uniments], 1923.

29 *C.I.P.M., 1327–36*, no. 557; *C.F.R. 1327–37*, 417–8; *C.C.R. 1339–41*, 352, 384; Berkshire R[ecord] O[ffice], D/EBp T 65/2.

30 *Register of Edward the Black Prince, 1346–8*, 21; Hon. G. Wrottesley, *Crécy and Calais* (Collections for a History of Staffordshire, xviii, 1897), pp. 98, 143, 162; A. R. Wagner, *A Catalogue of English Medieval Rolls of Arms* (Oxford, 1950), p. 60.

31 KB 27/255 m. 70^{d}.; *C.C.R. 1323–7*, 163.

32 CP 25 (1)/10/50/19, 54/38; N.C.M. 10352, 14056–7; CP 25 (1)/189/17/87.

33 N.C.M. 10347, 10354.

34 Lincolnshire A[rchives] O[ffice], Ancaster MSS., 2^{A}/18/6.

35 *The Scrope and Grosvenor controversy*, ed. N. H. Nicolas (London, 1832), i. 166–7, ii. 378; Lincs. A. O., Ancaster, 2^{A}/18/6.

36 *C.P.R. 1364–7*, 327; *C.C.R. 1364–8*, 249.

37 *C.P.R. 1361–4*, 190; *C.C.R. 1364–8*, 185; *ibid., 1369–74*, 611.

38 C 76/34 mm. 8, 15.

39 *Register of Edward the Black Prince, 1346–8*, 21, 31; C 61/79 m. 14, 83 m. 3; C 81/919/42; E 101/29/24.

40 *Life of the Black Prince, by the herald of Sir John Chandos*, ed. M. K. Pope and E. C. Lodge (Oxford, 1910), lines 4215–9; *Cal. Pap. Reg., Letters, 1362–1404*, 28, 93, 95; Archives départementales des Pyrénées-Atlantiques, E 742. I owe my knowledge of this last document to Dr. M. C. E. Jones.

41 C 81/959/24; E 101/33/25 mm. 1–3; E 364/9 m. 9; E 403/460 m. 13 (1374); C 81/456/304, 982/3; E 364/13 m. 3, 15 m. 6 (1378).

42 *Anglo-Norman Letters and Petitions*, ed. M. D. Legge (Anglo-Norman Text Society, Oxford, 1941), pp. 198–202; M. Jones, *Ducal Brittany, 1364–1399* (Oxford, 1970), pp. 148–50.

43 E 101/37/2, 30; 68/7 (10); E 364/13 m. 3.

44 CHES 2/48 m. 2.

45 *C.P.R. 1377–81*, 155; N. Orme, *From Childhood to Chivalry* (London, 1984), pp. 18–20.

46 Tout, *Chapters*, v. 431–40; *C.P.R. 1374–7*, 376; *Testamenta Vetusta* ed. N. H. Nicolas (London, 1826), p. 14.

47 E 101/398/8 m. 2.

48 Thomas Walsingham, *Historia Anglicana*, ed. H. T. Riley (Rolls Series, 1863–4), i. 330.

49 *C.P.R. 1377–81*, 155; E 101/401/2 f. 42; E 403/521 m. 6.

50 E 101/318/21 m. 2; E 403/472 m. 17, 478 m. 23; E 364/13 m. 4^{v}.

51 E 403/481 m. 13; E 364/15 m. 6; *The diplomatic correspondence of Richard II*, ed. E. Perroy (Camden Soc., 3rd series, xlviii, 1933), nos. 27, 28.

52 *C.C.R. 1381–5*, 135; *C.P.R. 1381–5* 263, 291, 335; *ibid., 1385–9*, 154; C 81/1349/8; *Issues of the Exchequer, Henry III–Henry VI*, ed. F. Devon (Record Commission, 1847), pp. 221–2.

53 E.g., E 403/465 m. 12; C 81/980/33; E 403/471 m. 3, 502 m. 10; *Select Cases Before the King's Council, 1243–1482*, ed. I. S. Leadam and J. F. Baldwin (Selden Soc., xxxv, 1918), p. 74; J. F. Baldwin, *The King's Council in England in the Later Middle Ages* (Oxford, 1913), pp. 507, 517.

54 C 81/980/39; *C.P.R. 1377–81*, 121; *C.F.R. 1377–83*, 50, 257; E 403/487 m. 22; *C.P.R. 1389–92*, 107.

55 Given-Wilson, *The King's Affinity*, pp. 169–73.

56 E.g., SC 6/773/4 m. 3, 6 m. 3, 8 m. 3, 10 m. 3, 12 m. 3.

57 *C.P.R. 1377–81*, 23, 155; C 47/9/57, mm. 9, 11.

58 *C.P.R. 1381–5*, 311; *ibid., 1385–9*, 15. It is difficult to disentangle the full details of Sir Richard's sale of his Sussex manors but, since he apparently received from Sir John Arundel, the purchaser, a life-interest in the manor of Stapleford (Wilts.) and the advowson of Aynho (Northants), besides 200 marks in cash, it seems likely that he misrepresented the extent of his financial loss to the King. *An abstract of feet of fines relating to the county of Sussex from 1 Edward II to 24 Henry VII*, ed. L. F. Salzman (Sussex Record Soc., xxiii, 1916), no. 2457; *C.C.R. 1374–7*, 432, 458; C 138/12/3; J. Bridges, *The History and Antiquities of Northamptonshire* (Oxford, 1791), i. 138.

59 E 101/401/2 f. 42; *Foedera, conventiones, litterae*, ed. T. Rymer (Hague, 1737–45), III. iii. 74, 77.

60 For fourteenth-century valuations of the Abberbury lands: C 133/26/8; C 135/37/20, 81/4. These inquisitions *post-mortem* give a maximum valuation of just over £100 p.a. but do not cover all the family manors.

61 Tout, *Chapters*, iv. 334–5; Tuck, *Richard II and the English Nobility*, p. 65.

62 *Chronicon Henrici Knighton*, ed. J. R. Lumby (Rolls Series, 1889–95), ii. 294 estimates this at 3000 marks a year, which may not be so far out. Tuck, pp. 74–5; C. J. Given-Wilson, 'Richard II and his grandfather's will', *E.H.R.*, xciii (1978), 327–30.

63 *C.P.R. 1377–81*, 70; *ibid., 1381–5*, 316, 339; *ibid., 1385–9*, 17, 18, 279.

64 *C.P.R. 1385–9*, 469; C 76/70 m. 15, 72 mm. 11, 12; *C.C.R. 1385–9*, 299.

65 *C.P.R. 1385–9*, 469; *ibid., 1388–92*, 134–5, 341.

66 *Oxfordshire Sessions of the Peace in the reign of Richard II*, ed. E. G. Kimball (Oxfordshire Record Soc., liii, 1983), pp. 60, 62, 65; cf. *ibid.*, p. 13 for the editor's suggestion that this roll of the Oxfordshire bench, which shows Sir Richard as the principal working justice, was prepared in response to demands made in the Cambridge Parliament for the better administration of justice. In which case, the picture it presents – Abberbury the responsible country gentleman, not the feckless and corrupt courtier – may not be entirely fortuitious.

67 Walsingham, *Historia Anglicana*, ii. 172; *The Westminster Chronicle, 1381–1394*, ed. L. C. Hector and B. F. Harvey (Oxford, 1982), p. 230; *Historia Vitae et Regni*

Ricardi Secundi, ed. G. B. Stow (Pennsylvania, 1977), p. 116; *Chronicon Henrici Knighton*, ii. 257, the most Lancastrian of the chronicles, omits Abberbury's name.

68 DL 28/1/2 ff. 16ᵛ, 26, 5ᵛ, 11ᵛ.

69 C 67/30, m. 12.

70 E 403/521 m. 6.

71 E 28/1 (unnumbered); *Calendar of Charter Rolls, 1341–1417*, 319; *C.P.R. 1389–92*, 374; *ibid., 1391–6*, 281; *C.C.R. 1385–9*, 681; *ibid., 1391–6*, 364.

72 *C.P.R. 1389–92*, 208, 210; *ibid., 1391–6*, 488, 731; *ibid., 1396–9* 245, 518.

73 *Proceedings and Ordinances of the Privy Council*, ed. N. H. Nicolas (London, 1834), i. 11, 17; E 403/530 m. 16; Perroy, *Diplomatic Correspondence of Richard II*, no. 120; C 76/74 mm. 5, 6.

74 E 403/548 m. 21, 551 m. 15; B.L., Royal 10 B IX f.2.

75 *Oxfordshire Sessions of the Peace*, p. 26; *Calendar of the General and Special Assize and General Gaol Delivery Commissions on the dorses of the Patent Rolls – Richard II* (Nendlen, 1977), nos. 422, 572; C 115/K2/6684 f. 150; *C.P.R. 1389–92*, 40, 47, 412, 425; *ibid., 1391–6*, 388; E 28/3 (5 June 1391).

76 *C.P.R. 1389–92*, 204; *ibid., 1391–6*, 489; *C.C.R. 1389–92*, 118; *ibid., 1396–9*, 34, 152; *C.P.R. 1391–6*, 526, 594; *ibid., 1396–9*, 136; *C.C.R. 1396–9*, 16, 25.

77 CP 25 (1)/12/74/5; Corporation of London R.O., Hustings Deeds Roll 105/20.

78 CP 25 (1)/191/23/1, 21, 38, 45.

79 *C.C.R. 1381–5*, 449; Cambridge University Library, Ms. Dd. III. 53 f. 132; W. Kennet, *Parochial Antiquities* (Oxford, 1695), ii. 73–4; *C.P.R. 1391–6*, 369.

80 *C.P.R. 1391–6*, 434, 438.

81 CP 25 (1)/12/78/5, 11.

82 SC 8/251/12546; *C.P.R. 1385–9*, 136.

83 M. Wood, *Donnington Castle (Berks.): Official Guide Book* (H.M.S.O., 1964), p. 16.

84 J. Evans, *English Art, 1307–1461* (Oxford, 1949), p. 121.

85 Given-Wilson, *The King's Affinity*, p. 169.

86 McFarlane, *Lancastrian Kings and Lollard Knights*, pp. 139–220.

87 C 143/342/19; *C.P.R. 1361–4*, 190; *ibid., 1399–1401*, 486.

88 C 143/356/5; *C.P.R. 1364–7*, 197; E 301/51/28.

89 N.C.M. 14035–6; *C.P.R. 1374–7*, 252; *Cal. Pap. Reg., Letters, 1396–1404*, 12–13.

90 H. F. Chettle, 'The Friars of the Holy Cross', *History*, xxxiv (1949), 204–20.

91 C 143/398/11; *C.P.R. 1391–6*, 209.

92 Bodleian Library, Oxford, Ms. Ch. Oxon. 403; B.L., Add. Ch. 7290; *C.P.R. 1391–6*, 267, 369.

93 'Laws, Statutes and Ordinances of Donnington Hospital', *Transactions of the Newbury and District Field Club*, iii (1875–6), 264–6.

94 J. Catto, 'Religion and the English Nobility in the late Fourteenth-century', *History and the Imagination*, ed. H. Lloyd-Jones, B. Worden, V. Pearl (London, 1981), p. 47. It is worth noting that the foundation of more almshouses was one of the avowed purposes of the Lollard disendowment bill put forward in 1410, and that the Crutched Friars were, with the Carthusians and the Bonshommes, one of the few religious orders exempt from the planned disendowment. A. Hudson, *Selections from English Wycliffite Writings* (Cambridge, 1978), pp. 135–7, 203–7.

95 B. H. Putnam, *The place in legal history of Sir William Shareshull, chief justice of the King's bench, 1350–61* (Cambridge, 1950), p. 7.

96 *C.C.R. 1381–5*, 449; *C.P.R. 1350–4*, 512.
97 The manors of Stainswick and Winterbourne Danvers, a sub-manor in South Denchworth and the advowson of the chapel of Chapelwick; Magdalen College, Oxford, Stainswick deeds, 7, 34[a], 83; SC 2/154/17 m. 1; *Cal. Ch. Rolls, 1341–1417*, 319. Lincs. A. O., Ancaster Mss., 2[A]/18/6, 7; *C.C.R., 1364–8*, 271 for earlier associations between the two families.
98 *C.C.R. 1389–92*, 162; JUST 3/216/4. The Abberburys were granted custody of the heir of John Baldington in 1393. *C.P.R. 1391–6*, 281.
99 C 1/29/62; *C.C.R. 1409–13*, 140, 141. The Arches also possessed a manor in East Hendred, where the Abberburys held land. *Victoria County History: Berkshire*, IV (London, 1924), 298.
100 F. W. Macnamara, 'Donnington Castle and its Ancient Lords', *Berkshire, Buckinghamshire and Oxfordshire Archaeological Journal*, iv (1898), 53–4; *Feudal Aids*, iv. 187; *C.P.R. 1391–6*, 276, 381.
101 *John of Gaunt's Register 1372–76*, ed. S. Armitage-Smith (Camden Soc., 3rd series, xxi, 1911), no. 969; C 81/988/1; *C.P.R. 1377–81*, 458; C 76/65 m. 7; *The Scrope and Grosvenor controversy*, i. 70–1.
102 East Sussex Record Office, Glynde Mss., GLY 3469 mm. 1–5; *John of Gaunt's Register, 1379–1383*, ed. E. C. Lodge and R. Somerville (Camden Soc., 3rd series, lvi, 1937), p. 7.
103 C 76/70 m. 17; DL 29/728/11975 m. 1; *John of Gaunt's Register 1379–1383*, nos. 1236, 1239; *Foedera*, III. iv. 28; DL 43/15/1 m. 4.
104 DL 43/15/3 m. 3.
105 DL 28/3/2 f. 6[v]; *C.C.R. 1392–6*, 544.
106 East Sussex Record Office, GLY 3469, mm. 6, 8, 10, 11, 12; DL 28/1/4 f. 18.
107 *Foedera*, III. iv. 28; *Proceedings and Ordinances of the Privy Council*, i. 14 c-d; A. Coville, *Pierre et Gontier Col* (Paris, 1934), pp. 26–7; R. Vaughan, *Philip the Bold* (London, 1962), p. 42 n. makes the identification of the English knight as Abberbury.
108 E 403/546 mm. 13, 16 (1393); E 159/173, Brevia Baronibus, Easter m. 1; E 403/549 mm. 2, 6; 551 m. 15; 556 m. 14; E 364/30 m. 4[v], 31 m. 5[v]; Perroy, *Diplomatic Correspondence of Richard II*, no. 230. B.L., Stowe Ms. 440 f. 20 suggests that it was originally intended to send both Sir Richard *le pere* and Sir Richard *le filz* on the German mission.
109 C 81/1078/17; C 76/82 m. 6; Perroy, nos. 233–4.
110 *Anglo-Norman Letters and Petitions*, ed. M. D. Legge, pp. 74–6; V. H. Galbraith, 'A New Life of Richard II', *History*, n.s., xxvi (1942), 231 for the correct date.
111 C 76/57 m. 13; E 403/496 m. 9; *The Stonor Letters and Papers, 1290–1483*, ed. C. L. Kingsford (Camden Soc., 3rd series, xxix–xxx, 1919), i. 23.
112 *C.F.R. 1383–91*, 16; *C.P.R. 1385–9*, 133.
113 E 101/68/10 (248); E 403/510 m. 30.
114 CP 25 (1)/223/105/8.
115 *C.P.R. 1391–6*, 535; *ibid., 1396–9*, 526; E 101/402/20 f. 10.
116 E 101/403/10 f. 43d; *C.P.R. 1396–9*, 107; E 403/559 m. 14; E 28/4 (95).
117 *C.P.R. 1396–9*, 469, 526.
118 N.C.M. 10373 establishes the relationship.
119 *C.P.R. 1381–5*, 140, 195; E 159/166, Brevia Directa Baronibus, Easter, m. 24; *Oxfordshire Sessions of the Peace*, pp. 25–6.
120 *C.F.R. 1391–9*, 124; *Manuscripts of St. George's Chapel, Windsor Castle*, ed. J. N. Dalton (Windsor, 1957), p. 172.

121 *C.C.R. 1392–6*, 278; *ibid., 1396–9*, 135.
122 DL 28/1/4 f. 18; S. Armitage-Smith, *John of Gaunt* (London, 1904), p. 428.
123 A. L. Brown, 'The reign of Henry IV: the establishment of the Lancastrian régime', *Fifteenth-century England 1399–1509*, ed. S. B. Chrimes, C. D. Ross, R. A. Griffiths (Manchester, 1972), pp. 15–19; F. R. H. du Boulay, 'Henry of Derby's Expeditions to Prussia, 1390–1 and 1392', *The Reign of Richard II*, ed. F. R. H. du Boulay and C. M. Barron (London, 1971), p. 172.
124 *C.P.R. 1399–1401*, 211; N.C.M. 14037; C 76/85 m. 14.
125 C 76/86 m. 11, 91 m. 2, 93 m. 17, 94 m. 17; N.C.M. 14040; *C.C.R. 1405–9*, 195; *ibid., 1409–13* 444.
126 DL 29/738/12098 m. 2, 12102 m. 2; DL 42/16 f. 180v.
127 CP 25 (1)/13/81/5, 6, 7, 8, 9.
128 C 1/29/62; Oxfordshire Record Office, Glympton deeds (unsorted); Bodleian, MS. Ch. Oxon. 2717; CP 25 (1)/191/26/6, 7, 8, 9. Chaucer had already secured the reversion of another Abberbury manor, Hook Norton; E 212/DS 79, printed in J. Hunter, 'The Seal of Chaucer', *Archaelogia*, xxxiv (1852), 43–4.
129 E.g., Sir John Cheyne, Sir Arnold Savage. J. S. Roskell, *Parliament and Politics in Late Medieval England*, ii. 82, iii. 73.
130 Roskell, iii. 28; J. D. Milner, 'Sir Simon Felbrigg, K. G.: the Lancastrian Revolution and personal fortune', *Norfolk Archaeology*, xxxvii (1978), 84–91.
131 Magdalen College, Oxford, Stainswick deeds, 83; CP 40/555 m. 3.
132 *C.P.R. 1399–1401*, 211; E 159/176, Communia, Adhuc Recorda, Hilary m. 16, Easter m. 1.
133 C 76/85 m. 14, 86 m. 11, 91 m. 2, 93 m. 17, 94 m. 17; Magdalen College, Stainswick deeds, 29. K. B. McFarlane, 'Henry V, Bishop Beaufort and the Red Hat', *E.H.R.*, lx (1945), 335 for Thomas Chaucer's extensive estates in Berkshire and Oxfordshire.
134 M. M. N. Stansfield, 'The Hollands, Dukes of Exeter, Earls of Kent and Huntingdon, 1352–1475' (Unpub. Oxford, D. Phil. thesis, 1987), p. 143, suggests Abberbury was implicated in the revolt of the earls in 1400. I have been unable to find any evidence to confirm this statement.
135 E 28/24 (8).
136 A. Molinier, 'Description de deux manuscrits contenant la règle de la "Militia Passionis Jhesu Christi" de Philippe de Mézières', *Archives de l'Orient Latin*, i (1881), 363–4; J. J. N. Palmer, *England, France and Christendom 1377–1399* (London, 1972), p. 206.
137 *C.C.R. 1405–9*, 195; *ibid., 1409–13*, 444.
138 E 101/509/19 f. 8^v.
139 DL 28/3/2 f. 6^v; E 403/549 m. 12; E 159/176, Communia, Adhuc Recorda, Hilary m. 16, Easter m. 1.
140 CP 25 (1)/12/76/14; W. N. Clarke, *Parochial Topography of the Hundred of Wanting* (Oxford, 1824), p. 102.
141 N.C.M., 14037.
142 *Stonor Letters and Papers, 1290–1483*, ed. Kingsford, ii. 98.
143 E 101/106/11; E 159/179, Brevia Baronibus, Michaelmas m. 10; E 404/17/790; *C.P.R. 1399–1401*, 364, 503.
144 E 404/16/54, 640; 17/298, 671; 18/137, 19/425; *Calendar of Signet Letters of Henry IV and Henry V, 1399–1422*, ed. J. L. Kirby (H.M.S.O., 1978), no. 592; E 404/22/475.

145 C 266/38/15; *C.P.R. 1408–13*, 94.
146 *Cal. Pap. Reg., Letters, 1396–1404*, 563, 569; *C.C.R. 1435–41*, 344, *ibid., 1454–61*, 294.
147 *C.F.R. 1430–7*, 119; *C.P.R. 1429–36*, 402.
148 E 326/7483/1, 2, 3; E 210/6125; *C.P.R. 1441–6*, 358; SC 12/5/59, 60; R. Faith, 'Berkshire: Fourteenth and Fifteenth Centuries', *The Peasant Land Market in Medieval England*, ed. P. D. A. Harvey (Oxford, 1984), pp. 144–5.
149 *C.P.R. 1446–52*, 169.
150 CP 25 (1)/13/84/21, 24; 85/16, 17; Lincs. A. O., Ancaster Mss. 2^A/19–22, 24.
151 N.C.M., 14025.
152 Lincs. A. O., Ancaster Mss., 2^A/26.
153 E 212/DS 60; Lincs. A. O., Ancaster Mss. 2^A/30–34; Berkshire R.O., H/R Ta 25; B.L., Add. Ch. 15764.
154 *A cartulary of the hospital of St. John the Baptist*, ed. H. E. Salter (Oxford Historical Soc., lxvi-lxix, 1914–17), iii. 266, 271, 275, 279.
155 *C.P.R. 1408–13*, 484; *C.F.R. 1399–1405*, 38, 45; CP 25 (1)/179/90/39, B.L., Egerton Ms. 1938 f. 84; P. Hyde, 'The Winchester Manors at Witney and Adderbury (Oxon.) in the Later Middle Ages' (Unpub. Oxford, B.Litt. thesis, 1954), p. 319.
156 A. B. Emden, *A biographical register . . . Oxford*, i. 1; B.L., Egerton Ms. 1938, ff. 85^v, 86.
157 B.L., Add. MS. 15644, f.3; B.L., Egerton MS. 1938, f. 87.
158 T. Fuller, *The History of the Worthies of England* (London, 1662), pp. 99–100, 112.
159 D. A. Carpenter, 'Was there a crisis of the knightly class in the thirteenth century? The Oxfordshire evidence', *E.H.R.*, xcv (1980), 724; N. Saul, 'The Social Status of Chaucer's Franklin: a reconsideration', *Medium Aevum*, lii (1983), 23; Clarke, *Parochial Topography of the Hundred of Wanting*, p. 102; CP 25 (1)/13/81/5 for lands bought by the Hydes from the Abberburys.
160 C 143/29/11; 73/23; 356/5; N.C.M. 14037.
161 Houlbrooke, *The English Family 1450–1700*, p. 40.
162 N.C.M. 14034; *C.C.R. 1389–92*, 510; *ibid., 1396–9*, 85.
163 C 1/29/62.
164 C 138/12/3.
165 Coss, *Langley Family and its Cartulary*, p. 10.
166 C. F. Richmond, 'After McFarlane', *History*, lxviii (1983), 60–1.
167 J. R. Maddicott, 'Thomas of Lancaster and Sir Robert Holland', *E.H.R.*, lxxxvi (1971), 449.
168 *A descriptive C[atalogue of] A[ncient] D[eeds]* (H.M.S.O., 1890–1915), ii. B3268–3271; *C.C.R. 1381–5*, 449; *ibid., 1385–9* 97, 297; *ibid., 1389–92*, 399, 401–2, 501 (Lovell); *C.C.R. 1385–9*, 224; *C.P.R. 1399–1401*, 348; *ibid., 1401–5* 172 (Holland).
169 *C.C.R. 1364–8*, 165; *ibid., 1377–81*, 126, 375, 377; *ibid., 1381–5*, 239–40; Winchester College Muniments, 1 (17 June 1393); *Cal. of General and Special Assizes*, no. 422 (Wykeham); *C.C.R. 1381–5*, 449; *ibid., 1389–92*, 399, 401–2, 501; M. Aston, *Thomas Arundel* (Oxford, 1967), p. 193 (Arundel).
170 *C.P.R. 1377–81*, 341. For the association between Abberbury and Vache, *C.P.R. 1391–6*, 331; *ibid., 1396–9*, 136; *C.C.R. 1377–81*, 203; *ibid., 1396–9*, 16, 25; CP 25 (1)/191/23/38; C.A.D., iii. D 390; C 115/K2/6684 f. 178^v.
171 G. G. Astill, 'The Medieval Gentry: a study in Leicestershire Society, 1350–99'

(unpublished University of Birmingham Ph.D. thesis, 1977), p. 314; Wright, *The Derbyshire Gentry in the Fifteenth Century*, p. 59.

172 *Calendar of Pleas and Memoranda Rolls, 1364–81*, ed. A. H. Thomas (Cambridge, 1929), p. 301; *C.C.R. 1364–8*, 182; *ibid., 1381–5*, 91; Corporation of London Record Office, Husting Deeds Roll 105/20 (Twyford); *C.C.R. 1389–92*, 334; C.L.R.O., Husting Deeds Roll 129/38 (Barentyn).

173 Westminster Abbey Muniments, 7396–7, 3852–3.

174 *C.A.D.*, i. C 987; Bodleian, Ms. Ch. Oxon. 403; *C.C.R. 1364–8*, 249; *ibid., 1377–81*, 375, 377.

175 E 101/37/2; *C.A.D.*, iii. B 3268–71; *C.C.R. 1381–5*, 449, 625; *ibid., 1385–9*, 97, 297; N.C.M. 14034.

176 *The Boarstall Cartulary*, ed. H. E. Salter (Oxford Historical Soc., lxxxviii, 1930), nos. 195–6; *C.C.R. 1377–81* 375, 377; *ibid., 1381–5*, 239–40; *ibid., 1385–9*, 297, 443; *ibid., 1389–92*, 334.

177 CP 25 (1)/12/78/4; C.A.D., iii. B 3268–71; *C.C.R. 1385–9*, 97, 297.

178 Bodleian, Ms. Ch. Oxon. 403; W.A.M. 7397; *C.P.R. 1377–81*, 444; *C.C.R. 1381–5*, 91; *ibid., 1385–9*, 115; *ibid., 1396–9*, 193; *Boarstall Cartulary*, nos. 195–6; JUST 3/172 m. 8.

179 N.C.M. 14034; CP 25 (1)/12/78/4; *C.F.R. 1391–9*, 136, 331; *C.P.R. 1391–6*, 331; *ibid., 1396–9*, 136, 586; *C.C.R. 1385–9*, 297; *ibid., 1399–1402*, 304–5 (Willicotes); *C.F.R. 1391–9*, 136; C.L.R.O., Husting Deeds Roll 129/38; *Boarstall Cartulary*, no. 196; *C.C.R. 1381–5*, 449; *ibid., 1385–9*, 443; *ibid., 1389–92*, 334, 510 (Barentyns).

180 E 364/13 m. 3; *C.C.R. 1374–7*, 528; *ibid., 1377–81*, 126, 138; *ibid., 1389–92*, 510; *C.A.D.*, iii. B 3268–71.

181 Given Wilson, *The King's Affinity*, p. 266.

182 *C.P.R. 1374–7*, 157, 220; *ibid., 1377–81*, 473, 628; *ibid., 1381–5*, 146, 195, 196, 197, 202, 247, 255, 284, 347, 426, 498; *ibid., 1385–9*, 80, 82; *ibid., 1389–92*, 208, 210, 214–5, 345, 516; *ibid., 1391–6*, 92, 434, 438; *ibid., 1396–9*, 99, 236, 371–2; *C.F.R. 1377–83*, 163; *C.C.R. 1381–5*, 176, 595; *ibid., 1399–1402*, 304–5.

183 E.g., E 101/37/2. The first two names on this retinue list are those of Sir Thomas Paynel and William Abberbury.

184 D. A. L. Morgan, 'The King's Affinity in the Polity of Yorkist England', *T.R.H.S.*, 5th series, xxiii (1973), 17.

3

Communities of the county in later medieval England*

The 'county community' in later medieval England enjoyed a brief but influential vogue during the 1980s, lasting roughly from Nigel Saul's *Knights and Esquires* (published in 1981), a study of the Gloucestershire gentry in the fourteenth century, to Simon Payling's *Political Society in Lancastrian England* (published in 1991), a study (despite its title) of the Nottinghamshire gentry in the first half of the fifteenth. This vogue was partly the consequence of a kind of intellectual overspill from the early modern period, then suffering from a glut of such county studies, but it also owed a good deal to the concise and vigorous case argued by John Maddicott, in a series of influential articles, for treating the fourteenth-century shire as an active and politically minded community, no longer predominantly the passive recipient of royal instructions, but 'electing representatives, petitioning, and expressing its views in parliament.'[1] From the first, however, there were dissentient voices. Susan Wright concluded, as early as 1983, that in fifteenth-century Derbyshire there was as yet 'no coherent county social group or "community" '. This scepticism gathered pace as historians digested the implications of Robert Palmer's demonstration that the development of the so-called 'viscontiel writs' had deprived the county courts of all effective jurisdiction by the 1330s, and his contention that, in their broader administrative work, those courts were largely dominated by trained lawyers acting as the attorneys and seneschals of the local aristocracy. During the 1990s, a more widespread reaction set in: Peter Coss warned against overemphasising the county as a factor for social cohesion during the century after the Angevin legal reforms; Michael Prestwich cast an unimpressed eye over the development of county consciousness in the thirteenth century, concluding that the counties were still largely institutions of royal government, serving the king more than local society; and Christine Carpenter, in her massive work on fifteenth-century Warwickshire, denied the existence of a *social* community of the county altogether. Left to their own devices, Carpenter suggests, the gentry formed associations that were determined by geographical, rather than administrative, divisions – hence, 'the forces that bound the gentry together served to pull the county apart'; only in the (relatively rare) cases that a nobleman proved both powerful and able enough to draw the disparate and localised gentry communities together could any sense of corporate consciousness be said to exist.[2]

My impression is that this scepticism is rapidly becoming professional orthodoxy: Richard Britnell has recently argued that, although the notion of a county community can be given 'some meaningful content for *some* administrative operations', it will not serve as a generally applicable framework for political history; Tony Pollard has similarly concluded that, while evidence undoubtedly exists to show that contemporaries had a sense of the body of the shire, it is doubtful whether the county community ever had the capacity or will to exercise independent collective political authority.[3] Ought we, then, to leave it at that? Admit the existence of social communities among the county gentry, created by ties of kinship and geographical proximity, but resist the notion of an effective county community, capable of imposing certain social norms within the shire and generally accepted as entitled to represent the corporate grievances and demands of its inhabitants in a variety of administrative and political contexts? This brief survey is an attempt to argue, in a somewhat schematic fashion, that there *is* more to the county community than that, and to suggest that, before we decide to ban the word 'community' from all academic writing,[4] we should take time to rescue the baby from the bathwater.

At the outset, two disclaimers need to be entered. The first concerns the unnecessary polarisation that has taken hold of the debate about the nature and significance of the later medieval county community. A lot of heat has been generated by the tendency to link belief in the influence of the county community with the argument for appreciable numbers of 'independent gentry', living outside the immediate embrace of magnate lordship. It is this group that some historians consider primarily responsible for the frequent petitions against noble maintenance and the abuses of livery put forward by the parliamentary Commons, while the persistence of the Commons' campaign against the abuses of lordship is seen as a major argument for the political significance of the shire communities who promoted the petitions.[5] Conversely, a belief in the predominance of noble authority as the normal organising principle within local society has come to be associated with a vigorous dismissal of the county community's claims to significance. Although the two issues – the 'independent gentry' and the county community – are obviously relevant to one another, they are also clearly separable. To argue for the importance of the county community is not necessarily to deny the simultaneous significance of magnate lordship.[6] As Susan Reynolds has commented, 'community did not involve equality'; even within a community that was not itself united by submission to a single lord, there was no incongruity in acknowledging seigneurial rights of consultation and representation. In practice, horizontal and vertical principles of social organisation often proved complementary rather than antagonistic.[7] Nigel Saul's recent study of the administration of the oath sworn in Sussex to uphold the acts of the Merciless Parliament in June 1388 shows that both the six rape courts of the shire and the powerful lordship of the earl of Arundel were at work in coralling as many as 90 of the lesser gentry of the shire into swearing their allegiance.[8] The second disclaimer is really only an amplification of the first; it is that, in discussing the county community, we should not envisage an organisation that made exclusive demands on the sentiment and attention of its members. It was one of a number of lesser solidarities – the parish, the hundred, the kindred, the affinity – which might each play a part of variable significance in the social, and occasionally the political, life of the later medieval gentry. The aim of this paper is to attempt to define what that part was and to suggest, briefly, how it may have changed over time.

A certain amount turns, of course, on what we mean by a 'community'. It is undeniable, I think, that the county community, the *communitas comitatum*, possessed considerable institutional significance in later medieval England. A county had a corporate personality and could legally both sue and be sued: the 'community of the whole county of Leicester' sued William Boyville in 1288–90, for example, for his misappropriation of certain buildings, intended to be the county gaol, that had been constructed with the proceeds of a general levy of the county during his shrievalty.[9] It is the community of the county, gathered in the shire court, that returns two representatives to Parliament and it was in the name of the community that those representatives granted the king a subsidy. It is also generally agreed that this institutional significance was enhanced by the changing administrative and fiscal requirements of the Crown during the fourteenth century. The system of fixed subsidy quotas introduced in 1334 required county representatives to apportion the fiscal burden between the shire's hundreds and towns, for example, while county representatives were similarly required to confer in 1352 with the justices of labourers and tax-collectors on the question of distributing the tax relief generated by fines imposed for labour offences.[10] The difficulty arises in determining how far the county's undisputed activity as an administrative territory *also* fostered a sense of social community, for 'community', in this sense, also carries with it a series of less precise meanings and expectations: a shared sense of values, a collective sense of purpose, a common agenda.

Some of the disagreement among historians about the existence and the significance of the county community springs from largely unacknowledged differences in their definition of 'community' in this context. Some proponents of the county community have tacitly adopted the notion of 'occasional community', for example, where the shire community is conceptualised *not* as a continuous state, but as one realised momentarily at particular junctures, either regularly, at the meetings of the shire court, or sporadically, at those especially afforced social gatherings, first identified by Michael Bennett as significant expressions of 'county consciousness', where a deliberate effort has apparently been made to bring together a large and representative body of local notables.[11] Eric Acheson has recently used a similar example, the 35 local gentry and clergy called to witness the birth and death of Robert Sherrard's daughter, Joan, in 1446, to suggest that the idea of a shire community was something that did not need to be constantly reaffirmed in commonplace transactions, since it was largely taken for granted and would surface naturally at times of difficulty or crisis.[12] The problem with this idea is to determine what keeps the sense of community in being during the periods of abeyance: *how*, exactly, is it 'taken for granted'? The 'occasional community' looks, in many respects, like a collective, whose communal meaning is exhausted once the action for which it was temporarily assembled is completed. An effective notion of community seems to require, rather, a sense of collective awareness, a set of shared assumptions that dispose the individual towards the group and, in doing so, transform collectivity into community.

One popular solution to this problem, latent in most discussions of the county community, is to identify a 'shire establishment' of leading gentry families, who take the most active part in county administration and representation, attract the lion's share of royal and baronial patronage, and foster a sense of identity within the county by their long-established social solidarity. Simon Payling points to the display of the arms of leading Nottinghamshire families in the window of archbishop Kempe's great hall at Southwell as evidence of the local superiority of one such group.[13] This convenient identification of an emotional and mental community (the 'county') with a social one has considerable empirical support: Henry Bracton made it, when he spoke of the *buzones*, the 'big shots', on whose nod the decisions of the shire court depended,[14] and there are plenty of late medieval examples of the same phenomenon; the dominance of Sir John Tiptoft and half a dozen associates in early Lancastrian Huntingdonshire, for example.[15] It has, though, also been the subject of severe criticism, essentially on two grounds: first, that the most prominent gentry families were often 'regional' rather than 'county' families, holding estates in several shires, with the result that it is not easy to demonstrate the county to be the *essential* focus of those families' identities; secondly, that since there was as yet no single focus of shire administration, such as the quarter sessions were to provide in the sixteenth century, a record of repeated office-holding cannot be fully identified, as it very often is, with local leadership.[16]

Neither of these objections seems to me to be especially powerful. Substantial gentry families did, indeed, hold land in several counties, but this did not preclude them identifying, or being identified, with one particular shire at any one time. The Hastings family of Slingsby, to take only one example, were a North Yorkshire family who acquired extensive estates, by marriage, in Leicestershire and traditionally elected to be buried at Sulby abbey in Northamptonshire, where they enjoyed the privilege of founders, yet there is no doubt that, at least until 1405, it was the shire community of Yorkshire that absorbed their local loyalties.[17] Nor were the Hastings untypical in this for, by the late fourteenth century, gentry identification with a single shire seems far advanced: 90 per cent of the county MPs elected between 1386 and 1421 sat for a single county while, of the remainder, a further 7 per cent were returned only in the two counties of a joint-shrievalty, where traditions of administrative co-operation were already well established.[18] The second objection, that there was no identifiable form of shire administration, underestimates the continuing significance of the county court. The court's judicial competence was certainly reduced by the mid-fourteenth century, but the meetings of the shire retained considerable administrative importance, as occasions when charters and statutes were proclaimed, petitions drafted, county rates fixed, and the visiting justices of assize informed of the disposition of the county; as a result, those gentry whose tenure of local office, as sheriff, escheator or justice of the peace, required their regular attendance at shire days inevitably acquired substantial influence over the decisions taken there. Local variations make it, in any case, hazardous to generalise too firmly. In a county like Cornwall, where there were few private hundreds to siphon off judicial business, where most of the substantial gentry attended a significant number of sessions of the peace, and where the county bench was exceptionally mobile, sitting in as many as 16 different locations within the shire, there is a reasonable case to be made for the quarter sessions already playing a significant role in the articulation of county sentiment, as early as Richard II's reign.[19]

The role of the 'shire establishment' in articulating and representing the sense of community within their counties does, therefore, seem a significant one, but this is not the same as saying that they *were* the county community. The sporadic but consistent evidence appearing throughout the later middle ages for occasional large gatherings at the shire court – the 170 distrainees and their mainpernors present at the Northumberland county court in 1278, or the 266 voters present at the Nottinghamshire parliamentary election in 1460 – points to the existence of a much broader group of lesser gentry and small freeholders who claimed some influence over the decisions of their social superiors.[20] There was clearly more to the county community than the concerns and ambitions of the 'hardcore of local political figures' who tended to dominate the meetings of the county court: but how much more? Answering this question requires some consideration of what contemporaries understood by 'the county' and of the degree of communal identity they invested in it. What needs to be established is whether contemporaries thought there was a sense in which the county could be imagined communally, *not* whether the social organisation of gentry society conformed to our own stringent standards of cohesion. All communities larger than primordial villages of face-to-face contact are, after all, in some sense 'imagined communities', to be distinguished from one another chiefly by 'the style in which they are imagined'.[21]

Identifying and defining the existence of a shared 'county consciousness' is a delicate, sometimes thankless, task. An attempt to evoke a 'Lincolnshire mentality' in the fourteenth century concluded that it was not really possible to speak of Lincolnshire as a unified county, 'for the integration of its parts to the whole into a recognizable whole was more real to crown administrators than to the local population'.[22] In most counties, however, a sense of the shire as a community of sentiment, endowed with a certain moral authority, was readily appealed to: John Hawley of Dartmouth sought to impugn the authenticity of certain (allegedly) forged evidences by claiming that the writings 'were never known in the county, nor known to any gentlemen of the county, until lately.'[23] Roger Virgoe's survey of the use of the word 'county' in the gentry correspondences of the mid-fifteenth century establishes clearly enough that the personification of the shire as a group of people was commonplace and that this social community commanded a degree of loyalty and affection: the best-known expression of such sentiments is John Jenney's comment on the outcome of the Norfolk election in 1455 – 'It is a evill precedent for the shire that a straunge man shulde be chosyn, and no wurshipp to my Lord off Yorke, nor to my Lord of Norffolk to write for hym; for yf the jentilmen of the shire will suffre sech inconvenyens, in good feithe, the shire shall not be called of seche wurshipp as it hathe be.' At a lower social level, the county demonstrated its continuing ability to embody the aspirations and loyalties of all its inhabitants during the great rising of 1381, when leaders like the captain of Norfolk, Geoffrey Lyster, sought to legitimate their sudden authority by building upon the established traditions of shire self-government.[24] The vision of 'the county' such evidence implies is not always a very precise one; 'county' and 'country' are largely used as interchangeable and equivalent terms, although 'county' can mean, in other contexts, a tract of territory either smaller or more extensive than the shire boundaries. *Some* notion of a county-based principle of social organisation seems, nevertheless, to lie at the heart of it.

A brief examination of some of the evidence for 'county consciousness' in Yorkshire, a shire larger and no less geographically diverse than Lincolnshire, may help to flesh out the content and significance of this notion.[25] At first glance, the results are discouraging. Election indentures in the Yorkshire county court were, unusually, witnessed only by the attorneys of the magnate suitors of the court until 1442, when quite large numbers of attestors suddenly begin to appear. This may simply be a question of diplomatic form, but it does, at least, call into question the extent to which the shire court provided the institutional focus for county sentiment. Equally, although there are a number of surviving petitions from 'the commons of the county of Yorkshire', requesting the remedy of its grievances – clarification of the sheriff's powers to hear indictments for homicide, or removal of obstructions from the river Ouse – these parliamentary petitions were often promoted by individuals or specific interest groups, who routinely claimed for their grievances a larger constituency than they could, in fact, command. They cannot really be used as evidence for the community of the shire as a consultative or corporate body. Non-administrative evidence, which is perhaps a safer guide to normal linguistic practice, proves to be a little more helpful. The Yorkshire deponents in the Scrope *vs* Grosvenor case, examined in 1386/7, referred most readily to a *regional* solidarity, the 'North country', by which they meant *both* Yorkshire and the counties of Durham and Northumberland, but they do, also, refer to the single county of Yorkshire, most frequently in the phrase 'all Yorkshire and Richmondshire'. There is some support for such a usage, which maintains a clear sense of county identity within an awareness of a broader regional community, in the anonymous libel posted against archbishop Neville *c.* 1386:

this attacks Neville, the 'bishop of Yorkshire', for acting as 'king in Yorkshire', but also invokes a more general distinction between 'northern men' and 'southern men'. The sense of a shire community, which can be called to witness in matters of dispute, seems well-developed in Yorkshire by the late fourteenth century, but it lies within a hierarchy of associations, encompassing both the larger, primarily social and dialectal, unit of the 'north country' and the smaller, principally tenurial, association of the lordship – Richmondshire, Hallamshire, the bishop of Durham's liberties of Howdenshire and Allertonshire.

Relations between these greater and lesser solidarities – region, county, lordship – were not always harmonious. Some of the violence that afflicted southern Yorkshire during the early 1390s sprang from the strength of local resistance to the attempted intervention of royal and shire officials into the affairs of what were, to the protestors, autonomous lordships – of Hatfield, Cottingham and so on. The persistence of such tensions should not be seen as a threat to the cohesion of the county community, so much as the condition of its existence. The strength and significance of the shire community did not lie in its embodiment of a spurious organic harmony, but in its effectiveness as a coercive organisation, restraining and attempting to resolve the tensions generated by the existence of a diverse collection of lesser groupings – social, administrative and tenurial – in its midst.[26] Every county was divided by the divergent and sometimes conflicting interests of its inhabitants. Most were kept together by the actions and decisions of the shire elite, whose regulatory and mediatory intervention was codified in the shire court as the will of the whole 'community of the county', for just as local society usually required and welcomed the exercise of magnate lordship, so it also needed to invoke the moral authority of its senior gentry. This authority was exercised in a variety of well-recognised ways: by the prominence of the leading gentry in conducting arbitrations, for example, and by their intervention on those rare occasions when it proved impossible to reach prior agreement as to the identity of the county's representatives in Parliament. In the disputed Huntingdonshire election of 1429, for example, the insistence of Sir Nicholas Stukeley and his associates on a second election seems intended as an assertion of the shire community's neutrality in the face of the concurrent hostilities between the earl of Huntingdon and the duke of Norfolk.[27] Another means to reimposing a certain social solidarity within a divided shire was by service as jurors on sensitive judicial enquiries, such as the commission of *oyer et terminer* that re-established order in Derbyshire in 1434. In this instance, many of the most influential shire gentry served on the two grand juries that returned a very comprehensive set of indictments, which, it was clearly hoped, would transcend existing factional divisions and act as the basis for a series of private compositions.[28]

Such a view of the nature and purpose of the county community has some obvious consequences. One is that, if the identity of the shire community was experienced most readily in the process of conflict resolution, then judicial proceedings will prove to be an especially fertile source for the expansion of county consciousness. Some time ago, the meagre attendance of the gentry at 'full' sessions of the shire court in late fourteenth-century Leicestershire was contrasted with their regular presence on assize juries of presentment – a duty that allowed the gentry jurors to demonstrate their local status as leaders of their hundreds before the itinerant royal justices.[29] Recent work seems to bear out the insight that such occasions fostered the expression of communal solidarity within the institutional framework of county government. A 'strong contingent of county society' backed the judicial process intended to pacify Leicestershire following the murder of Sir Roger Bellars in 1326 – 13 knights were named as presenting jurors at the resultant *oyer et terminer* sessions.[30] Equally, Edward Powell's work on the composition of gaol delivery juries on the Midland circuit affords a glimpse of the shire community active at more than one social level: among the higher officials of the shire administration who, in a county like Derbyshire, made up the single county jury, but *also* among the minor gentry who characteristically filled the posts of coroner and bailiff, whose service as trial jurors allowed them to claim a certain representative authority within their hundred or wapentake.[31]

A second consequence follows from this conclusion – which is, that our view of the county community has been, in certain respects, too restricted. Looked at from one direction, it appears to be clearly the case that the shire community was created and maintained in being by the obligation to respond to the demands constantly made upon local society by the king's government. But the shire was not only the instrument of royal action on local society. It was *also* the arena in which local status was confirmed and augmented – the affray that broke out in the Bedford shire hall in 1439, prompted by a dispute over the order of precedence within the commission of the peace, graphically demonstrates the extent to which gentry 'honour' was constituted and contested through the ordinary processes of shire administration.[32] For the 'shire establishment', this affirmation of their status lay in the ability to 'bear the rule' of the shire peacefully and effectively, while, for the parish gentry, an active career at county level added substance to their claims to social superiority over other freeholders. This is one of the crucial reasons, I think, that the county community became and remained a significant fact of political life in later medieval England: too many people had an investment in 'imagining' such an active and cohesive social body for it to be otherwise.

By taking these thoughts into account, I think it is possible to conclude by identifying, very schematically, three separate stages in the evolution of the county community. In the first stage, running roughly from *c.* 1300–50, the shire gained both definition and authority by its acquisition of a range of new administrative powers and responsibilities. This 'administrative' stage was the period in which the county was, in J. H. Baker's phrase, 'put into commission' among a group of influential local gentry,[33] although it is important to emphasise that these new powers were not simply ascribed to the shire communities on royal initiative, but were also acquired, in such cases as the increased gentry presence among the keepers and justices of the peace, by virtue of a lengthy campaign of parliamentary and extra-parliamentary lobbying. There was, at the same time, a move towards the *concentration* of this increased administrative responsibility within a smaller social group, now pursuing their official careers largely within a single county. In the decade 1290–1300, for example, 15 per cent of sheriffs served more than once in this office, but by 1330–40 the proportion is up to 44 per cent. Equally, 15 per cent of sheriffs had a record of service in more than one county, 1290–1399, while only 2 per cent did so between 1330 and 1340.[34]

These developments were accentuated during the second, 'social', phase of the county community's evolution, which took place, very roughly, from *c.* 1350–1430. The dynamic of change in this period was principally demographic, driven by high levels of plague-related mortality. Demographic decline increased the number of landed families failing in the male line and accelerated the transfer of estates through the marriage of heiresses, enabling those families that did succeed in producing male heirs to accumulate sufficient additional lands to consolidate their social position as a wealthy knightly elite, often at the expense of middling and lesser gentry lineages: the way in which a group of *c.* 45 knightly families in early fourteenth-century Nottinghamshire was reduced, by these means, to a smaller and richer shire elite, numbering no more than 13 families, by the start of the following century constitutes a particularly clear instance of this process.[35] A second consequence of the demographic crisis was a further delegation of the coercive power of the Crown to this emergent shire establishment by a government anxious to contain the widespread demand for social change by an insistence on the full enforcement of existing legal and tenurial obligations. The resulting consolidation of their local superiority was both documented and legitimated by the closer definition of armigerous status that developed during this same period. 'County' rolls of arms, listing the families entitled by ancestry to wear coat armour in each shire, have survived from Edward II's reign, but they become more common and more elaborate by the end of the fourteenth century. The institution of regular heraldic visitations, on a county-by-county basis, which is to be associated with the reform and rationalisation of the office of arms undertaken by Henry V and his brother, Thomas, duke of Clarence, between 1415 and 1421, marks the end-point in this process of social self-definition, whereby the armigerous elite in each county separated itself out from the broader shire community by acquiring a permanent mark of social distinction.[36]

In the third, chiefly political, phase of its development, county society responded to external pressures, principally the polarisation of national politics discernible from *c.* 1430 and the corresponding factionalism that threatened the cohesion of many localities, by an emphasis upon the independence and neutrality of the shire community that sought to avoid involvement in the divisive, and potentially disastrous, dynastic confrontations of mid-century. Norfolk, where the county establishment sought, with some success, to prevent its representation in Parliament being dominated by the nominees of either the duke of Norfolk or the earl of Oxford, provides the *locus classicus* for such expressions of independence, but Carpenter has identified a similar reaction in Warwickshire, where the gentry proved reluctant to commit themselves to the struggle for supremacy waged between the duke of Buckingham and the Neville earl of Warwick, and Rowney has commented on the 'masterly inactivity' displayed by the Staffordshire gentry during the same period.[37] Such self-reliance, based upon the mixture of administrative experience and social consequence acquired during the previous century and a half, served to give the shire a significance and self-definition that for the first time rendered 'the county' a legitimate object of historical enquiry. John Rous included, in his *Historia Regum Angliae*, an account of the origins of the shires which appears to have been the product of some independent historical research, while William Worcester's lost work, the *De Agris Norfolcensis Familiis Antiquis*, was (as far as we know) the first in that long line of self-regarding county histories by which the shire gentry celebrated both their own status and their collective significance as one of the essential components of England's *ancien régime* – what Henry James would call 'the long quietude of the respectable centuries, all cornfields and magistrates and vicars'.[38]

Notes

* The text of this paper was prepared for presentation at the International Medieval Congress held at the University of Leeds in July 1998 and was in the process of revision at the time of Simon Walker's death. References have been added, where possible, from his working notes. It is clear that the argument was being developed in at least three directions: a critical analysis of the concept of community, and the ways in which it was being used in late medieval studies; a closer reading of the uses of such terms as 'shire' and 'county' in order to recover contemporary consciousness of these identities; and the integration of local examples of the coalescence of political solidarities around county issues. No attempt has been made to reconstruct Walker's views on these issues, but the following works were evidently important to his thinking: David Carr, 'Narrative and the real world: an argument for continuity', *History and Theory*, 25 (1986), 117–31 (for the suggestion that 'a community exists where a narrative account exists of a *we* which persists through its experiences and actions', at p. 130); Jean-Philipe Genet's recovery of the importance of community in scholastic thinking (in contrast with Fortescue's emphasis on the need of every community to have a head: Sir John Fortescue, *On the Laws and Governance of England*, ed. Shelley Lockwood (Cambridge, 1997). This contrast reflected, Walker was inclined to suggest, a difference between the theoretical literature and the 'little tradition' of practical politics); Victor Turner, *The Ritual Process: Structure and Anti-Structure* (London, 1969) (in particular for the concept of 'communitas', ch. 3, esp. pp. 96 f.); Keith Wrightson, 'The social order of early modern England: three approaches', in Lloyd Bonfield, Richard M. Smith and Keith Wrightson (eds), *The World We Have Gained: Histories of Population and Social Structure Presented to Peter Laslett on his Seventieth Birthday* (Oxford, 1986), pp. 177–202 (in particular for the distinction between 'languages of differentiation' and 'languages of identification' at p. 196: the county was usually considered in terms of the latter, but might also be an

example of the former). Among the papers there were also notes on the following works which have not been referred to specifically: Peter Coss, 'Identity and the gentry *c.* 1200–*c.* 1340', in Michael Prestwich, R. H. Britnell and Robin Frame (eds), *Thirteenth Century England VI* (Woodbridge, 1997), pp. 49–60; Anthony Gross, 'Regionalism and revision' and J. R. Lander, 'The significance of the county in English government', in Peter Fleming, Anthony Gross and J. R. Lander (eds), *Regionalism and Revision: The Crown and its Provinces in England* (London, 1998), pp. 1–13, 15–27; Alison K. Gundy, 'The rule of Thomas Beauchamp, earl of Warwick, in the West Midlands, 1369–1401' (unpublished PhD thesis, University of Cambridge 2000); Simon Payling, 'The waning of noble lordship in late fifteenth-century England?', *Parliamentary History*, 13 (1994), 322–32; idem., 'County parliamentary elections in fifteenth-century England', *Parliamentary History*, 18 (1999), 237–59; Alan Rogers, 'The Lincolnshire county court in the fifteenth century', *Lincolnshire History and Archaeology*, 1 (1966), 64–78; Richard M. Smith, ' "Modernization" and the corporate medieval village community in England: some sceptical reflections', in A. H. R. Baker and D. Gregory (eds), *Explorations in Historical Geography: Interpretive Essays* (Cambridge, 1984), pp. 140–79; 234–45. I am very grateful to John Watts and Anthony Musson for their help in supplying footnotes to this chapter. Michael Braddick.

1 N. Saul, *Knights and Esquires: The Gloucestershire Gentry in the Fourteenth Century* (Oxford, 1981); S. Payling, *Political Society in Lancastrian England: The Greater Gentry of Nottinghamshire* (Oxford, 1991); J. R. Maddicott, 'The county community and the making of public opinion in fourteenth-century England', *Transactions of the Royal Historical Society*, 5th ser., 28 (1978), 27–43, quotation at p. 43; 'Magna Carta and the local community 1215–1259', *Past & Present*, 102 (1984), 25–65; 'Parliament and the constituencies, 1272–1377', in Richard G. Davies and J. H. Denton (eds), *The English Parliament in the Middle Ages* (Manchester, 1981), 61–87.

2 Susan M. Wright, *The Derbyshire Gentry in the Fifteenth Century*, Derbyshire Record Society, 8 (Chesterfield, 1983), p. 58; Robert C. Palmer, *The County Courts of Medieval England, 1150–1350* (Princeton, 1982), esp. p. 302; Peter R. Coss, *Lordship, Knighthood and Locality: A Study in English Society c. 1180–c. 1280* (Cambridge, 1991), p. 3; Michael Prestwich, *English Politics in the Thirteenth Century* (Basingstoke, 1990), esp. pp. 55–9; Christine Carpenter, *Locality and Polity: A Study of Warwickshire Landed Society, 1401–1499* (Cambridge, 1992), esp. ch. 9, quotation at p. 340.

3 R. H. Britnell, *The Closing of the Middle Ages? England, 1471–1529* (Oxford, 1997), quotation at p. 97; A. J. Pollard, 'Introduction: society, politics and the Wars of the Roses', in Pollard (ed.), *The Wars of the Roses* (Basingstoke, 1995), pp. 1–19, 221–3, esp. pp. 8–9.

4 The suggestion is Christine Carpenter's: 'Gentry and community in medieval England', *Journal of British Studies* 33 (1994), 340–80, at p. 340.

5 The argument for independent gentry is made by Saul, *Knights and Esquires*, esp. 258–62 and, for the independent gentry and the 'embrace' of bastard feudalism, see pp. 260–1. Walker accepted this case, with some reservations, in *The Lancastrian Affinity 1361–1399* (Oxford, 1990), see esp. pp. 247, 255–6, 258–60.

6 Carpenter, 'Gentry and community', pp. 356f.

7 Susan Reynolds, *Kingdoms and Communities in Western Europe, 900–1300* (2nd edn, Oxford, 1997), esp. introduction, pp. xi–lxvi, quotation at p. 247. See also

Mark W. Ormrod, *Political Life in Medieval England, 1300–1450* (Basingstoke, 1995), pp. 47–51.

8 Nigel Saul, 'The Sussex gentry and the oath to uphold the acts of the Merciless Parliament', *Sussex Archaeological Collections*, 135 (1997), 221–39.

9 It has not been possible to identify a source for this example.

10 Scott L. Waugh, *England in the Reign of Edward III* (Cambridge, 1991), pp. 167–8.

11 For occasional communities see David Gary Shaw, *The Creation of a Community: The City of Wells in the Middle Ages* (Oxford, 1993), pp. 2–8; see also the discussion in David Harris Sacks, *The Widening Gate: Bristol and the Atlantic Economy, 1450–1700* (Berkeley, CA, 1991), pp. 4–11; Michael J. Bennett, *Community, Class and Careerism: Cheshire and Lancashire Society in the Age of Sir Gawain and the Green Knight* (Cambridge, 1983), esp. ch. 2; see also idem., 'A county community: social cohesion amongst the Cheshire gentry, 1400–1425', *Northern History*, 8 (1973), 24–44.

12 Eric Acheson, *A Gentry Community: Leicestershire in the Fifteenth Century, c. 1442–1485* (Cambridge, 1992), pp. 89–92.

13 Payling, *Political Society*, p. 16

14 Alan Harding, *England in the Thirteenth Century* (Cambridge, 1993), p. 206; see also Prestwich, *English Politics*, pp. 53–4.

15 J. S. Roskell, Linda Clark and Carole Rawcliffe (eds), *The History of Parliament: House of Commons, 1386–1421*, 4 vols (Stroud, 1993), I, esp. pp. 447–8; see also Roskell, *The Commons in the Parliament of 1422: English Society and Parliamentary Representation Under the Lancastrians* (Manchester, 1954), pp. 70, 74, 150, 193, 234.

16 Carpenter, 'Gentry and community', esp. pp. 345–50.

17 Simon Walker, 'Hastings family (*per. c.* 1300–*c.* 1450)', *Oxford Dictionary of National Biography* (Oxford University Press, 2004) [http://www.oxforddnb.com/view/article/54526, accessed 11 March 2005].

18 Roskell, Clark and Rawcliffe, *Commons, 1386–1421*, I, appendix D_3, pp. 241–3.

19 For Cornwall see C. J. Tyldesley, 'The crown and the local communities in Devon and Cornwall from 1377 to 1422', unpublished PhD thesis, Exeter University, 1979, ch. 3, esp. pp. 75–7.

20 Northumberland: Maddicott, 'County community', p. 29; Nottinghamshire: Payling, *Political Society*, pp. 161–7.

21 Benedict Anderson, *Imagined Communities: Reflections on the Origins and Spread of Nationalism* (revised edition, London, 1991), p. 6.

22 Graham Platts, *Land and People in Medieval Lincolnshire* (Lincoln, 1985), esp. pp. 284–95, quotation at p. 292.

23 It has not been possible to identify a source for this example.

24 Roger Virgoe, 'Aspects of the county community in the fifteenth century', in Michael A. Hicks (ed.), *Profit, Piety and the Professions in Later Medieval England* (Gloucester, 1990), 1–13. For Jenney, see James Gairdner (ed.) *The Paston Letters A.D. 1422–1509*, 6 vols, (London, 1904), III, p. 39, quoted partially in Virgoe 'County community' at p. 5 and discussed more fully by K. B. McFarlane, 'Parliament and "bastard feudalism" ', in his *England in the Fifteenth Century: Collected Essays*, ed. G. L. Harriss (London, 1981), 1–21, at pp. 5–6. For Lyster and the 1381 rising, see Herbert Eiden, 'Joint action against "Bad" lordship: the Peasants' Revolt in Essex and Norfolk', *History*, 83 (1998), 5–30, at p. 20.

25 This discussion of Yorkshire is apparently based on another unpublished paper: 'National politics and local government in Yorkshire, 1386–1406', which exists

only in an unreferenced draft. For Walker's published work relating to Yorkshire see chapters 4 and 10 of this volume; and 'Les deux procès de Richard Scrope, archevêque de York, 1405–1406', in Brigitte Marin (ed.), *Les process politiques (XIVe–XVIIe siècles)*, Mélanges de l'École Française de Rome (forthcoming).

26 See the arguments of Christopher Dyer in relation to village communities in: 'Taxation and communities in late medieval England', in Richard Hugh Britnell and John Hatcher (eds.), *Progress and Problems in Medieval England: Essays in Honour of Edward Miller* (Cambridge, 1996), 168–90.

27 Roskell, *The Commons in the Parliament of 1422*, pp. 17–21.

28 Wright, *The Derbyshire Gentry*, p. 128.

29 Grenville G. Astill, 'The medieval gentry: a study in Leicestershire, 1350–1399' (unpublished PhD thesis, University of Birmingham, 1977), ch. 3, esp. pp. 190–3.

30 Anthony Musson, *Public Order and Law Enforcement: The Local Administration of Criminal Justice, 1294–1350* (Woodbridge, 1996), esp. pp. 266–9, quotation at p. 268.

31 E. Powell, 'Jury trial at gaol delivery in the late middle ages: the Midland Circuit, 1400–1429', in J. S. Cockburn and T. A. Green (eds), *Twelve Good Men and True: The Criminal Jury in England, 1200–1800* (Princeton, 1988), 78–116.

32 Philippa C. Maddern, *Violence and Social Order: East Anglia, 1422–1442* (Oxford, 1992), pp. 206–25.

33 This administrative phase was 'as identified' by Musson, *Public Order and Law Enforcement*, esp. chs. 1–7; J. H. Baker, *An Introduction to English Legal History* (3rd edition, London, 1990), quotation at p. 31.

34 Palmer, *The County Courts of Medieval England*, p. 33.

35 Payling, *Political Society*, ch. 3; and, for a slightly modified view, 'Social mobility, demographic change and landed society in late medieval England', *Economic History Review*, 45 (1992), 51–73.

36 Based on materials contained in Anthony Richard Wagner, *A Catalogue of English Mediaeval Rolls of Arms* (Aspilogia, being materials of heraldry, 1; Harleian Society, [100]), Oxford, 1950 for 1948; idem., *Heralds and Heraldry in the Middle Ages: An Inquiry into the Armorial Functions of Heralds* (2nd edn, 1956).

37 For Norfolk see McFarlane, 'Parliament and "bastard feudalism" ', pp. 4–12 and Virgoe, 'Aspects', pp. 8–11. For Warwickshire see Carpenter, *Locality and Polity*, p. 478ff, and, more generally, ch. 16. For Staffordshire see Ian Rowney, 'Government and patronage in the fifteenth century: Staffordshire, 1439–1459', *Midland History*, 8 (1983), 49–69, quotation at p. 65. Walker noted that this process can be identified earlier in some places, as in the dispute over the Huntingdonshire election in 1429 and, perhaps, in the high proportion of parliamentary 'novices' appearing in controversial parliaments (1388 and 1397/8: see Roskell, Clark and Rawcliffe, *The History of Parliament*, I, appendix D1, p. 239, and the comments of G. L. Harriss, 'The medieval parliament', *Parliamentary History*, 13 (1994), 206–26, esp. pp. 212–13).

38 Thomas Hearne (ed.), *Joannis Rossi Antiquarii Warwicensis Historia Regum Angliae* (Oxford, 1745), p. 66; Worcester's lost work is discussed in K. B. McFarlane, 'William Worcester: a preliminary survey', in *England in the Fifteenth Century*, pp. 199–224, at pp. 219–21; Henry James, *The Tragic Muse*, quoted in Richard W. Southern, 'Aspects of the European tradition of historical writing, 4: The sense of the past', *Transactions of the Royal Historical Society*, 5th ser., 23 (1973), 242–63, at p. 245.

4

Yorkshire justices of the peace, 1389–1413*

In later medieval England no institution better illustrates 'that collaboration of the well-to-do classes in power, so characteristic of the English political structure'[1], than the commission of the peace. The wide-ranging military and police powers originally committed on an emergency basis to small groups of royal officials, acting as keepers of the peace, in the early thirteenth century had evolved by Edward III's reign into a permanent commission of the peace in each county, that united magnates, royal justices and local gentry in discharging a variety of judicial and administrative duties.[2] The unusually extensive involvement of local elites in the exercise of government required by such commissions has long been recognized by historians as one of the defining characteristics of English state development.[3] This paper offers a detailed study of the justices of the peace in a single county during the years in which the commission of the peace took final – and very durable – form, in order to clarify the nature of that involvement and to examine its implications for the exercise of royal power.

Between 1389 and 1413 the powers and composition of the commissions of the peace, already the subject of more than half a century of discussion and negotiation between the Crown and the parliamentary Commons, underwent a further series of changes. The general peace commission of July 1389 drastically reduced each county bench in size, but simultaneously restored to the remaining justices power to determine all felonies and common law trespasses.[4] Further additions to the justices' responsibilities in cases of riot, forcible entry and breaches of the several contemporary statutes of livery followed in subsequent years, with the result that the justices of the peace enjoyed considerably increased powers of summary arrest and conviction by the end of Henry IV's reign.[5] It is usual to see these changes as a direct response to the repeated insistence of the parliamentary Commons that the task of maintaining law and order at the local level was best entrusted to the most substantial men of the shire, and to interpret them as one further episode whereby the degree of control exercised by successive kings over the institutions of local government was reduced and the powers of the county gentry correspondingly increased.[6] Historians have accordingly read considerable significance into this apparent shift in the balance of local authority, seeing in it a strategic resiting of the *locus* of class power, an explanation for the disorder of late medieval England, and one of the most damaging and permanent limitations on the powers of the English monarchy.[7]

Before such an interpretation, and the consequences that flow from it, can be fully accepted, certain objections, each of which casts doubt upon the degree of dominance the substantial gentry exercised over the commissions of the peace, need to be resolved. The first is a procedural one, for it has recently been suggested that the constant presence of the judges and officials of the Westminster courts on the commissions of the peace, acting in their capacity as assize justices, provided the king's ministers with a powerful and generally effective means of controlling the actions of the gentry justices.[8] The second objection is political, since there is some evidence that the kind of periodic revision of the commissions in favour of the servants and trusted supporters of the Crown, practised by Henry VI's government in the 1450s and more extensively by Edward IV in the 1470s, was already being attempted during the final years of Richard II's reign.[9] Henry IV's councillors certainly contemplated a very similar method of controlling the peace commissions when they advised him to nominate his retainers as justices in order to 'save the estate of the king and his people in their countries'.[10] A third reservation relates to the personnel of the commissions: Who were the 'best and most law-worthy'[11] men of the shire who the Commons insisted should be chosen as justices? Though they have frequently been supposed to be identical with the most substantial county gentry, from whom the shire knights who pressed these demands were themselves drawn, several studies have demonstrated that the work of the county bench was usually discharged by small groups of lawyers and officials drawn from the middling ranks of county society; this was certainly the case on the West Riding bench in the later fifteenth century. One writer goes so far as to suggest that such concentrations of judicial responsibility lent to the peace commission 'almost the air of a foreign court setting up quarterly in the shire'.[12]

This paper seeks to examine the strength of these reservations against the evidence available for the membership and activity of the commissions of the peace in the three Ridings of Yorkshire during the majority rule of Richard II and the reign of Henry IV. Within that period, 50 commissions were issued to a total of 94 justices, who can, with only a few problems of definition, be divided into four major categories: – 19 magnates, nine assize justices of the Northern circuit, 24 justices of the quorum and 42 gentry justices whose absence from the quorum suggests a lack of specialized legal knowledge.[13] By examining the personnel of each of these categories in turn and defining the part that each collectively played in the work of the Yorkshire justices of the peace, some understanding can be reached of the various pressures at work on the commissions and an estimate made of the extent to which the Crown was forced, in this period, to surrender a degree of its control over the local administration of criminal justice to private interests, whether those of the aristocracy or of the county gentry. Such a surrender has commonly been advanced as one of the principal explanations for the high incidence of disorder alleged to have characterized later medieval England; some consideration will consequently be given to the involvement of the three Riding benches in the creation and suppression of local violence. These conclusions will form the basis of a more general estimate of the place and significance of the justices of the peace in early Lancastrian England.

The position of the magnates on the commission of the peace and their influence on the administration of criminal justice remained controversial throughout this period. A determined campaign by the parliamentary Commons to lay the blame for much disorder in the localities at the door of the aristocracy culminated, between July 1389 and December 1390, in the complete exclusion of the nobility from the commissions of the peace. Even when political circumstances forced the abandonment of this policy, the Commons remained anxious to reiterate, in the livery legislation of 1399 and 1406, their belief that it was the maintenance and protection of evil-doers practised by the magnates which lay behind many contemporary breakdowns in public order.[14] By contrast, both Richard II and Henry IV welcomed the presence of magnates on the peace commissions, responding to any sign of political unrest, as in 1397 and 1405, by a swift increase in the number of aristocratic justices. Their attraction, in the Crown's eyes, lay in the physical resources they could command, the vested interest most magnates possessed in maintaining good order within their acknowledged sphere of influence, and the frequently close relationship between the king and individual noble justices. Aristocratic dominance of the bench was, in addition, less likely to arouse jealousy or faction than the pre-eminence of even the most substantial gentleman; contemporary social expectation ascribed to the nobility a natural leadership that local society was usually happy to accept. The same social expectations constrained the king and his advisers in their selection of magnate justices, setting limits to the freedom of their choice, though the Crown retained an important element of discretion. A few noblemen – John, Duke of Lancaster; Henry Percy, Earl of Northumberland; Ralph Neville, Earl of Westmorland – virtually commanded a place on the Yorkshire benches by virtue of their political eminence and their substantial estates in the county; a slightly larger group of baronial families might reasonably expect, if their residence and principal estates lay within one of the Ridings, consistent appointment as a justice of the peace there. In the North Riding, these families were the Scropes of Bolton, Roos of Helmsley and Fitzhughs of Ravensworth; in the East Riding, the Scropes of Masham and Mauleys of Mulgrave; in the West Riding, the Neville and Talbot lords of Hallamshire. Political considerations nevertheless retained some force, allowing Richard II discretion to omit a wealthy but negligible magnate like Edmund, Duke of York from the West Riding commission, despite his extensive estates in South Yorkshire,[15] and Henry IV to elevate a middling baron like Peter (VIII), lord Mauley – favoured by his kinship with the Nevilles – to a seat on the bench of all three Ridings.[16]

For the aristocracy, appointment as a justice of the peace did not entail constant attendance at the quarter sessions. Slightly later evidence suggests that peers were instead expected to maintain a general watch on the conduct of the bench and to hold themselves in readiness to intervene in cases of riot or serious disturbance.[17] By this criterion, though only six of the nineteen magnates appointed to the Yorkshire commissions between 1389 and 1413 can be shown to have sat as justices, noble oversight of the work of the Riding benches was relatively continuous. This was most clearly the case in the North Riding, where Richard, lord Scrope was active on the commission in the early years of the period.[18] Though he cannot be shown to have sat on the bench after 1392, Scrope's example was subsequently followed by both Henry, lord Fitzhugh, and Ralph Neville, Earl of Westmorland and lord of the honour of Richmond, who maintained a consistent interest in the work of the justices throughout Henry IV's reign.[19] That this was regarded as a desirable state of affairs is shown by the Chancery's efforts, over nearly a quarter of a century, to find a local magnate in the East Riding who was willing to involve himself in the work of the justices there in the same way. Peter, lord Mauley VI had been a consistent attender at sessions until his death in 1383,[20] but a suitable successor was hard to find. Though Henry Percy, Earl of Northumberland, occasionally presided at sessions, his commitments at court and on the border meant that he was never likely to become a regular presence.[21] In consequence, it was principally to the Scropes of Masham, resident within the Riding at Faxfleet, that the Chancery turned in search of steady oversight of the justices. Stephen, second lord Scrope, was added to the commission in March 1397 and his younger brother, Sir John Scrope, joined him on the bench in 1401. Sir John was active as a justice until his death in 1405 and Scrope influence over the East Riding bench was then maintained by the attendance of his nephew, Henry, third lord Scrope, first appointed to the commission in February 1407.[22] By contrast, the West Riding evidence for magnate attendance at the quarter sessions is much thinner; Thomas Neville, lord Furnivall, is the only peer known to have sat, and the single session he attended, in January 1402, was held on the edge of his own lordship of Hallamshire, at Doncaster.[23] Magnate influence was far from absent in the West Riding, however, for the well-articulated administrative structure of the Duchy of Lancaster allowed the greatest lord of the region to exercise a consistent influence over the personnel of the commission without requiring his physical presence. Between June 1394 and June 1395, for instance, the work of the West Riding bench was principally discharged by William Gascoigne and John Woodruff, respectively the Duke's chief steward and secondary justice in his palatinate of Lancaster, Sir John Savile of Eland, his constable at Pontefract, and Sir William Rilleston of Rilston, bailiff of his wapentake of Staincross in Craven.[24] The only active justice without a specific Lancastrian connection was Sir John Deepden of Helaugh, whose loyalties seem to have lain with the Nevilles.[25] The usurpation of 1399 did predictably little to modify this dominance of Duchy of Lancaster officials on the West Riding bench, which was effectively controlled throughout Henry IV's reign by Richard Gascoigne, chief steward of the Duchy in the North, and present as a justice at sixty-one of the sixty-four recorded peace sessions between October 1399 and December 1411.[26]

Although the resources of the Duchy of Lancaster allowed the Crown, after 1399, to maintain close and effective supervision of the West Riding commission, reliance on magnates like the Nevilles and Scropes to uphold social discipline both within their own 'countries' and on the county benches held its own dangers. Indeed, it was the close connection between the local agents of royal justice and the aristocracy that attracted the particular criticism of the Commons. Their suspicions were sometimes justified. When George Darell of Sessay was indicted before Ralph Neville and his fellows, justices of the peace in the North Riding, for the murder of Neville's servant, Sir Thomas Colville of Coxwold,[27] during the Scrope rising in May 1405, Darell failed to appear before the justices and, after repeated exactions, was eventually outlawed in the county court. Darell subsequently traversed the judgement on a writ of error on the grounds that, when exacted to answer the indictment, he had been unable to do so because he was kept prisoner in Neville's own castle of Richmond.[28] On this occasion, it seems very likely that Neville had temporarily subordinated his public capacity as a royal justice to his private concern to maintain and protect his own affinity. What is not so clear is whether such incidents were a regular occurrence. The evidence is rarely so direct, with the consequence that the attitude and ambitions of the county's magnates towards the peace commission must to a large extent be extrapolated from the presence or absence of their servants and retainers among the justices. The methodological problems with this approach are considerable, but not necessarily overwhelming. While it is wrong to assume that a gentry justice who was also the retainer of a magnate owed his appointment to the bench to the intervention of his patron or that, once on the commission, his actions were principally dictated by the resultant sense of obligation to his master, the simultaneous presence of several servants of a particular magnate on the peace commission at least indicates a lordship attractive and effective enough to appeal to the self-interest of an influential section of the Riding's gentry. It was such effective local lordship that the Crown was most anxious to harness or, in exceptional cases, to neutralize.

The prominence of estate stewards and men of law in the work of the Riding benches meant, of course, that any magnate with substantial estates in the county might include a number of justices of the peace among his servants. Among the Yorkshire justices receiving annual fees from Henry, lord Fitzhugh, for instance, were his steward, John Burgh, and several lawyers: John Conyers, Richard Norton, James Strangeways, William Lodington and William Waldeby.[29] This was equally the case for successive bishops of Durham, Walter Skirlaw and Thomas Langley, whose possession of the liberties of Howdenshire and Allertonshire, as well as their extensive estates in the North Riding, led them to employ several officials active on the Yorkshire peace commissions. Successive stewards of Howdenshire, John Aske of Ousthorpe and Peter del Hay of Spaldington, appear sporadically on the East Riding bench, while the episcopal steward in Allertonshire, John Conyers of Hornby, was one of the most active justices in the North Riding.[30] The extensive patronage available to the bishops within their own palatinate of Durham also allowed them to establish close links with the greater gentry of the North Riding and, as a consequence, to maintain the most consistent body of servants of any lord on the Riding's commission of the peace.[31] In neither case can the existence of such ties realistically be described as a threat to the proper conduct of the bench: Walter Skirlaw, an elderly crown servant with no discernible political inclinations beyond a desire for stability, and Thomas Langley, a confirmed Lancastrian loyalist, offered no threat to royal control of the justices in the North Riding, and the number of their servants among its justices of the peace very probably owed little to the deliberate lobbying of the bishops themselves. More problematic is the evidence for a growth in Percy representation among the justices of both the North and East Ridings after 1399. Among the Percy family's officials and annuitants, Sir John Colville of the Dale was appointed to the North Riding commission in March 1400, at the same time as John Aske returned to the East Riding bench after an absence of fifteen years.[32] Aske was subsequently joined, in May 1401, by Sir Robert Hilton and Sir John Scrope, who was linked by marriage and service to the Percies, and Colville by William Lasingby, one of the Percy family's regular attorneys and councillors.[33] Together with the consistent appointment of Sir Richard Tempest to the West Riding commission,[34] this gave the servants of the Percy family a presence on the benches of all three Ridings that, with the single exception of Sir Robert Hilton in the East Riding, they had lacked before Henry IV's accession. Yet even in the case of the powerful Percies, the presence of magnate retainers on the Yorkshire commissions of the peace cannot be said to constitute a genuine threat to royal control of the justices, for most of the Percy servants appointed to the Riding benches were servants of Henry IV as well. Tempest, Colville and Hilton were all knights of the king's affinity; Aske was a royal esquire and Lasingby an apprentice-at-law employed by the Duchy.[35] While this double allegiance is most obviously testimony to the considerable influence the Earl of Northumberland exercised on the distribution of crown patronage in the aftermath of the Lancastrian usurpation, it also indicates careful royal scrutiny of appointments to the commissions of the peace and a successful attempt to maintain some measure of discretion and control over the justices appointed. Alexander Neville, Archbishop of York, who managed to create a dangerously dominant role for his affinity in the North and East Ridings in 1385, was the only magnate to successfully evade this scrutiny and, even then, his triumph was short-lived.[36]

The pattern of noble involvement in the commissions of the peace suggested by the Yorkshire evidence is, therefore, reasonably clear. Though no more than a third of the magnates appointed to the Yorkshire commissions of the peace can be shown to have attended in person, those who did so included the most substantial regional magnates – the Nevilles, Scropes and Henry

Percy – while, among those who did not, several were active as justices of the peace in counties more central to their landed interests, as William, lord Roos was in Leicestershire and Thomas Holland, Duke of Surrey, (briefly) in Derbyshire.[37] The rapid accretion, at different times, of servants of Alexander Neville and Henry Percy on the North and East Riding benches indicates that some magnates also desired to exercise a more permanent supervision over the work of the justices than they could obtain by their personal presence alone, though their concern for the personnel of the commissions as yet lacked the jealous vigilance it was to acquire in the Yorkist period.[38] Yet neither expression of aristocratic power threatened, in practice, the considerable discretion the king and his advisers enjoyed over the nomination of the commissions, both in deciding which magnates should be appointed in Yorkshire and in approving the nominations and suggestions that those magnates, in turn, made.

The second category of justices of the peace to be considered, those automatically appointed by virtue of their office as a justice of assize on the Northern circuit,[39] is smaller and considerably more homogeneous than the group of noble justices already analysed, though the conclusions that emerge from such a consideration are not dissimilar. Nine Yorkshire justices of the peace fall into this category, and all were either judges of the central courts at Westminster or king's sergeants-at-law, possessed of a strong expectation of appointment as a justice of King's Bench (hereafter JKB) or Common Pleas (hereafter JCP). Between 1389 and 1411 these assize justices visited Yorkshire thirty-six times in twenty-three calendar years, usually in spring or late summer.[40] They might, in their secondary capacity as justices of gaol delivery, make further appearances in the county as well: forty-three sessions of gaol delivery were held at York during the same period,[41] usually at the same time as the assizes, though a sudden flurry of activity early in Henry IV's reign, coincident with the appointment of William Gascoigne as a justice of gaol delivery,[42] saw seven additional sessions held between the assizes in the space of two years. Two justices of the Westminster courts – usually John Markham and Hugh Huls under Richard II, then William Gascoigne and Thomas Tildesley for most of Henry IV's reign – therefore visited Yorkshire about twice a year throughout this period for sessions of assize and gaol delivery.

Automatically appointed to the quorum and statutorily required to be present when the bench was considering certain categories of difficult offences,[43] these central court justices on the commissions of the peace possessed, in theory, considerable opportunity to influence the actions and decisions of the local justices. The attendance payments made to the justices suggest, though, that in practice they made little use of this opportunity. John Markham (JCB, 1396–1408) was paid for two sessions on the North Riding bench between 1397 and 1399, John Cokayn (chief baron of the Exchequer, 1400–6) for one session in the West Riding early in Henry IV's reign, and William Gascoigne (CJKB, 1400–13), whose Yorkshire lands gave him more reason than any of the other assize judges to sit with the justices of the peace, was paid for only four sessions on the West Riding bench while Chief Justice.[44] To rely on the evidence of such payments alone would, however, be misleading; they appear to relate only to those occasions when the justices sat on the Riding benches outside their assize sessions. William Gascoigne, in particular, is recorded as sitting as a justice of the peace on many further occasions while the assizes themselves were in progress.[45] The influence of the assize justices on the conduct of the Riding benches and, in all likelihood, on their composition (since they were an obvious source of information when the Chancellor and his advisers sought to review the membership of the commissions) was therefore greater than the meagre record of their attendance payments would imply. The precise relationship between the regular quarter sessions and the sessions attended by the assize justices is not easy to recover, but it seems that, while the justices of the peace did not deliberately arrange their sessions to coincide with the arrival of the assizes in the county,[46] joint sessions of assize and of the peace were, in practice, held often enough to provide the assize justices with a good knowledge of the abilities and conscientiousness of the Yorkshire justices of the peace – eight joint sessions were held in the course of the twenty-six assize sessions for which sufficiently comprehensive information survives. This oversight was not the limit of the assize justices' influence on the Yorkshire benches, for the fact that all surviving recognizances to keep the peace entered into before the justices of the peace were, in fact, entered into before the assize justices acting in their secondary capacity as justices of the peace[47], suggests that the regular justices frequently looked to their professional colleagues in the more serious cases of disorder, referring them from the quarter sessions to await the next assize.

A further indication of the increasingly close connection between quarter sessions and the visits of the central court justices to the county lies in the growing proportion of gaol delivery business occupied by indictments originally taken before the justices of the peace. As in other counties with large private liberties still active, the Yorkshire justices' quarter sessions had yet to pre-empt all the criminal business traditionally dealt with at the half-yearly leets.[48] Consequently, the sheriff's tourn still provided the bulk of the work for the justices of gaol delivery throughout this period (see Appendix, Table 1), just as it continued to yield the greatest volume of Yorkshire business called into King's Bench.[49] Yet the growing importance of the quarter sessions in providing gaol delivery business, at the expense of the independent jurisdiction of the county coroners and the stewards of the private liberties, is clearly marked in Henry IV's reign. It is a development which indicates that the association of personnel fostered by the joint sessions of assize and of the peace also encouraged an increased integration of their business. The corresponding rise in the number of appeals of felony heard at the assizes might further suggest that behind this structural convergence lay individual initiative, a positive effort on the part of the assize judges to increase their cognizance of criminal justice in the county. It is hard not to associate such an initiative with William

Gascoigne, whose career as a West Riding justice of the peace prior to his elevation to King's Bench, just as much as the more regular sessions of gaol delivery he instituted at York in March 1401, suggests that, at least in the hands of an influential and determined justice, the assize sessions could indeed become a 'highly successful vehicle for the transmission of central government to the provinces.'[50]

The closest colleagues of the assize justices on the commission of the peace were the members of the quorum, those justices of the peace whose presence was necessary on the bench to determine felonies, trespasses and all other offences cited in the commission. The period saw some significant changes in the composition and powers of the quorum. Until November 1389, the peace commissions lacked any statutory authority to determine offences, though in practice many certainly did so, and the powers of the quorum were limited merely to the hearing of indictments. This system was abandoned in November 1389 for a double quorum, one consisting of the assize justices alone, to whom was reserved the power to determine felonies, and the other associating with them two or more lawyers competent to deal with trespass and the other offences over which the justices of the peace enjoyed jurisdiction. This double quorum lasted until July 1394 when it was replaced by a single body, including both the assize justices and local men of law, with power to determine both felony and trespass offences. It was this form of commission that remained in force, except for a brief reintroduction of the double quorum in December 1405, until it was further modified in 1417 and, more substantially, in 1424.[51] The durability of the compromise arrived at in 1394 indicates that it was generally acceptable to all the parties concerned, though the reintroduction in 1405 of the double quorum, which removed from the gentry justices the power to determine felonies, and the reservation of the task of enquiry into breaches of the livery statutes of 1399 and 1401 to the justices of assize, made by statute in 1406, suggest that Henry IV and his advisers may still have felt too much judicial authority had been surrendered to the gentry justices of the peace. As a group, the gentry members of the quorum, usually no more than two or three justices in each Riding, were the most frequent attenders at quarter sessions, accounting for a little more than half the justice-days for which a record of payment survives; the precise level of attendance varies from 51 per cent of the total in the East Riding (158 out of 309 justice-days) to 56 per cent in the West Riding (158 out of 272 justice-days) and 60 per cent (80 out of 134 justice-days) in the North Riding.[52] The quorum alone exercised the power to determine the more serious category of criminal offences, felony; and even when lesser matters were at stake, the legal knowledge and experience of the men of law on the county benches made it likely that those gentry justices appointed more for their social eminence than their administrative abilities would follow the lead of their lawyer-colleagues. It was consequently important for the efficient working of each county bench that suitable members of the quorum be found to direct its activities in the absence of the assize justices, and it was to this end that the Chancery devoted much thought to the selection of the twenty-four justices appointed, at one stage or another of their careers, to the quorum of the three Ridings.

In essence, the justices of the quorum were drawn from two distinct groups: lawyers of Yorkshire origin who practised successfully enough in the Westminster courts to earn themselves crown office of one kind or another; and men with some legal training whose expertise was exercised, sometimes at Westminster but more usually within Yorkshire itself, on behalf of predominantly local clients. The period saw something of a shift in the relative importance of these two groups within the Yorkshire commissions, with the Westminster practitioners gaining ground at the expense of their provincial colleagues. There is some evidence that, especially under Henry IV, this was the result of a deliberate Chancery policy, instituted in December 1405, which sought both a reduction in the size of the quorum and the exclusion from it of all those justices who did not depend on the Crown for some form of office. At the general reissue of the peace commissions made in June 1394, for instance, four of the nine quorum justices appointed to the Yorkshire benches were primarily local administrators; by May 1401 the number had risen, in line with a general inflation in the number of those appointed as justices, to six out of fourteen; but by February 1412 this had been reduced to only one of the eight quorum justices. In practice, however, the supply of able lawyers with good local connections who were prepared to ride from Westminster to Yorkshire and spend their time on the comparatively ill-rewarded and occasionally dangerous work of the bench was not endless. Those with ambitions of social ascent might welcome the enhanced status within their Riding that a career as an active justice brought; while others, like the sergeants-at-law, might be cajoled into the work as an unwelcome but unavoidable obligation of the lucrative royal appointment they held. Neither of these expedients was sufficient to remove all need for reliance upon the local men of business, and the differing character and effectiveness of each of the Riding benches owed much to the precise mix between these two groups of quorum justices.

Such fluctuations in the composition of the quorum can be most clearly illustrated in the North Riding, where the displacement of local lawyers by Westminster practitioners was only uncertainly effected. Between June 1389 and June 1394 the gentry justices appointed to the quorum were John Burgh of Brough, Queen Anne's bailiff at Richmond,[53] and John Frithebank of Manfield, another employee in the estate administration of the honour of Richmond, who subsequently rose to be steward of the neighbouring Beauchamp lordship of Barnard Castle.[54] By 1397, however, this partnership had been broken up in favour of a new pairing between Richard Norton and John Conyers of Hornby, both apprentices-at-law practising in the Westminster courts.[55] The advantage the Crown hoped to gain by this transformation in the personnel of the quorum was twofold: a stricter adherence to the limits of the peace commission's powers, which the king's judges consistently suspected the justices of exceeding,[56] and a greater resistance to the influence of private interests on the decisions of the bench. This was not because men like Norton and Conyers were innocent of such interests: their standing within the profession ensured that both of them, while active as justices of the peace, maintained a longer and more influential list of clients than men like Burgh or Frithebank could ever have hoped for.[57] But the Crown had at least the assurance, which it lacked in the case of lesser men whose careers revolved around the service of a single lord, that as the most lucrative of their many employers and possessor of the most damaging financial sanctions in the case of disloyalty, it had the most effective claim on their obedience. Norton and Conyers' dominance of the quorum held good for a decade but, following Norton's appointment as a justice of assize on the East Anglian circuit in 1406 and the subsequent omission of Conyers from the North Riding bench in February 1407, it proved impossible to find immediate replacements of a similar standing. A local quorum consequently re-emerged to fill the vacuum, in the persons of the durable John Burgh, now chief steward of lord Fitzhugh's lands in Yorkshire,[58] and William Lambard of Ingleby, an estate steward with some legal training.[59] Though John Burgh's place on the quorum was eventually filled, after his death in 1412, by Norton and James Strangeways of West Harsley, a newly-created serjeant-at-law,[60] it was the local man among the justices, William Lambard, who remained the most frequent attender at sessions to the very end of Henry IV's reign.

The situation was rather different in the West Riding, where the Westminster lawyers always predominated. Between 1389 and 1397 the partnership of William Gascoigne of Gawthorpe and John Woodruff of Wooley, both created sergeant-at-law at the same call in 1388, discharged the bulk of the commission's work and, on Woodruff's death in 1397,[61] his place was filled by Richard Gascoigne of Hunslet. An apprentice-at-law who had been marshal of the Exchequer since 1384 and became chief steward of the northern estates of the Duchy of Lancaster between 1400 and 1407,[62] Richard Gascoigne discharged the duties of the quorum more or less single-handed after his brother's elevation as Chief Justice of King's Bench in November 1400. Of the six other gentry justices appointed to the West Riding quorum, four[63] did not sit at all, while the other two – Robert Tirwhit, a busy serjeant-at-law with pre-existing commitments to the bench in Lindsey and the East Riding,[64] and John Ingleby of Ripley, a substantial gentleman of pronounced personal piety who probably owed his presence on the quorum to the reputation of his father, Sir Thomas Ingleby (CJKB)[65] – attended only sporadically. The active gentry members of the West Riding quorum thus consisted of no more than three men, but their legal distinction and regular attendance at quarter sessions ensured that the local bench posed few problems for the Chancery. This was reflected in the comparatively greater stability of its personnel: 12 commissions nominating 46 justices were issued for the Riding between July 1389 and February 1412, compared with 17 commissions to 45 justices in the North Riding and 21 commissions to 50 justices in the East Riding during the same period.

The marked instability in the composition of the East Riding bench stemmed in large part from the Chancery's inability to find the kind of settled and regular quorum acceptable to itself, that had emerged in the West Riding. The basis for such a quorum existed, in the regular pairing of William Hungate and Hugh Ardern, two local stewards and men of business who were the most consistent attenders at quarter sessions. Yet while Ardern was appointed to the quorum of every East Riding commission after June 1394, Hungate, little different in experience and reputation[66] and very nearly as assiduous in his attendance at sessions, did not become his regular partner as a quorum justice until as late as May 1401. The Chancery's obvious reluctance to appoint Hungate to the quorum sprang from its increasing unwillingness to allow any county bench to be dominated by local men of law, without the additional element of expertise and surveillance provided by the presence of a Westminster practitioner. It proved difficult to find a suitable candidate for such a role, however: some of the justices appointed, like Robert Tirwhit and Richard Gascoigne, were too busy elsewhere to attend more than an occasional session; others lacked the independent standing, necessary even for a place on the quorum, to maintain their seat on the bench. Nicholas Rosselyn of Cotness, for instance, appointed to both commission and quorum in November 1397, lost his status as a justice as soon as he lost the office, as clerk of the foreign estreats of the Exchequer, that had justified his appointment.[67] Yet the supply of local men capable of discharging the duties of a quorum justice was itself not so copious that the claims of a well-qualified candidate could be permanently overlooked. Besides Hugh Ardern, only the experienced William Holme,[68] who had borne much of the quorum's work in the early 1390s, satisfied the Chancery's requirements. Henry IV's advisers experimented with the appointment of two other local men to the quorum, Richard Beverley and Walter Rudstane of Hayton, and quickly discarded them both. Though an active and influential local attorney, Beverley occupied too prominent and controversial a position within the burgess oligarchy of Beverley to be entirely trustworthy,[69] while Rudstane's legal practice, largely confined to knightly families like the Ughtreds of Kexby, proved too modest to justify a regular place on the bench.[70] Both men were consequently dropped from the quorum after a year, while a third Beverley lawyer, Richard Tirwhit,[71] received even shorter shrift, losing his place on the quorum the day he was appointed to it. In the end, it was this shortage of suitably qualified justices willing to take an active role on the East Riding quorum which ensured that William Hungate was, in the summer of 1401, restored to the partnership with Hugh Ardern that his experience and frequent attendance at quarter sessions had always suggested. As a result, a measure of stability was restored to the East Riding bench: after July 1401 no new peace commission was issued for the Riding for three and a half years, in contrast to the five commissions issued within the previous two years.

Tensions remained, however, especially between the burgess oligarchy at Beverley and the East Riding justices. The burgesses' consistent ambition throughout this period was to gain the right to have the town's own officers act as justices of the peace within the liberty, as the mayor and aldermen of

York had been empowered to do since 1393, without interference from the East Riding bench.[72] Progress was made towards this goal in June 1397, when a peace commission was issued to eight of the keepers of Beverley, and in 1407 a determined attempt was made to gain a new commission excluding the county justices from the town entirely.[73] The pursuit of this private agenda only reinforced the Chancery's latent distrust of local men of business as justices and eventually provoked a remodelling of the East Riding quorum in line with the growing preference for Westminster lawyers. When Hugh Ardern's long career on the bench finally ended in January 1408, his leading role among the justices was taken over by William Waldeby of Portington, a clerk of King's Bench who was also a justice of gaol delivery in Yorkshire, clerk of the Crown in the palatinate of Lancaster and an associate justice of assize on the Midland circuit.[74] He was joined on the quorum the following year by John Ellerker of Risby, deputy chamberlain of the Exchequer,[75] and for the next two years these two recreated the administrative partnership exercised for so long by Hungate and Ardern. The change in attitude and priorities this implied was not great – both Waldeby and Ellerker came from the East Riding, used the profits of the law to buy further lands there, and maintained contact with the region while pursuing their careers at Westminster[76] – but their presence and activity on the East Riding bench finally made possible the greater degree of central surveillance over the work of the justices that, this survey of the justices of the Yorkshire quorum has suggested, it was the policy of Henry IV's advisers to promote. The growing predominance of Westminster practitioners on the Yorkshire benches that they achieved was nevertheless short-lived: under Henry V, Richard Gascoigne was replaced as doyen of the West Riding bench by the lesser figure of John Dawnay, under-steward of the duchy honour of Tickhill;[77] while the partnership of Waldeby and Ellerker in the East Riding soon gave way to a quorum dominated once again by two local lawyers, Guy Rouclif and Robert Rudstane.[78] Without persistent Chancery pressure, it was perhaps inevitable that this should be the case; the significant point is that it was deliberate policy, not accident, which dictated the composition of the quorum justices under Henry IV. As a policy, fine-tuning the existing institutions by a detailed scrutiny of their personnel lacked some of the appeal of Henry V's more spectacular initiatives. It was not necessarily a less fruitful approach to the problem of law enforcement.

By the reign of Richard II the qualifications desirable in the remaining group of justices of the peace to be considered, those gentry justices not appointed to the quorum, were well-established: they should be 'of good fame and good condition', resident in their counties, and neither barettors nor maintainers of quarrels.[79] These were uncontroversial demands, on which both the royal administration and the parliamentary Commons were prepared to agree, though the Commons sought, unsuccessfully, to impose certain further restrictions upon the type of justice appointed at the start of Richard II's majority: chiefly, that magnate stewards were to be excluded from the commissions and that the justices were to be 'assigned and nominated' in

Parliament rather than, as was usual, chosen by the Chancellor and the Council.[80] In reality, the gentry justices in Yorkshire were, like the quorum justices, drawn from two distinct social groups. The first group came from the social elite of county society and consisted of men for whom a seat on the bench was only one rung on the *cursus honorum* of county government: men such as Sir John Savile of Eland and Sir Robert Neville of Hornby in the West Riding, or Sir Robert Hilton of Swine and Sir Robert Constable of Flamborough in the East Riding.[81] The second group, drawn from outside the ranks of the greater gentry, owed their place either to their administrative experience, usually acquired in the service of one of the county's magnates, or to some legal knowledge. Edmund Fitzwilliam of Wadsworth, John Aske of Ousthorpe and Peter del Hay of Spaldington, for example, were respectively stewards of the Duke of York, Earl of Northumberland and Bishop of Durham,[82] while the North Riding justice, Henry Pudsey, occasionally acted as an attorney in Common Pleas.[83] What distinguished this latter group from the men of law on the quorum was, principally, their unquestionably gentle birth, though the important position on the Yorkshire commissions occupied by quorum lawyers drawn from established gentry families, such as Richard Gascoigne or John Conyers of Hornby, clearly suggests that this was not an immutable distinction.

While it has recently been concluded that, on the Yorkist and early Tudor commissions of the peace, 'many of the gentry were in practice idle and negligent',[84] the gentry justices of Yorkshire in this period usually made more than a token effort to attend the quarter sessions. More than half (25 out of 42) of the gentry justices appointed to the three commissions can be shown to have attended the sessions at least once, while in terms of justice-days for which payment was made, only in the North Riding did the attendance levels of the gentry justices (39 per cent) fall significantly below those of the quorum lawyers; in the West Riding the figure was 42 and in the East Riding 49 per cent. Most of the non-attenders were occasional justices, appointed to only one or two commissions at times of political uncertainty; the general expectation seems to have been that any gentry justice regularly appointed to the peace commissions regarded at least occasional attendance as an obligation upon him. It would be surprising if this were not the case; appointment as a justice of the peace was valued as a formal acknowledgement of the standing a justice enjoyed within county society, but also for the practical authority with which it endowed him, the exercise of which would, in turn, further advance his social standing. In a society where court-keeping was one of the most common statements of the public exercise of legitimate authority, to keep the courts of the county was to act, in one sense, as the embodiment and representative of the shire. Those gentlemen appointed as justices were, in consequence, usually eager to exercise their authority in as public a manner as possible. Already steward of Henry, Earl of Derby's household when he was added to the East Riding commission in August 1395, Sir Peter Buckton nevertheless valued the additional social status the appointment gave him highly enough to attend the next eight sessions of the peace subsequent to his appointment;[85] although Sir Thomas Brounflete's duties as controller and keeper of Henry IV's wardrobe detained him in London for most of the year and caused him to shift his principal residence to Bedfordshire, he was still careful to maintain his worship in his native East Riding by continuing to attend occasional sessions of the peace there.[86] In both the East and West Ridings, only one regular gentry justice failed to attend any sessions: in the West, it was Sir Roger Swillington, a wealthy Lancastrian annuitant who took up residence on his East Anglian estates soon after his appointment;[87] in the East, William Mowbray of Kirklington, whose death just over two years after his initial appointment suggests ill-health as the reason.[88] The rate of absenteeism was significantly higher in the North Riding, however: there, Sir Thomas Boynton of Acklam, who sat on the bench in the early 1390s[89], and Sir Robert Conyers of Ormesby, active during the later years of Henry IV's reign,[90] are the only two justices from the upper gentry of the Riding who can be shown to have sat, while eight further gentry justices never attended at all. It is in respect of this virtual absence of substantial gentry active on the bench that the North Riding commission, characterized by an unusual degree of magnate participation in its sessions and a dominant quorum on which the stewards and legal advisers of those magnates were prominent, is most clearly distinguished from the rest of Yorkshire.

The pattern of gentry attendance in the East and West Riding is, by contrast, fairly uniform and underwent roughly the same changes over time.[91] At the start of the period both Ridings saw a single prominent gentleman, working in partnership with a couple of quorum justices, discharging most of the bench's work: in the West Riding this was Sir John Savile of Eland; in the East Riding, Sir Robert Constable of Flamborough. By *c.* 1395, however, both Savile and Constable had retired from active work as a justice and no single gentleman emerged in either Riding to take their place; instead, while the quorum justices began to take on more of the bench's business, the task of attendance at quarter sessions was shared out amongst a wider group of gentry justices. In the East Riding this consisted principally of Sir Robert Hilton and Sir Peter Buckton, joined after 1399 by John Aske, John Routhe and, most notably, Peter del Hay. A similar group of active justices took rather longer to form in the West Riding, where Sir William Rilleston and Sir John Deepden attended only occasional sessions between Savile's retirement and the usurpation of 1399. The accession of Henry IV brought something of a revival of interest among the greater gentry in the work of the bench, however, with nine gentry justices taking a part in its work during his reign, compared to only four in the previous decade. This undoubtedly owed something to Henry's desire to mobilize the considerable resources his large affinity, in conjunction with the estate administration of the Duchy of Lancaster, put at his disposal in the principal institutions of local government,[92] but concern for the effective discharge of the bench's duties among the West Riding gentry is not to be ascribed to royal initiative alone. The diligent Sir Nicholas Middleton possessed no such straightforward incentive for his frequent attendance at sessions,[93] while the presence on the peace commission of Nicholas Gascoigne of Lasingby and Edmund Fitzwilliam, previously prominent in the service of former favourites of Richard II,[94] argues that political and factional considerations remained of less importance in determining which gentry were appointed to the bench than appetite and enthusiasm for the work of a justice.

This participation in the work of the bench by a substantial proportion of the gentry nominated to a place on the Yorkshire peace commissions was in line with the demands of the parliamentary Commons during much of Richard II's reign. For the Commons, the greater responsibility for the work of the bench shown by the 'wiser and more discreet' of the county, with a corresponding decline in the influence exercised by the 'poorer and less sufficient' justices,[95] was an essential precondition for the better maintenance of public order. Yet it remains open to question how far the reforms initiated by the parliamentary Commons between 1388 and 1390 either altered existing patterns of attendance at the quarter sessions or increased the county gentry's control over the activity and composition of the commissions. The Yorkshire evidence suggests that the central plank of the Commons' demands for reform, that the work of the county bench be discharged by substantial and independent gentry justices, met with only partial success: while some of the justices chosen in response to the Commons proposals proved willing to shoulder the burdens of office, most notably in the East Riding, where all the knightly justices – Sir John Goddard, Sir John Constable, Sir Robert Hilton – attended sessions, others proved more reluctant. Two of the Commons' new breed of justice, Sir William Aldeburgh of Harewood and Sir Ralph Pigot of Clotherholme, relinquished their responsibilities within a year of their initial appointment in May 1389, while the choice of Sir John Wadsley of Ecclesfield, from the very south of the county, to serve on the North Riding bench suggests a serious dearth of more suitable knightly candidates in that Riding. This was compounded by the drastic reduction in the size of the commissions – from twenty-two justices in the West Riding in 1386 to only eight in 1389 – which placed an impractically heavy administrative burden on those who remained on the bench; by May 1391, Richard II was having to respond to complaints that the justices were failing to hold even their statutory sessions.[96]

In consequence the Commons' ideal of a bench of knightly magistrates was, within a couple of years of their parliamentary victory, upheld only in a minority of counties. In many cases it had dissolved, as in the East and West Ridings, into the reality of a single knight discharging the work of the commission in partnership with a couple of local lawyers, or into a county bench dominated by the quorum justices and without a significant upper-gentry presence, as was the case in the North Riding. In terms of those justices who actually attended sessions, the Commons' campaign to reform the peace commission therefore brought only marginal changes to the Yorkshire benches. The replacement of John Dronsfield of West Bretton, an apprentice-at-law who was the central figure in the work of the West Riding commission throughout the minority of Richard II,[97] with the more substantial partnership of Savile and Gascoigne represented the most considerable movement in the direction of the Commons' ideal. The active gentry justices in the East Riding, William Holme and Sir Robert Hilton, may in addition have enjoyed a slightly freer hand after 1389 than before, though this was more the result of the political misfortunes that overcame their professional colleagues on the commission – principally John Lockton and Roger Fulthorpe[98] – than the consequence of the institutional changes demanded by the Commons. In the North Riding, the outcome of the reforms was the exact opposite of the intention behind them: established county gentry like Sir John Marmion of Tanfield and Sir William Percy of Levisham were more active as justices before 1389 than in any subsequent years.[99]

The Yorkshire evidence thus suggests that the Commons' campaign to ensure a greater gentry presence on the county benches enjoyed, at best, a limited success; only relatively slight changes in the composition of the active justices were effected by the reforms begun in May 1389. More significant in shaping the character of the bench in this period was the considerable effort expended by the king and his advisers to ensure the appointment of gentry justices of proven diligence and loyalty. Richard II had shown himself anxious to secure peace commissions in conformity with his wishes as early as 1386,[100] but there is little sign of direct royal influence on the personnel of the Yorkshire commissions before the political crisis of 1397. Until then, the only knight of the king's affinity to serve as a justice of the peace, Sir John Goddard, had left the East Riding bench by the time the king retained him.[101] Following the fall of the former Appellants, however, there are some indications that Richard began to seek more systematically to ensure a body of gentry justices in Yorkshire, as in several other counties,[102] upon whose loyalty he could rely. The commissions issued in July 1397 saw the addition of the king's knight, Sir James Pickering, as well as the Exchequer official, Richard Gascoigne, to the West Riding bench; Pickering's appointment, followed by his election to Parliament the following September and subsequent nomination as sheriff, was clearly intended to establish him as the king's chosen lieutenant in the Riding.[103] In the East Riding the existing justices were also afforced by the appointment of two royal officials, Nicholas Rosselyn and Thomas Lumbard of Beverley, a former teller of the Exchequer who had spent several years as controller of the Bordeaux garrison.[104] Modest though such changes appear, they contributed to the complaint of the Commons in October 1399 that justices of the peace had been appointed *par brocage*.[105] Yet in Yorkshire they constituted no more than a prelude to the more radical remodelling of the Riding benches undertaken by Henry IV in line with the policy enunciated by his advisers in the spring of 1400. The extent of the dominance exercised over the Yorkshire commissions by the king's affinity as a result of this policy can be briefly stated: between 1399 and 1413, nineteen of the twenty-seven gentry justices appointed to the Yorkshire commissions were either members of the king's household and affinity or in receipt of an annuity from the revenues of the Crown and the Duchy of Lancaster. Though the true extent of the influence exerted by the king's affinity is somewhat inflated by the policy of appointing additional Lancastrian loyalists to the commissions during the disturbances of 1405 – justices like Sir William Fulthorpe, John of Lancaster's councillor, and the royal sergeant-at-arms, John Drax,[106] were dropped from the benches to which they had been added as soon as the crisis was passed – the contrast with the decade before Henry IV's accession nevertheless underlines the change in policy that the usurpation of 1399 brought in its wake: between 1389 and 1399 only three of the twenty-three gentry justices appointed had been royal annuitants. Though an analysis of the Lancastrian presence on the commissions of the peace throughout the country suggests a relatively brief period of sustained royal influence on the selection of justices, between the autumn of 1404 and spring 1406, it seems clear that in Yorkshire the build-up of Henry's supporters on the benches started earlier and lasted longer.[107]

For the Crown, this increased ability to maintain control over one of the principal instruments of local government was an important end in itself, especially to be valued in a county like Yorkshire, which saw its full share of disturbances in this period. The vulnerability of the bench to intimidation or corruption had been clearly acknowledged in March 1386, when the Council had sought to forestall the reported danger of insurrection in the county by the anachronistic measure of appointing a powerful body of magnate keepers of the peace to assist the regular justices in their duties.[108] The reasoning behind the measure was soon revealed in a series of attacks on two East Riding justices, William Holme and Stephen del Fall; Fall's assailants were the servants of the powerful Howdenshire knight, Sir Thomas Metham, and the incident precipitated a prolonged prosecution in King's Bench that involved two further justices, William Gascoigne and John Woodruff, in the threats of Metham and his followers.[109] One response to such attacks on the king's local agents was to reinforce their authority by the dispatch of powerful *ad hoc* commissions, such as the Duke of Lancaster's 'trailbaston' visitation in 1390 and the journeys of Kings Bench to York at Michaelmas 1392 and Easter 1393.[110] More permanent solutions depended, however, on the increased effectiveness of the justices of the peace themselves, in conjunction with the sheriff, in discharging their peace-keeping duties. There is some evidence to suggest that the degree of control the Crown achieved over the personnel of the Yorkshire commissions in this period was reflected in some progress towards this end. Sessions of the peace were held with more than statutory frequency – on average, six times a year in the West Riding, seven in the East Riding. The justices were conscientious in their itineration around the shire, holding their sessions in most of the major settlements in the county; five different venues for the bench are known in the North Riding, ten in the East and as many as fourteen in the West.[111]

Whenever statutory powers were conferred upon the commissions of the peace, the Yorkshire justices were quick to exercise them: they assigned coroners and heard the appeals of approvers, though both actions were technically reserved to the sheriff; delivered royal gaols; remitted suspected felons to prison by their record; and exacted sureties of the peace.[112] On occasion, the justices' enthusiastic use of their powers ran counter to the Crown's expressed desire for impartiality; when a group of villagers was indicted, in the course of an enclosure dispute, for breaking Sir Robert Conyers' close at Upsall in Cleveland, it was Conyers himself who heard the initial indictment.[113] Though common, such sectional applications of the powers of the peace commission had their own tacitly-agreed limit, and when a member of the gentry transgressed that limit the Riding benches could act as an effective initiator of legal action against him. The murder of a canon of Bolton Priory was clearly a case in point and the culprit in that instance, John Rilleston, son of the West Riding justice Sir William Rilleston, received no special consideration from his father's former colleagues on the bench, undergoing the full process of indictment, exaction in the county court and subsequent outlawry.[114] Such attitudes contributed towards a modest improvement in the standard of public order in the shire. Yorkshire still experienced sporadic outbursts of disorder at the end of Henry IV's reign: there was opposition to Sir Robert Plumpton's authority as steward of Knaresborough, and the gentry family of Routhe led resistance to the sheriff's officials in the East Riding.[115] These were relatively isolated incidents, however, lacking the persistence or the widespread popular support that had rendered the Beckwith confederacy and the associated disturbances, such as the riots in the Duke of York's lordship at Wakefield and Conisburgh, so threatening in the early years of Richard II's majority.[116] The institutional innovations of the period were perhaps less important in creating this improvement than the commissions' more efficient execution of their existing powers, made possible by the greater integration of their personnel and the increased co-ordination of their work effected by the oversight of William Gascoigne and his assize colleagues at York.

From an examination of each of the four groups of justices which constituted the Yorkshire commissions of the peace, the same conclusion seems justified: prosopographical analysis supports the procedural evidence in suggesting that the changes in the composition and powers of the commission in this period neither surrendered the initiative in local government to the county gentry nor weakened its resistance to the claims of ambitious magnates; rather, they considerably increased the ability of the royal administration to enforce its will in the localities. This ability was exercised in several ways: by the attendance of magnates closely associated with the king, such as Ralph Neville, at occasional sessions; by the increasingly close control the justices of assize maintained over all aspects of the bench's work; by the policy of seeking, whenever possible, to place the work of the quorum in the hands of Westminster practitioners, dependent on royal favour for further advancement within their profession; and by the steady accretion of crown servants among the gentry justices, a development especially marked under Henry IV. The obstructions to these centripetal pressures were slight and generally ineffective: though an individual magnate might occasionally turn his oversight of the bench to his own private advantage, none possessed the resources to outbid the Crown when it came to securing the loyalty of the justices; the reforms in the personnel of the commissions demanded by the parliamentary Commons, intended to ensure the predominance of the established county gentry in the deliberations of the bench, were, in addition, shortlived and generally negligible in their consequences, confirming an existing balance of power rather than creating a new one.

How far do these conclusions hold good for the rest of the country? While there can be no final answer to the question without a similarly intensive investigation of the evidence available for other shires, there is at least sufficient information to allow some preliminary observations. The active involvement of the region's magnates in the work of the Yorkshire benches at this period is significantly at variance, for example, with the pattern that has emerged from the study of a series of Midland and East Anglian counties in the mid-fifteenth century, in each of which it appears that, as far as the administration of justice was concerned, 'the local gentry, unhindered by the nobility, ran the shire'.[117] The crucial variable in this case seems as much chronological as geographical, for aristocratic participation in the ordinary business of the county benches remained commoner in Richard II's reign than it was later to become, both among the great nobles, like the Beauchamps in Warwickshire, and by lesser peers such as John, lord Strange, in Shropshire.[118] Equally, although few studies of the work of the later medieval peace commission have yet paid adequate attention to the supervision and co-ordination of the bench's activities provided by the justices of assize and gaol delivery, the central role these justices played on the East Anglian commissions under Henry VI suggests that the prominence assumed by the assize justices in the work of the Yorkshire bench may not have been exceptional.[119] Although few justices attained as dominant a position within their native counties as William Gascoigne, the powerful influence exercised by the justices and sergeants of the Westminster courts on the quorum of the Yorkshire commissions was nevertheless replicated in several other counties. In Devonshire, John Hill (JKB 1389–1408), Robert Hill (JCP 1408–25) and Sir William Hankford (JCP 1398–1413) were all among the most diligent justices of the peace, while the prominence of Sir John Cassy (CBEx. 1389–1400) on the Gloucester bench, of William Rickhill (JCP 1389–1407) and John Colepeper (JCP 1406–14) in Kent, and of Sir Hugh Huls (JKB 1394–1415) in Staffordshire ensured that local justice in each of these counties was subject to careful regulation by a highly experienced royal servant.[120]

Among the gentry justices with whom such Westminster lawyers were expected to work, two main conclusions stand out from the Yorkshire evidence: the relatively high level of gentry participation in the work of the bench and the rapid accretion of crown servants among the justices after 1399. Establishing the general applicability of these conclusions is especially difficult, for no single aspect of the commissions of the peace varied as much from county to county as the character and diligence of the gentry justices; the range of possibilities runs from the situation in Huntingdonshire, where two justices discharged the entire work of the bench throughout the 1390s, to that in Wiltshire, where threats of popular disturbance compelled the attendance at sessions of all the eligible gentry justices.[121] The commonest configurations in Yorkshire nevertheless form two of the most characteristic patterns to be found in the country at large: the domination of the North Riding bench by the quorum justices found a parallel in both Kent and Hampshire, for example, while the close working relationship between a single knightly justice and a couple of lesser companions, observable in the East and West Riding during the 1390s, was replicated in counties like Cambridgeshire and Oxfordshire.[122] As a result, the kind of attendance levels prevalent among the gentry justices in Yorkshire – 54 per cent for the county as a whole, going as low as 36 per cent in the North Riding but rising to 58 per cent in the West Riding and to 67 per cent in the East – fall within the range of figures which can be established for other counties over the same period, suggesting that it was not only in Yorkshire that the dominance of the bench by lesser gentry and lawyers – a standard pattern by the mid-fifteenth century – was significantly mitigated by the continued presence of some upper-gentry justices.[123] Less typical, however, were the marked changes in the personnel of the Yorkshire commissions during Henry IV's reign; they were a solution to the particular problems created by the county's involvement in the Percy rebellions of 1403 and 1405, and one made possible largely by the extensive resources of the Duchy of Lancaster estates in the region. But while the rapid increase in the number of royal servants among the justices more closely resembles developments in other 'Duchy' counties than in the country at large,[124] Henry IV's concern for the composition and control of the county benches is observable elsewhere, whether in the elevation of suitable knights of the king's affinity – such as Sir Payn Tiptoft in Cambridgeshire[125] – to a predominant position among the justices of their native county, or in the more traditional policy of alliance with leading regional families, like the Courtenays in Devon, resurgent after a decade of disfavour, in order to harness the resources of their lordship to the interest of the Crown.[126]

If the development of the Yorkshire commissions of the peace in these years was not, then, untypical of the changes taking place in the rest of the country, some more general observations seem to follow from the resolution of the questions with which this study began. The first concerns the respective attitudes of Richard II and Henry IV towards the kind of self-regarding local sentiment embodied in the parliamentary Commons' aspirations to control the county bench. It seems clear that Richard II's appointments to the peace commissions, in particular his preference for a strong magnate presence among the justices and his promotion of the influence of a small group of royal servants in November 1397, had little effect on the actual conduct of the sessions. By contrast, Henry IV was able to maintain an impressively close grip on the personnel, both nominal and active, of the Yorkshire commissions, through the agency of several trusted noblemen and his own extensive affinity. If this seems unremarkable, granted the considerable local influence the £1500-worth of annuities charged on the Duchy of Lancaster estates in the county brought him,[127] it should not obscure the skill with which Henry IV managed to marry the local aspirations of the gentry to his own cause. The chief instruments of this marriage of sentiment and convenience, the Gascoigne brothers, illustrate the point. Their connection with the new king dated as far back as Michaelmas 1387, when Richard Gascoigne was retained by Henry of Derby as his attorney at the Exchequer; his elder brother had joined him on the Lancastrian payroll by 1391 and soon became an indispensable figure in the administration of the Duchy.[128] Yet the Gascoignes, like many gentry families, looked to more than one magnate for advancement and, for much of Richard II's reign, the royal favourite, Thomas Holland, Duke of Surrey, had been one of their principal patrons. Richard Gascoigne owed his appointment as marshal of the Exchequer to Holland and continued to act as his attorney there; William Gascoigne was Holland's counsel in King's Bench by Easter 1388; Nicholas Gascoigne of Lasingcroft, the most closely involved in Holland service of the three, acted as steward of the Duke of Surrey's household and took a substantial retaining fee from the Holland manor of Cottingham.[129] It was not, therefore, inevitable that the Gascoigne family should cleave so promptly and firmly to the Lancastrian cause on Henry's return to England in June 1399[130], yet the new king was tactful and generous enough to make the transition appear a natural extension of their previous loyalties. In doing so he was securing for himself the services of just such 'gentz plus suffisantz et de bone fame' as both the Commons and his own Council urged him to employ, while avoiding the charge of excessive interference in the affairs of the county community preferred against Richard II.

The relationship between William Gascoigne and the new king soon developed beyond the purely official; he became one of Henry's most trusted advisers, summoned to his presence in July 1401 'pur chivacher en nostre compaignie pur certaines treschargeantes matires touchante lestat de nous et de nostre roiaume' and singled out by the Council in 1405 as one of those in whom the king put special confidence.[131] His reward was an unprecedented elevation from king's sergeant to Chief Justice of King's Bench in November 1400, but the resulting responsibilities went beyond the strictly judicial. In Yorkshire, his possession of the threefold commission of assize, gaol delivery and the peace, vigorously exercised on his usually biannual visits to the county and bolstered by further *ad hoc* commissions issued to him in times of unrest or rebellion[132], gave him overall responsibility for the execution of criminal justice in the county and made him one of Henry's principal lieutenants in preserving the peace of the North. His close relations with his brother Richard, whose duties as chief steward of the Duchy in the north and principal justice of the West Riding bench required frequent itinerations around the county,[133] provided him with an excellent source of information on the disposition of the region. The best measure of the influence these powers gave Gascoigne is the resentment they generated. When the Parliament of November 1411 requested a statute specifically prohibiting the Chief Justice of King's Bench from sitting on assizes in his own county, apparently on the grounds that he might be required to sit in error on a case he had already tried at first instance, the petition drew upon a long tradition of complaint on the issue, but it was clearly against Gascoigne and his local influence that the resulting legislation was principally aimed.[134]

A second general observation suggested by this study concerns the opposition between central government and local autonomy, royal authority and gentry independence that is assumed in much writing on the subject of the justices of the peace. It is an opposition that the Yorkshire evidence cannot really sustain. Those justices who appear to be most clearly the delegates of central authority, the magnates, assize judges and Westminster practitioners among the quorum lawyers, usually possessed strong and continuing ties in Yorkshire itself. It could hardly have been otherwise; to be effective, government had to be local government and the Crown's agents had necessarily to be well acquainted with the local forum in which they exercised their authority. The assumption that they were perceived as the agents of a distant and intrusive power rests on a model of physical and intellectual distance between capital and province which underestimates the sophistication and mobility of later medieval English society. Even amongst the county knights, familiarity with London and Westminster was commonplace, though rarely so intimately expressed as by Sir John Deepden's bequest to an ale-wife in Holborn.[135] Consequently, to say that 'the county establishment . . . was almost a law unto itself and difficult to control from Westminster'[136] is to place due weight on the importance and resilience of the gentry communities of the shire, but to underestimate the extent to which those communities were anxious to share in the many benefits the king and his advisers had to offer. The prominence of men like Richard Norton or William Waldeby in the administration of local society was more often welcomed than resented; as the local brokers of central authority, they and their fellow lawyers were a source of counsel and advice sought after by both individuals and communities. William Hungate and Richard Gascoigne were asked by their fellow gentry to assist in the execution of royal commissions; Hugh Ardern received a special payment from the grateful community of Beverley 'for his counsel in the time of litigation and insurrection'.[137] The county gentry were far less exclusive in their pursuit of local autonomy than some of the demands of the parliamentary Commons might suggest; they needed the expertise of the lawyers, just as they cultivated the influence of the magnates, though they were anxious to set a limit to both. When the commission of the peace functioned effectively, as it did in Yorkshire for much of this period, it did so by maintaining an equilibrium between the interests and expectations of each of those groups. What characterized these years was not a decisive shift in the balance of judicial power towards the local communities, for this had never been the exclusive object of their petitioning, but a modest increase in the oversight of local society maintained by the king's government, achieved by the creation of a balance between professional and amateur justices on which both the Crown and the parliamentary spokesmen of the gentry could agree. It was the embodiment of an enduring ideal of local government, already enshrined in Magna Carta and reiterated in the second Statute of Westminster, which associated the knights of the shire with the itinerant justices in hearing assizes and attaints in each county.

Appendix

Table 1 Source of Indictments before Yorkshire Justices of Gaol Delivery[1]

	1389–99	*1399–1413*
Sheriff	287 (44%)	226 (39%)
Justices of the Peace	156 (24%)	213 (37%)
Private liberties	118 (18%)	59 (10%)
Coroners	71 (11%)	39 (6%)
Appeals	26 (4%)	47 (8%)
	658	586

1 [PRO], JUST 3/176, 183, 184, 191.

Table 2 Attendance Payments for the Justices: East Riding

	1	*2*	*3*	*4*	*5*	*6*
Sir John Goddard	7					
Sir Robert Constable	21	3				
William Holme	13					
William Hungate	24	16	10	14		
Hugh Ardern		16	12	21	2	
Sir Robert Hilton		5	6	1	2	2
Sir Peter Buckton		7			2	
Robert Tirwhit		3	1	6	6	
Nicholas Rosselyn				2		
John Aske				4		
Walter Rudstane				1		
Peter del Hay				4	10	10
Sir Thomas Brounflete				1	2	
William Waldeby				1	25	8
Sir John Routhe					6	
John Ellerker					18	5
Richard Beverley					7	
(Robert Rudstane)						8
(Guy Rowcliffe)						7
No. of session days:	24	17	12	29	30	14

1. 20 Mar. 1391–23 April 1394. E 101/598/28; E 372/244, Adhuc Item Ebor.
2. 21 Sept. 1394–5 Sept. 1396. E 137/49/2A mm. 1–4; E 372/254, Res' Ebor.
3. 21 Sept. 1396–17 Dec. 1397. E 101/598/50, fo. 1; E 372/244, Westml'. The record of payments made to the justices differs slightly from the record of their presence at sessions, which is: Hungate 9; Ardern 11; Hilton 5; Buckton 1; Tirwhit 1.

4. 14 Jan. 1399–14 Mar. 1403. E 372/248, Adhuc Item Ebor.
5. 20 June 1407–17 Oct. 1412. E 370/160/2 m. 13; E 372/258, Adhuc Res' Ebor.
6. 19 Dec. 1412–10 Jan. 1415. E 372/260, Res' Ebor.

Table 3 Attendance Payments for the Justices: North Riding

	1	*2*	*3*	*4*
Richard Norton	10	10	9	5
John de Burgh	20	9	4	
William Newsome	4			
John de Frithebank	3			
William Lambard	9	7	1	10
John Markham		2		
John Conyers		6	12	
John Barton				9
James Strangeways				4
(Christopher Boynton)				3
No. of session days:	22	13	12	10

1. 2 Mar. 1395–11 Dec. 1396. E 372/254, Item Ebor.
2. 25 June 1397–17 Mar. 1399. E 372/247, Item Ebor.
3. 6 Oct. 1399–4 Aug. 1401. E 372/254, Item Ebor.
4. 19 Aug. 1412–30 Aug. 1414. E 372/260, Res' Ebor.

Table 4 Attendance Payments for the Justices: West Riding

	1	*2*	*3*	*4*	*5*	*6*
Sir John Savile	15	16				
William Gascoigne	15	15	11	11	2	2
John Woodruff	11	17				
Sir William Rilleston		2	2			
Sir John Deepden		1	2	9		
John Ingleby		1	1	4		
Richard Gascoigne			4	25	26	15
Sir Richard Tempest				2	3	1
Sir William Dronsfield				9		
Sir Nicholas Middleton				11	7	
Sir John Cokayn				1		
Robert Tirwhit				1		
Nicholas Gascoigne				1	8	
Robert Waterton					1	1
Sir Robert Neville					6	5
Sir Richard Redman					1	
Edmund Fitzwilliam						7
No. of session days:	15	20	13	31	26	15

1. 18 Aug. 1390–3 Oct. 1392. E 101/598/28; E 372/242 Adhuc Item Ebor.
2. 7 Oct. 1392–6 June. 1395. E 370/160/1, fo. 4; E 372/242 Adhuc Item Ebor.
3. 21 Dec. 1395–8 Jan. 1399. E 101/598/28; E 372/247 Item Ebor.
4. 3 Mar. 1399–6 Oct. 1402. E 137/49/2B mm. 1–14; E 372/248, Adhuc Item Ebor.
5. 21 Dec. 1402–4 Mar. 1409. E 372/254, Item Ebor.
6. 23 May. 1409–23 Dec. 1411. E 372/259, Res' Ebor.

Notes

* Work on this article was assisted by a Small Personal Research Grant from the British Academy.

1 M. Bloch, *Feudal Society* (London, 1962), ii. 371.

2 A. Harding, 'The Origins and Early History of the Keepers of the Peace', *T[ransactions of the] R[oyal] H[istorical] S[ociety]*, 5th ser. x (1960), 85–109; H. Ainsley, 'Keeping the Peace in Southern England in the Thirteenth Century', *Southern History*, vi (1984), 13–35; A. L. Brown, *The Governance of Late-Medieval England, 1272–1461* (London, 1989), pp. 122–6.

3 F. W. Maitland, *The Constitutional History of England* (Cambridge, 1908), pp. 206–9, 495; M. Powicke, *Medieval England, 1066–1485* (London, 1931), pp. 209–13; P. Corrigan and D. Sayer, *The Great Arch. English State Formation as Cultural Revolution* (Oxford, 1985), p. 16.

4 R. L. Storey, 'Liveries and Commissions of the Peace, 1388–1390', in *The Reign of Richard II*, ed. F. R. H. du Boulay and Caroline M. Barron (London, 1971), pp. 131–52; J. B. Post, 'The Peace Commissions of 1382', *EHR*, xci (1982), 98–101.

5 J. G. Bellamy, *Bastard Feudalism and the Law* (London, 1989), pp. 17–23.

6 B. H. Putnam, 'The Transformation of the Keepers of the Peace into Justices of the Peace, 1327–1380', *TRHS*, 4th ser. xii (1929), 24–41; *Proceedings before the Justices of the Peace in the Fourteenth and Fifteenth Centuries: Edward III to Richard III*, ed. B. H. Putnam (Ames Foundation, London, 1938), pp. xxxvi–lvi. For a concise and recent restatement of Putnam's views, see N. Saul, 'Conflict and Consensus in English Local Society', in *Politics and Crisis in Fourteenth-Century England*, ed. J. Taylor and W. Childs (Gloucester, 1990), p. 39.

7 R. H. Hilton, 'A Crisis of Feudalism', in *The Brenner Debate. Agrarian Class Structure and Economic Development in Pre-Industrial Europe*, ed. T. H. Aston and C. H. E. Philpin (Cambridge, 1985), p. 135; A. Harding, *The Law Courts of Medieval England* (London, 1973), p. 94; J. R. Lander, *The Limitations of the English Monarchy in the Later Middle Ages* (Toronto, 1989), pp. 21–37.

8 E. Powell, 'The Administration of Criminal Justice in Late-Medieval England: Peace Sessions and Assizes', in *The Political Context of Law*, ed. R. Eales and D. Sullivan (London, 1987), pp. 49–59; id., *Kingship, Law and Society: Criminal Justice in the Reign of Henry V* (Oxford, 1989), pp. 56–62.

9 R. A. Griffiths, *The Reign of Henry VI* (London, 1981), pp. 801–2; J. R. Lander, *English Justices of the Peace, 1461–1509* (Gloucester, 1989), pp. 109–12; R. Virgoe, 'The Crown and Local Government: East Anglia under Richard II', in *The Reign of Richard II*, pp. 238–9; N. Saul, *Knights and Esquires: The Gloucestershire Gentry in the Fourteenth Century* (Oxford, 1991), pp. 131–2.

10 *Proceedings and Ordinances of the Privy Council*, ed. Sir N. H. Nicolas (1834), i. 109.

11 *The Westminster Chronicle, 1381–1394*, ed. L. C. Hector and B. F. Harvey (Oxford, 1982), p. 358.

12 Virgoe, 'The Crown and Local Government', p. 237; J. B. Post, 'Criminals and the Law in the Reign of Richard II' (Oxford D. Phil. thesis, 1976), pp. 140–1; I. Rowney, 'Government and Patronage in the Fifteenth Century: Staffordshire 1439–1459', *Midland History*, viii (1983), 59; C. Arnold, 'The Commission of the Peace for the West Riding of Yorkshire, 1437–1509', in *Property and Politics: Essays in Later Medieval English History*, ed. T. Pollard (Gloucester, 1984), pp. 116–38; R. B. Goheen, 'Social Ideals and Social Structure: Rural Gloucestershire, 1450–1500', *Histoire Sociale – Social History*, xii (1979), 266–7.

13 *[Calendar of] P[atent] R[olls], 1388–92*, pp. 137, 138, 343, 345, 525; ibid., *1391–6*, pp. 292, 439, 588, 727; ibid., *1396–9*, pp. 97, 235–6; ibid. *1399–1401*, pp. 566–7; ibid., *1401–5*, p. 521; ibid., *1405–8*, pp. 499, 500; ibid., *1408–13*, pp. 486–7. No commission of appointment survives for Edmund Fitzwilliam, who attended seven sessions of the West Riding bench between May 1409 and December 1411. In addition, some justices continued to sit for several months after they were removed from the commission, e.g. Richard Beverley, who lost his place on the East Riding bench on 20 February 1412, but attended a session on the following 30 May: P[ublic] R[ecord] O[ffice], E 370/160/2 m. 13.

14 J. M. W. Bean, *From Lord to Patron. Lordship in Late Medieval England* (Manchester, 1989), pp. 202–8.

15 *Inquisitions Post Mortem Relating to Yorkshire of the Reigns of Henry IV and V*, ed. W. P. Baildon and J. W. Clay (Yorks[hire] Arch[aeological] Soc., record ser., vol. lix, 1918), pp. 24–5.

16 T. Madox, *Formulare Anglicanum* (London, 1702), no. 575; *The Complete Peerage*, ed. G. E. Cokayn (London, 1910–57), viii. 569–70.

17 *Proceedings and Ordinances of the Privy Council*, iii. 302; *Letters of Queen Margaret of Anjou and Bishop Beckington and Others, written in the Reigns of Henry V and Henry VI*, ed. C. Munro (Camden Soc., old ser., vol. lxxxvi, 1863), p. 69.

18 PRO, JUST 3/176 mm. 13, 14d.; Putnam, *Proceedings*, pp. 449–55.

19 PRO, JUST 3/176 m. 16d.; Putnam, *Proceedings*, pp. 453–5; PRO, JUST 3/191 mm. 24, 25, 38, 41d. (Neville); ibid., JUST 3/191 m. 24 (Fitzhugh).

20 Ibid., KB 9/142 m. 2; ibid., JUST 3/169 mm. 4, 10d.

21 Ibid., E 137/49/2A mm. 2, 4d. For Henry Percy's activity as a JP in Cumberland, see ibid., KB 27/564 Rex m. 1.

22 Ibid., JUST 3/191 mm. 30d., 32, 32d., 36, 39.

23 Ibid., E 137/49/2B m. 9.

24 R. Somerville, *History of the Duchy of Lancaster* (London, 1953), pp. 468, 472; S. Walker, *The Lancastrian Affinity, 1361–1399* (Oxford, 1990), p. 289; PRO, JUST 3/185 mm. 3d., 5.

25 *C[alendar of] C[lose] R[olls], 1385–9*, p. 150; ibid., *1392–6*, p. 76; *C[alendar of] F[ine] R[olls], 1391–9*, p. 283.

26 Somerville, *Duchy of Lancaster*, p. 418; PRO, E 137/49/2B mm. 5–14; ibid., E 372/254/Item Ebor, 259/Res Ebor.

27 *CFR, 1391–9*, p. 196; ibid., *1399–1405*, p. 29; *CPR, 1391–6*, p. 624; PRO, E 372/248/Item Ebor.

28 Ibid., KB 27/592 Rex m. 14, 594 Rex m. 2.

29 N[orth] Y[orkshire] C[ounty] R[ecord] O[ffice], Northallerton, ZJX 3/2/45, 51.

30 *CPR, 1385–9*, p. 414; PRO, JUST 3/176 mm. 3, 9 (Aske); ibid., DURH 3/33 m. 12, JUST 3/191 m. 43 (Hay); ibid., DURH 3/33 m. 14; ibid., JUST 3/191 mm. 5, 6d., 9d., 23d. (Conyers).

31 Sir Thomas Boynton, sheriff of the palatinate of Durham, 1391–1401, Sir Robert Conyers, sheriff, 1401–6, Sir Ralph Eure, steward of the palatinate, and Sir William Fulthorpe, master forester, were all nominated as North Riding justices while in the service of the bishops of Durham: ibid., DURH 3/33 mm. 11, 24, 7, 6*d.*; 34 m. 2. For Conyers' close relations with Bishop Skirlaw, see NYCRO, ZPQ 36.

32 *CPR, 1401–5*, p. 297; *The Chronicle of John Hardyng*, ed. H. Ellis (London, 1812), p. 163 (Colville); J. M. W. Bean, *The Estates of the Percy family, 1416–1537* (Oxford, 1958), p. 93; *CPR, 1385–9*, pp. 243, 354; ibid., 1401–5, pp. 297, 324; ibid., *1405–8*, p. 67; *CCR, 1385–9*, p. 682; *CFR, 1383–91*, p. 339; ibid., *1391–9*, p. 5 (Aske).

33 *CPR, 1401–5*, p. 297; ibid., *1405–8*, p. 53; *CCR, 1402–5*, p. 326; *C[alendar of] I[nquisitions] M[iscellaneous], 1399–1422*, no. 232 (Hilton); *CCR, 1389–92*, pp. 367–8; ibid., *1399–1402*, pp. 525–6; PRO, E 101/43/4 (Scrope); *CPR, 1405–8*, p. 30; *Rotuli Parliamentorum*, iii. 605–6; Bod[leian Library, Oxford], MS Dodsworth 70, fo. 54 (Lasingby).

34 *CPR, 1399–1401*, p. 125; ibid., *1405–8*, p. 48; *CFR, 1399–1405*, p. 12; PRO, E 372/246/Adhuc Item Ebor.

35 *CPR, 1401–5*, p. 28; PRO, DL 28/27/3 m. 4 (Tempest); *CPR, 1401–5*, p. 42 (Colville); *CCR, 1402–5*, p. 326 (Hilton); *CPR, 1399–1401*, p. 311; ibid., *1408–13*, p. 93; *CCR, 1399–1401*, p. 349 (Aske); Somerville, *Duchy of Lancaster*, p. 453 (Lasingby).

36 *CPR, 1381–5*, p. 593; *CCR, 1381–5*, p. 635.

37 PRO, KB 27/582 Rex m. 8d.; Putnam, *Proceedings*, pp. 87–108 (Roos); PRO, KB 27/560 Rex m. 5d., 561 Rex m. 23d. (Holland).

38 *Plumpton Correspondence*, ed. T. Stapleton (Camden Soc., old ser., vol. iv, 1839), pp. 31–3.

39 Appointment of the justices of assize as justices of the peace was not quite automatic, in fact; John Preston was commissioned as an assize justice on the Northern circuit on 24 June 1411, but is not nominated as a Yorkshire justice of the peace until Henry V's reign: PRO, JUST 1/1517 m. 52.

40 Ibid., JUST 1/1500, 1507, 1509, 1517.

41 Ibid., JUST 3/176, 183, 184, 191.

42 On 12 February 1401: ibid., JUST 3/191 m. 1.

43 R. Sillem, 'Commissions of the Peace, 1380–1485', *Bulletin of the Institute of Historical Research*, x (1938), 96–7.

44 Details of these payments, and of all others made to the justices, can be found in the Appendix.

45 PRO, JUST 1/1517 mm. 10–13.

46 E.g. Nicholas Middleton and Richard Gascoigne held a session of the West Riding bench at Leeds on 22 September 1402, while William Gascoigne and William Waldeby were sitting at York: PRO, E 137/49/2B m. 14d.; ibid., JUST 3/191 m. 10d.

47 Ibid., JUST 1/1517 mm. 10–13.

48 J. B. Post, 'Local Jurisdictions and Judgement of Death in Later Medieval England', *Criminal Justice History*, iv (1983), 13–15.

49 During Henry IV's reign the justices of King's Bench took cognizance of eighteen Yorkshire presentments originally made before the sheriff, eleven before the justices of the peace and five before the coroners of the county: PRO, KB 27/554–607.

50 E. Powell, *Kingship, Law and Society: Criminal Justice in the Reign of Henry V* (Oxford, 1989), p. 56.

51 Post, 'Peace Commissions of 1382', 98–101; Putnam, *Proceedings*, pp. xxv–vi; Powell, 'Administration of Criminal Justice', p. 56; Sillem, 'Commissions of the Peace', 95.

52 For the composition of the quorum in all three Ridings: PRO, C 66/328 mm. 24–5d., 331 mm. 31d., 33d., 333 m. 8d., 337 m. 21d., 339 m. 20d., 341 m. 34d., 343 m. 29d., 345 m. 14d., 347 m. 25d., 358 mm. 36–7d., 363 mm. 13–14d., 372 mm. 33–4d., 374 m. 24 d., 376 m. 38 d., 380 m. 23d., 384 mm. 26–7d., 385 m. 31d.

53 NYCRO, ZRL 1/17; PRO, JUST 3/176 mm. 7, 9d., 183 mm. 3, 3d. For further details of Burgh's career, see A. J. Pollard, 'The Burghs of Brough Hall', *North Yorkshire County Record Office Journal*, vi (1978), 11–13.

54 *CCR, 1409–13*, p. 100; M. C. E. Jones, *Ducal Brittany, 1364–1399* (Oxford, 1970), p. 178, n. 4; *CIM, 1392–99*, nos. 339, 346–7; NYCRO, ZRL 7/9.

55 For Norton, see J. H. Baker, *The Order of Sergeants at Law* (Selden Soc. suppl. ser., v, 1984), p. 160. John Conyers, *apprenticius*, was retained by Henry of Derby at a fee of one mark in 1391–2; PRO, DL 28/3/3 m. 4.

56 *Les Reports del Cases en Ley . . . les Roys Henry le IV et Henry le V* (London, 1679), 2 H. IV, p. 19, 9 H. IV, p. 1.

57 Norton was steward of the liberty of Ripon under Archbishop Scrope and acted on behalf of the Scropes of both Bolton and Masham; he counselled Elizabeth, lady Clifford and the earls of Northumberland and was paid a fee by the Mowbrays, Beauchamps, Fitzhughs and the dean and chapter of York. Conyers owed his initial advancement to the Scropes of Bolton, but maintained close relations with the Neville family, acting as steward of their honour of Richmond. Besides his employment by the dukes of Lancaster, he was also steward of the bishop of Durham's liberty of Allerton and took fees from the dean and chapter of York and Henry, lord Fitzhugh. PRO, JUST 3/82/2 m. 1, 191 m. 32; B[orthwick] I[nstitute of] H[istorical] R[esearch], York, Archbishops' Registers, 5A fo. 333; *CPR, 1391–6*, pp. 232, 295; *CCR, 1396–9*, p. 216; Bod., MS Dodsworth 70, fo. 54; B[ritish] L[ibrary], Add. Charter 16556, m. 15, Egerton MS 8772 m. 2d.; NYCRO, ZJX 3/2/45; Y[ork] M[inster] L[ibrary], E 1/38 (Norton); BL, Egerton MS 3402, fo. 90; *CPR, 1396–9*, p. 509; *CCR, 1392–6*, pp. 360, 362; *Yorkshire Inquisitions Post-Mortem*, p. 68; PRO, E 326/4517; ibid., JUST 1/1517 mm. 25, 38; ibid., JUST 3/191 mm. 5, 6d., 9d., 23d.; ibid., DURH 3/33 m. 14; YML, E 1/28–38; NYCRO, ZJX 3/2/45 (Conyers).

58 Ibid., ZJX 3/2/45, 46.

59 Bailiff of the liberty of the priory of Guisborough, Lambard was sufficiently well-qualified as a lawyer to be joined with William Gascoigne in hearing a *nisi prius* case at York: PRO, JUST 3/191 m. 43; *CCR, 1409–13*, p. 25; PRO, KB 27/592 Rex m. 14.

60 J. S. Roskell, *Parliament and Politics in Late Medieval England* (3 vols., London, 1981–3), ii. 280–1.

61 BIHR, Probate Register 2, fos. 5–6.

62 *Officers of the Exchequer*, comp. J. C. Sainty (List and Index Soc., vol. xviii, 1983), p. 154; Somerville, *Duchy of Lancaster*, pp. 386, 418.

63 John Scardeburgh, a Chancery clerk with Yorkshire connections; Robert Newton, apparently appointed as a deputy for Scardeburgh; John Foljambe, a household esquire from a prominent Derbyshire family appointed in December 1405, when loyalty was at a premium; and William Lodington, king's attorney in Common Pleas since 1399, promoted to sergeant-at-law in 1412.

64 N. Ramsay, 'Retained Legal Counsel, *c. 1275–c. 1475*', *TRHS*, 5th ser., xxxiv (1985), 105, for Tirwhit's many clients, to whom may be added the abbot of Ramsey and the keepers of Beverley; BL, Add. Roll 34349; H[umberside] CRO, BC II/6/3, 4, 5. For Tirwhit's activities as a JP: PRO, E 370/160/4, fo. 7, E 101/598/50, fos. 1–2.

65 A. J. Pollard, *North-Eastern England during the Wars of the Roses* (Oxford, 1990), pp. 181–2; W. T. Lancaster, *The Early History of Ripley and the Ingleby Family* (Leeds, 1918), pp. 17–18.

66 Ardern was escheator for the county in 1391–2 and 1394–5; he was a member of Archbishop Neville's affinity and steward of Mary, lady Roos' lands in Yorkshire, but was most influential around Beverley, where he was simultaneously steward for the burgesses and the archbishop. Hungate was escheator in 1401–2; he was one of the *gens de curia* retained by the chamberlains of York, an attorney at the Exchequer for Queen Anne, and deputy-steward of Holderness throughout Thomas, Duke of Gloucester's tenure of the lordship: *List of Escheators for England and Wales* (List and Index Soc., vol. lxxii, 1972), p. 191; *CCR, 1381–5*, p. 635; *Test[amenta] Ebor[acensia]* (Surtees Soc., vol. iv, 1836), i. 202; Magdalen College, Oxford, MS Candlesby 56 b; HCRO, BC II/6/4, 5; PRO, JUST 3/82/1 m. 1, 3, m. 6; *CIM, 1392–9*, nos. 342, 348; *York City Chamberlains' Account Rolls, 1396–1500*, ed. R. B. Dobson (Surtees Soc., vol. cxcii, 1980), pp. 2, 8; PRO, E 368/156, Michaelmas, Recorda, m. 5.

67 *CPR, 1391–6*, p. 385; *Officers of the Exchequer*, p. 88; Rosselyn was last paid for his office on 21 February 1400 and omitted from the East Riding commission issued on 1 June 1400. He was still alive in 1409: *Yorkshire Deeds*, vol. ix, ed. M. J. Hebditch (Yorks. Arch. Soc., vol. cxi, 1948), no. 184.

68 Escheator in 1386/7 and 1394, dying during his second term of office: BIHR, Prob. Reg. 1 fo. 69.

69 Beverley was briefly the archbishop's steward within the town of Beverley, as his father had been, and took fees from the community there, from the chamberlains of Hull and from the abbot and convent of Meaux: PRO, JUST 3/82/1 m. 1; HCRO, BC II/2, fo. 8, II/6/3, 4, 5, 6; K[ingston upon] H[ull] R[ecord] O[ffice], BRF 2/345; *Chronica Monasterii de Melsa*, ed. E. A. Bond (Rolls Ser., 1868), vol. iii, p. lxvii. For the actions of the Beverley family in 1381, see R. B. Dobson, 'The Risings in York, Beverley and Scarborough, 1380–1381', in *The English Rising of 1381*, ed. R. H. Hilton and T. H. Aston (Cambridge, 1984), pp. 127–8, 130.

70 *Yorkshire Inquisitions Post-Mortem*, p. 22; *Test, Ebor.*, i. 244–5; *Yorkshire Deeds*, vol. ii, ed. W. Brown (Yorks. Arch. Soc., vol. i, 1914), p. 127, n. 7.

71 HCRO, BC II/6/3, 5.

72 E. G. Kimball, 'Commissions of the Peace for Urban Jurisdictions in England, 1327–1485', *Proceedings of the American Philosophical Society*, cxxi (1977), 465–7.

73 HCRO, BC I/36, BC II/6/5.

74 *Select Cases in the Court of King's Bench*, vol. vii, ed. G. O. Sayles (Selden Soc., vol. lxxxviii, 1971), pp. lxvii–lxx; Somerville, *Duchy of Lancaster*, p. 486; PRO, JUST 1/1501, 1514; ibid., JUST 3/184, 191.

75 *Officers of the Exchequer*, comp. Sainty, p. 23.

76 Waldeby acted as attorney in King's Bench for many Yorkshire clients, including lord Fitzhugh, the dean and chapter of York, the abbey of St Mary's, York, the prior of Malton, and the abbot of Selby. Ellerker was steward of Thomas of Lancaster's lordship of Holderness, attorney for the baronial families of Mauley

and Fauconberg, and counsel to the burgesses of Hull and Beverley: NYCRO, ZJX 3/2/51; YML, E 1/13, 17; PRO, JUST 1/1517 mm. 14 d., 52; ibid., KB 27/508, attornies, m. 1, 570 Rex m. 16; J. H. Tillotson, *Monastery and Society in the Late Middle Ages* (Woodbridge, 1988), p. 55 (Waldeby); PRO, SC 6/1083/12 mm. 1, 4; *CPR, 1408–13*, p. 422; ibid., *1416–22*, p. 363; *Yorkshire Inquisitions Post-Mortem*, pp. 115–16; PRO, CP 25 (1)/150/49, 151/1; KHRO, BRF 2/346; HCRO, BC II/6/7 (Ellerker).

77 Somerville, *Duchy of Lancaster*, p. 528.

78 PRO, E 372/264, Item Ebor.

79 Putnam, *Proceedings*, p. lxxix.

80 Storey, 'Liveries and Commissions of the Peace 1388–90', esp. pp. 147–9.

81 Their careers are outlined in *The Parliamentary Representation of the County of York, 1258–1832*, ed. A. Gooder (Yorks. Arch. Soc., vol. xci, 1935), pp. 123–5, 126–9, 145–6.

82 *CPR, 1413–16*, p. 377; PRO, JUST 3/191 mm. 12, 30, 40d. (Fitzwilliam); *CPR, 1401–5*, p. 324 (Aske); PRO, DURH 3/33 m. 12; ibid., JUST 3/191 m. 43 (Hay).

83 Ibid., CP 40/544, attornies, m. 8d., 574 m. 453d.

84 Lander, *English Justices of the Peace*, p. 177.

85 *Expeditions to Prussia and the Holy Land Made by Henry, Earl of Derby*, ed. L. Toulmin Smith (Camden Soc., new ser. vol. lii, 1894), pp. 126, 201; PRO, DL 28/1/4, fo. 17v, 1/6, fo. 26; ibid., E 137/49/2A.

86 C. Given-Wilson, *The Royal Household and the King's Affinity* (New Haven, 1986), pp. 57, 107; *Victoria County History, Bedfordshire* (London, 1912), iii. 118.

87 C. Richmond, *John Hopton* (Cambridge, 1981), pp. 7–11.

88 *Calendar of Inquisitions Post-Mortem, 1391–9*, nos. 96–7. Mowbray's influential position as a quorum justice in the East Riding was recognized by the dean and chapter of York, who paid him an annual fee between 1389 and 1391: YML, E 1/13–17.

89 PRO, JUST 3/176 mm. 4d., 12.

90 Ibid., KB 27/590 Rex m. 9, 596 Rex m. 11, 608 Rex m. 5.

91 See Appendix, Tables 2–4, for details of attendance.

92 Given-Wilson, *The Royal Household and the King's Affinity*, pp. 226–34, 245–54.

93 For Middleton's activity as a coroner, in addition to his duties as a justice of the peace: PRO, JUST 3/176 m. 18d., 184 mm. 2, 2d.

94 Gascoigne had been steward of the household of Thomas Holland, Duke of Surrey; Fitzwilliam had been Edmund, Duke of Aumale's steward in his lordship of Holderness and was briefly constable of Pontefract Castle while the honour was in Aumale's hands. His independent standing was recognized by the dean and chapter of York who paid him 'and others of the country' the substantial sum of £4 6s. 8d. for past and future services in 1403: J. B. Post, 'Courts, Councils and Arbitrators in the Ladbroke Manor Dispute, 1382–1400', *Medieval Legal Records*, ed. R. F. Hunnisett and J. B. Post (London, 1978), pp. 321–2; *Chronica Monasterii de Melsa*, iii. 263; PRO, DL 42/15, fo. 61; YML, E 1/35.

95 *Rot. Parl.*, iii. 17, 44.

96 *CCR, 1389–92*, pp. 252–3.

97 J. Hunter, *South Yorkshire: The History and Topography of the Deanery of Doncaster* (London, 1828–31), ii. 241–2; 'Rolls of the Collectors in the West Riding of the Lay Subsidy (Poll Tax) 2 Richard II', *Yorkshire Archaeological and Topographical Journal*, v (1879), 424; PRO, JUST 3/169 mm. 13, 17, 19, 22–25, 28d.

98 Putnam, *Proceedings*, pp. 441–2; PRO, JUST 3/169 mm. 16, 18, 20d., 27d., 28d., 30; ibid., KB 27/507 Rex m. 33d. Lockton and Fulthorpe were among the six justices exiled to Ireland by the Appellants in the Merciless Parliament.
99 Ibid., JUST 3/169 mm. 12, 29d., 30.
100 Ibid., C 81/1352/17: a signet letter to the Chancellor, dated 7 July 1386, nominating the entire commission of the peace in Leicestershire. The commission issued the following day contained some significant alterations, however: *CPR, 1385–9*, p. 254.
101 *CPR, 1391–6*, p. 31.
102 Virgoe, 'The Crown and Local Government', pp. 238–9; Saul, *Knights and Esquires*, pp. 131–2.
103 Roskell, *Parliament and Politics*, iii. 22–4.
104 *Officers of the Exchequer*, p. 225; *CPR, 1399–1401*, p. 161; *CCR, 1399–1402*, p. 18; BIHR, Prob. Reg. 3, fo. 59.
105 *Rot. Parl.*, iii. 444.
106 R. R. Reid, *The King's Council in the North* (London, 1921), pp. 36–7 (Fulthorpe); *CPR, 1405–8*, p. 203; PRO, CP 25 (1)/279/150/82, 151/30 (Drax).
107 A. Rogers, 'The Royal Household of Henry IV' (Nottingham Ph.D. thesis, 1966), pp. 596–9.
108 *CPR, 1385–9*, p. 172; cf. ibid., *1381–5*, p. 592.
109 PRO, KB 27/526 Rex m. 19; Sayles, *Select Cases in the Court of King's Bench*, vii. 83–5; *CPR, 1391–6*, p. 249; PRO, KB 27/507 Rex mm. 33–7, 509 Rex mm. 10, 17; *CCR, 1385–9*, pp. 200, 236, 322, 436, 491–2; *CPR, 1385–9*, p. 319.
110 *Westminster Chronicle*, p. 422; Sayles, *Select Cases in the Court of King's Bench*, vii. p. lvi.
111 Putnam, *Proceedings*, pp. 455–7; PRO, E 137/49/2, E 370/160/1 fo. 4, 2 m. 13, E 101/598/50, fo. 1. One estimate suggests there were about thirty towns in the county at this time: R. B. Dobson, 'Yorkshire Towns in the Late Fourteenth Century', *Thoresby Society Miscellany*, xviii (1) (1985), 4–11.
112 PRO, JUST 3/176 m. 15d., 183 m. 6; *CCR, 1399–1402*, p. 345; R. F. Hunnisett, *The Medieval Coroner* (Cambridge, 1961), p. 71; PRO, JUST 1/1517 mm. 10–13.
113 Ibid., KB 27/590 Rex m. 9; cf. J. B. Post, 'Some Limitations of the Medieval Peace Rolls', *Journal of the Society of Archivists*, iv (1970–3), 635–6.
114 PRO, KB 27/587 Rex m. 6; ibid., C 260/125/3.
115 Ibid., KB 9/205/1 mm. 1–14.
116 J. G. Bellamy, 'The Northern Rebellions in the Later Years of Richard II', *Bulletin of the John Rylands Library*, xlvii (1965), 255–61; PRO, JUST 1/1146/17, KB 9/144 m. 31.
117 S. M. Wright, *The Derbyshire Gentry in the Fifteenth Century* (Derbyshire Record Soc., vol. viii, 1983), p. 94, for the quotations; S. J. Payling, *Political Society in Lancastrian England. The Greater Gentry of Nottinghamshire* (Oxford, 1991), pp. 171–2; E. Acheson, *A Gentry Community. Leicestershire in the Fifteenth Century, c. 1422–1485* (Cambridge, 1992), p. 131; P. Maddern, *Violence and Social Order. East Anglia, 1422–1442* (Oxford, 1992), pp. 62–3, 249–54 (but note the activity of John, lord Fanhope in Bedfordshire).
118 *Rolls of the Warwickshire and Coventry Sessions of the Peace, 1377–1397*, ed. E. G. Kimball (Dugdale Soc., vol xvi, 1939), pp. xxi, xxxi, xlviii; PRO, KB 27/542 Rex m. 24 d., 551 Rex m. 3, 587 Rex m. 8 (Beauchamp); ibid., E 370/160–4, fo. 2 (Strange).

119 Maddern, *Violence and Social Order*, pp. 48–54.

120 C. J. Tyldesley, 'The Crown and the Local Communities in Devon and Cornwall, 1377–1422' (Exeter Ph.D. thesis, 1979), pp. 71–2 (Devon); *Rolls of the Gloucestershire Sessions of the Peace, 1361–1398*, ed. E. G. Kimball (Transactions of the Bristol and Gloucestershire Archaeological Soc., vol. lxii, 1940), pp. 56–7, 142–65 (Gloucestershire); PRO, E 101/567/2, 34; ibid., E 370/160/1, fo. 3; ibid., E 372/241/Item Kanc., 242/Item Kanc., 246/Item Kanc.; ibid., E 352/197/Item Kanc.; ibid., E 372/253/Item Kanc., 257/Item Kanc. (Kent); ibid., E 372/257/Res' Stafford (Staffordshire).

121 Ibid. E 372/239/Cant. et Hunt., 245/Cant. et Hunt. (Huntingdonshire); *Victoria County History of Wiltshire*, vol. v, ed. R. B. Pugh and E. Crittall (1957), pp. 34–5 (Wiltshire).

122 Above, n. 120 (Kent); J. B. Post, 'Criminals and the Law in the Reign of Richard II' (Oxford D. Phil. thesis, 1976), pp. 140–1 (Hampshire); PRO, E 101/553/6, 7, 8; 598/50 fo. 5; ibid., E 137/4/1 mm. 8–12; ibid., E 370/160/1, fo. 1 (Cambridgeshire); *Oxfordshire Sessions of the Peace in the Reign of Richard II*, ed. E. G. Kimball (Oxfordshire Record Soc., vol. liii, 1983), pp. 33–5 (Oxfordshire).

123 Wright, *Derbyshire Gentry*, p. 98; Maddern, *Violence and Social Order*, pp. 61–4; C. Arnold, 'A Political Study of the West Riding of Yorkshire, 1437–1509' (Manchester Ph.D. thesis, 1984), pp. 334, 339; C. Carpenter, *Locality and Polity. A Study of Warwickshire Landed Society, 1401–1499* (Cambridge, 1992), pp. 267–9. Percentage attendance levels of eligible gentry justices in other counties over the same period include Devon, 52, Worcestershire, 52, Cornwall, 67, and Cambridgeshire, 78.

124 Carpenter, *Locality and Polity*, pp. 274–5.

125 PRO, E 372/247/Res. Cant., 248/Item Cant., 252/Item Cant., 254/Item Cant., 256/Item Cant.; *CIM, 1399–1422*, no. 235.

126 M. Cherry, 'The Crown and the Political Community in Devonshire, 1377–1461' (Univ. of Wales Ph.D. thesis, 1981), pp. 154–98.

127 Annuities assigned on the Duchy of Lancaster honours in Yorkshire stood at £504 in 1389/90, rising to £788 by 1394/5 and a peak of £1565 by 1401/2; by 1408/9 this sum had declined by a third to £1015: Walker, *The Lancastrian Affinity*, pp. 305–8; PRO, DL 29/738/12097 mm. 2–4, DL 28/27/3 mm. 3–4.

128 Ibid., DL 28/1/2, fo. 16, DL 28/3/3 m. 4; Somerville, *Duchy of Lancaster*, pp. 373, 408. William Gascoigne was also steward of Pontefract in the early 1390s, in succession to Sir Robert Swillington, before being replaced by William Skipwith and Sir Robert Neville: PRO, JUST 3/183 m. 1d., 184 mm. 4 d., 6d.

129 *CPR, 1381–5*, p. 482; *Rot. Parl.*, iii. 344; *Year Books of Richard II, 12 Richard II*, ed. G. F. Deiser (Ames Foundation, 1914), p. 180; *CPR, 1399–1401*, p. 287; *CCR, 1399–1402*, p. 245.

130 Richard Gascoigne was one of the first of the Yorkshire gentry to declare for Henry of Lancaster: PRO, DL 42/15, fo. 70.

131 Ibid., E 404/16/742; *Proceedings and Ordinances of the Privy Council*, i. 262.

132 *CPR, 1401–5*, pp. 129, 284, 294, 297, 361; ibid., *1405–8*, pp. 59, 65, 75, 405. For Gascoigne acting under these powers in 1408: PRO, JUST 1/1517 m. 12 d., KB 27/592 Rex m. 14.

133 E.g., Richard Gascoigne was at Knaresborough on 14 March and 12 August 1401 in his capacity as duchy steward, and again on 14 September as a justice of the peace in the West Riding. PRO, DL 30/128/1915, E 137/49/2B m. 8.

134 *Rot. Parl.*, ii. 334, iii. 139, 200, 661; J. S. Cockburn, *A History of English Assizes, 1558–1714* (Cambridge, 1972), p. 21.

135 *Test. Ebor.*, i. 298.

136 A. L. Brown, 'The Reign of Henry IV', *Fifteenth-Century England, 1399–1509*, ed. S. B. Chrimes *et al.* (Manchester, 1972), p. 23.

137 PRO, SC 1/51/65; HCRO, BC II/6/4.

5

Janico Dartasso: chivalry, nationality and the man-at-arms*

When Richard II, disguised as a priest, arrived at Conway castle in August 1399 the army he had brought back from Ireland a fortnight before had dwindled to a band of about fifteen companions. Among the bishops and peers who accompanied him were three commoners, whose presence in the royal party argues for a particular intimacy with the king: Sir Stephen Scrope, under-chamberlain of the household; William Ferriby, the king's notary; and an esquire of the household, Janico Dartasso.[1] It was the last of these three who caught the imagination of the young Frenchman, Jean Creton, who now joined the royal party. Creton reports that Janico was 'reputed to be a good fighter [*qui tenoit pour bon routier*], for it was said of him that he had performed great feats of arms'. Repeatedly required to take off Richard's livery badge, the collar of the white hart, by the ascendant Lancastrians, Janico consistently refused to do so, until his obduracy came to the attention of Henry, duke of Lancaster, himself, who had him imprisoned in Chester castle where, Creton concluded, he lived in daily fear of execution.[2] Creton had reasons of his own for emphasizing the loyalty of the 'Gascon esquire', using his steadfast conduct as a rhetorical device to reproach the innate perfidy of Richard's English-born subjects, but the prominence accorded Janico in Creton's narrative of the king's deposition seems faithfully to reflect his contemporary reputation. Janico Dartasso was something of a minor chivalric celebrity, who attracted the admiring epithets of chroniclers and was remembered, even half a century after his death, as 'a noble man of arms among the esquires of all England and France'.[3] His long and picaresque career has several times caught the eye of historians but, apart from a survey of its Irish dimension,[4] the scattered evidence for his life has never been systematically assembled. It seems worthwhile to do so, partly because the career of a man who was the intimate of both Richard II and Henry IV has its own intrinsic interest, and partly for what the investigation suggests about the continuing vitality of an international chivalric culture and the limits of the social world such a culture encompassed. There is much that is typical in the several constituent elements of Janico's experience – as man-at-arms, courtier and Anglo-Irish official – but their combination within a single career is unusual, perhaps unique, while the opportunities and obstacles that he encountered, as a plausible outsider seeking to establish himself in English landed society, provide a revealing angle of approach to the social and political realities of later medieval England.

Janico Dartasso first appears in English sources as the joint-master of an important prisoner of war, Olivier du Guesclin, the accident-prone brother of the constable of France.[5] Du Guesclin was ambushed and captured outside Cherbourg, as he reconnoitred the fortifications of the town in January 1379, by a force commanded by Sir John Arundel and a Navarrese esquire, called Jean Cok by Froissart in his account of the incident.[6] They were acting together on this occasion because the castle of Cherbourg had been leased by Charles of Evreux, king of Navarre, to the English crown in July 1378 and the garrison was thereafter a joint Anglo-Navarrese one. Arundel was the new English commander and Jean Cok, perhaps, his Navarrese counterpart.[7] Though he is customarily described as a Gascon, English administrative sources consistently identify Janico Dartasso as Navarrese during his early years in England, which suggests that Froissart's Jean Cok was simply his phonic version of the captor's first name, Janico.[8] His surname is likely to be a toponymic, indicating family origins at Artaxo, a royal castle on the Navarrese frontier with Castile, in the *merindad* of Estella. One source plausibly describes him as a Basque.[9] What is known of Janico's early career seems, in any case, to tally with Froissart's picture of Jean Cok as an already experienced soldier, well versed in the geography of lower Normandy: Janico appears as a man-at-arms in the Cherbourg garrison as early as April 1367, when most of the Cotentin peninsula was still in the possession of Charles of Navarre, engaged in skirmishes with the duke of Brittany's forces around the marcher towns of Champeaux and Gennes. Something of the life he led is indicated by the payment of 300 francs to Janico and his companions, including the evocatively named Perrin 'Ratstooth', in October 1368 'so that they will not plunder the countryside'.[10]

For a professional soldier of Janico's sort, the capture of a prisoner as prominent as Olivier du Guesclin was a major triumph, offering the prospect of a permanent prosperity from the ransom that could be demanded of such a captive. In the short term, however, it created almost as many problems as it promised to solve. The kings of England and Navarre both had a claim to a third of the ransom money, which had first to be adjudicated; the claims of lesser men to a share of the spoils had to be resisted, and du Guesclin himself had, finally, to be induced to raise the necessary sums as quickly as possible. By November 1379 the first two of these issues had been settled: the crown had remitted its claim to the sovereign's third part of the ransom, set at 40,000 gold francs, in favour of Charles of Navarre and a committee of three English knights had split the remainder three ways between Arundel, Dartasso and a third party, Amcot de Solle – a settlement which promised each captor about £1,500 sterling.[11] Receiving full satisfaction from du Guesclin for such a large sum was bound to take some time and it was no doubt in order to protect his investment in the prisoner, currently detained in London, that Janico first transferred from Navarrese to English service. By December 1380 he had moved from Cherbourg to the pale of Calais, where he was serving under the command of Sir Robert Ashton in the garrison of Guines.[12] In the following month, he contracted with Sir Thomas West to join the reinforcements being sent to Thomas, earl of Buckingham, in Brittany. In the event, West's men never got further than Dartmouth, where they were ordered to return to London to help in the suppression of the commons' rising.[13] It was at this point, in June 1381, that Janico and his partner, Amcot de Solle, decided that the volatility of the situation in the capital justified a relaxation of their demands against du Guesclin: they cut his ransom to 25,000 francs – reducing their own expectations to about £950 each – and allowed him immediate licence to return to France to supervise the collection of the money himself.[14] The condition of du Guesclin's release was that he should surrender himself at Calais whenever he was required to do so, and it was at Calais, accordingly, that Janico took up his own residence. He was serving in the Calais garrison by December 1381 and remained there until, at least, December 1382.[15]

Once established at Calais, Janico's innate opportunism was quickly in evidence when he attempted to repeat, on a lesser scale, the financial success of his capture of du Guesclin. In January 1382 he detained Bernardo Lippi, a Florentine merchant travelling from Bruges to Calais on his way to England, on the pretext that he was a subject of the king of France, and demanded a ransom for his release. Lippi had been travelling under royal letters of protection and the affair was, in consequence, quickly brought to Richard II's attention, who ordered the captain of Calais, Sir John Devereux, to bring Janico before the council at Westminster to explain his conduct.[16] An experienced ransom-taker such as Janico was unlikely to relinquish his prize so easily however, and in October the council was compelled to repeat the order, this time offering additional guarantees that, if Lippi absconded, Janico would receive the 1,850 francs he was claiming from him. Lippi's continuing detention was a diplomatic embarrassment for the English government and the pressure for his release began to mount after a powerful commission of *oyer et terminer* was sued out on his behalf in November.[17] By April 1383 the case was under active investigation in the court of the constable and marshal. It took a further petition to parliament, and the association of several magnates with the existing commissioners, to secure a final resolution of the dispute and the release of Lippi in December 1383.[18] No final sentence in the case has survived and Janico's gains from the affair, if any, must remain conjectural, but the incident provides an early indication of the tenacity and resourcefulness that were to be characteristic of his whole career.

Between 1379 and 1383, therefore, Janico had made the transition from Navarrese to English allegiance and, it seems likely, had acquired a considerable capital sum to finance his further advancement. By the summer of 1387 he was beginning to make a name for himself at the highest levels of English society. He was able to do so for several reasons. In general, the political crisis of 1386–8 shook the framework of political society sufficiently to create new opportunities for the enterprising and sure-footed, while the advent of an Appellant regime, dominated by Richard II's noble opponents and committed to a more aggressive foreign policy, provided employment for experienced professional soldiers. In particular, Janico's close association with the Percy earls of Northumberland allowed him to take full advantage of the opportunities thus presented. Janico was in the service of the Percies as early as the autumn of 1383, accompanying the earl of Northumberland to the march in order to strengthen the garrison of Berwick-upon-Tweed. By October 1384, Northumberland was confident enough of his loyalty to name Janico as his attorney to receive custody of an important prisoner. Subsequently, Janico rose to further prominence in the service of the earl's eldest son, Henry 'Hotspur'.[19] When the council nominated Hotspur as captain of the fleet assembled in August 1387 to relieve the siege of Brest, Janico acted as one of his retinue leaders, with a company of 20 men-at-arms and 20 archers under his command, while his conduct in the course of the well-received campaign was sufficiently striking to earn him an *ex gratia* payment of £40 from the council.[20] This was only one of several marks of trust and favour bestowed on Janico by the continual councillors[21] and further confidential employment was found for him in December, when it came to the Appellants' attention that the attorneys of Robert de Vere, the disgraced duke of Ireland, were due to receive an instalment of the ransom of Jean de Bretagne on de Vere's behalf. Janico was commissioned to go to Calais in order to claim the ransom payments for the new regime.[22] Another commission followed in February 1388, when Janico was appointed to survey the fortifications of Calais and all the king's other castles in Picardy and report back to the council on the defects found. If these appointments suggest that the Appellants were looking to use Janico as their confidential agent at Calais, a town of considerable strategic significance but uncertain political allegiance,[23] their suspicions were soon shown to be justified when Janico was himself arrested and imprisoned, apparently by elements in the garrison still loyal to Richard II and de Vere – though this was not before he had successfully secured a portion of the ransom instalment for the Appellant regime.[24] Released from his captivity in April 1388, Janico returned to England and was soon acting on Henry Hotspur's behalf once more. When Hotspur, in his capacity as warden of the east march, moved northwards to defend the march against an unexpected Scottish incursion, Janico went with him and was, in consequence, one of the many members of his master's company captured by the Scots following Hotspur's defeat at Otterburn in August.[25] Imprisoned for the second time in six months, Janico soon secured his liberty once more, though at the price of a sizeable ransom.[26]

Despite the uncertain fortunes of politics and war, the period of Appellant domination had allowed Janico to achieve a new prominence and brought him considerable *ad hoc* rewards. Although Richard II's resumption of power in May 1389 and the conclusion of a general Anglo-French truce in the following July closed down his previous avenues of advancement, Janico was now in possession of sufficient funds to participate in a series of chivalric ventures that would add further weight to his reputation. In March 1390 he travelled to the Calais marches, together with many other English knights and esquires, in order to participate in the jousts at St Inglevert. Janico fought on the third day of the festivities, in a series of combats completed 'not without bloodshed'.[27] At St Inglevert there was much talk among the assembled knights concerning Louis, duke of Bourbon's projected expedition to north Africa. Though Henry, earl of Derby, and the main English contingent were eventually thwarted in their intention of accompanying Bourbon, a smaller group, including John, lord Clifford, Sir John Cornwall and Janico himself, sought and successfully obtained the duke's permission to join his Barbary crusade. Embarking from Marseilles in June, Bourbon's army landed at the Tunisian port of al-Mahdiya and began a siege of the city. Janico distinguished himself in the two-month conflict and, when mounting casualties obliged Bourbon to contemplate lifting the siege in September, he was vocal in urging acceptance of the treaty terms offered by al-Mahdiya's Hafsid rulers.[28] The campaign had taken its toll on many of the English crusaders, a dozen of whom died of disease on the way home, but Janico continued undaunted. Landing at Genoa in October, he immediately journeyed north to join Henry Bolingbroke in Prussia, where he was campaigning with the Teutonic knights against the Lithuanians. He caught up with Derby in his quarters at Königsberg, but, since there was to be no winter campaign that year, Janico was sent back almost immediately to England with the earl's instructions to his council.[29] By May 1391 he was back in the service of his old masters, the Percy family, serving with the earl of Northumberland in his capacity as captain of Calais.[30]

These chivalric exploits brought Janico's virtues to the attention of a new and influential group of patrons. One of them was John Waltham, bishop of Salisbury and treasurer of England, whose household esquire Janico now became.[31] Waltham's household included a number of esquires who were also in royal service and it was perhaps by this means that Janico gained the vital recommendation that brought him entry to the king's affinity, when he was retained by Richard II, at a fee of 40 marks per annum, around Michaelmas 1392.[32] His cosmopolitan experience was immediately put to use by the king, who sent him, via Cologne and Vienna, with diplomatic letters for the city states of northern Italy. Janico was certainly in Venice by February 1393, where he cashed a letter of credit on behalf of Henry, earl of Derby, who was then on his way back from Jerusalem, and evidently discharged his whole mission to Richard's satisfaction, for he received a gift of £40 from the king on his return in August 1393 and had his retaining fee increased, from 40 marks to £40 per annum, in the following October.[33] When Richard transformed his largely civilian household into the nucleus of an expeditionary force for his Irish campaign in 1394, Janico's long military experience allowed him to recommend himself still further. His initial contribution to the household force was a small one, consisting of himself and three mounted archers, but he began to distinguish himself soon after the king's landing in Ireland by leading a successful punitive raid against the O'Neills. Janico was in consequence promoted to the command of a larger detachment of ten men-at-arms and twenty mounted archers until the expedition's end.[34] He was rewarded for his good service with a large grant of confiscated land in the south of county Dublin – which, he reported to Waltham, 'would be worth more than a thousand marks a year, if it had been near London, but . . . I have such trouble keeping it that I would not want to live such a life for long, for a quarter of the whole land [of Ireland]' – and, more concretely, with a further increase in his annuity in November 1395, from £40 to 100 marks per annum.[35]

The easy fluency of his letter to Waltham suggests something of the qualities that made Janico a frequent choice as envoy and agent for both his royal and magnate masters.[36] The king, in particular, used him for a series of confidential diplomatic missions: to Paris, in October 1396, just before Richard's marriage to Isabella de Valois; to Paris again in March 1397 and then, once it became clear that Charles VI's state of mind would render him incapable of transacting business, onwards to Poitiers to consult with John, duke of Berry;[37] and then, immediately on his return, to the Rhineland with Thomas Merks, bishop of Carlisle, to consult with the archbishop of Cologne regarding the possibility of Richard's election as Holy Roman Emperor.[38] Such regular employment makes it clear that, despite the pardon for his actions during the time of Appellant supremacy that Janico prudently sought in March 1398, he enjoyed a growing intimacy with the inner circle of the king's councillors and companions, reflected in the stream of small favours and rewards – usually grants of minor wardships or forfeitures, held jointly with other members of the household – that continued to flow his way.[39]

Such grants were important to Janico for, despite the royal favour he enjoyed, he continued to suffer from the insecurity of the landless man throughout these years, dependent upon the generosity and reliability of his various patrons for the capital to defray the heavy expenditure that a man with ambitions to shine at the king's court had necessarily to incur. The Appellant regime had been generous to Janico in this regard, adding the keeping of the manor of Dedham (Essex), a forfeited de la Pole property, to the frequent cash rewards they gave him, while Janico obtained a further grant of forfeited land, the manor of 'Daubeneys' in Tottenham, formerly held by Sir John Beauchamp of Holt, in November 1389.[40] Properties of this kind tended to have more than one claimant, however, and usually proved hard to retain: Janico's tenure of 'Daubeneys' lasted only two years and Dedham was certainly out of his hands by midsummer 1393.[41] The manor of Huntspill Marreys, which Janico was granted in October 1395, seemed for a time a better prospect and, by allowing Janico to describe himself as 'of Somerset', it briefly provided him with that foothold in county society he had hitherto lacked. It had become clear by 1399, however, that James Butler, earl of Ormond, had a powerful claim to the estate and, despite a long rearguard action in the courts, Janico had eventually to concede possession of this property as well.[42] The green-acred respectability that was the essential preliminary to permanent acceptance in English political society continued to elude him.

Yet Janico's aspirations for further advancement were always underwritten by the undeniable fact of his military prowess. At the Smithfield jousts held in December 1396 to honour the king's marriage, he was one of the company of twenty knights and esquires chosen to hold the field against all-comers,[43] and in 1399, when the rapid disintegration of Richard's Irish settlement compelled the king to undertake a second expedition there, Janico again played a significant part in the short campaign. Sent on ahead of the main royal army, Janico acted as field-commander for his latest patron, Thomas Holland, duke of Surrey, the new lieutenant of Ireland, and when the king arrived in June he covered the northward advance of the royal army by a series of vigorous raids into Carlow and Kildare against Art Macmurrough's forces.[44] These successes cemented his relationship with Thomas Holland, who granted Janico the estates of the barony of Norragh – optimistically valued at £40 per annum – as his retaining fee, and won him further favour from the king, who promised him an additional 100 mark annuity, partly to defray the expenses Janico had incurred on his raids and partly to finance his forthcoming marriage to a wealthy Anglo-Irish widow, Joan Taafe.[45] A promising campaign was cut short, however, by the news of Henry of Lancaster's landing in England and Janico hastened back to Dublin in order to embark with the main royal army.[46] Thereafter, his path followed the king's, as Richard sought safety among the castles of north Wales, until their final separation at Chester, where Janico's fate eventually proved somewhat less drastic than Creton's imaginings. On 20 August, probably within a day or two of his initial arrest, Sir Thomas Gray and Sir John Stanley offered sureties for his release from confinement, on condition that he stay within the city walls 'until he is reasonably delivered of his arrest by the duke and his council' – as indeed he was, a fortnight later.[47]

Despite his brief imprisonment at Chester, Janico was quickly able to make his peace with the new Lancastrian regime. At first, it was to his old connection with the Percy family that he looked to recover and consolidate his position. In October 1399 he was acting as the earl of Northumberland's attorney at the exchequer and, in the following December, Percy influence secured for Janico appointment as one of the English commissioners assigned to settle infractions of the fragile Anglo-Scottish truce at a march day.[48] Henry of Lancaster was enough of an idealist to appreciate the display of conspicuous fidelity that Janico had staged at Flint, however, and quickly welcomed his old acquaintance into the royal household. Retained by the new king in November 1399, all his fees were confirmed – including the 100 marks from Drogheda that Richard had promised him in the summer, though Janico had had the signet letters authorizing the grant stolen from him during his captivity at Chester – and a further £40 per annum from the issues of Dublin were added to recompense him for his surrender of the barony of Norragh. This run of Irish preferment continued in May 1400, when Janico was granted custody of the valuable Mortimer lordship of Trim during the minority of the heir.[49]

The scale of these rewards was testimony to a growing intimacy with the king and his advisers that others were quick to recognize and call upon. When the mayor and burgesses of Waterford sought exemption from the requirement to make the dangerous journey to Dublin in order to swear their oaths of office in person, they turned to Janico to put their case to the king and council;[50] and when the post of gaoler of Newgate fell vacant, Robert Frye, one of the clerks of the privy seal, sought to use Janico's credit with the chancellor in order to secure his own client's appointment.[51]

Janico's stock rose still further following a notable feat of arms in July 1400. As Henry IV assembled his troops for the forthcoming Scottish campaign at York, a French knight and esquire presented themselves before the king and issued a challenge to the assembled company. Janico's reputation as a 'good fighter' was high enough to ensure that he was one of the two champions chosen, with his old crusading companion, Sir John Cornwall, to defend the English honour.[52] More was at stake in this encounter than knightly reputation alone, for at a time of mounting Anglo-French tension there was a sense in which the combat could be seen as a trial by battle of the validity of Henry's title to the English throne. Defeat for his champions in so public a forum would have represented a considerable propaganda triumph for the king's enemies.[53] Henry was consequently so pleased by the English victory that he remitted his displeasure at Cornwall's unlicensed marriage to his sister, Elizabeth Holland, and showered Janico with a further series of preferments: an additional £100 per annum as his retaining fee; custody of the manor of Ardbracken (Meath) and the lands of the alien priory of Fore (West Meath); and a grant of the provostry of Ombrière, seat of the royal administration in Gascony, with power to discharge the post by deputy.[54]

For all the hardships he had suffered during the summer of 1399, therefore, the change of dynasty had had little immediate effect on the direction of Janico Dartasso's career. Like many others, he simply exchanged one royal master for another, though he showed an unusual ability to maintain the momentum of his personal advancement in the process. A more permanent change took place in April 1401, however, when Janico set out once more for Ireland, this time in the suite of the new lieutenant, Thomas of Lancaster, the king's second son. In contrast to his previous visits, this trip was to mark the beginning of Janico's permanent residence in the lordship. The general disposition of the grants made to Janico since October 1399 suggests that, following his marriage to Joan Taafe, his future was ultimately expected to be an Irish one, but it is equally clear that, while his run of luck at court held good, Janico was in no hurry to enter into this portion of his inheritance. In November 1399 he had obtained a royal licence to occupy all his Irish grants by attorney for the next eight years.[55] His decision to take up more permanent residence in Ireland was apparently a response to a shift in the climate of English public opinion, for it was taken immediately after the Hilary 1401 parliament, in which Henry IV's generosity towards his courtiers and his dependence upon the advice of a small group of intimates had incurred heavy criticism. More specifically, hostility towards aliens within the realm, such as the Navarrese Janico, was growing: the minute of a council meeting held in April reported a rumour that certain aliens around the king were being paid pensions by the French in order to betray his secrets; the next two items on the council agenda were a general recommendation that patents of exemption, such as Janico held, from the provisions of the absentee statutes should be revoked and all Irish landowners required to reside on their estates, and a specific complaint that, because the king had granted Janico Dartasso the castle of Trim without any stipulation concerning responsibility for its maintenance, the castle was in a state of ruinous disrepair.[56] It seems clear from the idiosyncratic direction of this discussion that the general prominence of aliens around the king, and the favour shown to Janico in particular, was attracting hostile attention from some of Henry's councillors. It may well have been this hostility that persuaded Janico, always sensitive to a change in the direction of the winds of fortune, to depart for his Irish estates. He was hastened on his way by a further series of royal grants, designed to establish his position among the Anglo-Irish governing elite: appointment as deputy to the king's admiral in Ireland was added to a grant of all the revenues of the lordship of Trim, while Janico invested some of the proceeds of royal favour in purchasing for himself the constableship of Dublin castle.[57]

Once arrived in Ireland, Janico quickly came to play an important part in the government of the lordship, both as a member of Thomas of Lancaster's council and as one of his principal military commanders.[58] Lancaster's original intention, signalled in the unexpected winter campaign that Janico, together with Sir Stephen Scrope and Sir Edward Perrers, conducted in January 1402, was to regain the military initiative from the Gaelic chieftains and push back the frontiers of English rule.[59] A chronic shortage of funds soon forced his advisers to plan, less ambitiously, for a stabilization and pacification of the existing marches. Janico's efforts in this regard were initially centred around his wife's estates in the western marches of the lordship. As a keeper of the peace in Meath and Louth, he was commissioned to negotiate with both rebels and the king's faithful subjects for the good governance of Meath during 1403 and had permission, in the same year, to fortify his manor of Liscartan (Meath) with a tower-house 'in aid of the defence of [the king's] faithful lieges'.[60] Increasingly, however, Janico's tenure of a substantial portion of the Mortimer estates in Ireland during the minority of Edmund, earl of March, drew his attention northwards to the earldom of Ulster.[61] By 1407 he was acting as steward of Ulster and, early in the following year, he was put in possession of the Mortimer coastal strongholds at Greencastle and Carlingford by the lieutenant.[62]

This new sphere of responsibility fitted well with his principal military duty, from July 1404, as admiral of Ireland, since the increasing severity of the Scottish naval raids along the coastline of Ulster was steadily undermining the stability of the region.[63] Janico did his best to provide an adequate defence, equipping a balinger to patrol the Irish Sea coasts and, when this vessel was stolen by a group of Genoese, building another at his own expense.[64] His diligence brought some military success: a Scottish raiding party was defeated off Greencastle in May 1405 and its commander captured, while an effective campaign was launched into Ulster in June 1409.[65] He was engaged, at the same time, in negotiations intended to bring a more permanent pacification to the region. In September 1407 Janico was commissioned, with John Dongan, bishop of Down, to treat for a final peace and alliance with Donald, lord of the Isles, and John Mór his brother. The talks continued for some time and, although no formal treaty between the two parties was concluded, the issue of a royal licence for Janico to celebrate a double marriage between his children and those of John Mór in April 1410 facilitated a private resolution of hostilities along the Ulster coastline.[66] The projected marriages held out the prospect of strategic benefits for the Dublin government for, as 'constable of the Irish of Ulster', and now a major landowner in Antrim in the right of his wife, John Macdonald was a powerful figure in the politics of the lordship. For Janico and his family there were additional attractions. The Macdonald lords of the Isles were a force to be reckoned with in the kingdom of Scotland, grandchildren of Robert II and possessed of a plausible claim to the Scottish crown themselves. Alliance with such a kindred brought with it prestige that was well worth the price of the solid match for his children among the Anglo-Irish gentry that Janico thereby forsook.[67]

The important part Janico now played in the defence of the lordship was recognized by his appointment, following the sudden death of the lieutenant, Sir John Stanley, as one of three 'governors of the king's wars' in Ireland in January 1414. The ceaseless skirmishing such a post involved offered much danger and little profit, however. Janico and his men, campaigning in County Down, had themselves recently sustained heavy casualties at the hands of Magennis of Iveagh, while his lands in western Meath were coming under increasing pressure from the expansionist ambitions of the O'Connors.[68] The resumption of full Anglo-French hostilities soon promised, in contrast, a more attractive campaigning ground, and Janico was quick to join Henry V's first expedition to northern France, contracting with the king in April 1415 to serve with a company of ten men-at-arms and thirty mounted archers.[69] It may be that, following the fall of Harfleur, Janico, familiar with the routines of garrison duty along the Norman coastline, remained in the captured town. He was certainly part of the garrison there from January 1416, and, in the following March, he joined a foraging expedition led from the blockaded town by its captain, Thomas Beaufort, earl of Dorset. In the course of this foray, Beaufort's men were unexpectedly confronted at Valmont by a superior French force, which the English with difficulty held at bay until nightfall. On the advice of his lieutenants, Janico and Sir Thomas Carew, Beaufort then retreated and, by marching along the shoreline, managed to evade all further French efforts to prevent his troops regaining the safety of Harfleur.[70] Janico had long and valuable experience of this kind of fighting, a warfare of siege, raid and ambush, and it seems that he spent most of the rest of Henry V's reign in Normandy. He was with the king at Louviers in June 1418 and served throughout the siege of Rouen (July 1418–January 1419), where he was principally engaged in mustering the Welsh troops commanded by Sir Thomas Carew.[71] Still in France in October 1419, he also took out letters of protection for the king's third and final campaign there in 1421.[72]

It was not until July 1423, when he was commissioned to investigate reports concerning the smuggling of counterfeit coins into Ireland, that Janico resumed his official career within the lordship.[73] His prolonged absence had been partly a matter of choice, for Henry V's Norman campaigns provided a welcome opportunity to engage once more in the *grandes journées* that had made his reputation, but it sprang, too, from a recognition that his own place within the governing establishment of Ireland was becoming noticeably less secure by 1415. During Henry IV's reign Janico had used his wealth and talents to consolidate an influential local position: his custody of the Mortimer lordship of Trim, together with his wife's estates in Meath and Down, made him a considerable landowner in the north of the lordship, while part of the proceeds of his royal annuities, which promised an income of nearly £350 per annum by Henry IV's death,[74] was devoted to the acquisition of further lands, especially in County Down, where the bishop and chapter of Down were only one of several ecclesiastical landowners persuaded to sell out their interests in marcher manors of uncertain value.[75] The unusual strength and diversity of Janico's interests and contacts outside the lordship was also called into play: trading ventures to Bordeaux, Bayonne and, later, Harfleur were planned to provide an additional source of revenue, while he was careful to maintain his standing at Henry IV's court by frequent visits there during the early days of his Irish residence.[76] This growing regional influence was underwritten by Janico's friendship with the lieutenant, Thomas of Lancaster, and his usual deputy, Sir Stephen Scrope, while the knowledge that he enjoyed these influential protectors meant that his services were, in turn, sought after by others. James Butler, second earl of Ormond, the most influential of the Anglo-Irish magnates, granted Janico an annuity of 40 marks per annum in June 1404.[77] As a result, Janico enjoyed considerable latitude in the informal exercise of his official powers. An aggrieved petitioner complained, for instance, that Scrope had suddenly ordered him to surrender his possession of the Mortimer castles at Carlingford and Greencastle in January 1408 and delivered them to Janico, in his capacity as steward of Ulster, who had then secured his title to the properties by collusive litigation in the Irish chancery, and was now ignoring the council's order to give up the castles once more.[78] Scrope's death in September 1408 and the formal termination of Thomas of Lancaster's patent of appointment as lieutenant in March 1413 reduced the scope for such instances of collaboration, however, while Janico was compelled to surrender a substantial portion of his local power base when Edmund Mortimer, earl of March and Ulster, came of age and was granted full livery of his inheritance in June 1413.

The implications of this shift in the centre of political gravity within the lordship began to become apparent once John Talbot, Lord Furnivall, took up his post as the new lieutenant in November 1414. Talbot was anxious to increase the Irish revenues at his disposal and, as one means to this end, suggested to him by 'the sinister information of certain officers of the land of Ireland', he had the barons of the Irish exchequer order the cessation of all annuity payments to Janico, on the grounds that he had obtained the patents granting them by 'sinister and false suggestion'.[79] Janico countered with a petition to the English parliament in November 1417 and secured a confirmation of the validity of his grants and an order to the Irish exchequer to pay the outstanding arrears, then estimated at £844.15.0. This seems to have had little practical effect, for Janico was moved to seek a royal exemplification and confirmation of the judgment in his favour in June 1418 and then submitted a further petition to the king at Vernon in April 1419, asking that Henry's confirmation, passed under the great seal of Normandy, be now confirmed by the chancellor in England.[80] Such precautions were well advised, for Janico experienced considerable difficulty in re-establishing his rights. At Drogheda, for instance, the mayor and sheriffs of the new shire-incorporate refused in January 1418 to resume payment of the annuity of 100 marks assigned to Janico from their communal revenues and took their case to the king's bench at Westminster, where it remained unresolved three years later.[81] Satisfaction of a kind was provided by February 1420, when payment of Janico's annuity at the Irish exchequer was restored, though he continued to pursue the issue of arrears, complaining in July 1421, like other victims of Talbot's highhanded policies, that the former lieutenant held no Irish lands and so could not be distrained for payment within the lordship.[82]

Several larger issues were involved in this bout of high-profile petitioning and litigation: the exhaustion of Irish exchequer revenues and the fragile financial state of the lordship; the growing hostility between Talbot and James Butler, earl of Ormond, here directed against an annuitant of Butler's; a lingering suspicion of Janico as an alien courtier who had wormed his way into royal affections.[83] It is also clear that Janico's service in the Lancastrian army in France, and the relatively easy access to the king that this conferred, proved vital to him in carrying his main point, on this as on other issues.[84] Though Henry was finally reluctant to alienate John Talbot, now himself serving with some distinction in France, to the extent of allowing distraint on his English lands for the arrears of Janico's pension, he provided his loyal, and now aged, esquire with generous compensation, in the form of a life-grant of several manors in County Dublin, to the value of £100 per annum.[85] Fortified by these renewed tokens of royal favour, Janico was able to resume some of his old prominence within the lordship before his death in November 1426: re-appointed as a keeper of the peace in Louth, he was granted his former office of steward of Ulster, together with the custody of Carlingford and Greencastle, in July 1425, during the minority of the new heir to the Mortimer lands, Richard, duke of York.[86]

In one sense, Janico Dartasso's long career appears a successful fulfilment of Froissart's optimistic conception of social mobility, whereby 'many knights and esquires have advanced themselves, more by their prowess than their lineage.' If he had not been 'ennobled by the power of gold and silver', his experience had, at least, confirmed Geffroi de Charny's more realistic axiom that 'the practice of arms always gives back what is put in it, whatever the delay.'[87] Many of the Navarrese lesser nobility, badly affected by the fourteenth-century crisis of seigneurial revenue, began entering into agreements for paid military service during the 1350s, both with the king of Navarre and with other rulers, as a means of restoring their fortunes.[88] As a man-at-arms, Janico spent most of his military career on the peripheries of the Plantagenet dominions – at Cherbourg, Calais, Berwick and Harfleur – before finally establishing himself in another borderland, the marches of English lordship in Ireland. Yet the values and practice of chivalric society kept him closely in touch with the centres of cultural influence and political authority. A noted tourneyer and crusader, present at such knightly set pieces as Otterburn and al-Mahdiya,[89] Janico's reputation for prowess in arms warranted his claim to gentility and eased his access to the royal court. The credit and acquaintance he had acquired among the French nobility by his service with the duke of Bourbon made him, for example, a shrewd choice as Richard II's envoy to Paris in 1396–7. Some commentators have discerned a new, and more cynical, tone in the expression of chivalric sentiments by the late fourteenth century. There is little doubt that, for Janico, as for his former master Henry Hotspur, 'his chivalry was a hard core of war',[90] but, however tenuous and pragmatic his adherence to knightly ideals of military conduct, they continued to serve him as an effective means of social advancement.

Yet the axioms that governed knightly conduct no longer went uncontested in the wider political arena. In contrast to the cosmopolitan fellowship of arms, the growing sense of national identity evident in later medieval England demanded an ever-sharper definition of the differences between aliens and loyal subjects, together with a greater differentiation in their respective treatment. A parliamentary resolution at Hilary 1404 thus envisaged a literal marginalization of those born outside the king's obedience: adherents of the Avignonese anti-pope should leave the realm immediately; 'Catholic aliens' might stay, but they should be assigned to the borders of the kingdom, in garrisons, as in the time of Edward III; the households of the king and queen were, in any case, to be purged of all foreigners, whether schismatic or not: French, Bretons, Lombards, Italians and Navarrese.[91] Such hostility towards aliens had a long pedigree in English political society but exception had usually been made, in the past, for those foreigners who followed the king to war. Both Edward I and Edward III were able to show considerable favour to selected foreign captains without inducing any adverse reaction. As recently as 1377 the Poitevin knight, Sir Guichard d'Angle, had been raised to the highest rank of English society by his creation as earl of Huntingdon.[92] Above a certain social level, therefore, these currents of parliamentary opinion still had little force. Alien knights with dual allegiances, like the Silesian Hartung van Klux or the Hainaulter Louis Robessart, continued to enjoy successful and honourable careers in Lancastrian service.[93] For Janico, a man-at-arms of obscure family who, despite his prowess in battle, always remained an esquire, such sentiments were less easy to ignore. The growing legal and linguistic uniformity of the Plantagenet dominions proved an obstacle to his permanent acceptance into English society. The apparently enviable facility with which he acquired one new patron after another was really a testimony to his marginal status, his rootlessness, for Janico's efforts to establish a durable landed base on the English mainland all met with disappointment, while the favour shown him by Henry IV attracted some of the hostility especially reserved for aliens in the royal entourage.[94] Ireland had not seemed an attractive proposition to Janico on first acquaintance, the people false and untrustworthy, the life of a landowner there unacceptably strenuous, yet that was where he ended up, for it proved to be the only place within the English dominions still flexible enough in its social and territorial structure to offer him the prospect of permanence.

Janico's own identity as a Basque, a people without a territory, and his early experience of Navarre, where a fluid ethnic mix of servants gathered around the French-born ruler of a multiple kingdom, inclined him towards a looser pattern of lordship.[95] He sought to maintain the integrity of his lands on the western edge of English rule by a series of expedients that used to the full his cosmopolitan contacts and experience: frequent trips to the English mainland; military service in France; commercial ventures to Aquitaine; a projected marriage into the Scottish aristocracy. His was a lesser version of the transregional colonial lordships, knit together by the sea, that the Anglo-Norman conquerors had first established in Ireland two centuries before. At a time when the Plantagenet dominions were slowly dissolving into their constituent communities, it proved a solution still well adapted to life on the margins.[96]

Notes

* I am grateful to Professor Christopher Allmand, Dr. Anne Curry, Professor Michael Jones and Professor Beatrice Leroy for responding to my speculative enquiries on a variety of issues with helpful advice and relevant references.

1 Jean Creton, 'Metrical History of the Deposition of King Richard the Second', ed. J. Webb, *Archaeologia*, xx (1824) [hereafter Creton, 'Metrical History'], 322; C. Given-Wilson, *The Royal Household and the King's Affinity: Service, Politics and Finance in England, 1360–1413* (New Haven, Conn., 1986), pp. 164–5 (Scrope); A. B. Emden, *A Biographical Register of the University of Oxford to 1500* (Oxford, 1958), pp. 678–9 (Ferriby). Something of Scrope's qualities as a courtier can be gauged by his gift to the king of a live white hart, captured near Cherbourg: Public Record Office, London [hereafter PRO], King's Remembrancer, Accounts Various, E 101/403/22 f. 15.

2 Creton, 'Metrical History', 369. *Chronique de la Traison et Mort de Richart Deux Roy Dengleterre*, ed. B. Williams (English Historical Society, 1846), pp. 192, 196, 198, 210 repeats the story, with some minor embellishments, but is not an independent authority for this episode: J. J. N. Palmer, 'The Authorship, Date and Historical Value of the French Chronicles on the Lancastrian Revolution', *Bulletin of the John Rylands Library* [hereafter *BJRL*], lxi (1978–9), 145–81.

3 *The Chronicle of John Hardyng*, ed. Henry Ellis (1812) [hereafter *Hardyng*], p. 344 ('Iamco saunz fayle'); *Historical Collections of a London Citizen*, ed. James Gairdner (Camden Society, n.s., 1876) [hereafter *Historical Collections of a London Citizen*], xvii. 9 ('Janygo . . . A grete Squyer for to prove'); *William Worcestre: Itineraries*, ed. J. H. Harvey (Oxford, 1969), p. 348.

4 Edmund Curtis, 'Janico Dartas, Richard the Second's "Gascon Esquire": his Career in Ireland, 1394–1426', *Journal of the Royal Society of Antiquaries of Ireland*, lxiii (1933), 182–205.

5 *Calendar of Plea and Memoranda Rolls of the City of London, 1364–1381*, ed. A. H. Thomas (Cambridge, 1929) [hereafter *Cal. Plea and Memoranda Rolls, 1364–1381*], pp. 297–300; *Calendar of Select Pleas and Memoranda of the City of London, 1381–1412*, ed. A. H. Thomas (Cambridge, 1932), pp. 8–9.

6 *Oeuvres Complètes de Froissart*, ed. Kervyn de Lettenhove (28 vols., Brussels, 1867–77) [hereafter *Oeuvres de Froissart*], ix. 93–6; *Chronique des Quatre Premiers Valois*, ed. Simeon Luce (Paris, 1862), pp. 275–6. The incident and its repercussions are analysed in detail in C. Given-Wilson, 'The Ransom of Olivier du Guesclin', *Bulletin of the Institute of Historical Research* [hereafter *BIHR*], liv (1981), 17–28.

7 English reinforcements had been sent to Cherbourg, *ad opus regis Navarre*, on 17 June: PRO, Foreign Accounts, E 364/13 m. H; P. E. Russell, *The English Intervention in Spain and Portugal in the Time of Edward III and Richard II* (Oxford, 1955), pp. 255–61. Ramón de Esparza, the captain of Cherbourg in March 1378, had been replaced by the following August: *Archivo General de Navarra. Catalogo de la Seccion de Comptos. Documentos*, xi (1378), ed. José Ramón Castro (Pamplona, 1955), nos. 163, 165, 576.

8 PRO, Treaty Rolls, C 76/65 m. 19 (Johannes Darcascho de Navarre); 66 m. 8 (Janco Dartaisso, *naverner*); 67 m. 22 (Johan Cowe de Navarre); Ancient Correspondence, SC 1/56/104 (John Dartaisso, *naverner*). As these examples indicate, it was not only Froissart who had difficulty with the orthography of Janico's name. Where the divergence is wide enough to raise a question of identification, it is recorded in the footnotes.

9 *Archivo General de Navarre. Catalogo de la Seccion de Comptos. Registros, 1258–1364*, li, ed. F. Idoate (Pamplona, 1974), nos. 376, 563; *Chronique du Religieux de Saint-Denys, contenant le Regne de Charles VI, de 1380 à 1422*, ed. L. Bellaguet (6 vols., Paris, 1839–52) [hereafter *Chronique du Religieux de Saint-Denys*], i. 676 (Jankobasque).

10 *Le Compte des Recettes et Dépenses du Roi de Navarre en France et en Normandie de 1367 à 1370*, ed. E. Izarn (Paris, 1885), pp. 137–8, 276, 279; A. Vallez, 'Un aspect du conflit entre Charles V et Charles de Navarre: le noyautage du Clos de Contentin par le Roi de France, 1365–1378', *Receuil d'Études offert en hommage au doyen Michel de Bouard* (2 vols., Caen, 1982), ii. 533–48.

11 *Calendar of the Patent Rolls Preserved in the Public Record Office* [hereafter *Cal. Pat. Rolls*], *1377–81*, p. 362; *Calendar of Close Rolls Preserved in the Public Record Office* [hereafter *Cal. Close Rolls*], *1377–81*, p. 356; *Cal. Plea and Memoranda Rolls, 1364–1381*, pp. 297–300.

12 PRO, C 76/65 mm. 19, 20.

13 PRO, Chancery Warrants, C 81/1001/29; J. W. Sherborne, 'Indentured Retinues and English Expeditions to France, 1369–1380', *English Historical Review*, lxxix (1964), 732–3.

14 *Cal. Plea and Memoranda Rolls, 1364–1381*, pp. 297–300; PRO, C 76/66 m. 15.

15 PRO, C 76/66 m. 8, 67 m. 19.

16 PRO, C 76/66 mm. 8, 11. Calais was a dangerous border town for those not of unequivocally English allegiance. In a similar case, Hankyn Loreyn, a Fleming, complained that, despite spending six years in service in England, he was lured into detention there and claimed as a prisoner of war: PRO, Chancery Miscellanea, C 47/6/5.

17 PRO, C 76/67 m. 22; *Cal. Pat. Rolls, 1381–5*, p. 202. The affair of Janus Imperial, a Genoese envoy murdered in London in August 1379 while under the king's protection, would have been fresh in the council's mind: Benjamin Z. Kedar, *Merchants in Crisis: Genoese and Venetian Men of Affairs and the Fourteenth-Century Crisis* (New Haven, Conn. 1976), pp. 31–7.

18 PRO, SC 1/56/104; *Cal. Pat. Rolls, 1381–5*, p. 357; PRO, C 76/68 m. 14.

19 PRO, Scotch Rolls, C 71/63 m. 8; *Cal. Close Rolls, 1381–5*, p. 467 (John Dartasoun); PRO, Issue Rolls, E 403/517 m. 16.

20 PRO, E 403/517 m. 14, 518 m. 7. For the favourable judgements of the chroniclers on this campaign: Thomas Walsingham, *Historia Anglicana*, ed. H. T. Riley (2 vols., Rolls Series, 1863–4), ii. 156–7; *The Westminster Chronicle, 1381–1394*, ed. L. C. Hector and Barbara F. Harvey (Oxford, 1982), p. 196.

21 He was chosen, for instance, to deliver a prisoner to the constable of Brest and when, in the preparations for the embarkation of Hotspur's flotilla, the exchequer failed to honour an advance due to Janico, this routine default was covered by the issue of letters patent, granting him the unusual privilege of repayment direct from the parliamentary subsidy: *Cal. Close Rolls, 1385–9*, pp. 428, 652; PRO, E 403/517 m. 14; Receipt Rolls, E 401/568 (27 July); *Cal. Pat. Rolls, 1385–8*, p. 346.

22 PRO, C 76/72 mm. 10, 17; M. C. E. Jones, 'The Ransom of Jean de Bretagne, Count of Penthièvre: an Aspect of English Foreign Policy 1386–88', *BIHR*, xlv (1972), 7–26.

23 PRO, E 403/519 m. 15; C 76/72 m. 10; J. J. N. Palmer, *England, France and Christendom 1377–1399* (1972), pp. 109–12.

24 PRO, C 76/72 m. 8; E 403/518 m. 22. Janico did not go unrewarded for his trouble, receiving £20 in cash and a bolt of silk valued at a further 5 marks; ibid., m. 23.

25 PRO, E 403/519 m. 14; Anthony Goodman, 'Introduction', *War and Border Societies in the Middle Ages*, ed. Anthony Tuck and Anthony Goodman (1992), pp. 21–2.

26 PRO, E 403/519 m. 21, 521 m. 2.

27 *Chronique du Religieux de Saint-Denys*, i. 676 (Jankobasque).

28 *La Chronique du Bon Duc Loys de Bourbon*, ed. A. M. Chazaud (Société de l'Histoire de France, Paris, 1876) [hereafter *Chronique du Bon Duc*], pp. 222, 238, 248–9 (Jeannicot d'Ortenye); Léon Mirot, 'Une expédition française en Tunisie au XIVe siècle: le siège de Mahdia (1390)', *Revue des études historiques*, xcvii (1931), 357–406.

29 *Expeditions to Prussia and the Holy Land made by Henry Earl of Derby*, ed. Lucy Toulmin-Smith (Camden Society, n.s., 1894), liii. 108; F. R. H. du Boulay, 'Henry of Derby's Expeditions to Prussia 1390–1 and 1392', *The Reign of Richard II*, ed. F. R. H. du Boulay and C. M. Barron (1971), pp. 162–5. Janico was not alone among the Barbary crusaders in travelling directly from Tunisia to Prussia; Geoffrey le Maingre, Marshal Bouciquaut's brother, and Gadifier de la Salle were among those who made the same trip: *Le Livre des fais du bon messire Jehan le*

Maingre, dit Bouciquaut, ed. Denis Lalande (Paris, 1985), p. 75; *Le Canarien: cronicas francescas de la conquista da Canarias*, ed. E. Serra Rafols and A. Cioranescu (3 vols., Las Palmas, 1959–65), i. 354–5.

30 PRO, C 81/1057/28.

31 *The Register of John Waltham, Bishop of Salisbury 1388–1395*, ed. T. C. B. Timmins (Canterbury and York Society), lxxx (1994), 216. For some comment on Waltham's influence with the king, see Simon Walker, 'Richard II's Views on Kingship', *Rulers and Ruled in Late Medieval England: Essays Presented to Gerald Harriss*, ed. Rowena E. Archer and Simon Walker (1995), pp. 54–6.

32 PRO, E 403/546 m. 10.

33 *The Diplomatic Correspondence of Richard II*, ed. Edouard Perroy (Camden Society, 3rd series), xlviii (1933), no. 165; PRO, Duchy of Lancaster, Accounts Various, DL 28/3/2 f. 19^{v}, 4 f. 33^{v}; ibid., E 403/543 m. 20; *Cal. Pat. Rolls, 1391–96*, p. 320; PRO, E 403/548 m. 11.

34 PRO, E 101/402/20 f. 37^{v}; Edmund Curtis, 'Unpublished Letters from Richard II in Ireland', *Proceedings of the Royal Irish Academy*, xxxvii (1927) [hereafter Curtis, 'Unpublished Letters'], no. III.

35 *Rotulorum Patentium et Clausorum Cancellarie Hibernie Calendarium, Henrici II–Henrici VII* (Dublin, 1828) [hereafter *Rot. Pat. Hib.*], p. 154 (52); Curtis, 'Unpublished Letters', no. VI; *Cal. Pat. Rolls, 1391–6*, p. 671; PRO, E 403/562 m. 7.

36 For example, the gift of a mark made to *cuidam valetto Janekow*, bringing Roger Mortimer, earl of March, a black courser from an unnamed lord, April 1393–4: B[ritish] L[ibrary], Egerton Roll 8739.

37 PRO, E 364/31 m. A; *Chronique de Religieux de Saint-Denys*, ii. 528, 544; F. Lehoux, *Jean de France, Duc de Berri* (3 vols., Paris, 1966), iii. 481.

38 PRO, E 403/555 mm. 19, 27; E 364/31 m. A; *Johannis de Trokelowe et Anon., Chronica et Annales* [hereafter *Chronica et Annales*], ed. H. T. Riley (Rolls Series, 1866), ii. 199–200.

39 PRO, Supplementary Patent Rolls, C 67/30 m. 3; *Cal. Pat. Rolls, 1396–9*, pp. 323, 279; *Calendar of the Fine Rolls Preserved in the Public Record Office* [hereafter *Cal. Fine Rolls*], *1391–9*, p. 245; PRO, E 101/403/10 f. 44.

40 *Cal. Fine Rolls, 1383–91*, pp. 211, 302.

41 PRO, King's Remembrancer, Memoranda Rolls, E 159/169, Trinity, brevia directa baronibus, m. 12; *Victoria County History, Middlesex*, vol. 5, ed. T. F. T. Baker (Oxford, 1976), p. 325; *Cal. Close Rolls, 1392–6*, p. 237.

42 *Cal. Close Rolls 1396–9*, p. 323; *Cal. Fine Rolls, 1391–9*, p. 164; PRO, E 159/173, Easter, brevia directa baronibus, m. 3*d*; *Calendar of Inquisitions post mortem, 1377–84*, no. 525; ibid., *1392–99*, no. 1258; *Cal. Close Rolls, 1399–1405*, pp. 526–7; ibid., *1402–05*, 433; *Cal. Fine Rolls, 1399–1405*, pp. 300–1.

43 *Hardyng*, p. 344.

44 PRO, C 81/1081/1; *Chronica et Annales*, p. 239; 'Annales breve Hiberniae', *The Annals of Ireland by Fr John Clyn and Thady Dowling*, ed. R. Butler (Dublin, 1849), p. 25; Dorothy Johnston, 'The Interim Years: Richard II and Ireland, 1395–1399', *England and Ireland in the Later Middle Ages*, ed. J. F. Lydon (Blackrock, 1981), pp. 189–90.

45 PRO, Warrants for Issue, E 404/16/400; *Cal. Pat. Rolls, 1399–1401*, p. 154; *Documents on the Affairs of Ireland before the King's Council*, ed. G. O. Sayles (Dublin, 1979) [hereafter *Documents on the Affairs of Ireland*], pp. 269–70; *Rot.*

Pat. Hib., p. 242 (30). Norragh was a very questionable asset, since Art Macmurrough claimed the barony in the right of his wife and had declared his intention never to make peace until it was restored to him: *A Roll of the Proceedings of the King's Council in Ireland, 1392–93*, ed. James Graves (Rolls Series, 1877), pp. 261–2; Robin Frame, 'Two Kings in Leinster: The Crown and the MicMhurchadha in the Fourteenth Century', *Colony and Frontier in Medieval Ireland: Essays Presented to J. F. Lydon*, ed. T. B. Barry, Robin Frame and Katharine Simms (1995), pp. 171–2.

46 *Calendar of Ormond Deeds, ii: 1350–1413*, ed. Edmund Curtis (Dublin, 1934), no. 341.

47 PRO, Palatinate of Chester, Enrolments, CHES 2/73 m. 7.

48 *Ancient Kalendars and Inventories of the Treasury of His Majesty's Exchequer*, ed. Sir Francis Palgrave (3 vols., 1836), ii. 26–7; *Rotuli Scotiae* (2 vols., 1814–19), ii. 152–3.

49 *Cal. Pat. Rolls, 1399–1401*, pp. 74, 154, 247; *Cal. Close Rolls, 1399–1402*, p. 14; *Documents on the Affairs of Ireland*, pp. 269–70; *Cal. Fine Rolls, 1399–1405*, p. 62.

50 *Cal. Pat. Rolls, 1399–1401*, p. 248; *Cal. Close Rolls, 1399–1402*, pp. 74–5; James Lydon, 'The City of Waterford in the Later Middle Ages', *Decies*, xii (1979), 5–9.

51 *Anglo-Norman Letters and Petitions*, ed. M. Dominica Legge (Anglo-Norman Text Society), iii (1941), 80–2, 88–9; A. L. Brown, 'The Privy Seal Clerks in the Fifteenth Century', *The Study of Medieval Records*, ed. D. A. Bullough and R. L. Storey (Oxford, 1971), pp. 272–5 for Frye's prominence as a patronage-broker.

52 *Duo Rerum Anglicarum Scriptores Veteres*, ed. Thomas Hearne (2 vols., Oxford, 1732), i. 230; *Issues of the Exchequer, Henry III-Henry VI*, ed. Frederick Devon (1837), p. 278. BL, Add. MS 21357, f. 4 is a copy of the response of Cornwall and Janico to the original challenge, agreeing to a contest of ten courses with the lance, followed by further combat with sword and dagger, *a leyde de dieu et de saint Jorge*.

53 Anthony Tuck, 'Henry IV and Europe: a Dynasty's Search for Recognition', *The MacFarlane Legacy: Studies in Late Medieval Politics and Society*, ed. R. H. Britnell and A. J. Pollard (Stroud, 1995), pp. 107–9. The French challengers, Charles de Savoisy and Ector de Pontbirant, were notably hostile to Lancastrian claims: *Foedera, Conventiones, Litterae*, ed. Thomas Rymer (20 vols., 1727–35) [hereafter *Foedera*], viii. 140, 151; *El Victorial. Crónica de Don Pedro Niño, conde de Buelna*, ed. Juan de Mata Carriazo (Collección de Crónicas Españolas, i, 1940), pp. 186 ff., 264, 269.

54 A. C. Reeves, *Lancastrian Englishmen* (Washington, DC, 1981), pp. 143–4; *Cal. Pat. Rolls, 1399–1401*, p. 354; *Rot. Pat. Hib.*, p. 159 (4); PRO, Gascon Rolls, C 61/107 m. 6. The Ombrière grant proved problematic; Janico later claimed that he had derived no profit from it and sold out all his rights in the office in April 1404: PRO, Patent Rolls, C 66/368 m. 25, C 61/109 m. 3.

55 *Cal. Pat. Rolls, 1399–1401*, pp. 466, 131.

56 A. Rogers 'The Political Crisis of 1401', *Nottingham Medieval Studies*, xii (1968) [hereafter Rogers, 'Political Crisis'], 85–96; *Proceedings and Ordinances of the Privy Council of England*, ed. Sir Harris Nicolas (7 vols., 1834–7), i. 181–3. For the correct dating of this minute: Rogers, 'Political Crisis', 92.

57 *Cal. Pat. Rolls, 1399–1401*, pp. 475, 488, 446; PRO, C 66/368 m. 25.

58 *Royal and Historical Letters during the Reign of Henry IV*, ed. F. C. Hingeston

(2 vols., Rolls Series, 1860), i. 76; H. G. Richardson and G. O. Sayles, *The Irish Parliament in the Middle Ages* (Philadelphia, 1952), pp. 166–7.

59 BL, MS Cotton Tiberius B XI (44); Art Cosgrove, 'The Emergence of the Pale, 1399–1447', *A New History of Ireland, II: Medieval Ireland 1169–1534*, ed. Art Cosgrove (Oxford, 1992), pp. 537–8.

60 *Rot. Pat. Hib.*, pp. 160 (17), 165 (222), 166 (15), 169 (21).

61 Besides the lordship of Trim itself, he was granted the keeping of all the Mortimer lands in Co. Meath in November 1405; *Cal. Fine Rolls, 1399–1405*, p. 62; ibid., *1405–13*, 21; *Rot. Pat. Hib.*, p. 186 (75).

62 PRO, Ancient Petitions, SC 8/331/15761; C 47/10/26/1.

63 *Cal. Pat. Rolls, 1401–5*, p. 406; ibid., *1405–8*, p. 309; A. J. Otway-Ruthven, *A History of Medieval Ireland* (1968) [hereafter Otway-Ruthven, *Medieval Ireland*], p. 344.

64 PRO, Council and Privy Seal Records, E 28/6, unnumbered; *Rot. Pat. Hib.*, p. 193 (184).

65 'Henry Marlborough's Chronicle of Ireland', *Ancient Irish Histories* (2 vols., Dublin, 1809), ii. 19, 23. The ransom of the captured Scottish commander, Sir Thomas Maconlagh, was still under discussion in 1409: *Rot. Pat. Hib.*, p. 193 (160).

66 *Cal. Pat. Rolls, 1405–8*, p. 361; *Foedera*, viii. 527; *Cal. Pat. Rolls, 1408–13*, p. 183; *Acts of the Lords of the Isles 1336–1493*, ed. Jean Munro and R. W. Munro (Scottish Historical Society, 4th ser.), xxii (1986), lxxvi–lxxvii. For the wider diplomatic significance of these negotiations, see Ranald Nicholson, *Scotland: The Later Middle Ages* (Edinburgh, 1974), p. 234.

67 T. E. McNeil, *Anglo-Norman Ulster: The History and Archaeology of an Irish Barony* (Edinburgh, 1980), pp. 118–21; Edmund Curtis, *Richard II in Ireland 1394–5 and the Submission of the Irish Chiefs* (Oxford, 1927), pp. 87–8; John Bannerman, 'The Lordship of the Isles', *Scottish Society in the Fifteenth Century*, ed. Jennifer M. Brown (1977), pp. 211–17.

68 *Rot. Pat. Hib.*, p. 203 (37); Ralph Holinshed, *The Chronicles of England, Scotlande and Irelande*, ed. Henry Ellis (6 vols., 1807–8), vi. 264; Cormac O'Cleirigh, 'The O'Connor Faly Lordship of Offaly, 1395–1513', *Proceedings of the Royal Irish Academy*, xcvi (1996), 89–90.

69 PRO, E 101/69/3/370; C 76/98 m. 12; *Cal. Pat. Rolls, 1413–16*, p. 356.

70 PRO, E 101/47/39 m. 5; 'Chronicle of John Strecche for the reign of Henry V (1414–1422)', ed. Frank Taylor, *BJRL*, xvi (1932), 156–7 (dominum Johannem Jenico); *Gesta Henrici Quinti*, ed. Frank Taylor and John S. Roskell (Oxford, 1975), pp. 115–21; Janico's son, *Janico le fitz*, also served in the Harfleur garrison.

71 PRO, C 76/101 m. 11; Norman Rolls, C 64/9 mm. 32d., 18d., 11d., 8d., 6d.; *Historical Collections of a London Citizen*, p. 9. For the duties involved in these musters, see R. A. Newhall, *Muster and Review: A Problem of English Military Administration, 1420–1440* (Cambridge, Mass., 1940), pp. 3–4.

72 PRO, C 76/102 m. 6, 104 m. 11.

73 *Rot. Pat. Hib.*, p. 229 (109b).

74 *Cal. Pat. Rolls, 1413–16*, pp. 74–6 conveniently lists these, to which should be added the grant of the manor of Ardmulghan (Meath), valued at £35 p.a.; *Rot. Pat. Hib.*, p. 186 (75). Janico's good standing with the king allowed him to apply some leverage at the exchequer, with the result that his annuities assigned on English sources of revenue, at least, did not fall seriously into arrears until the end of Henry IV's reign: PRO, E 404/21/25, 27/436.

75 *Rot. Pat. Hib.*, p. 242 (29–31); *Inquisitionum Cancellarie Hiberniae Repertorium* (2 vols., Dublin, 1826), i. Lough, II. VI (1); *Statute Rolls of the Parliament of Ireland, Henry VI*, ed. H. F. Berry (Dublin, 1910), pp. 194–202.

76 PRO, C 61/109 m. 4; *Cal. Pat. Rolls, 1416–22*, p. 59; ibid., *1401–5*, p. 436; ibid., *1405–8*, pp. 149, 247. Janico was with the king, and preparing to return to Ireland, in July 1404, November 1405 and March 1407.

77 PRO, C 66/374 m. 29; *Cal. Pat. Rolls, 1405–8*, p. 101.

78 PRO, SC 8/331/15671; C 47/10/26/1; *Rot. Pat. Hib.*, p. 188 (116). For the original grant to the petitioner, John More: *Cal. Pat. Rolls, 1399–1401*, p. 449.

79 PRO, SC 8/105/5245; *Rotuli Parliamentorum* (6 vols., 1783) [hereafter *Rot. Parl.*], iv. 161–2; PRO, Placita Coram Rege, KB 27/628 m. 61. Talbot's policies while lieutenant are discussed in more detail by Otway-Ruthven, *Medieval Ireland*, pp. 348–58; A. J. Pollard, 'The Family of Talbot, Lords Talbot and Earls of Shrewsbury, in the Fifteenth Century', unpublished PhD thesis (University of Bristol, 1968), pp. 112–25.

80 PRO, C 64/9 m. 20; *Cal. Pat. Rolls, 1416–22*, p. 331; PRO, SC 8/331/15678; *Calendar of Signet Letters of Henry IV and Henry V (1399–1422)*, ed. J. L. Kirby (1978), no. 860.

81 PRO, KB 27/628, m. 61, partly printed in *Select Cases in the Court of King's Bench, vii: Richard II, Henry IV, Henry V*, ed. G. O. Sayles (Selden Society), lxxxviii (1971), 240–2; *Calendar of the Charter Rolls Preserved in the Public Record Office, 1341–1417*, pp. 447–50, 476–7. The case turned on the sensitive issue of the acceptability of English letters of warrant at the Irish exchequer; compare the discussion in *Select Cases in Exchequer Chamber, 1377–1461*, ed. M. Hemmant (Selden Society), li (1933), pp. 81–4.

82 PRO, E 364/57 m. G; *Rot. Parl.*, iv. 161–2; *Rot. Pat. Hib.*, p. 219 (61, 62). Full payment of the annuity was still far from guaranteed. Between 24 Feb. 1420 and 27 Nov. 1424 Janico received £70.7.8, approximately 15 per cent of the sum due to him: PRO, E 364/60 mm. C, D.

83 James F. Lydon, *The Lordship of Ireland in the Middle Ages* (Dublin, 1972), pp. 258–60; M. C. Griffiths, 'The Talbot–Ormond Struggle for Control of the Anglo-Irish Government, 1414–47', *Irish Historical Studies*, ii (1940–1), 376–97.

84 *Cal. Signet Letters, Henry IV and Henry V*, no. 840; *Cal. Close Rolls, 1413–19*, p. 496.

85 *Cal. Pat. Rolls, 1416–22*, p. 316; *Rot. Pat. Hib.*, p. 220 (80).

86 *Rot. Pat. Hib.*, p. 239 (116); *Cal. Pat. Rolls, 1422–9*, pp. 287–8; *Inquisitionum Cancellarie Hiberniae Repertorium*, i, Louth, Henry VI (1).

87 *Oeuvres de Froissart*, ii. 8; K. McRobbie, 'The Concept of Advancement in the Fourteenth Century in the Chroniques of Jean Froissart', *Canadian Journal of History*, vi (1971), 1–19 (quotation at n. 27); Richard W. Kaeuper and Elspeth Kennedy, *The Book of Chivalry of Geffroi de Charny: Text, Context and Translation* (Philadelphia, 1996), p. 126.

88 J. A. Fernàndez de Larrea Roja, *Guerra y sociedad en Navarra durante la edad media* (Bilbao, 1992).

89 Competent judges considered Otterburn to be 'as hard an encounter and as well-fought a battle as there could ever be' and the siege of al-Mahdiya to be as honourable an exploit as three mortal battles: *Oeuvres de Froissart*, xiii. 219; *Chronique du Bon Duc*, p. 248. For the significance of such judgements, see Howard Kaminsky, 'Estate, Nobility and the Exhibition of Estate in the Later Middle Ages', *Speculum*, lxvii (1993), 705–9.

90 Peter F. Ainsworth, *Jean Froissart and the Fabric of History* (Oxford, 1990), pp. 81–5, 304–6; Edward Miller, *War in the North: The Anglo-Scottish Wars of the Middle Ages* (Hull, 1960), p. 15.

91 R. A. Griffiths, 'The English Realm and Dominions and the King's Subjects in the Later Middle Ages', *Aspects of Government and Society in Later Medieval England: Essays in Honour of J. R. Lander* (Toronto, 1986), pp. 83–105; Christopher Allmand, *Henry V* (1992), pp. 414–25; J. W. McKenna, 'How God became an Englishman', *Tudor Rule and Revolution*, ed. Delloyd J. Guth and John W. McKenna (Cambridge, 1982), pp. 25–43; *Rot. Parl.*, iii. 527–8; and note the further Commons' petition for the expulsion of aliens in 1406; ibid., iii. 578.

92 M. T. Clanchy, *England and its Rulers 1066–1272* (1983), pp. 241–62; Michael Prestwich, *Edward I* (1988), pp. 151–2; *The Complete Peerage*, ed. G. E. Cokayne (12 vols., 1910–57), vi. 650–3.

93 Pierre Chaplais, *English Medieval Diplomatic Practice, Part I* (2 vols., 1982), i. 100, 353; David Morgan, 'From a Death to a View: Louis Robessart, Johan Huizinga and the Political Significance of Chivalry', *Chivalry in the Renaissance*, ed. Sidney Anglo (Woodbridge, 1990), pp. 93–106.

94 Rosemary Horrox, 'Personalities and Politics', *The Wars of the Roses*, ed. A. J. Pollard (Basingstoke, 1995), pp. 95–6; Robert Bartlett, *The Making of Europe: Conquest, Colonization and Cultural Change 950–1350* (1993), pp. 230–2.

95 Roger Collins, *The Basques* (Oxford, 1986), pp. 234–48; Beatrice Leroy, *Le royaume de Navarre à la fin du Moyen Age: gouvernement et société* (Aldershot, 1990), I. 87–8, VIII. 240–1.

96 Robert Bartlett, 'Colonial Aristocracies of the High Middle Ages', *Medieval Frontier Societies*, ed. Robert Bartlett and Angus MacKay (Oxford, 1989), pp. 23–47; Robin Frame, *The Political Development of the British Isles 1100–1400*, revised ed. (Oxford, 1995), pp. 199–224.

II

Political culture

6

Richard II's views on kingship

Few aspects of the reign and personality of Richard II have attracted as much attention as the related questions of his views on the rights and duties of kingship and the effect that these views had on his conduct of government. The range of opinion among historians on the issue remains unusually wide, from those who maintain that Richard was animated by a clear and consistent set of absolutist principles that anticipated the Divine Right theories of the Renaissance monarchies, to those who insist upon the unremarkably traditional nature of his thinking, his 'conscientious misunderstanding . . . of the rights and duties of kingship'.[1] In part, this diversity of opinion springs from the narrow range of the evidence from which judgement must be made. There are a few comments in the chronicles, mainly concentrated in the last two years of the king's reign; a handful of explicit statements by the king or his closest advisers; and a rather larger body of indirect evidence, concerning the king's artistic and literary patronage, as well as the size and expense of his household, from which something about Richard's attitude to the 'burden of the government of the English' may be deducible. In part, however, it arises from the overly direct relationship between intellectual training and political attitudes on which historians, lacking any extended statement of the king's theoretical position, have been forced to insist. Neither the suggestion that Richard strove to rule his people by the maxims of the civil law, nor the hypothesis that he and his advisers were especially influenced by the writings of Giles of Rome, have been judged to possess much foundation.[2] Yet Richard's actions as king cannot be explained solely as reactions to his previous political experiences; actions need to be justified and, even when the king's choice of justification appears to be a purely instrumental one, designed only to legitimate decisions already taken, it is a reasonable expectation that the arguments chosen will influence the future formulation of policy, reducing the available courses of action to those compatible with the lines of argument already advanced. A detailed analysis of Richard's thinking on the subject of kingship consequently remains essential to a proper understanding of his reign.

This essay attempts to reach some preliminary conclusions by concentrating on one of the fullest, but least-studied, reports of Richard's views on kingship. It is Sir William Bagot's account of a conversation he had with the king at Lichfield, most probably in June 1398,[3] when Richard reportedly said to him:

> that he desired neuer lenger to levyn thanne that he myht se the Crovne off Englond in al so hyh prosperyte, and so lowely be obeyed off alle his lieges, as hit hadde ben in eny other kyngis tyme; havyng consideracion how he hadde ben oppressed and dysobeyed as well by his lordes as by his comvnes; so that hit myght be cronycled perpetuelly that with wytte and wysdome and manhode he hadde recouered his dignyte, Regalye, and honourable estate; with that condicion that he Renounced the Crowne on the morowe. Seyyng, more ouer, that yiff he wolde Renounce, the most able man off wysdom and off manhode that he knew to Renounce hit to, were The Duk off Aumarle, and askyng myn avys, I seyde: 'be my trouthe I wyst wele the peple wolde nat obeye to him.' And the kyng seyde, my wille were bettir to the Duk off Hereford. 'And yff he be kyng, he wole be as wilde a Tyraunte to holy Cherche as euer was eny.' And I helde my pees, and durste speke no more; yitt seyde the kyng: 'meny goode confessours haue ben off his auncestres and off myn, that neuer wrouht ayens hooly chirche'.[4]

Bagot was brought from the Tower to present the Bill which contains this account on 16 October 1399. He was, in fact if not formally, on trial for his life and everything he said needs to be considered in that context. There are, all the same, good reasons for giving credence to the substance of his statement. Bagot was prepared to make some damaging admissions about his own conduct yet resisted the temptation to implicate others, exonerating the duke of Norfolk, now dead, from any responsibility for the death of the duke of Gloucester. Most significant, his claim that he had been sending intelligence to the exiled Henry of Lancaster was independently confirmed, while Bagot's subsequently lenient treatment at Henry's hands suggests that the new king recognised a debt of gratitude towards him.[5] While these considerations can themselves provide no guarantee of the accuracy of Bagot's report, they do mean that his account cannot be dismissed out of hand. He was talking to an audience that knew the former king intimately and it was in his interest to be credible. Except in those areas where the rest of the available evidence seems to call his statement strongly into question, therefore, it can provisionally be treated as an accurate rendering of the king's opinions.

From this account, four cardinal points in Richard's thinking on the subject of kingship seem to emerge. First, the importance of obedience: Richard sees the obedience of his subjects as the touchstone of his kingdom's prosperity and the standard against which kings, in general, and himself in particular, will be judged. Secondly, the influence of precedent and history: Richard presents his task as one of restoration, recovering for the Crown rights of which it had been deprived by its rebellious subjects. Thirdly, renunciation: Bagot claimed that Richard declared himself willing to renounce the Crown once he had fully regained for his successors all the rights and powers of kingship. That he could contemplate such a surrender must imply that Richard adhered to some version of the doctrine of capacities, with its insistence on the distinction between the person of the king and the institution of the Crown. Lastly, Richard laid great emphasis upon the protection of the church as one of the essential duties of kingship and displayed a lively awareness of the spiritual prestige – the *many good confessors* – of the Plantagenet lineage. In the rest of this essay I shall examine these four points in greater detail in order to establish whether they are reconcilable with Richard's statements on the subject of royal authority on other occasions and if, between them, they amount to a coherent and comprehensible theory of kingship.

The importance of obedience in Richard's thinking is clearly marked. Past disobedience and future obedience form the twin poles around which Richard appears to have formulated his policy towards his subjects and the topic appears consistently in the royalist rhetoric of persuasion. As early as November 1383, Michael de la Pole had sought to explain the great rebellion of 1381 as the culmination of many acts of petty disobedience towards the king's ministers.[6] A more elaborate exposition of the necessity of obedience was canvassed in the tract on kingship presented to Richard II soon after March 1392, the *De quadripartita regis specie*.[7] The plan of this work was simple – first to outline the virtues necessary to good kingship, then to enumerate the obstacles to its exercise and to add some practical suggestions on overcoming them – and its first, positive, half is largely an abridged version of the pseudo-Aristotelian *Secreta secretorum*.[8] The second half, dealing mainly with the obstacles to good kingship, contains apparently original material and dwells at length on only two such obstacles – disobedience and *stultitia*. Disobedience is especially deprecated; nothing more gravely afflicts the hearts of earthly princes or moves kings more greatly to impose penalties or vengeance upon their subjects. *Stultitia* is defined as popular sovereignty, the people declaring 'we do not want this man to rule over us'; the author helpfully adds that, among the people, the *stultus* is by custom deprived of all his hereditary possessions. Whoever wrote this tract, whether a political exile in Ireland or an Irish visitor to the court, was seeking royal favour and clearly intended to flatter the king's known prejudices; his work may reasonably be taken as a guide to the direction of royalist thinking early in Richard's majority.

It was not long, in any case, before the royalist insistence on the necessity of obedience got a more public airing. In his opening address to parliament in February 1395, for instance, the chancellor urged that by his conduct in Ireland the king had earned the honour and obedience of his subjects. In September 1397 Edmund Stafford explained to the Commons that three things were necessary for good government: that the king should be strong enough; that his laws be justly executed; and that the subjects of his kingdom be duly obedient.[9] What constituted true obedience was, of course, more controversial. Stafford sought to base the king's claim to obedience on his possession of the *patria potestas*; Richard's subjects should obey him as sons obey their father and be ready to submit themselves, if necessary, to the chastisement ordained by his laws. The king himself seems to have preferred a biblical analogy: his epitaph announces that, in defeating those who had violated royal authority, he had trampled the proud underfoot (*elatos suppeditavit*).[10] He was clearly attached to the image, for he informed the Emperor Manuel II that, by defeating his rebellious subjects, he had trodden on the necks of the proud and haughty.[11] It is hard to miss the reminiscence of the Magnificat – 'He has put down the mighty from their seats' (Luke 1:55) – in such phrases. Richard seems to have been reaching for a justification of his rule grounded in the drama of human salvation. Disobedience was founded upon pride, the sin of Lucifer, just as the king's reduction of his subjects to obedience was the temporal counterpart of God's retributive justice.

How this notion was, in practical terms, to be implemented is foreshadowed by Richard's longstanding interest in Ireland. It was as a land *in rebellion* that the Irish problem presented itself to the king and his policy there 'was based upon the acceptance of the political concept of Ireland as one lordship, with its inhabitants being in theory all liege subjects, and in practice either rebel or loyal, whatever their racial distinction'. Richard's identification of the 'rebel Irish, our enemy' as the particular target of his expedition in 1394 owed less to his growing appreciation of the intricacies of Irish politics than to the fact that, of all his subjects within the British Isles, they were the most conspicuously disobedient to his authority; in explaining the objectives of his expedition to Philip, duke of Burgundy, the king characteristically placed 'the punishment and correction of our rebels' before 'the establishment of good government and just rule'.[12] The short-term success of the king's first Irish expedition was consequently important in confirming the centrality of the obedience/disobedience polarity in his thinking. The 'respect and reverence for your exalted Crown' that the Irish chieftains promised to Richard,[13] and the liege-homage that they performed in person to him, created a relationship of submission that served as a model to be imposed on the rest of his subjects.

On the second point raised by Bagot's testimony, there is plenty of evidence to support the contention that Richard was highly conscious of his royal ancestors and their achievements and that he had a good, if selective, knowledge of political and administrative precedent. As a 'curious investigator of the relics of his ancestors',[14] Richard's concern centred principally on the vindication of the actions of his great grandfather, whose canonisation he sought,[15] and the promotion of the cult of Edward the Confessor,[16] though his interest in his royal ancestors was not confined to these two kings alone. Besides encouraging the veneration of two royal saints of the Anglo-Saxon past, Edmund of the East Angles and Edward the Martyr,[17] Richard was also anxious to situate himself and his policies firmly within the traditions of their Anglo-Norman successors. In 1385 he commissioned a series of thirteen royal statues, presumably forming a complete iconographic programme from the Confessor to the present day, to decorate the refurbished Westminster Hall.[18] It is wholly characteristic of Richard that, in berating the Commons for their presumption in submitting the reformist petition associated with Thomas Haxey, he should describe them as having done offence to the king, his liberty and that of his royal progenitors.[19] Richard's royal ancestors remained a living presence, by whose exacting standards he was acutely aware that his own regime would be judged.

In the hands of the king's advisers this concern for royal rights and their recovery, based upon a grasp of legal and historical precedent, was a potentially powerful weapon. Richard himself possessed a statute collection, presented to him in 1389, and the Exchequer copy of the statutes of England was brought up to date in 1392. At much the same time, the statement on royal rights of wardship and forfeiture known as the *Prerogativa regis* was copied on to a spare leaf in the Exchequer statute-book.[20] A document of uncertain status and date, the *Prerogativa* seems originally to have been a private compilation, made between 1272 and 1285, that gained a quasi-official authority by virtue of its incorporation in the early statute collections. Though well enough known to contemporary lawyers, its great days lay in the future, when its doctrines were ruthlessly applied by Henry VII's councillors to bolster their campaign to increase the prerogative revenues of the Crown.[21] There are some signs that Richard's advisers were also eager for a more general application of the principles, consistently favourable to the interest of the Crown, found in the *Prerogativa*. The Chancery maintained a close interest in the king's potential feudal and prerogative rights, compiling memoranda on several occasions as to the king's right to present to vacant ecclesiastical benefices.[22] Farms owed to the Crown and reversions scheduled to fall due were also carefully monitored. Lists of such potential sources of revenue, together with the names of Crown debtors, were routinely extracted from the memoranda rolls after 1389.[23] Close attention was paid, too, to the profits of justice; outlawry rolls, consisting of the names of those outlawed each term in King's Bench and Common Pleas, and whose goods were thereby forfeit to the Crown, began to be returned to the Exchequer late in the reign.[24] A still more thoroughgoing application of the concerns of the *Prerogativa* occurred in the king's treason legislation in 1398, with its 'reversion to Bracton's view of forfeiture as total deprivation of the traitor and his family'.[25]

Behind this new rigour in the enforcement of the Exchequer's claims lay, in all probability, the initiative of the treasurer, John Waltham, bishop of Salisbury. As keeper of the privy seal (1386–9) and treasurer of the Exchequer (1391–5), contemporary opinion recognised his considerable influence with the king, holding him responsible both for the elaboration of the council's *sub pena* jurisdiction that is so marked a feature of Richard's majority and for the king's decision to take the City of London into his own hands in July 1392.[26] If Waltham's involvement in ecclesiastical controversy suggests a temperamental disposition towards authoritarian legalism, willing to enforce and defend the rights of his episcopal dignity to the last,[27] his successful reform of the customs administration, inaugurated in December 1391, and his imaginative sponsorship of an export scheme designed to revive the wool-production of north-west England show him capable of a flexible and inventive response to the problems of government.[28] His services were certainly highly valued by the king, who, at Waltham's death, had his body abstracted from the grasp of an indignant dean and chapter of Salisbury by William Lescrope and buried among Richard's most faithful and favoured servants at Westminster.[29] As the great-nephew of Edward III's chancellor, John Thoresby, and the last member of Thoresby's great clerical affinity to hold important administrative office,[30] Waltham was an appropriate architect for a policy of royalist renewal based upon a close knowledge and selective exploitation of existing precedents. In his vindication of 'the royal liberty of the Crown' precedent provided the king with a legitimating consensus, while leaving him considerable freedom to set an authoritarian agenda; Richard had to go no further back than his grandfather's reign to find repeated assertions that the Crown had the right to amend and repeal statutes without the consent of Parliament, as well as the declaration that the king could choose whomsoever he willed as his minister.[31]

Yet Richard's thinking on the subject of kingship was not wholly bounded by the authority of precedent. This emerges most clearly from a consideration of the third point raised by Bagot's Bill: the king's statement that he would willingly renounce the Crown once his work as the restorer of the royal prerogative was accomplished. Problematic though Bagot's testimony is in general, it is nowhere more problematic than on this point. Bagot was on trial for his life in a Parliament that had, a fortnight earlier, been informed of the king's *actual* renunciation of the Crown. Evidence that the former king had voluntarily contemplated such a renunciation was obviously welcome to the Lancastrian regime that would eventually decide Bagot's own fate and that supreme opportunist clearly had a pressing motive for supplying it. What he claimed Richard had told him was, in its implications, remarkable. It appears to suggest that the king held to a version of the doctrine of capacities close to that declared by Edward II's magnates in 1308, that separated, as well as distinguished, the person of the king from the institution of the Crown. This was at odds with the generally-accepted view that, as a corporate entity composed of the rights and interests of *both* the king and his subjects, 'in the Crown the whole body politic was present'.[32] It is not easy to reconcile with Richard's declared belief in the inalienable character of royal authority, clearly expressed in the protestation he made in the Tower, that by his renunciation of the government of the kingdom (*regimen regni*) he did not wish or intend to surrender the spiritual qualities conferred upon him by the rite of unction at his coronation.[33] Richard's plans for a second anointing, with the newly-discovered oil of St Thomas of Canterbury, indicate how much store he set by those qualities.[34]

Nothing Richard said to Bagot is, on the other hand, incompatible with an interpretation of his protestation in the Tower that sees him as intending 'at least to remain a titular king, while delegating the conduct of affairs to others and securing the rights of succession' upon them.[35] By insisting that he could dispose unilaterally of his crown Richard was seeking to extend the scope of royal action. Implicitly, he was denying that the Crown was a bearer of public rights, inalienable without the consent of the magnates as well as the king, and instead asserting the identity of the Crown with the interests and the wishes of the king alone. It was a more theoretical formulation of the opinion he had expressed in 1385, that the nobility were 'gems and precious stones' adorning the Crown – desirable but dispensable decorations – and one quite consistent with his declared desire to 'dispose of his own goods at his own will, wherever and whenever he pleased'.[36] The changes in court ceremonial in the final years of Richard's reign embodied, at a practical level, the same movement of ideas; an increasing distinction between the king's public and private persons which simultaneously conferred upon him a greater degree of discretion in his courses of action. While his public person became increasingly sacralised, to the extent that courtiers were required to drop to their knees whenever the royal glance lighted upon them, the privilege of familiar access to the king was increasingly personalised, with the king's own will regarded as sufficient, in the notorious case of the yeomen of the Cheshire Watch, to dissolve the barriers of social and ceremonial hierarchy.[37] In this vision, the Crown was to become the repository of Richard's restored sovereignty, an independent and undying guarantor of the permanence of his political achievements. Anyone who raised the people or rose against the king within his kingdom in manner of war was declared in 1398 to be adjudged 'as traitor of high treason against the Crown'.[38]

The importance Richard attached to the rite of unction and the spiritual qualities it imparted helps to explain some of his concern to defend the church against its enemies, reflected in the doubts he expressed to William Bagot over the probable conduct of Henry of Lancaster. Informed opinion held that a duly-anointed king enjoyed a special character, part layman and part clerk.[39] Richard was very ready to acknowledge the duties this special status laid upon him: as he explained to the Commons, if he came to know of anyone who sought by tyranny to subjugate and destroy the Christian people in any place, then he was bound, out of reverence for God and by his status as a king, to seek to destroy the tyrant and to restore the oppressed and desolated people to their former estate.[40] Yet Richard's aspiration to the title 'most Christian king' sprang from more than a sense of royal duty.[41] Both the Evesham and Westminster chroniclers remark approvingly on the favour he showed the church.[42] This was seemingly born of a lively personal devotion, which welcomed the latest news of miracles performed at English shrines and rejoiced at the gift of rather minor relics.[43] Richard chose to express this devotion in a characteristically embattled way by emphasising his position as the defender of orthodoxy against the assaults of its enemies; 'he obliterated heretics and destroyed their friends' was the claim he chose for his epitaph and, despite the presence of a group of heterodox fellow-travellers around his own person, Richard did indeed use the expanding jurisdiction of the council to take cognisance of cases involving suspected heresy.[44]

Two of the most strongly-marked characteristics of Richard's thinking about kingship were the importance he attached to this defence of the church and the sense of inter-dependence between Crown and church that it bred. He was naturally encouraged to make this connection by much of the advice and admonition he received from ecclesiastical sources. One regular source of this advice was the sermons preached before the king and court at the major feasts of the liturgical year.[45] The prominent English mendicants called upon to deliver these sermons were also deeply engaged in the examination and extirpation of theological error.[46] Though not every court preacher proved a blind royalist (one was later imprisoned for 'speaking the truth' concerning Richard's tyranny),[47] their intellectual and devotional concerns were evidently close to the king's own interests. At least three of the known court preachers – Alexander Bache, Thomas Cranly,[48] and John Depyng – were promoted to bishoprics. Depyng, prior of the London Dominican house, appears to have been a particular favourite; his frequent sermons on the feasts of Edward the Confessor, rewarded by a pension and a licence of non-residence in his Irish see, were delivered during the years of Richard's rapidly-maturing devotion to the saint.[49] In general, the mendicants' teaching on the tasks and duties of kingship seems to have combined an unexceptional but welcome emphasis upon the necessity of obedience with an injunction to the king to 'walk in the footsteps of his holy predecessors',[50] although in the case of one court preacher, Roger Dymoke, it is possible to be more precise. In his *Liber contra XII errores Lollardorum*, presented to the king in 1396, Dymoke argued at length that it was by the defence of the church that kings could best bring peace and stability to their kingdoms.[51] Showing a well-tuned sense of his audience, Dymoke developed his argument by defining heresy as a form of treason – since the Lollards were born of the church they were, like vipers, devouring their own mother – and making good use of the double-edged scriptural *exemplum* of Amon, king of Judah, himself a traitor, since he encouraged the worship of idols at the royal court, but also the victim of treachery, killed by conspirators after only two years on the throne. The implication is clearly that one treason led inevitably to the other; treachery to God bred treachery to the king.

Richard was prepared to accept such arguments, writing to Archbishop Arundel in terms that make a direct connection between his increasing freedom of political action and his ability and intention to do more on behalf of the church; obedience to the king would breed obedience to God.[52] He had made a similar elision, between the vitality of the Catholic faith and the prestige of his kingship, in a letter sent to Arundel's predecessor, William Courtenay, two years earlier, thanking the archbishop for news of a new miracle worked by St Thomas of Canterbury. Writing from Corfe, scene of the murder of Edward the Martyr, he added that it seemed to him that his noble and holy predecessors would, at this present time, be more glorified than they had been for many years, for the Christian faith and belief now had more enemies than had been the case for time out of mind, who would be converted to the way of salvation by the exhibition of these miracles.[53] Just how far Richard was prepared to identify his own interests with those of Catholic orthodoxy emerges from his letter to Albert of Bavaria, count of Holland, late in 1397. After informing the count that 'by the just judgement of God, our avenging severity' had condemned and executed certain members of the nobility, the king warns Albert to take heed of the example – 'that the faces of those who contrive wickedness against the king Christ our Lord may be hammered back into confusion and prevented from doing the like by the enormity of the punishment'.[54] Rebellion against the ruler is here presented, in the terms Dymoke had suggested, as rebellion against God, while the former sufferings of the king find their type in the sufferings of Christ. The *imitatio Christi* was a mode of action routinely urged on late medieval rulers, as it was urged on the king at his reconciliation with the City of London in 1392,[55] but few of them seem to have adopted it so literally and personally as Richard II.

Do the hopes and fears Richard expressed to William Bagot add up, when taken together with his other statements on the subject of his kingship, to a coherent and comprehensible set of views? In general, historians have concluded that they do not. Even those reasonably sympathetic to the king argue that 'his theory of kingship was as untidy as his absolutist programme . . . his exposition wanted consistency in both definition and purpose'.[56] In expounding his conception of the royal office Richard was certainly eclectic in his choice of argument. His demand for obedience was based as much upon an appeal to legal and historical precedent as upon a developing theory of royal rights that was, at least as regards the suggested status of the Crown, largely novel. It was justified both by reference to civil law doctrines, such as the *patria potestas*, and by an instinctive emphasis upon the need to defend ecclesiastical orthodoxy. His presentation of these views was, if not confused, not always clear; the vehemence with which he chose to express himself occasionally makes his position appear more radical than it really was. Faced with criticism of his policy towards the local offices of sheriff and escheator in February 1397, for example, Richard responded in person with a thoroughgoing rebuttal of the Commons' cherished belief in the annual appointment of local men to such posts. He argued instead that a year was not long enough for a layman to gain sufficient experience in his office to discharge it effectively and that only a longer term of service would give those appointed sufficient security 'to serve the king and do right' by acting, if necessary, against the interests of their neighbours and patrons.[57] This sounds like the blueprint for a radical break with existing administrative practice, yet in reality Richard was doing no more than restating the Crown's accepted position on the length of the escheators' terms of office; at the time that he spoke, none of the current escheators had exceeded the statutory three-year term established in 1378. As for the sheriffs, every county – except those held in fee by the nobility – had a new incumbent appointed in December 1396 and only two, Staffordshire and Wiltshire, did not receive one the following November.[58]

A further difficulty is that there are some elements in Richard's thinking that remain too inchoate in their expression for their significance to be fully evaluated. When the king described himself in 1397 as 'entire emperor', exercising a plenitude of power within his realm, he was, in all likelihood, doing no more than asserting that no superior jurisdiction or authority existed within the boundaries of the kingdom.[59] This was an uncontroversial proposition, ringingly endorsed by Archbishop Courtenay in 1393 when he declared that 'the Crown of England hath been so free at all times, that it hath been in no earthly subjection, but immediately subject to God in all things touching the regality of the same Crown, and to none other'. Yet these claims were capable of further expansion, such as they received in later medieval France, to the point where the king's vassals were reduced in status to his subjects, on the grounds that the royal claim to sovereignty, now said to rest on an *imperium*, was unconditionally binding on all who lived in the kingdom.[60] The submission of one of the rebel Irish chieftains to Richard in 1395 as his 'faithful liege subject and vassal',[61] rather than in the more usual form of submission as a faithful liegeman, provides an intimation of such a doctrine of imperial sovereignty in England but it is a line of thought that, at least on the surviving evidence, Richard and his advisers developed no further.

Yet such hesitations and inconsistencies in Richard's views on kingship were not necessarily a hindrance to the success of the policies based upon them. If the king was not an analytical political thinker, there were few others in the world of high politics who were. Even among those higher clergy who possessed the necessary intellectual training, there was a notable reluctance to expound their views at any length. 'Political theology' of the type Richard seems at times to have been espousing was in full-scale retreat before the pragmatic citation and selective interpretation of precedent that, for the most part, constituted the substance of political debate in later medieval England.[62] While it is possible to construct, from the words and actions of the king and his opponents, a clear-cut conflict between the king's *voluntas* and those who took their stand on the *leges et consuetudines regni*, in reality everyone operated within 'a loose framework of ideas', largely common to both sides, in which 'practice was not matched by theory'.[63] This very unclarity in the nature of practical political dialogue worked to the king's advantage, for virtually every aspect of his claims and policy could, if articulated at the appropriate level of generality, call upon a broad measure of consent. Richard's use of the appeal to precedent to bolster royal authority carried considerable resonance, for there were few elements in the theory and practice of his kingship that could be described as completely novel; even the hieratic ceremonial of his court had its roots in the practice of his father in Aquitaine, *si hauteyn et de si grant port* that all who came into his presence had to kneel before him for hours at a time.[64]

Equally, although the administrative changes of the 1390s were, with the benefit of hindsight, denounced as oppressive, they appealed to, and appeared to satisfy, a contemporary demand for institutional reform originally associated with the king's opponents. The reorganisation of Chancery personnel carried out in 1388–89 originated in a petition presented to the Merciless Parliament, for instance, and aimed at the reduction of improper curial influence on the 'business of the lord king and the republic', while the streamlining of council procedures in 1390 had as its object not only the more efficient dispatch of conciliar business but also the closer scrutiny of Crown patronage by the chancellor and the king's uncles.[65] Waltham's reforms appeared as the natural extension of the scope of these initiatives but their success allowed for a simultaneous and uncontroversial consolidation of royal authority. A good example is the administrative advantage to which the Crown's concession in the Cambridge Parliament that justices of the peace would, in future, be paid daily wages was turned.[66] Payments to the justices were claimed by the sheriffs of each county as an allowance against the farm of their shires and indentures detailing such payments were submitted at the Exchequer. From these particulars of account the Exchequer was able to draw up consolidated lists of the active justices in each county, listing the session days term by term and the justices sitting at each session; details that served no direct financial purpose, yet provided the king's ministers with a precise overview of the personnel of local justice.[67] The ability this gave them to manage the quarter sessions more effectively was in line with the general policy, pursued throughout Richard's majority, of seeking to extend the scope of Crown surveillance over proceedings before courts of inferior but independent status.[68]

On occasion, Richard made deliberate use of the consensual nature of most political thinking to stigmatise his opponents. He turned the rhetoric of pacification and concord, associated with the many schemes to heal the divisions of Christendom, against them, denouncing Thomas Arundel, for instance, as 'impatient of peace', his very existence a threat to the stability and security of the kingdom.[69] Such claims were neither very profound nor very original, but they did not need to be. What Richard attempted to do in the last two years of his reign was so unusual, so far outside the normal boundaries of royal action, that it is easy to assume that the ideas underpinning them were equally uncommon. There are certainly some distinctive elements in Richard's views on kingship, not least the personal intensity of belief with which he maintained them, but it was the traditional nature and unremarkable formulation of much of his thinking on the subject that allowed him to move so far towards implementing his vision. What he sought was, in contemporary terms, neither unjustified nor unattainable; it was the manner of his seeking that betrayed him.

Notes

1 J. N. Figgis, *The Divine Right of Kings* (2nd edn, Cambridge, 1914), pp. 73–80; V. H. Galbraith, 'A New Life of Richard II', *History*, xxvii (1942), p. 223; C. Barron, 'The Art of Kingship: Richard II', *History Today* (June 1985), pp. 30–7; J. W. Sherborne, 'Aspects of Court Culture in the Later Fourteenth Century', *English Court Culture in the Later Middle Ages*, ed. V. J. Scattergood and J. W. Sherborne (London, 1983), p. 5. J. Taylor, 'Richard II's Views on Kingship', *Proceedings of the Leeds Philosophical and Literary Society*, xiv (1971), pp. 189–205 adopts a middle position, arguing that it was only in 1397 that Richard

began to put his autocratic principles of kingship into action. An earlier version of this paper was presented at the Twenty-Seventh International Congress on Medieval Studies, Western Michigan University, Kalamazoo, in May 1992. I would like to thank the audience there, particularly Nigel Saul and Chris Given-Wilson, for their comments upon it.

2 Sir John Fortescue, *De laudibus legum anglie*, ed. S. B. Chrimes (Cambridge, 1942), pp. 79–81; R. H. Jones, *The Royal Policy of Richard II: Absolutism in the Later Middle Ages* (Oxford, 1968), pp. 154–63; A. Tuck, *Richard II and the English Nobility* (London, 1973), pp. 203–4.

3 The king was at Lichfield in mid January 1398 and again towards the end of June (*CPR, 1396–99*, pp. 258, 292, 313, 376, 381–2; *CCR, 1396–99*, pp. 318, 386, 392, 397; *CFR, 1391–99*, p. 271). The conversation Bagot recounted might have taken place on either occasion, though Richard's allegedly hostile attitude towards Henry Bolingbroke seems to suit the situation in June 1398 better.

4 *Chronicles of London*, ed. C. L. Kingsford (Oxford, 1905), p. 52, which provides a marginally better text of Bagot's Bill than *The Great Chronicle of London*, ed. A. H. Thomas and I. D. Thornley (London, 1938), p. 76. Walsingham reports the contents of the bill in J. de Trokelowe et anon., *Annales Ricardi Secundi et Henrici Quarti*, ed. H. T. Riley (RS, 1866), pp. 303–4.

5 *HC, 1386–1421*, ii. 99–103 is now the best short account of Bagot's career. Note, in addition, the payment of 100 marks made to Bagot by Henry of Lancaster just before going into exile; PRO, DL 28/1/10 f. 3v.

6 *RP*, iii. 150.

7 *Four English Political Tracts of the Later Middle Ages*, ed. J.-P. Genet, Camden Society 4th series, xviii (1977), pp. 22–39. The authorship of this tract and its relationship to the other items found in the same manuscript (Bodleian Library, MS Bodley 581) remain disputed. Genet's edition should be consulted in the light of the comments of W. C. Jordan, *Speculum*, liv (1979), pp. 801–2, and H. M. Carey, *Courting Disaster: Astrology at the English Court and University in the Later Middle Ages* (Basingstoke, 1992), pp. 98–104.

8 R. F. Green, *Poets and Princepleasers: Literature and the English Court in the Late Middle Ages* (Toronto, 1980), pp. 140–2, for the widespread popularity of the *secreta secretorum* and its derivatives.

9 *RP*, iii. 329, 347.

10 Royal Commission on Historical Monuments, *An Inventory of the Historical Monuments in London*, i, *Westminster Abbey* (London, 1924), p. 31.

11 *Official Correspondence of Thomas Bekynton*, ed. G. Williams (2 vols., RS, 1872), i. 285.

12 D. Johnstone, 'Richard II and the Submission of Gaelic Ireland', *Irish Historical Studies*, xxii (1980), p. 2; *Anglo-Norman Letters and Petitions*, ed. M. D. Legge (Oxford, 1941), p. 48.

13 E. Curtis, *Richard II in Ireland* (Oxford, 1927), p. 132.

14 Thomas Walsingham, *Historia Anglicana*, ed. T. Riley (2 vols., RS, 1864), ii. 239.

15 *The Westminster Chronicle, 1381–1394*, ed. L. C. Hector and B. F. Harvey (Oxford, 1982), pp. 158, 436–8; *The Diplomatic Correspondence of Richard II*, ed. E. Perroy (Camden Society, 3rd series, xlviii, 1933), p. 210.

16 M. V. Clarke, *Fourteenth Century Studies* (Oxford, 1937), pp. 274–6; J. H. Harvey, 'The Wilton Diptych: A Re-Examination', *Archaeologia*, xcviii (1961), pp. 5–6.

B. Harvey, *Westminster Abbey and its Estates in the Middle Ages* (Oxford, 1977), pp. 43–5, points to the limited popularity of the Confessor's cult.

17 D. Gordon, *Making and Meaning: The Wilton Diptych* (London, 1993), pp. 53–4; *Literae Cantuarienses*, ed. J. B. Sheppard (3 vols., RS, 1889), iii. 40–1. As early as 1385 Richard had granted his favourite, Robert de Vere, the privilege of augmenting his arms with the mythical arms of St Edmund: *CPR, 1385–89*, p. 78; J. H. Round, *Peerage and Pedigree* (2 vols., London, 1910), ii. 353.

18 H. M. Colvin, R. A. Brown, A. J. Taylor, *The History of the King's Works: The Middle Ages* (2 vols., London, 1963), i. 528–32.

19 *RP*, iii. 339.

20 *A Descriptive Catalogue of the Manuscripts in the Library of St John's College, Cambridge*, ed. M. R. James (Cambridge, 1913), pp. 8–9; PRO, E 164/9, ff. 157–79v, 220v, 221v. This volume can be identified as the Exchequer's *liver destatues* by the description of the position of the *Prerogativa* given in *Prerogativa regis*, ed. S. E. Thorne (New Haven, 1949), pp. 2–3.

21 F. W. Maitland, *Collected Papers*, ed. H. A. L. Fisher (3 vols., Cambridge, 1911), ii. 182–9; S. B. Chrimes, *Henry VII* (London, 1972), pp. 208–11.

22 PRO, C 270/26/22, 24, 26; C 255/8/3/15.

23 PRO, E 370/141/8, 9; 143/3.

24 PRO, E 370/3/1, 2, 24, 27.

25 C. D. Ross, 'Forfeiture for Treason in the Reign of Richard II', *EHR*, lxxi (1956), p. 574.

26 *RP*, iv. 84; W. M. Ormrod, 'The Origins of the Sub Pena Writ', *Historical Research*, lxi (1988), pp. 11–20; *The Brut*, ed. F. W. Brie (EETS, o.s., cxxxvi, 1908), ii. 345; C. M. Barron, 'The Quarrel of Richard II with London', *The Reign of Richard II*, ed. F. R. H. du Boulay and C. M. Barron (London, 1971), pp. 180–1.

27 J. Dahmus, *William Courtenay, Archbishop of Canterbury, 1381–1396* (Pennsylvania, 1966), pp. 149–56; K. Edwards, *The English Secular Cathedrals in the Middle Ages* (2nd edn, Manchester, 1967), pp. 102, 114, 122, 130–1.

28 *RP*, iii. 437; S. H. Rigby, 'The Customs Administration at Boston in the Reign of Richard II', *BIHR*, lviii (1985), pp. 12–24; H. Summerson, 'Responses to War: Carlisle and the West March in the Later Fourteenth Century', *War and Border Societies in the Middle Ages*, ed. A. Goodman and A. Tuck (London, 1992), pp. 168–9.

29 PRO, C 270/36/18, SC 8/141/7050; for further comment on the burial of Richard's servants at Westminster, N. Saul, 'The Fragments of the Golafre Brass in Westminster Abbey', *Transactions of the Monumental Brass Society*, xv (1992), pp. 24–5.

30 A. H. Thompson, 'The Registers of the Archdeaconry of Richmond, 1361–1442', *Yorkshire Archaeological Journal*, xxv (1920), pp. 257–60; T. F. Tout, *Chapters in the Administrative History of Medieval England*, iii (Manchester, 1928), pp. 215–16.

31 *RP*, ii. 139, 140, 203, 241.

32 For the theoretical status of the Crown at this period, E. Kantorowicz, *The King's Two Bodies* (Princeton, 1957), pp. 336–83 (quotation at p. 362); W. Ullmann, *Principles of Government and Politics in the Middle Ages* (4th edn, London, 1978), pp. 178–82.

33 H. G. Wright, 'The Protestation of Richard II in the Tower in September 1399', *Bulletin of the John Rylands Library*, xxii (1943), pp. 157–9.

34 Walsingham, *Historia Anglicana*, ii. 239; T. A. Sandquist, 'The Holy Oil of St Thomas

of Canterbury', *Essays in Medieval History Presented to Bertie Wilkinson*, ed. T. A. Sandquist and M. R. Powicke (Toronto, 1969), pp. 330–44.

35 G. O. Sayles, 'The Deposition of Richard II: Three Lancastrian Narratives', *BIHR*, liv (1981), p. 259.

36 *Reports from the Lords Committees Touching the Dignity of a Peer* (5 vols., London, 1820–29), v. 64–5; *RP*, iii. 338.

37 *Eulogium historiarum sive temporis*, ed. F. S. Haydon (RS, 3 vols., 1858–63), iii. 378; Clarke, *Fourteenth-Century Studies*, p. 98; for parallels with the development of the Burgundian court, W. Paravicini, 'The Court of the Dukes of Burgundy: A Model for Europe?', *Princes, Patronage and the Nobility: The Court at the Beginning of the Modern Age, c. 1450–1650*, ed. R. Asch and A. Birke (Oxford, 1991), pp. 71–86.

38 *Statutes of the Realm* (Record Commission, 1810–28), ii. 98–9.

39 S. B. Chrimes, *English Constitutional Ideas in the Fifteenth Century* (Cambridge, 1937), pp. 7–8.

40 *RP*, iii. 338.

41 R. A. Griffiths, 'The Crown and the Royal Family in Later Medieval England', *Kings and Nobles in the Later Middle Ages*, ed. R. A. Griffiths and J. Sherborne (Gloucester, 1986), p. 25 n. 34.

42 *Historia vitae et regni Ricardi Secundi*, ed. G. B. Stow (Philadelphia, 1977), p. 167; *The Westminster Chronicle*, pp. 326–7.

43 *Calendar of Charter Rolls, 1341–1417*, p. 288; *Literae Cantuarienses*, iii. 26–28; *Anglo-Norman Letters and Petitions*, pp. 67–8; *CPR, 1385–89*, p. 194, *1396–99*, p. 329.

44 H. G. Richardson, 'Heresy and the Lay Power under Richard II', *EHR*, li (1936), pp. 10–25.

45 Details of preachers before the king are preserved in the surviving household books, from which the names of all those mentioned in this paragraph are, unless otherwise stated, drawn; PRO, E 101/401/2, ff. 37–38; E 101/402/5, ff. 26–27; BL, MS Add., 35115, ff. 33–4; PRO, E 101/403/10, ff. 35–6.

46 E.g., Thomas Palmer; John Kynyngham; John Tille; *Registrum Johannis Trefnant, episcopi Herefordensis*, ed. W. W. Capes (Canterbury and York Society, xx, 1916), pp. 396–401; *Fasciculi Zizaniorum*, ed. W. W. Shirley (RS, 1858), pp. 4–104, 453–80; M. Deanesley, *The Lollard Bible and other Medieval Biblical Versions* (Cambridge, 1920), pp. 294, 443–4.

47 John Paris; *Annales Ricardi Secundi et Henrici Quarti*, p. 223.

48 Cranly's sermon is noted in R. L. Storey, 'The Foundation and the Medieval College', *New College, Oxford, 1379–1979*, ed. J. Buxton and P. Williams (Oxford, 1979), pp. 9, 22.

49 *CPR, 1396–99*, pp. 44, 220, 223; Depyng is recorded as preaching five times on the feasts of Edward the Confessor and once on the feast of Edward the Martyr.

50 A. Gwynn, *The English Austin Friars in the Time of Wyclif* (Oxford, 1940), pp. 201–7.

51 *Rogeri Dymmok liber contra XII errores et hereses Lollardorum*, ed. H. S. Cronin (Wycliffe Society, 1912), pp. 4–7. Dymoke had preached before the king on Whit Sunday 1391; PRO, E 101/402/5, f. 26v.

52 *Literae Cantuarienses*, iii. 50–1.

53 Ibid., iii. 36–41.

54 *Letters and Papers Illustrative of the Wars of the English in France during the Reign of Henry VI*, ed. J. Stevenson (2 vols., RS, 1861), i. lxxv–lxxvi.

55 G. Kipling, 'Richard II's "Sumptuous Pageants" and the Idea of the Civic Triumph', *Pageantry in the Shakespearean Theatre*, ed. D. M. Bergeron (Athens, Ga., 1985), pp. 83–103.
56 Jones, *Royal Policy of Richard II*, pp. 174–5.
57 *RP*, iii. 339.
58 Ibid., iii. 44; *List of Escheators for England and Wales* (PRO Lists and Indexes, lxxii, 1971), pp. 3–198; *List of Sheriffs for England and Wales* (PRO Lists and Indexes, ix, 1898), pp. 1–165.
59 *RP*, iii. 343; W. Ullmann, ' "This Realm of England is an Empire" ', *Journal of Ecclesiastical History*, xxx (1979), pp. 175–203.
60 *RP*, iii. 304; A. Bossuat 'La formule "le roi est empereur en son royaume": son emploi au XVe siècle devant le parlement de Paris', *Revue historique de droit français et étranger*, 4th series, xxxix (1961), pp. 371–81.
61 Curtis, *Richard II in Ireland*, p. 61.
62 J.-P. Genet, 'Ecclesiastics and Political Theory in Late Medieval England: The End of a Monopoly', *The Church, Politics and Patronage in the Fifteenth Century*, ed. R. B. Dobson (Gloucester, 1984), pp. 23–44.
63 Ullmann, *Principles of Government and Politics*, p. 183; A. L. Brown, 'Parliament, *c.* 1377–1422', *The English Parliament in the Middle Ages*, ed. J. H. Denton and R. G. Davies (Manchester, 1981), p. 131.
64 *The Anonimalle Chronicle, 1333–1381*, ed. V. H. Galbraith (Manchester, 1927), p. 56.
65 *RP*, iii. 250; B. Wilkinson, *The Chancery under Edward III* (Manchester, 1929), pp. 214–23; *PPC*, i. 18a.
66 R. L. Storey, 'Liveries and Commissions of the Peace, 1388–90', *The Reign of Richard II*, p. 139.
67 PRO, E 101/598/50; E 370/160/1, 4.
68 PRO, C 255/5/4. This file of warrants to do justice shows the range of the Crown's intervention, previously confined largely to the county courts, widened to include urban jurisdictions and the admiralty courts during Richard's reign.
69 D. Wilkins, *Concilia Magna Brittaniae et Hiberniae* (4 vols., London, 1737), iii. 232; A. L. Brown, 'The Latin Letters in MS All Souls 182', *EHR*, lxxxvii (1972), pp. 572–3.

7

Rumour, sedition and popular protest in the reign of Henry IV

I

On 21 September 1405 two local esquires fell into conversation with a traveller from the north at Little Walsingham in Norfolk. Asked what tidings there were, the stranger replied that there had been a great debate and battle between the earls of Northumberland and Westmorland, and that Westmorland was now the earl of Northumberland's prisoner.[1] Intrigued, as well they might be by this startling news, which was very nearly the precise opposite of the truth, the two esquires went on to ask the traveller what news there was of Wales and of Glyn Dŵr. The answer was equally forthcoming. Glyn Dŵr was strong and would get stronger, for he offered wages of nine pence a day to any man who would come to him, so that forty, sixty, even eighty men were joining his company every day. The traveller had chosen bad company in which to utter such inaccurate and potentially seditious rumours. Both his interlocutors were longstanding Lancastrian partisans, loyal members of the king's affinity; both had been with the king at Pontefract two months earlier when he put down the Yorkshire rising, and were likely to have known as much about conditions in the north as their informant.[2] They had little hesitation, in any case, in calling upon the village constable to arrest the stranger, with instructions that he should be carried off to Norwich castle and kept in prison there until, 'upon such words', the king and council should decide his fate.

For John Kingsley, the man they had just arrested, the outlook was bleak. Since 1402 Henry IV and his advisers had been accustomed to construe words which incited the king's subjects to act against their liege lord, as Kingsley's enthusiastic endorsement of the pay and conditions offered by Owain Glyn Dŵr might be thought to do, as falling within the compass of the Statute of Treasons.[3] Nor was this an isolated instance of questionable loyalties on Kingsley's part. A former esquire of the deposed Richard II, Kingsley had joined Henry Percy in rebellion in 1403, and fought against the king at Shrewsbury. In addition, his status as a servant and annuitant of Thomas Mowbray, earl of Norfolk – an ally of the earl of Northumberland's in the rebellion of 1405 – rendered his current behaviour all the more suspect to a government already wary of the power of disinformation.[4] Pardoned in 1403, Kingsley was lucky to be released from custody a second time, following examination before the council, in January 1406.[5] Yet within a month of his release he was allegedly at work fomenting rebellion again: this time he told a group of sworn accomplices in his native Nantwich, Cheshire, that King Richard was still alive and living in Scotland 'in as good estate and prosperity as ever he was'; when certain magnates gave the word to rise up against the present king, Kingsley and his companions would rise with them.[6]

John Kingsley's indiscretions were unusual only in the detailed nature of their misinformation. All over the country during the early years of Henry IV's reign, groups and individuals freely expressed their dissatisfaction with the rule of the new king. At Oxford, a group of Welsh clerks spoke badly of the king in March 1401, saying that he would rule for only two years because he occupied the crown unjustly, and wished him a short life and a bad end.[7] At Bishop's Lynn, the justices of the peace were told in June 1402 that at the time of Henry's return from exile in July 1399, William Ashbourne had called him a false traitor and said that all those who prayed for him were worthy to be hanged. More recently, another townsman had gloomily forecast that the Scots, Welsh and French would all rise together against England within the next two years, and cursed the king for it ('the devel hym al to-dasshe').[8] At Twywell in Northamptonshire, one of the local gentry was arrested late in July 1403 for predicting the date of the battle of Shrewsbury with suspicious accuracy and for claiming that after the battle Sir Henry Percy would be crowned king, 'saying, most sovereign lord, that you were not a loyal king'.[9] A prisoner in the abbot of Bury St Edmunds's gaol went further in November 1405, telling a fellow inmate that Henry had the guidance of 'a spirit, a devil by whom he knows if any man does aught against him', and forecast that, with the help of this diabolic advice, Henry would reign for eleven or thirteen years but that his rule would 'bring battle to every man's door', and that after him there would never be another king in England.[10]

Such conversations were part of the 'infrapolitics' of later medieval England, the broad area of discussion, complaint and dissent that fell somewhere between wholehearted consent and open rebellion. Within this arena of popular debate, politics remained the art of the possible: action was constrained by an acknowledgement of the established patterns of dominance and a desire to avoid the worst consequences of defiance.[11] What was new about these exchanges was not the open criticism voiced of the king and his government, for which earlier evidence haphazardly survives,[12] but the frequency with which such utterances were recorded. The rising volume of criticism reflected an atmosphere of social unrest generated by rapid economic change and sharpened by the exceptional instability of dynastic politics between 1397 and 1406, as first Richard II and then Henry IV were confronted with repeated rebellions against their authority.[13] Anxiety at the scope and effect of such seditious comments led to a relaxation, sanctioned by Henry IV and his judges, in the definition of what was legally admissible as evidence in certain cases directly affecting the person and security of the king: the evolution of the doctrine of 'treason by words'. Among claims of this type the Ricardian rumour – that the deposed King Richard II had somehow escaped from captivity, was still alive, and would soon return into England – was a particularly fertile source of accusations and indictments. It proved so fecund because it satisfied the requirements of 'infrapolitical' protest so well, couching resistance in the idiom of consent to legitimate authority while offering, in the uncertainties that came to cluster around the central figure of the returning king, a ready means of disavowal in the face of reprisals. A detailed consideration of its provenance and chronology consequently provides a fruitful starting point for a study of the place and purpose of such potentially seditious rumours within the political culture of early Lancastrian England. Though the general outlines of the 'false Richard' episode have long been known to historians, and its interpretation is currently the subject of some debate,[14] the full extent of the Ricardian rumour has never been documented, while its place within the broader context of the abundant evidence for popular protest and discontent in the early years of Henry IV's reign remains to be considered in detail. This has distorted understanding of the whole episode in certain important respects.

Some caution needs to be exercised of course in analysing the hearsay material on which much of this study is based. Some of it derives from the appeals of approvers, criminals who had already confessed to a capital felony before a coroner and were, to avoid execution, systematically informing on as many of their accomplices and co-conspirators as they could bring to mind. The dangers of elaboration, exaggeration and outright invention in such material are obvious and were well-recognized by contemporaries.[15] It is also clear that, even when accusations of treasonable or seditious words originate from a jury of presentment rather than an approver, they may be no more than devices to attract the attention of the authorities to an especially unpopular or disruptive individual in the midst of a community. Richard Pennyfeather, chaplain, indicted before the steward of the household in September 1406 for 'falsely and treasonably' comparing the lord king to a hedge sparrow (*haysugge*) while predicting that he would reign no more than six years, may or may not have said the words imputed to him but, as an allegedly incontinent priest in dispute with his parishioners, he was precisely the sort of unpopular local figure against whom such accusations were laid.[16] Sometimes the inaccuracies in such material are easily demonstrable: Henry Clee, one of the 'Welsh clerks' of Oxford accused of having spoken disparagingly of the king, cleared himself in court by showing that he was English, not Welsh, and born in the City parish of St Peter's, Breadstreet.[17] On other occasions the private compulsions that lay behind an allegation can only be suspected.[18] Uncertain and misleading though this material can be, with careful contextualization there remains much to be learned from it. Recent work on the appeals of approvers has confirmed their value and, whatever the inconsistencies of a particular accusation, whether certain words were actually uttered is usually less significant than the fact that it was thought plausible that they might have been. Both approvers and local juries of presentment required a certain degree of credibility in their claims in order to catch the disapproving attention of the authorities. Regardless of the truth that lies behind them, such allegations retain their value in indicating the topics and actions popularly recognized as best calculated to exploit the current anxieties of government.[19] It is important, in consequence, to establish the precise dimensions and chronology of the Ricardian rumour before examining, in more detail, its significance.

II

The first and, for the Lancastrian regime, most threatening phase of the rumour followed its initial emergence, virtually without prior warning, in the spring of 1402. What is most striking at this stage is the nearly simultaneous appearance of the survival story in several widely separated locations. Charles VI, king of France, who had been happy to accept the fact of his son-in-law's death without question for the previous two years, spoke in April 1402 of the 'common report' that Richard was still alive, and despatched one of his valets to Scotland to investigate.[20] In the same month Franciscan friars from the Midland houses of Aylesbury, Leicester and Northampton began to spread the word that Richard was alive, calling on his loyal lieges to assemble together and join him when he returned to the kingdom on Midsummer day.[21] The same story was abroad in Suffolk and the north-west. John Lancaster, a piper, told an audience at Winnington in Cheshire on 14 May, that he had himself seen the former king alive at Berwick-upon-Tweed, while the council received a report from the diocese of Carlisle in the same month that clerks and laymen were going about disturbing the people, telling them that Richard was still alive in Scotland and would soon be invading the country with an army of Scots. A Lancashire man, William Balshalf, was arrested in Hertfordshire for repeating the rumour.[22]

Once established, the story of Richard's survival and his imminent return continued to give Henry IV and his councillors concern for several years, playing a part in several of the major rebellions against his authority. The earl of March's uncle, Sir Edmund Mortimer, announced to his tenants in December 1402 that he was joining the Welsh rebels commanded by Owain Glyn Dŵr in order to vindicate the right of King Richard, if he was still alive.[23] In July 1403 Henry Percy sought to rally support for his rebellion among the commons of Cheshire by proclaiming that the former king would appear before them with a great army. The multitudes that rallied to the advertised meeting-places, in Delamare forest in Cheshire and at Prees in Shropshire, seem to confirm the opinion expressed a month earlier by the abbot of the Praemonstratensian house of Revesby, Lincolnshire, that there were ten thousand men in England who thought King Richard was still alive.[24] Despite the denials of the Lancastrian regime, the very public circulation of letters purporting to come from Richard during the January 1404 parliament can only have augmented their numbers. Maud de Vere, countess of Oxford, consequently sought to mobilize such sentiments between November 1403 and May 1404 as one element in her plan to offer assistance to a planned French invasion force. During these months, members of her household spread the word through Suffolk and Essex that Richard would soon return from the north in order to join forces with the duke of Orleans and the count of St Pol at Northampton, distributing livery badges of the former king's device, the white hart, as an earnest of their intent.[25]

Yet the continued belief in Richard's return did not solely depend upon such active proselytizing. At Southampton, the recorder of the town allegedly offered the French a joyful welcome if they came in the name of King Richard.[26] In November 1404, at Winchester, a Dominican friar, John Huchon, was said to have told two of his colleagues that he had seen the former king in the custody of the duke of Albany in Scotland, and claimed that but for the fear of the damage it would wreak on his order he would publicly preach as much. Huchon went on to encourage his companions to spread the news and to advise all those they told to make their way to Cheshire next midsummer, going two by two in order to avoid arousing suspicion, where they would join with a great army of Cheshiremen and their helpers in order to restore Richard to his throne. He added that more than two thousand friars, as well as many magnates and gentlemen, were already sworn together in this matter.[27]

Fr Huchon's tale, like John Kingsley's alleged conspiracy in February 1406, indicates the continued prevalence of belief in Richard's survival, which the author of the *Continuatio Eulogii*, an exceptionally well-informed source on this episode, describes as continuing to increase even after the capture and execution of its principal publicist, William Serle, in July 1404.[28] In the middle years of Henry IV's reign, however, the Ricardian rumour began to acquire a different character. While its content remained more or less identical, its incidence was less widespread, becoming increasingly confined to a relatively small group of malcontents kept under regular surveillance by the Lancastrian government, who nevertheless operated with comparative immunity from the sanctuary at Westminster. In May 1407, Benedict Wolman, John Tange and others, were said to have leagued together at Westminster to affirm wherever they went that the man known to the English authorities as Thomas Warde of Trumpington was in reality King Richard, and that he would soon be returning from Scotland to reclaim his kingdom once again. They swore to be 'faithful in their heart and works' to him, and were further alleged to have travelled to Scotland themselves in order to confer with the English traitors, Henry Percy, earl of Northumberland, and Thomas, lord Bardolf, as well as with the former king himself, and then to have distributed letters and signs on his behalf following their return to England.[29] More charges of a similar kind followed over the next two years. William Denton, a monk of St John's, Colchester, was accused of sending out letters to the same effect from Westminster in May 1408, and Fr John Huchon, still at large, was engaged in similar activities in March 1409. In May Thomas Goodlak entertained a messenger returning from Scotland, and a new batch of letters was put into circulation, while in the following August John Longe, cobbler, and his brother welcomed another Scottish agent, this time sent on Richard's behalf by Gavin Dunbar, younger son of the earl of March, in order to discuss the extent of continued Ricardian loyalties in England.[30] Late in 1409 a large group of dissidents, which included several monks of Westminster and two Franciscan friars, as well as several known maintainers of the Ricardian claim, was indicted for sending out messengers to France, Scotland, Wales and Flanders announcing that Richard would return into England before next Christmas. For the Lancastrian authorities there was no doubt that these incidents were related to one another. Each took place at Westminster or in its immediate environs, and the protagonists of the Ricardian claims were identified as a single, precisely located, group: 'all the traitors within the sanctuary at Westminster'.[31] Despite the gap of three and a half years, it seems clear that John Whitelock, indicted in 1413 for distributing bills in Westminster, London and Bermondsey during Henry V's first parliament, offering to prove the familiar assertion that Richard II was alive in Scotland and in the keeping of the duke of Albany, was drawn from the same group of sanctuary-men. Definitely identified as a Ricardian activist since 1410, he was said to have been in hiding with his accomplices at Westminster and elsewhere for the previous seven years.[32]

It was during Henry V's reign that the Ricardian rumour entered the final phase of its existence, when the continued decline in the number of its apparent adherents was partially offset by the renewed notoriety it gained through association with two prominent conspiracies to overthrow the king. In May 1415 Henry Talbot of Easington in Yorkshire, a committed gentry supporter of the Ricardian cause, brought his activities forcibly to the attention of the authorities by attempting to liberate one of the king's most valuable prisoners, Murdoch of Fife, the eldest son of the alleged King Richard's chief protector, the duke of Albany, in order to win Scottish backing for an invasion of the north in Richard's name. In September, the noble plotters involved in the 'Cambridge conspiracy' to kill Henry V admitted in their confessions that their initial intention had been to replace him with the man the Scots asserted to be Richard II.[33] The visit of Sigismund, king of the Romans, to England in the following year provoked a further flurry of activity on the part of the Ricardians, who saw in Sigismund's imperial authority a last chance to right a dynastic wrong. Thomas Lucas, a former subwarden of Merton College with a past history of Lollard sympathies, was indicted for spreading handbills addressed to Sigismund (with the help of Benedict Wolman and John Whitelock) in April 1416, outlining the Ricardian case and calling for the disendowment of the religious orders, while Wolman's own career of agitation was finally brought to a close when together with an accomplice, John Beckering, he was found guilty of treason in September 1416. His crime was to have petitioned Sigismund to depose the reigning king by force of arms and to restore Richard to his rightful throne.[34] Undeterred, Henry Talbot was active once more in the early months of 1417, seeking to recruit a force to support Richard's return among the villagers of Yorkshire and Northumberland, while in the same year the Ricardian claim received its last and most public affirmation when the Lollard leader, Sir John

Oldcastle, refused to recognize the authority of parliament to pass judgement on him on the grounds that his liege lord, King Richard, was still alive.[35]

Oldcastle's is the last surviving declaration of belief in the reality of the Scottish claims on behalf of their client, and after his execution the Ricardian rumour swiftly receded, its demise further hastened by the incontestable death of the man the English knew as Thomas Warde in December 1419.[36] Henry V had still been apprehensive earlier that year that the alleged Richard might be used as the figurehead for a Scottish-led attempt to free the duke of Orleans from his captivity at Pontefract, while the government's anxieties remained well enough known for a group of forgers to pick on a Scottish raid into England in the name of King Richard as a plausible subject for a fabricated inquisition.[37] Yet the death of the Scottish Richard was certainly known in London by September 1420, when a fishmonger, Thomas Cobbold, was arrested in the City on suspicion of his sympathy with the Ricardian claims. Questioned by the mayor, Cobbold admitted that he had recently been in Scotland and said that Thomas Warde was known there as King Richard. He added that whoever Warde was, he had died before Cobbold left again for England. Cobbold's own sympathies, and his motive for travelling to Scotland in the first place, remain unclear, since he refused the mayor's invitation to deny the statement that the Scottish claimant was indeed King Richard. Given his association with suspected Lollards, Cobbold's journey may have been an attempt on the part of a group of religious dissidents to re-establish the kind of contact with Albany's regime that Benedict Wolman, himself a possessor of suspect books, and his associates in the Westminster sanctuary had cultivated a decade earlier in order to keep the Ricardian rumour alive.[38]

Considered chronologically, and in all its manifestations, the Ricardian rumour appears to consist of two virtually separate episodes. In the first, running from 1402 to 1406, the rumour drew strength from a constituency that was both geographically and socially diverse, appearing simultaneously in several areas of the country and appealing to a spectrum of support broad enough to encompass the countess of Oxford, the learned theologian Roger Frisby and John Sparrowhawk, 'wandering man of Wales'.[39] In the second phase, clearly identifiable by 1407, the rumour was confined to London, and even within the capital it was only reported in and around the Westminster sanctuary. Those unquestionably associated with the dissemination of the rumour in this second phase were relatively few in number, repeatedly indicted for the same set of offences, and drawn from a fairly uniform social background in which the common denominator was past service in the royal household. Besides Henry Porter 'of the king's household', the most prominent members of this group were Simon Warde, an esquire of Richard II's household before he entered the service of the de Vere family; John Whitelock, 'groom and afterwards yeoman with King Richard throughout thirty winters' (though he had initially been happy enough to serve Henry IV in the same capacity); and Benedict Wolman, described in one indictment as 'late undermarshal of the marshalsea of the household', and certainly trusted enough at one time to be among the party chosen to accompany Henry IV's new queen, Joan of Navarre, to England in November 1402.[40] Whereas the rumour in its early stages was generalized and protean in content, nourished in the fertile ground of prophetic speculation and spread by word of mouth, in the second phase of its life the belief in Richard's continued survival was fixed, even stereotyped, in form, and in need of constant reiteration through the circulation of letters and tokens and by the intermittent encouragement of the Scottish court. Equally, while the overwhelming priority behind the early manifestations of the rumour was perceived to be the restoration of Richard II, with correspondingly little time devoted to canvassing support for alternative claimants, the sanctuary-plotters saw their task as principally the removal of Henry IV. The further elaboration of their plans beyond that simple goal was from the first conditional upon proof of the old king's survival. If he was dead, they were willing to advance the claims of the young Edmund Mortimer, earl of March, in his stead.[41]

In the light of these comparisons, the contrast between the scope and preoccupations of the two phases of the Ricardian rumour seems clear. It has been acutely remarked that '[a]lthough the government of Henry IV had searched for evidence of conspiracy, it seems likely that there was often little more than a coincidence of common purpose and exculpation among those who espoused Richard's cause',[42] and for the period from 1402 to 1406 there is much truth in this contention. Though the activities of William Serle and the acquiescence of the Scottish court in the imposture of Thomas Warde fanned the flames of Ricardian loyalties, a widely disseminated sense of expectation seems to have existed quite independent of their efforts. But after 1406 it seems difficult to deny that conspiracy among a small but homogeneous group of recusants, inspired as much by their dislike of the new king as by their sense of personal loyalty to the old one, was what kept the claims of Richard's survival alive. In discussing the progress and significance of the Ricardian rumour, therefore, a clear distinction between the two phases of its existence needs to be drawn. The first was an important element in the very generalized protests against the rule of Henry IV that marked the early years of his reign; the second was genuinely marginal in terms of its location and social composition, and owed much of its continuing public prominence to its growing association with a Lollard activism that, as a shrill but isolated voice of dissent against a widely held orthodoxy, it came increasingly to resemble. By 1407, certainly by Henry V's reign, political debate had moved on: doubts about the legitimacy of the Lancastrian dynasty no longer focused on the survival of Richard II; while criticism of the king himself was shifting from the fundamental question of his right to rule, towards more specific complaints about the cost and conduct of his wars.[43]

III

This conclusion has some obvious implications for the broader topic of the nature of popular political culture in early Lancastrian England. In seeking to explain the rumour's cultural significance, historians have tended to treat it as one instance of a well-recognized and geographically widespread phenomenon in medieval and early modern Europe: belief in a 'hidden king', the lost ruler who will return – from prison, death or exile – to remedy the wrongs of his oppressed but faithful subjects. England was not the only later medieval monarchy to be troubled by such apparitions: between 1354 and 1360 the Sienese merchant Giannino Baglioni had gained some credence for his claim to be, as the posthumous son of Louis X, the true king of France; Louis the Great, king of Hungary, had been troubled by the appearance in 1357 of a man claiming to be his younger brother, Andrew, murdered a dozen years earlier; Henry IV's own ambassadors kept him informed of the fate of a pretender to the Scandinavian kingdoms who was eventually burned to death by the regent Margaret in 1402.[44] Such lost kings and sleeping heroes characteristically inhabit the gap between legitimation and legitimacy, between the assertion of a claim to rule and the naturalization of dynastic authority. The most recent synthesis on the subject has argued that an insistence on a return to the 'true' line of royal descent was often the only recourse open to the poor and dispossessed, who believed that by restoring the legitimate succession they would inevitably restore a natural and healthy balance within the body politic.[45] Recent interpretations of the false Richard episode have broadly followed this line of argument, seeing it as an indication that the new Lancastrian dynasty had failed to establish an effective monopoly over the symbols and sources of legitimacy, while suggesting that by providing an emblem of justice against which the rule of Henry IV could be measured and found wanting, the figure of the former king offered Henry's political opponents the chance to define themselves within a tradition of loyalist rebellion.[46] Yet if belief in the survival and imminent return of Richard II was in fact widespread only for the space of two or three years, then the relevance of longer-lasting and better-supported pretender episodes, and indeed the general explanatory category of naïve monarchism, to an understanding of the significance of the Ricardian rumour, remains an open question. The interpretative emphasis laid in the analysis of such episodes upon the issue of dynastic legitimacy, may prove in the case of Richard II to be misplaced. A close reading of the available evidence seems to suggest that the rumours of Richard's survival were principally important for providing the medium in which, for reasons of prudence, the groundswell of criticism against the defects of Henry IV's government expressed itself.

My starting point is the extent to which the contents of the Ricardian rumour appear to have departed from the normal expectations surrounding such returning rulers. Two features stand out as especially distinctive. The first is the physical absence of the king. In many of the comparable instances – the pseudo-Baldwin, count of Flanders, who appeared in 1225, or the man known as Dietrich Holzschuh, the most convincing of the several Frederick IIs to appear in the German lands during the 1280s – the pretender's success seems to have depended principally upon his physical resemblance to the king or ruler he claimed to be.[47] Even the brief and fitful rumour that Edward II, Richard's greatgrandfather, had successfully escaped from his captivity threw up an actual claimant, who confronted Edward III in person at Cologne in 1338.[48] The claims of the Ricardian pretender in Scottish custody do not seem to have been strong in this respect. Even some Scottish sources were alarmed by a lack of royal dignity in his manner, describing him as showing little devotion, seldom hearing mass and often behaving like a halfwit or a madman.[49] *A fortiori*, all the rituals of confirmation normally associated with a successful claim to royal status – the display of a distinctive birthmark; the air of natural nobility and unconscious royal grace; the gradual dawning of recognition among the old king's servants and intimates – were conspicuously absent in his case. It is not surprising that his sponsors never allowed him to appear in England to put his claims to the test. This does not mean that the sudden emergence of the report that there was a man in Scotland who claimed to be King Richard was without significance, for it clearly served to crystallize previously inchoate expressions of discontent around a single issue. But the Ricardian rumour, unlike many of its European counterparts, flourished independent of the authenticity of its figurehead. Some of its adherents may, like William Serle, have eventually become disenchanted with the impostor, but in general his physical absence did not hamper the appeal and circulation of the rumour. There were many who shared the opinion of the copyist of the *Dieulacres Chronicle*, who explained that Richard had not appeared in Delamere forest in 1403 'because his time had not yet come', and glossed his continuing absence by an apposite quotation from the *Prophecies of Merlin*.[50]

The second distinctive feature of the Ricardian rumour is that no defined political programme seems ever to have been associated either implicitly or explicitly with the return of the exiled king. This is another contrast with most pretender episodes, where such a programme was either asserted, as in many of the Russian risings in the name of Tsar Dimitri, which usually articulated a variety of popular grievances and proposed some kind of reform programme,[51] or assumed, as in the case of the Emperor Frederick, who would reform the Church and establish in the Last Days a reign of peace and plenty.[52] It is possible that there was an element of chiliastic expectation in some of the beliefs surrounding Richard: John Lancaster said in 1402 that he had seen Richard alive at Berwick, 'and soon we will have a new world'; John Longe and his father looked forward to the former king's return in 1409, 'and then it would be a new world in England'.[53] In general, however, asserting the fact of Richard's continued existence and imminent return was sufficient for his partisans, who saw no reason to elaborate further. One action only was required from those who sought his favour, which was to go to meet him at the appointed time and place. This was usually at Midsummer eve (the vigil of the nativity of St John the Baptist), though the site of his epiphany was less certain: at Atherstone, Northampton, Sandiway or on the plain of Oxford.[54] Later apostles of the Ricardian gospel were forced to acknowledge the fact of the king's continued absence only to the extent of urging their audience to join Richard in Scotland.[55]

These features of the false Richard episode seem to suggest that the focus of the rumour on the person and fate of Richard himself was comparatively rather weak. His physical presence was evidently not essential to the rumour's vitality, his authority was insufficient to validate a programme of reform. In life Richard II had been neither popular nor charismatic enough to serve in his own person as a talisman of good order, and he lacked the allure of youth and piety that would later support the unlikely claims of Perkin Warbeck to the throne of England and make of Sebastian, king of Portugal, so enduring an icon of royalty.[56] It was to his royal status, his ceremonial body, that Richard's partisans appealed, though what they sought was something both less specific and more valuable than a vindication of the general principle of dynastic legitimacy. While the rumour of Richard's survival clearly draws strength from the widespread popular dissatisfaction felt for the rule of Henry IV during the early years of his reign, that discontent was already being cogently and effectively expressed before the first reports that the former king was still alive appeared. The Ricardian rumour formed only one strand in the rich array of complaint and protest that Henry IV was required to address, and its importance was, to that extent, tactical rather than strategic, more significant for enabling protest than for legitimizing it.

It was not always necessary in early Lancastrian England to invoke one king in order to criticize another. Some of Henry IV's new subjects were content with a simple rejection of his claims; during the Epiphany rising (January 1400) the rebels' slogan was simply 'we do not want King Henry to reign over us' ('nolumus regem Henricum regnare super nos').[57] Others were prepared to look beyond the established lines of descent for their sovereign; during the same rebellion the prior of Launceston in Cornwall allegedly promised to give up all his goods 'to see if the earl [of Huntingdon] be made king of England'.[58] Such outright denials of a well-established claim to royal authority were rare, save in moments of open rebellion, but they were underlain by a more general reluctance to recognize the king's overriding authority on particular issues, and this reluctance was, inevitably, fed by Henry's perceived lack of royal charisma. Taking advantage of the confusion of government in August 1399, the townsmen of Frome in Somerset rose against the king's ministers in the town, imprisoned them, and destroyed the town's guildhall, 'publicly saying among themselves that they did not wish any longer to be governed or judged there by the laws of England'. It took a further six months for the disturbances there to die down.[59] Serious rioting broke out in London at Lent 1400, when the apprentice boys 'banded together in their thousands to choose their kings'.[60] Resistance to Henry IV's authority was generally less pointed than this, but it could nevertheless enjoy considerable success. At Shrewsbury, the new king's attempt to resolve a long-running dispute over the government of the town in September 1400 ran counter to the townsmen's sense of their communal rights – in this instance, to congregate together for 'some honest deed', like feasting, wrestling, archery or listening to a lord's letter – with the result that he found himself unable to impose a lasting composition on the burgess factions.[61]

Some of the early resistance to Henry IV's rule sprang, therefore, less from a refusal to recognize his dynastic right, than from a general resentment at the imposition of any form of royal authority upon the communal preference for self-regulation. This was a constant element in the relations between the Crown and the various local communities of the realm, that was given a particular prominence in the aftermath of 1399 by the weakness of Henry of Lancaster's title. The problems this created for the new Lancastrian regime were greatly compounded by a further consequence of the usurpation: Henry's promise to live, as far as possible, 'of his own'.[62] This allowed every subsequent demand for taxation to be portrayed as a breach of the king's faith and sparked off a rash of fiscal protests. The commons of Chester rose in 1400 'on account of a tallage',[63] and in 1401 there were riots against the collection of the aulnage on cloth throughout the south-west: at Dartmouth, Norton St Philip and at Bristol, where the king's aulnager was attacked and wounded and the bells of the city's churches were rung to gather support for further attacks on royal officials.[64] Each of these riots was pacified, but each added to a climate of discontent in which Henry's continued right to the throne came to seem increasingly debatable. In July 1403 a London tailor, John Freston, discussing the rebellion of Henry Percy, allegedly remarked that Hotspur came 'for you and for me, in order to stop the taxes and the tallages', and recalled that when the present king was crowned he had promised to levy no taxes on his people. He was a traitor to King Richard and unworthy to be king.[65]

Popular extra-parliamentary criticism of Henry IV and his government was demonstrably widespread and confident, capable of articulating its grievances effectively and concisely without recourse to the legitimation offered by the memory of a former king. It follows that adherents to the Ricardian survival legend were not simply seeking a vehicle for the expression of their discontents, for popular political culture was already diverse enough to furnish several strategies of protest from which to choose; rather, they were attracted by the particular method and vocabulary of protest it provided. One such attraction of the Ricardian rumour was simply the arcane nature of the intelligence it conveyed, since this conferred on the disseminators of the rumour the status that went with a knowledge of great and secret events.[66] Another was the anonymous nature of the rumour itself, spread as much by the exchange and interpretation of prophecies as by individual assertions of fact and allegiance. This reliance on the medium of prophecy was common to all social levels of dissent: the learned glosses of the educated, who showed 'by prophecy' that Richard II was still alive, and 'by chronicle and prophecy' that he would enjoy his realm once more, had their counterpart in the dogmatic predictions of John Sparrowhawk and his like that 'no collar [of the king's livery] shall be seen within half a year, and we shall have a new king for seven and a half years'.[67] Such prophecies and predictions were a crucial part of the Ricardian rumour's appeal, for they placed a vital distance between their seditious message and the messenger who bore them: they were neutral texts, apt for idiosyncratic elaboration, that furnished a supernatural authority for action while allowing individual exegetes to disclaim direct responsibility for their interpretations. One final advantage attaching to the prophecies of Richard's return was that they could command belief without compelling a decisive commitment. The time for action on the former king's behalf was itself displaced to some future date – 'in brief time'; before Christmas; within the next six months.[68] Most characteristically however, the king's return was predicted for Midsummer eve (23 June, the vigil of St John the Baptist), a customary holiday in town and countryside, when bonfires were lit to mark the turning of the year.[69] Though the commotion that inevitably accompanied these gatherings offered certain practical advantages to prospective insurgents, the ritual connotations of the appointed day – a time of feasting and reconciliation among neighbours – were equally significant. By placing the advent of the king within the context of the communal activity associated with midsummer, the Ricardian rumour maintained about itself a crucial aura of ambivalence, equating the return of the king with the limited and licensed disorders of the 'summer games'.[70]

The broad appeal of the Ricardian rumour during the early years of Henry IV's reign lay as much in what it left unsaid as in what it asserted. It lay somewhere in the middle of the spectrum of political resistance, occupying the ground between silent obstruction of the king's officials and declaration of outright support for his enemies. It was an effective vehicle for the demonstration of discontent that stopped short in the eyes of most people of genuine sedition. The 'shoals of fools' who gathered in Delamere forest in July 1403 to greet the returning king were nevertheless shrewd enough to decline the opportunity to involve themselves in the course of more direct and more dangerous political action offered them by Henry Percy, while the Welshmen who joined him at Lichfield, bearing Richard II's livery badge of the white hart, carried their alibis on their sleeves.[71] It does less than justice to the flexibility and effectiveness of popular protest in later medieval England to take the widely professed belief in the survival of Richard II as evidence that the ideology of hereditary monarchy provided the only idiom in which popular dissent could be expressed, still less to consign beliefs in lost kings and sleeping heroes to a traditionalist universe 'where innovation has to be disguised as a return to the past and where the fact of change is essentially unrecognized'.[72] By invoking the former king, popular criticism of Henry IV made use of the figure of Richard II to evolve a cogent rationale of protest that, by its association with prophecy and festive ritual, remained sufficiently unspecific in its claims to offer a reasonable prospect of minimizing the consequences of failure.

The sophistication of popular political attitudes is equally evident in the details, as well as the overall object, of the beliefs surrounding the survival of Richard II. One view of the episode, favoured by Henry IV and his advisers, and subsequently adopted by some historians, sees its origin in a form of black propaganda originating at the Scottish court in 1402 and deliberately disseminated with the intention of destabilizing the new Lancastrian dynasty.[73] The chief agents of this dissemination in the initial phase of the rumour were a group of highly educated publicists, the mendicant friars. The sanctuary-conspirators who succeeded them continued to employ the characteristic techniques of literate culture by circulating letters and posting handbills in order to advertise their message of dissent. In this perspective, the whole episode seems to provide a clear-cut instance of the concerns and agendas of elite culture imposing themselves upon and giving shape to the previously inchoate grievances of popular politics. Moreover, they did so in a form that while disputing the *locus* of dynastic legitimacy, nevertheless reaffirmed the right of those bearing legitimate authority to rule. Yet popular political culture seems often to have been significantly less dependent on the motifs of elite discourse, and more creative in its reaction to them, than this view would imply.[74] Different elements in the cluster of beliefs that gathered around the figure of Richard II appealed to significantly different constituencies. Many of the friars involved in the 1402 agitation do seem to have been genuinely exercised by the issue of legitimacy: Fr John Lakenheath told an audience at Thetford in Norfolk that if he were a secular man he would prove with his body that King Henry was not the rightful king of England, while a friar of the Aylesbury convent, confronted by the king himself, told Henry that he did not wish him any harm, only to see him as duke of Lancaster again.[75] Among the sanctuary-conspirators, concern on this score mingled with a deep-seated distrust of the motives of all those in authority: by 1416 Benedict Wolman was seeking to advertise the scandal of collusion between the *de facto* rulers of England and Scotland that was depriving both realms of their rightful kings, alleging that the duke of Albany would not allow King Richard to regain his inheritance as long as James I was safely held in English custody.[76] Yet the audience to which these appeals and protests were addressed treated the dynastic issue as only one element in a more extended critique of Lancastrian government. This took a variety of forms, each allegation drawing on a diverse pool of grievances and each calculated to exploit a particular weakness in Lancastrian claims: the simple assertion that Henry IV was not a 'loyal king'; that he was the son of a butcher's son and so not worthy of the throne; that Henry had not been elected and chosen by the estates of the realm, but only by the rabble (*villanos*) of the City of London; that he was gathering up the resources of the kingdom by his taxation before fleeing overseas to Brittany; even that he was ruled by diabolic advice.[77] Such opinions themselves indicate the range and retentiveness of popular political debate: the claim that the king's father, John of Gaunt, was a Flemish changeling had first surfaced in his confrontation with the City of London in 1376–7, while the view of Henry IV as the Londoners' king owed something to contemporary French propaganda against the new dynasty. Henry's attendant devil may recall the anti-papal polemic of Philip the Fair and his publicists, but it had a more immediate analogue in the 'prophecy of the White Hermit', which predicted that the king would be succeeded by a devil.[78]

The charge of diabolic possession, a mirror-image of the accusations of sorcery the Lancastrian regime sought to make against Owain Glyn Dŵr,[79] is a good instance of the skill with which critics of Henry's rule adapted the idiom of public political discourse for their own purposes. In claiming that the duke of Lancaster, 'who calls himself king of England', was only the provost and bailiff of King Richard and would soon be required to render account to him and the kingdom, Nicholas Louthe, hanged in 1402, was neatly turning against its proponent the claim to exercise authority as steward of England that had served as an important initial justification of Henry's invasion.[80] Equally, the rumour that Richard II was alive and dwelling 'in a castle of the duke of Rothesay called Albion', reported by the author of the *Continuatio Eulogii*, immediately placed the former king within the context of the national foundation myth, where the land of Albion represented the pre-contractual state of nature, invaded, conquered and ultimately reduced to order by the Trojan Brutus, from whom all kings of England subsequently traced their descent.[81] It was a reminder to Henry, hailed by his supporters as 'conqueror of Brutes Albyon', that the issues of justice and legitimacy his actions had raised could not simply be neutralized by their transposition to legendary history.[82] At the same time, the report characteristically attributed to Richard's survival a significance that went beyond a simple rebuke to the new royal regime, in order to invoke a broader and more prophetic vision of the future. Richard's return from such a location sometimes came to assume an ominous and threatening character, representing less a guarantee of good government than an earnest of the dissolution of all effective authority. As one Ricardian supporter told the husbandmen of Essex, there was no longer any need to bother ploughing and sowing their fields, for the former king would return by midsummer with a multitude of foreigners, and no Englishman would occupy his own lands thereafter.[83]

The complex nature of the beliefs that clustered around the figure of the absent Richard II appears consistent with the rest of the evidence that can be recovered for the nature of popular political debate in later medieval England. Where the records allow a sufficiently detailed view of the tactics of popular protest, it seems that the vocabulary of ritual gesture and defiance, familiar from the better-documented early modern period, was already in place. Female participation in tax and food riots, intended to emphasize the damaging domestic effects of royal fiscal demands, was a feature of the Bristol disturbances in 1401. Adam of Usk's comment on the incident, that 'the wives, acting the part of their husbands, gave the tax-collectors a similar beating, giving and receiving wounds', seems intended to set it within the context of the widespread Hocktide rituals of role reversal, when married women claimed for a day temporary possession of the customary male monopoly of violence.[84] At Bishop's Lynn, it was the townsmen's attempt to implement their version of a 'moral economy' that caused disorder in October 1405: a section of the *mediocres* paraded through the town with trumpets blowing before them, in order to enforce their demand that the grain on board a ship bound for Bordeaux be sold to them instead, at 5*d* a bushel. Offered the grain at 6*d* a bushel by the mayor – which was the price the shippers expected to get in Bordeaux – the rioters refused, 'violently saying that they wished to choose a new government', and threatening to assault anyone bearing royal letters patent for the delivery of the cargo.[85]

Such evidence suggests that it would be inappropriate to draw too sharp a distinction between the attitudes and concerns of governors and governed in later medieval England. The false Richard episode indicates, rather, that political criticism and debate was generally articulated through a common stock of beliefs and attitudes, albeit one appropriated and interpreted according to individual circumstances and predilections. It was as much a part of the widespread pattern of resistance to the initial imposition of Lancastrian authority as the fiscal riots that disturbed the south-west and the sporadic aristocratic support for the claims of Edmund Mortimer, earl of March, to be the true heir of the former king. The conventional differentiation of this resistance as expressions of either popular or baronial concerns, couched in terms of fiscal or dynastic protest, obscures both the unity and the complexity of English political culture. Just as those who protested at Henry's broken promises with regard to taxation were contesting the *demands* of the new regime, so the proponents of the Ricardian rumour were contesting its *claims*. Just as the occasional violent resistance to Henry's tax-gatherers expressed a more continuous and widespread resentment, so the expression of adherence to a lost King Richard spoke of a general unease at the means and claims by which Henry of Lancaster had secured his throne. It was a protest against the 'symbolic taxation' that was exacted through demonstrations of public acquiescence to Henry's authority, as dangerous in its way as the refusal to meet the actual fiscal demands of a Crown threatened by the rebellions of Henry Percy in 1403 and of Richard Scrope in 1405. The metaphorical connection between the two forms of resistance had been articulated as early as 1401, when Geoffrey Taylor predicted that the kingdom would be suddenly changed within two years, 'as a tally in the Exchequer is changed'.[86]

It follows from this that the Ricardian rumour should not be judged solely by its failure to achieve its stated objective, the restoration of Richard II, or even by its inability to assemble a critical mass of support for this end. It was not an ineffective attempt at rebellion, a popular movement that repeatedly sought and failed to imitate more impressive baronial initiatives. Rather, it was a protest against the exactions of royal government that provided, in the figure of Richard, both an effective symbolic justification for acts of resistance and insubordination, and a prophylactic against the more drastic consequences of failure. The myth of the returning king issued an open invitation to resist the agents and demands of the *de facto* ruler in the name of his legitimate predecessor, while keeping open an obvious avenue of retreat. If belief in Richard's continued existence could be shown to be unfounded, as the Lancastrian authorities were repeatedly anxious to demonstrate it was, then actions taken in his name could be disowned as acts of mistaken good faith. It was a comforting formula, as attractive to Henry's regime in its assurance that discontent rested on an irrational and erroneous premise, as it was to those dissidents who could use it to portray themselves as overzealous supporters of monarchical legitimacy, faithful subjects who had loved not wisely but too well.

IV

It is this double quality to the Ricardian rumour, at once protest and excuse, that explains some of the apparent contradictions in the Lancastrian government's response to it. A brief survey of the measures taken by Henry IV and his advisers to counteract the rumour may serve to confirm the force of the argument offered above. Their most instructive feature is the contrast between the speed with which Henry and his advisers elaborated an effective symbolic strategy against the claims of the Ricardian dissidents, and the casual inconsistency that attended its administrative enforcement. Central to this strategy was the well-recognized technique of associating sedition with heresy and allowing each to stigmatize the other, consummated by the inclusion of a provision in the statute against the Lollards passed in 1406 for the punishment of 'evil men and women', who 'as far as they are able, publicly and falsely spread abroad among the people of England, by false oaths and signs, that Richard, formerly king of England . . . is still alive'.[87] In addition, the abject figure of Thomas Warde was seized on for further marginalization and caricature. To the English government, he was a fool, an idol to be worshipped by the misguided, a nullity.[88] None of these epithets was randomly chosen. *Ydolum* (and its vernacular equivalent, *mawmet*) depicted the pretender as a pagan deity, worshipped for his oracular powers, and sought to turn to advantage the entanglement of the Ricardian rumour in the luxuriant growth of contemporary prophecy by depicting Warde as the source, not the fulfilment, of such prophecies.[89] His characterization as a fool or madman amplified the suggestion of ritual inversion at which some of the beliefs surrounding the false Richard, such as the location of his return within the festivities of midsummer, already hinted, intimating that he was to be treated no more seriously than a midsummer king, a festive sovereign and licensed fool whose rule was for a day.[90]

In the early years of the rumour this programme of ideological exclusion was ruthlessly enacted. In 1401 William Clerk, a scrivener of Canterbury, had his tongue cut out and his right hand severed for circulating libels about the king; in June 1402 sixteen men were convicted and executed for disseminating rumours of Richard's return; in 1404 William Serle, the architect of much of the early Ricardian agitation, was condemned to suffer 'great number of pains, more severe than other traitors heretofore', in an act of theatrical cruelty designed to provide a cathartic closure to the whole episode of imposture.[91] After this initial bout of rigorous repression, however, the Lancastrian authorities seemingly showed little further concern to bring the remaining Ricardian activists to book. As Henry's grip on royal power tightened, so his attitude towards dissent appears to have grown more tolerant. Between 1404 and 1416, when Benedict Wolman made the mistake of embarrassing

Henry V in front of the Emperor Sigismund, only one man – the Dominican friar, John Alford – was executed for involvement in disseminating the Ricardian rumour, and this was, technically, because he had failed to make good his accusations as an approver.[92] Wolman's own career is instructive in this respect: the pattern of repeated arrest and release that characterizes it suggests that neither public opinion nor the king's justices regarded him as a serious threat to national security.[93] It seems likely that this attitude was extended to the whole body of Ricardian activists. One indication of this lies in the anomalous episode that occurred at Michaelmas 1409, when an unusually comprehensive set of indictments was taken against all known or suspected Ricardians, evidently with the intention of breaking up the cell of conspirators in the Westminster sanctuary. The indictments themselves, however, had been carelessly compiled, omitting such standard details as the names of the jurors and the dates on which the indictments had been taken, and the whole process arising from them was cancelled on the grounds of these irregularities at the parliament of Hilary 1410.[94] The names of those indicted are, all the same, informative. Some had apparently been obtained by trawling the files of past indictments for suspect individuals: the appearance of three Westminster monks, two of them previously indicted during the Minorite agitation, is best explained on these grounds;[95] as is the indictment of Geoffrey, abbot of St John's, Colchester – implicated in the countess of Oxford's rising but dead before September 1405.[96] Others, like the Franciscan astronomer John Somer, were seemingly projected into the group of the accused by their general notoriety.[97] But despite these anomalies, whoever drew up the indictments showed some prescience in identifying Ricardian sympathizers: John Whitelock, Elias Lynet and Henry Talbot, all prominent in the renewed agitation that followed the accession of Henry V, were first publicly identified as suspect individuals on this occasion.[98] Yet there was no attempt made after Hilary 1410 to rectify the shortcomings of the original indictments in order to pursue these individuals further. The whole episode seems to confirm what the details of Benedict Wolman's career suggest: that after 1404 the Lancastrian authorities combined a good knowledge of the identities and actions of the surviving Ricardians with a certain half-heartedness, even leniency, in pursuing them.

Why were Henry IV and his advisers prepared to tolerate the presence of a group of seditious plotters whose continued existence around Westminster was apparently well known to them for so long? Part of the answer lies in the Council's unwillingness to apply the blunt instrument of treasonable words too broadly and in the reluctance of juries to convict on such grounds. The Lancastrian authorities had already encountered considerable difficulty in empanelling a jury to find the Minorite friars guilty in June 1402.[99] But the king and Council's disposition to leniency was based on more than purely practical considerations, for several of the sanctuary-conspirators found no more difficulty than Benedict Wolman in obtaining a royal pardon.[100] Pardon was in itself preferable to punishment as a means of closure. By accepting a pardon the offender acknowledged that a crime had indeed been committed, and recognized the authority of the king to exercise his prerogative of mercy. As the legitimacy of this authority was precisely the issue at question in many of the cases of seditious rumour with which Henry IV and his counsellors had to deal, there was a strong incentive to be merciful in their treatment of all but the most dangerous offenders. Beyond these immediate calculations, however, it seems that the Lancastrian authorities saw the claims of the Ricardians for what they really were, a rhetoric of protest rather than overt statements of political intent, and acted in accordance with that recognition. Though Archbishop Arundel wished to call the dissidents' bluff in 1407, advising that the return of the Scottish-sponsored pretender be made the precondition for any further talks on the release of James I from English captivity,[101] the general aspiration of Henry IV's government was for the containment, not the eradication, of the Ricardian rumour. For both sides there was something to be gained from such an accommodation: the Ricardians retained the freedom to dream their dreams, while their activities allowed the Lancastrian authorities to translate a private obsession into a public threat and to depict any degree of legitimist speculation as offering aid and comfort to the nation's enemies.

Naturally, such a conclusion does not exhaust the significance of the false Richard episode. Like Mario Vargas Llosa's fictional 'short-sighted journalist', sent to cover the supposedly Sebastianist rebellion that broke out at Canudos in the Brazilian backlands in 1896, the historian must confront the likelihood that the familiar concepts of conspiracy and subversion are inadequate to explain something so 'diffuse, timeless and extraordinary'.[102] Although this article has sought to identify and to emphasize the immediate purposes served by belief in Richard II's survival and imminent second coming within the everyday world of political debate, it remains no less the case that much of the appeal of such myths of return lay in their ability to ascribe to the puzzling accidents of contemporary experience a clear metahistorical meaning.[103] For contemporaries, however, there was more than one such meaning. Close examination of the myth of Richard's survival and return suggests that it was less a static body of beliefs than a claim that was subject to constant, and sometimes competing, acts of appropriation and accommodation. Much of the durability of the Ricardian rumour lay in this quality of plasticity. By its ability both to subvert and to affirm the dominant discourse of monarchical authority, the rumour provided a framework within which various shades of political dissent could safely express themselves. It was the practical safeguards the rumour offered to the dissidents who espoused it, by virtue of its protean and inchoate character, that explains its widespread early appeal. To that extent, the apparent weaknesses in content – the physical absence of the king; the lack of a defined programme of political action; the festive undertones – became, by fostering a crucial ambiguity, one of the rumour's greatest strengths: they allowed damaging criticism of Henry IV to be advanced and then, when necessary, disowned. Such safeguards were especially valued during the 'time of troubles' that disturbed the English polity between 1397 and 1406.[104] They became less essential once the political and dynastic situation restabilized. The changes in the content and incidence of the Ricardian rumour consequently allow us to document the evolving process of accommodation between the first Lancastrian king and his new subjects. By 1406 it had largely ceased to articulate a widespread discontent and became instead a vehicle for the irreconcilable grievances of a small but active rump of dissidents.

Placing the rumour within the broader context of popular dissent reveals the continuities between the tactics and claims of the Ricardians and of those who focussed their protests on more specific issues. The study of popular political culture in later medieval England has principally concentrated upon the more abundant evidence thrown up by the rising of 1381, but the course and content of the Ricardian rumour suggest that some of the conclusions emerging from that material, pointing to the existence of a flexible and self-sufficient discourse of protest that allied a confident acquaintance with the dominant notions of hierarchical authority to a creative adaptation of its injunctions, have a more general applicability.[105] Although the slogans of 1381 were largely laid aside, the traditions of resistance and dissent on which that rising had drawn remained strong, fostered by the long-established involvement of village society in the discharge of administrative and judicial responsibilities at the crown's behest. Shared responsibilities bred a broad and relatively inclusive political culture in later medieval England, in which the claims and merits of successive kings and their advisers were widely known and discussed.[106] The Ricardian rumour was part of this common language of politics, adding damaging questions about the legitimacy and mandate of the new sovereign to the complex idiom of protest that Henry IV was compelled to confront. Henry's wary but ultimately indulgent attitude towards all but the most incorrigible of his detractors, even the mercurial John Kingsley,[107] sprang from a realistic recognition that the need to accommodate and allay such criticism now constituted a permanent constraint upon the exercise of royal power.

Notes

1 Public Record Office, London (hereafter PRO), Chancery, Parliamentary and Council Proceedings, C 49/48/6.

2 They were John Payn and William Plumstead. Both men had had their annuities increased by the king at Pontefract, 19 July 1405: Simon Walker, *The Lancastrian Affinity, 1361–1399* (Oxford, 1990), 277, 278; Norfolk Record Office, Norwich (hereafter NRO), NRS 11061 m. 2.

3 J. G. Bellamy, *The Law of Treason in England in the Later Middle Ages* (Cambridge, 1970), 116–23; C. A. F. Meekings, 'Thomas Kerver's Case, 1444', *Eng. Hist. Rev.*, xc (1975), 340–2.

4 'Calendar of Recognizance Rolls of the Palatinate of Chester', in *Thirty-Sixth Report of the Deputy Keeper of Public Records* (London, 1875), 273; *Cal. Pat. Rolls, 1401–5*, 257; PRO, SC 6/1092/18 m. 4. Kingsley's prompt petition for royal confirmation of his Mowbray annuity, granted at Ripon on 9 June 1405, suggests

that he was present in Yorkshire at the time of the rising: PRO, Exchequer, Council and Privy Seal Records, E 28/22/5.

5 *Cal. Pat. Rolls, 1401–5*, 264; *Cal. Close Rolls, 1405–9*, 27.

6 PRO, Palatinate of Chester, Indictment Rolls, CHES 25/10 mm. 34–34d. Kingsley remained one of the most disruptive local figures in Cheshire, his long vendetta against the former king's clerk, John Macclesfield, leading to frequent violence: PRO, CHES 25/11 m. 12; A. E. Curry, 'The Demesne of the County Palatine of Chester in the Early Fifteenth Century' (Univ. of Manchester M.A. thesis, 1977), 223.

7 R. A. Griffiths, 'Some Partisans of Owain Glyndwr at Oxford', *Bull. Board of Celtic Studies*, xx (1964); PRO, King's Bench, Placita Coram Rege, KB 27/566 Rex mm. 5d., 29; King's Bench, Controlment Rolls, KB 29/46 m. 5.

8 PRO, Chancery, Miscellanea, C 260/196/4.

9 PRO, KB 27/571, attornies, m. 2d.; KB 29/47 m. 10d.

10 PRO, KB 29/48 m. 9d.

11 James C. Scott, *Weapons of the Weak: Everyday Forms of Peasant Resistance* (New Haven, 1985), ch. 7; also his *Domination and the Arts of Resistance: Hidden Transcripts* (New Haven, 1990), 17–23, 198–201.

12 Note, for instance, the allegation that Thomas Austin several times said, between October 1384 and May 1385, that things would never be well in England while Richard II was king, or the opinion of Peter Mildenhall that Richard was unable to govern any kingdom and should stay in his privy: A. J. Prescott, 'The Accusations against Thomas Austin', in Paul Strohm, *Hochon's Arrow: The Social Imagination of Fourteenth-Century Texts* (Princeton, 1992), appendix 1; *Cal. Close Rolls, 1389–92*, 527.

13 J. Ambrose Raftis, *Warboys: Two Hundred Years in the Life of an English Medieval Village* (Pontifical Inst. Medieval Studies, Studies and Texts, xxix, Toronto, 1974), 220–1; Marjorie K. McIntosh, *Autonomy and Community: The Royal Manor of Havering, 1200–1500* (Cambridge, 1986), 209–11; Christopher Dyer, 'Small-Town Conflict in the Later Middle Ages: Events at Shipston-on-Stour', *Urban Hist.*, xix (1992), 198–204, 207–10; John B. Gillingham, 'Crisis or Continuity? The Structure of Royal Authority in England, 1369–1422', in Reinhard Schneider (ed.), *Das Spätmittelalterliche Königtum im europaïschen Vergleich* (Sigmaringen, 1987), 59–60.

14 Thomas Amyot, 'An Inquiry Concerning the Death of Richard II', *Archaeologia*, xx (1824); Patrick F. Tytler, 'Historical Remarks on the Death of Richard II', in his *History of Scotland*, 9 vols. (Edinburgh, 1828–43), iii, 325–86; Thomas Amyot, 'A Reply to Mr Tytler's "Historical Remarks on the Death of Richard the Second" ', *Archaeologia*, xxiii (1831); P. W. Dillon, 'Remarks on the Manner of the Death of King Richard II', *Archaeologia*, xxviii (1840); *Rotuli Scaccarii Regum Scotorum: The Exchequer Rolls of Scotland*, ed. George Burnett, 23 vols. (Edinburgh, 1878–1908), iv (1406–36), lxv–lxix; J. H. Wylie, *History of England under Henry IV*, 4 vols. (London, 1884–98), i, 265–80, 416–28. For the recent revival of interest in the topic, see Peter McNiven, 'Rebellion, Sedition and the Legend of Richard II's Survival in the Reigns of Henry IV and Henry V', *Bull. John Rylands Univ. Lib.*, lxxvi (1994); Philip Morgan, 'Henry IV and the Shadow of Richard II', in Rowena E. Archer (ed.), *Crown, Government and People in the Fifteenth Century* (Stroud, 1995); Paul Strohm, 'The Trouble with Richard: The Reburial of Richard II and Lancastrian Symbolic Strategy', *Speculum*, lxxi (1996); reprinted, with additions,

in his *England's Empty Throne: Usurpation and the Language of Legitimation, 1399–1422* (New Haven, 1998), ch. 4.

15 The parliamentary Commons were already exercised by the danger of false appeals by approvers in 1402 and a statute limiting their scope was passed in 1404: *Rotuli Parliamentorum*, 6 vols. (London, 1783), iii, 511, 539; *Statutes of the Realm*, 11 vols. (London, 1810–28), ii, 144. On the general issue of approvers, see F. C. Hamil, 'The King's Approvers', *Speculum*, xi (1936); R. F. Hunnisett, *The Medieval Coroner* (Cambridge, 1961), 69–74.

16 PRO, KB 27/582 Rex m. 3d. He was acquitted of all charges against him by a jury. The appearance of another accusation of treason at the same sessions, against Richard Bird, for allegedly carrying letters of Lord Bardolf and the earl of Northumberland and 'imagining . . . and counselling in what manner the said King Henry could be destroyed', certainly suggests that the passage of the royal household through Northamptonshire had prompted an outbreak of local score-settling in the court of the verge: PRO, KB 27/584 Rex m. 9; KB 29/48 m. 10d. W. R. Jones, 'The Court of the Verge: The Jurisdiction of the Steward and Marshal of the Household in Later Medieval England', *Jl Brit. Studies*, x (1970–1). For 'community' use of legal procedure against disruptive social elements, see Thomas A. Green, *Verdict According to Conscience: Perspectives on the English Criminal Trial Jury, 1200–1800* (Chicago, 1985), 53–9; Bernard William McLane, 'Juror Attitudes toward Local Disorder: The Evidence of the 1328 Lincolnshire Trailbaston Proceedings', in J. S. Cockburn and Thomas A. Green (eds.), *Twelve Good Men and True: The Criminal Trial Jury in England, 1200–1800* (Princeton, 1988), esp. 47–9; Edward Powell, 'Jury Trial at Gaol Delivery in the Late Middle Ages: The Midland Circuit, 1400–29', *ibid.*, esp. 101–4.

17 PRO, KB 27/566 Rex m. 5d.; A. B. Emden, *A Biographical Register of the University of Oxford to 1500*, 3 vols. (Oxford, 1957), i, 431.

18 For instance, William Ashbourne, accused at Bishop's Lynn of calling the king a false traitor, was clerk of the bishop of Norwich's courts in the town. The allegation of treasonable words was contemporary with another against him in King's Bench, concerning his enforcement of the bishop's unpopular commercial privileges, and both were made at a time of particular tension between the bishop and the burgess community. PRO, C 260/196/4; KB 27/565 Rex m. 1; *William Asshebourne's Book*, ed. Dorothy M. Owen (Norfolk Record Soc., xlviii, Norwich, 1981), 60–2.

19 H. J. Röhrkasten, 'Some Problems of the Evidence of Fourteenth-Century Approvers', *Jl Legal Hist.*, v (1984); J. B. Post, 'The Evidential Value of Approvers' Appeals: The Case of William Rose, 1389', *Law and Hist. Rev.*, iii (1985). Cf. the sudden efflorescence of reports of seditious speech against Henry VI after 1444: Bertram Wolffe, *Henry VI* (London, 1981), 16–18; I. M. W. Harvey, *Jack Cade's Rebellion of 1450* (Oxford, 1991), 31–2.

20 S. P. Pistono, 'Henry IV and Charles VI: The Confirmation of the Twenty Eight Year Truce', *Jl Medieval Hist.*, iii (1977), 357–60; J. J. N. Palmer, 'The Authorship, Date and Historical Value of the French Chronicles of the Lancastrian Revolution', *Bull. John Rylands Lib.*, lxi (1978–9), 153–4.

21 *Eulogium Historiarum sive Temporis*, ed. F. S. Haydon, 3 vols. (Rolls Ser., London, 1858), iii, 389–94, is the fullest account, probably compiled before the end of Henry IV's reign; S. N. Clifford, 'An Edition of the Continuation of the *Eulogium Historiarum*, 1361–1413' (Univ. of Leeds M.Phil. thesis, 1975), 29–38. The episode

is further discussed in D. W. Whitfield, 'Conflicts of Personality and Principle: The Political and Religious Crisis in the English Franciscan Province, 1400–1409', *Franciscan Studies*, xvii (1957); R. L. Storey, 'Clergy and Common Law in the Reign of Henry IV', in R. F. Hunnisett and J. B. Post (eds.), *Medieval Legal Records* (London, 1978), 353–61.

22 *Cal. Close Rolls, 1399–1401*, 548; PRO, CHES 25/10 m. 10d.; Special Collections, Ancient Petitions, SC 8/119/5945; *Cal. Pat. Rolls, 1401–5*, 125; *Select Cases in the Court of King's Bench*, vii, *Richard II, Henry IV and Henry V*, ed. G. O. Sayles (Selden Soc., lxviii, London, 1971), 126–8; PRO, KB 29/45 m. 29. The strength of the rumour in the north-west is further confirmed by the choice of Lancaster as the place of execution for one of the Minorite friars convicted of treason in 1402: *Incerti Scriptoris Chronicon Angliae*, ed. J. A. Giles (London, 1848), 28.

23 *Original Letters Illustrative of English History*, 2nd ser., ed. Henry Ellis, 4 vols. (London, 1827), i, 24.

24 'Chronicle of Dieulacres Abbey, 1381–1403', in M. V. Clarke and V. H. Galbraith, 'The Deposition of Richard II', *Bull. John Rylands Lib.*, xiv (1930), 177–8; PRO, Exchequer, King's Remembrancer, Miscellanea, E 163/6/28 m. 8.

25 *Eulogium Historiarum*, ed. Haydon, iii, 400; *Select Cases*, ed. Sayles, vii, 151–5; Morgan, 'Henry IV and the Shadow of Richard II', 19–22, discusses this conspiracy in greater detail.

26 PRO, E 163/6/28 m. 16.

27 PRO, KB 27/579 Rex m. 2. The Council took a close interest in this case, sending a serjeant at arms into Hampshire to bring two of the Dominicans implicated in the affair to London: PRO, Exchequer, Issue Rolls, E 403/585 (3 Feb. 1406).

28 *Eulogium Historiarum*, ed. Haydon, iii, 402–3; Thomas Walsingham, *Historia Anglicana*, ed. H. T. Riley, 2 vols. (Rolls Ser., London, 1863–4), ii, 263–4. For a contrasting judgement: *Duo Rerum Anglicarum Scriptores Veteres*, ed. Thomas Hearne, 2 vols. (Oxford, 1732), i, 49.

29 PRO, King's Bench, Ancient Indictments, KB 9/196/1 m. 13; KB 27/593 Rex m. 13d; *The St Albans Chronicle, 1406–20*, ed. V. H. Galbraith (Oxford, 1937), 11. Thomas Warde, 'who pretends to be King Richard', was first publicly identified as the royal impostor by the Lancastrian authorities in January 1404. The messuage and eight acres of land he inherited from his mother at Trumpington (Cambs.) were subsequently taken into the king's hands on account of his treason: *Rot. Parl.*, iii, 544; *Cal. Close Rolls, 1402–5*, 363–4; PRO, Special Collections, Ministers Accounts, SC 6/770/6 m. 2.

30 PRO, KB 27/595 Rex m. 11d. (Denton); KB 29/50 m. 13 (Huchon); Justices Itinerant, Assize Rolls, JUST 1/554 m. 8 (Goodlak); KB 9/198 m. 28, KB 27/595 Rex m. 8 (Longe).

31 PRO, JUST 1/554 mm. 6–8; KB 27/594 Rex mm. 17, 21, 23; KB 29/50 mm. 7d., 8d. The quotation is from PRO, JUST 1/554 m. 8. On the extent and character of the sanctuary at Westminster, see I. D. Thornley, 'Sanctuary in Medieval London', *Jl Brit. Archaeol. Assoc.*, new ser., xxxviii (1932), 299–308; Gervase Rosser, *Medieval Westminster, 1200–1540* (Oxford, 1989), 155–8, 217–21.

32 PRO, KB 9/203 mm. 1–4; *Select Cases*, ed. Sayles, vii, 213–14; PRO, JUST 1/554 m. 8.

33 *Select Cases*, ed. Sayles, vii, 236–7; T. B. Pugh, *Henry V and the Southampton Plot of 1415* (Southampton Records Ser., xxx, Southampton, 1988), appendix 2.

34 PRO, KB 27/624 Rex m. 9; Anne Hudson, *The Premature Reformation: Wycliffite Texts and Lollard History* (Oxford, 1988), 88–91; Corporation of London Record Office, London (hereafter CLRO), Letter Book I, fos. 180–1. By 1416 Thomas Lucas was practising as a common lawyer, while John Beckering was a cadet of a well-established Nottinghamshire family, the Beckerings of Tuxford: Maureen Jurkowski, 'Heresy and Factionalism at Merton College in the Early Fifteenth Century', *Jl Eccles. Hist.*, xlviii (1997), 673–81; S. J. Payling, *Political Society in Lancastrian England: The Greater Gentry of Nottinghamshire* (Oxford, 1991), 43.

35 *Select Cases*, ed. Sayles, vii, 237–9; *St Albans Chronicle*, ed. Galbraith, 116–17.

36 Walter Bower, *Scotichronicon*, 9 vols., ed. D. E. R. Watt (Aberdeen, 1987–), viii, 28–9, 114–15.

37 *Original Letters Illustrative of English History*, 1st ser., ed. Henry Ellis, 3 vols. (London, 1825), i, 2; *Select Cases*, ed. Sayles, vii, 248–53.

38 PRO, KB 27/646 Rex m. 22; KB 29/56 m. 4d.; CLRO, City Journal 1, fo. 83[v]. For Wolman's possession of a psalter glossed in English, see Maureen Jurkowski, 'New Light on John Purvey', *Eng. Hist. Rev.*, cx (1995), 1188.

39 A. B. Emden, *A Biographical Register of the University of Cambridge to 1500* (Cambridge, 1963), 244–5, for Frisby's career; the description of Sparrowhawk is at PRO, KB 9/189 m. 27.

40 PRO, JUST 1/554 m. 8 (Porter); Exchequer, Accounts Various, E 101/403/10 fo. 44; E 163/6/28 m. 2 (Warde); *Select Cases*, ed. Sayles, vii, 213; PRO, E 101/403/10 fo. 45, 404/21 fo. 45[v] (Whitelock); CLRO, Letter Book I, fo. 180[v]; PRO, C 76/87 m. 27 (Wolman). The sanctuary-plotters thus conform quite closely to the characterization of a criminal association as 'not . . . a band, but . . . a group, united by ties of acquaintanceship that were extensive but quite loose, and by ties of collaboration that were stronger, but limited to certain people': Bronislaw Geremek, *The Margins of Society in Late Medieval Paris* (Cambridge, 1987), 123.

41 PRO, KB 9/196/1 m. 13; KB 27/593 Rex m. 13d.

42 Morgan, 'Henry IV and the Shadow of Richard II', 22.

43 For instance, the alleged opinions of Richard Burton, canon of Wells, accused in October 1415 of offering to spend £6,000 of his own goods to help depose Henry V, because he was not the rightful king of England ('non est justus Rex Angliae'), and of Henry Glomyng of Southwark, committed to the Fleet in October 1418 for suggesting that Henry was dependent on the support of the duke of Burgundy for his success in France: PRO, KB 9/208 m. 97; Exchequer, Parliamentary and Council Proceedings, E 175/3/21 m. 2.

44 L. Bréhaut, 'Giannino Baglioni, roi de France', *Revue contemporaine*, 2nd ser., xvii (1860), 8–14, 257–8; M. de Ferdinandy, 'Ludwig I von Ungarn', in S. B. Vardy, Giza Grosschmid and Leslie S. Domonkos (eds.), *Louis the Great, King of Hungary and Poland* (New York, 1986), 7–12; *Royal and Historical Letters during the Reign of Henry IV*, ed. F. C. Hingeston, 2 vols. (Rolls Ser., London, 1860–1965), i, 117.

45 Yves-Marie Bercé, *Le Roi Caché: sauveurs et imposteurs: mythes politiques populaires dans l'Europe moderne* (Paris, 1990). Beside the studies of particular episodes cited below, the phenomenon is given general consideration in Keith Thomas, *Religion and the Decline of Magic* (London, 1971), 493–501; Peter Burke, *Popular Culture in Early Modern Europe* (London, 1975), 150–5; Maureen Perrie, *Pretenders and Popular Monarchism in Early Modern Russia: The False Tsars of the Time of Troubles* (Cambridge, 1995), 239–50; Adam Fox, 'Rumour, News and Popular Political Opinion in Elizabethan and Early Stuart England', *Hist. Jl*, xl (1997), 614–16.

46 Strohm, 'The Trouble with Richard', 90, 103; Morgan, 'Henry IV and the Shadow of Richard II', 11.

47 R. L. Wolff, 'Baldwin of Flanders and Hainault, First Latin Emperor of Constantinople: His Life, Death and Resurrection, 1172–1225', *Speculum*, xxvii (1952), 294–301; Tilman Struve, 'Utopie und gesellschaftliche Wirklichkeit: Zur Bedeutung des Friedenkaisers im späten Mittelater', *Historische Zeitschrift*, ccxxv (1977); Tilman Struve, 'Die falschen Friedriche und die Friedenssehnsucht des Volkes im späten Mittelalter', in *Fälschungen im Mittelalter*, 6 vols. (Monumenta Germaniae Historica, Schriften, xxxiii, Hanover, 1988–90), i.

48 *The Wardrobe Book of William de Norwell, 12 July 1338 to 27 May 1340*, ed. Mary Lyon, Bryce Lyon and Henry S. Lucas (Brussels, 1983), 212–13; G. P. Cuttino and T. W. Lyman, 'Where is Edward II?', *Speculum*, liii (1972). Henry III had been similarly confronted in September 1238 by a man claiming to bear 'the mark of royalty upon his shoulder', who demanded that Henry resign the kingdom he had so long usurped and now unjustly detained: Matthew Paris, *Chronica Majora*, ed. H. R. Luard, 7 vols. (Rolls Ser., London, 1872–83), iii, 497.

49 *The Original Chronicle of Andrew of Wyntoun*, ed. F. J. Amours, 6 vols. (Scot. Text Soc., lvii, 1908), vi, 390–1; Bower, *Scotichronicon*, viii, 66–7, also notes that 'King Richard' would not be persuaded to grant an interview to Henry Percy, earl of Northumberland, after he fled to Scotland in 1405.

50 Walsingham, *Historia Anglicana*, ii, 264; 'Chronicle of Dieulacres Abbey', 177–8.

51 Perrie, *Pretenders and Popular Monarchism*, 63, 74, 128, 171–2, 190; Philip Longworth, 'The Pretender Phenomenon in Eighteenth-Century Russia', *Past and Present*, no. 66 (Feb. 1975); Daniel Field, *Rebels in the Name of the Tsar* (Boston, 1976, repr. 1989), 1–17.

52 Norman Cohn, *The Pursuit of the Millennium*, revised edn (London, 1970), ch. 6; Marjorie Reeves, *The Influence of Prophecy in the Later Middle Ages* (Oxford, 1969), 306–19.

53 PRO, CHES 25/10 m. 10d.; KB 9/198 m. 28.

54 *Select Cases*, ed. Sayles, vii, 127 (Atherstone), 154; PRO, E 163/6/28 m. 15 (Northampton); 'Chronicle of Dieulacres Abbey', 177 (Sandiway); *Eulogium Historiarum*, ed. Haydon, iii, 391 (plain of Oxford). For the favoured date, St John's eve, see below, n. 69.

55 Fr John Huchon, speaking in November 1404, is the first Ricardian apostle advising this course of action: PRO, KB 27/579 Rex m. 2.

56 James Gairdner, *History of the Life and Reign of Richard III*, revised edn (Cambridge, 1898), 263–335; S. B. Chrimes, *Henry VII* (London, 1972), 81–92; Mary Elizabeth Brooks, *A King for Portugal: The Madrigal Conspiracy, 1594–95* (Madison, 1964), chs. 1–3; Bercé, *Le Roi Caché*, ch. 1.

57 PRO, Exchequer, Court of the Marshalsea, E 37/28 m. 1.

58 *Cal. Inq. Misc., 1399–1422*, no. 101.

59 PRO, KB 9/184/1 m. 14; KB 27/557 Rex m. 19; KB 27/558 Rex mm. 12, 27; KB 29/44 m. 18. Further process in this case is at KB 27/559 Rex m. 19; KB 27/561 Rex m. 2.

60 *The Chronicle of Adam Usk, 1377–1421*, ed. Chris Given-Wilson (Oxford, 1997), 94–6.

61 PRO, KB 9/191 m. 10; KB 27/570 Rex m. 3. For previous disturbances at Shrewsbury, see PRO, KB 9/189 m. 45; KB 27/564 Rex m. 13; KB 29/45 m. 20d. The background to these disputes is summarized in J. S. Roskell, Linda

Clark and Carole Rawcliffe (eds.), *The History of Parliament: The House of Commons, 1386–1421*, 4 vols. (Stroud, 1993), i, 582–3.

62 *Rot. Parl.*, iii, 419; *Concilia Magna Britanniae et Hiberniae*, ed. David Wilkins, 4 vols. (London, 1737), iii, 238.

63 'Chronicle of Dieulacres Abbey', 172; the rising is discussed in Peter McNiven, 'The Cheshire Rising of 1400', *Bull. John Rylands Lib.*, lii (1970).

64 *Chronicle of Adam Usk*, ed. Given-Wilson, 130; *Cal. Pat. Rolls, 1401–5*, 516–17; PRO, KB 27/562 Rex m. 22. Earlier instances of regional resistance to the collection of the aulnage suggest that these riots were expressing long-standing grievances: Maryanne Kowaleski, *Local Markets and Regional Trade in Medieval Exeter* (Cambridge, 1995), 23.

65 PRO, KB 27/593 Rex m. 18.

66 An attraction embodied most clearly in the person of William Blithe, whose attempts to pass himself off as a knight were immediately discounted by his listeners, despite his 'grete gylde girdil', yet came to be accounted 'a perilouse man' by virtue of his knowledge of King Richard's fate: PRO, E 163/6/28 mm. 12, 15.

67 Storey, 'Clergy and Common Law', 358–9; PRO, KB 9/189 m. 27. Sparrowhawk's prediction about a new king was omitted from the King's Bench enrolment.

68 PRO, KB 9/198 m. 28; KB 27/594 Rex m. 17; KB 27/595 Rex m. 11d.

69 Storey, 'Clergy and Common Law', 360; *Select Cases*, ed. Sayles, vii, 127, 153; *Eulogium Historiarum*, ed. Haydon, iii, 391; PRO, E 163/6/28 m. 13. The king and his advisers recognized the significance of the date for Ricardian sympathizers, choosing to display the severed head of Master Roger Frisby to the assembled University of Oxford on Midsummer eve: *Eulogium Historiarum*, ed. Haydon, iii, 394. For the frequent coincidence of popular risings and festivals of the church, see Thomas Pettit, ' "Here Comes I, Jack Straw": English Folk Drama and Social Revolt', *Folklore*, xcv (1984); Margaret Aston, 'Corpus Christi and Corpus Regni: Heresy and the Peasants' Revolt', *Past and Present*, no. 143 (May 1994), 10–12.

70 G. C. Homans, *English Villagers of the Thirteenth Century* (London, 1941), 369–70; P. D. A. Harvey, *A Medieval Oxfordshire Village: Cuxham, 1240 to 1400* (Oxford, 1965), 148; Charles Phythian-Adams, 'Ceremony and the Citizen: The Communal Year at Coventry', in Peter Clark and Paul Slack (eds.), *Crisis and Order in English Towns, 1500–1700: Essays in Urban History* (London, 1972), 65–6; Ronald Hutton, *The Rise and Fall of Merry England: The Ritual Year, 1400–1700* (Oxford, 1994), 37–40.

71 'Chronicle of Dieulacres Abbey', 178; *Eulogium Historiarum*, ed. Haydon, iii, 396.

72 Burke, *Popular Culture in Early Modern Europe*, 170–5; Thomas, *Religion and the Decline of Magic*, 507; F. Graus, 'Social Utopias in the Middle Ages', *Past and Present*, no. 38 (Dec. 1967), 14–17.

73 Storey, 'Clergy and Common Law', 360; *Eulogium Historiarum*, ed. Haydon, iii, 403; Alexander Grant, *Independence and Nationhood: Scotland, 1306–1469* (London, 1984), 44.

74 E. H. Kantorowicz, 'Zu den Rechtsgrundlagen der Kaisersage', in his *Selected Studies* (Locust Valley, NY, 1965); Burke, *Popular Culture in Early Modern Europe*, ch. 2; Robert Muchembled, *Culture populaire et culture des élites dans la France moderne (XVe–XVIIIe siècles)* (Paris, 1978), 11–13; Roger Chartier, 'Culture as Appropriation: Popular Cultural Uses in Early Modern France', in Steven L. Kaplan (ed.), *Understanding Popular Culture: Europe from the Middle Ages to the Nineteenth*

Century (Berlin, 1984); Aaron Gurevich, *Medieval Popular Culture: Problems of Belief and Perception* (Cambridge, 1988), 221–4.

75 PRO, C 260/196/4; *Eulogium Historiarum*, ed. Haydon, iii, 390. On examination, Lakenheath expressed several equally suspect opinions, including the view that though King Richard was said to be dead he would arise again, but he was subsequently pardoned: PRO, KB 9/190 m. 36; *Cal. Close Rolls, 1399–1402*, 529.

76 CLRO, Letter Book I, fo. 180^{v}.

77 PRO, KB 29/47 m. 10d; KB 27/595 Rex m. 13; E 163/6/28 m. 6; *Select Cases*, ed. Sayles, vii, 127; PRO, KB 29/48 m. 9d.

78 *The Anonimalle Chronicle, 1333–1381*, ed. V. H. Galbraith (Manchester, 1927), 104–5; *Chronicon Angliae*, ed. E. M. Thompson (Rolls Ser., London, 1874), 107, 398; Jean Creton, 'Metrical History of the Deposition of King Richard the Second', ed. John Webb, *Archaeologia*, xx (1824), 231–2; *Chronique de la traison et mort de Richart Deux roy Dengleterre*, ed. Benjamin Williams (London, 1846), 212–15; *Documents relatifs aux états généraux et assemblées réunis sous Philippe le Bel*, ed. Georges Picot (Paris, 1901), 36–45; Bower, *Scotichronicon*, viii, 28–9.

79 *Johannis de Trokelowe . . . Chronica et Annales*, ed. H. T. Riley (Rolls Ser., London, 1866), 343; 'Chronicle of Dieulacres Abbey', 176; R. R. Davies, *The Revolt of Owain Glyn Dwr* (Oxford, 1995), 334–6.

80 Storey, 'Clergy and Common Law', 358; J. W. Sherborne, 'Perjury and the Lancastrian Revolution of 1399', *Welsh Hist. Rev.*, xiv (1988–9), 221–3, 231–4.

81 *Eulogium Historiarum*, ed. Haydon, iii, 401; *The Historia Regum Britannie of Geoffrey of Monmouth, i, Bern, Bürgerbibliothek, MS. 568*, ed. Neil Wright (Cambridge, 1985), 13–15; R. W. Hanning, *The Vision of History in Early Britain: From Gildas to Geoffrey of Monmouth* (New York, 1966), 156–60.

82 *The Complete Works of Geoffrey Chaucer*, ed. F. N. Robinson, 2nd edn (Oxford, 1974), 539–40; Paul Strohm, 'Saving the Appearances: Chaucer's Purse and the Fabrication of the Lancastrian Claim', in Barbara A. Hanawalt (ed.), *Chaucer's England: Literature in Historical Context* (Minneapolis, 1992).

83 PRO, E 163/6/28 m. 13; Robert E. Lerner, *The Powers of Prophecy: The Cedar of Lebanon Vision from the Mongol Onslaught to the Dawn of the Enlightenment* (Berkeley, 1988), 192–4, for the place of such predictions within the 'deep structure' of medieval prophecy.

84 *Chronicle of Adam Usk*, ed. Given-Wilson, 130; E. P. Thompson, *Customs in Common* (London, 1991), 305–36; Charles Phythian-Adams, *Desolation of a City: Coventry and the Urban Crisis of the Late Middle Ages* (Cambridge, 1979), 90–1. Adam's statement is confirmed by the overwhelmingly female composition of the indicted rioters: PRO, KB 27/562 Rex m. 1.

85 PRO, KB 27/580 Rex m. 5; KB 27/582 Rex m. 10; KB 27/583 Rex m. 8; E. P. Thompson, 'The Moral Economy of the English Crowd in the Eighteenth Century', *Past and Present*, no. 50 (Feb. 1971). The riot was the culmination of a summer of unrest in the town. One of its leaders, Edmund Basile, a goldsmith, was reported to be harassing the mayor and burgesses in July: NRO, KL/C10/2 fo. 19^{v}.

86 PRO, KB 9/178 m. 1; *Dialogus de Scaccario*, ed. Charles Johnson (London, 1950), 23, for the point of the comparison, which likens Henry IV to the temporary 'memoranda tally' issued at the Easter view of account, but subsequently broken and discarded.

87 *Rot. Parl.*, iii, 583–4; Margaret Aston, 'Lollardy and Sedition, 1381–1431', *Past and Present*, no. 17 (Apr. 1960). The garbled account of the Minorite agitation

preserved in Bodleian Library, Oxford, Digby MS 196, fo. 157v, which claims that eight friars were executed for necromancy, having plotted to kill the king and his lords with a poisonous ointment, suggests this technique enjoyed some contemporary success.

88 British Library, London (hereafter Brit. Lib.), Cotton MS Vespasian F VII, fo. 94 ('illud fatuum . . . illud ydolum'); *Original Letters*, 1st ser., ed. Ellis, i, 2 ('the mawmet'); *Rot. Parl.*, iii, 584 ('celuy fool'), iv, 65 ('ideotam'); *Select Cases*, ed. Sayles, vii, 211 ('ut falsa ficta persona').

89 *Middle English Dictionary*, ed. Sherman M. Kuhn and John Reidy (Ann Arbor, 1956–), *s.v.* 'maumet'; and note the description of Geoffrey Litster, leader of the Norfolk rebels in 1381, as 'idolum Northfolkorum': Walsingham, *Historia Anglicana*, ii, 8.

90 Sandra Billington, *Mock Kings in Medieval Society and Renaissance Drama* (Oxford, 1991), ch. 3.

91 *Chronicle of Adam Usk*, ed. Given-Wilson, 122; Storey, 'Clergy and Common Law', 357; *Cal. Close Rolls, 1402–5*, 203, 354, 357; Richard van Dülmen, *Theatre of Horror: Crime and Punishment in Early Modern Germany* (Oxford, 1990), esp. 134. Serle was hanged, cut down while still alive, then dragged through the streets in nearly every major town between York and London; he seems to have suffered these penalties at Doncaster, Lincoln, King's Lynn, Norwich and Colchester, at least: PRO, Exchequer, Foreign Accounts, E 364/38 m. 3; Exchequer, Sheriffs Accounts, E 199/55/6; E 364/39 mm. 1, 3d.

92 PRO, KB 27/579 Rex m. 2.

93 Already under suspicion in January 1404, when he was examined in the court of the constable, the intervention of the parliamentary Commons offered him the chance to clear himself in King's Bench; rearrested in October 1404 and imprisoned at Kenilworth, the Commons again petitioned on Wolman's behalf. He was indicted again, for treasonable correspondence with the Scots, in Hilary 1408 but when he eventually appeared in court at Trinity 1409 Wolman produced a royal pardon and went without day. He was immediately indicted again on the same charges and, at Hilary 1410, was described as 'one of the principal traitors of the lord king' but, despite this notoriety, he remained at large until his conviction for participation in the Oldcastle rising in 1415. Pardoned and released once more, it was another year before he finally met his fate. *Rot. Parl.*, iii, 580; PRO, SC 8/148/7362; *Cal. Pat. Rolls, 1401–5*, 503; PRO, KB 9/196/1 m. 13; KB 27/593 Rex m. 13d.; *Cal. Pat. Rolls, 1405–8*, 46; PRO, JUST 1/554 m. 8; KB 27/595 Rex m. 3d.; KB 27/611 Rex m. 13.

94 PRO, JUST 1/554 m. 8d. Only eleven of the forty-eight men indicted were eventually judged to be worthy of further examination by the Council. The Commons subsequently expressed their disapproval of the whole initiative, petitioning that those responsible for procuring the indictments should be punished. *Cal. Pat. Rolls, 1405–8*, 177; *Rot. Parl.*, iii, 624.

95 John Botlesham, John Karlill and Master Ralph Selby: E. H. Pearce, *The Monks of Westminster* (Cambridge, 1916), 123, 127, 128; A. B. Cobban, *The King's Hall within the University of Cambridge* (Cambridge, 1969), 282–3.

96 PRO, KB 27/595 Rex m. 11d.; *Les Reports del Cases en ley . . . les Roys Henry le IV et Henry le V* (London, 1679), Hilary 11 H. IV, 41. Abbot Geoffrey had fallen under suspicion of treason again at Lent 1405, when he was arrested and imprisoned in Nottingham castle: *The Red Paper Book of Colchester*, ed. W. G. Benham (Colchester, 1902), 35.

97 A. G. Little, *The Grey Friars in Oxford* (Oxford Hist. Soc., xx, Oxford, 1892), 244–5; Hilary M. Carey, *Courting Disaster: Astrology at the English Court and University in the Later Middle Ages* (Basingstoke, 1992), 80–1.
98 PRO, JUST 1/554 m. 8; *Select Cases*, ed. Sayles, vii, 212–15, 236–9; Edward Powell, *Kingship, Law and Society: Criminal Justice in the Reign of Henry V* (Oxford, 1989), 136–9.
99 *Eulogium Historiarum*, ed. Haydon, iii, 393–4; Edward Powell, 'The Strange Death of Sir John Mortimer: Politics and the Law of Treason in Lancastrian England', in Rowena E. Archer and Simon Walker (eds.), *Rulers and Ruled in Late Medieval England: Essays Presented to Gerald Harriss* (London, 1995), 92–4.
100 PRO, KB 27/595 Rex m. 8; *Cal. Pat. Rolls, 1405–8*, 231 (John, son of Henry Longe; John Longe, junior); PRO, KB 27/593 Rex m. 13d. (John Tange). John Huchon and John Hewett were released on bail at Hilary 1410 and there was apparently no further process on their cases: PRO, KB 29/50 m. 13.
101 Brit. Lib., Cotton MS Vespasian F VII, fo. 94.
102 Mario Vargas Llosa, *The War of the End of the World* (London, 1985), 258.
103 Mircea Eliade, *The Myth of the Eternal Return*, trans. Willard R. Trask (London, 1955), 141–2.
104 Brit. Lib., Egerton Roll 8769 m. 3, for the *tempore tribulacionis*.
105 Rosamond Faith, 'The "Great Rumour" of 1377 and Peasant Ideology', in R. H. Hilton and T. H. Aston (eds.), *The English Rising of 1381* (Cambridge, 1984); Richard Firth Green, 'John Ball's Letters: Literary History and Historical Literature', in Hanawalt (ed.), *Chaucer's England*; Lawrence R. Poos, *A Rural Society after the Black Death: Essex, 1350–1525* (Cambridge, 1991), 231–52; Paul Strohm, ' "A Revelle!": Chronicle Evidence and the Rebel Voice', in his *Hochon's Arrow*, ch. 2; Christopher Dyer, 'The Rising of 1381 in Suffolk: Its Origins and Participants', in his *Everyday Life in Medieval England* (London, 1994), 232–3; Steven Justice, *Writing and Rebellion: England in 1381* (Berkeley, 1994), esp. ch. 1. Cf. the conclusions in John J. McGavin, 'Robert III's "Rough Music": Charivari and Diplomacy in a Medieval Scottish Court', *Scot. Hist. Rev.*, lxxiv (1995).
106 R. B. Goheen, 'Peasant Politics? Village Community and the Crown in Fifteenth-Century England', *Amer. Hist. Rev.*, xcvi (1991), 52; G. L. Harriss, 'The Dimensions of Politics', in R. H. Britnell and A. J. Pollard (eds.), *The McFarlane Legacy: Studies in Late Medieval Politics and Society* (Stroud, 1995), 14–16.
107 PRO, SC 6/774/13 m. 6; Privy Seal Office, Warrants, PSO, 1/9/455, for Kingsley's subsequent employment in Lancastrian service as an annuitant of Henry, prince of Wales, and then Thomas, duke of Clarence.

8

Remembering Richard: history and memory in Lancastrian England[1]

In 1409, Walter Somery, called as a witness to the inquest held to determine whether Thomas Montague, earl of Salisbury, was now of full age, replied that indeed he was, and that he knew this to be so because on the day the earl was born, 25 May 1388, he had ridden in haste from St. Albans to Shenley, where the baptism was to take place, with Sir Richard Sturry, 'talking of rumours concerning King Richard'.[2] There would have been much to talk about. The 'Merciless Parliament' was still in session at Westminster, but it had already convicted five of the king's closest advisers of treason and there was still much unfinished business, most notably the fate of Sir Simon Burley, to be concluded. Sir Richard Sturry was one of the great survivors of the late fourteenth century but, as one of the king's longest-serving chamber knights, he must have been a little anxious about his own future. Since the king's chief opponent, Thomas, duke of Gloucester, was also invited to the christening, it promised to be a somewhat fraught social occasion. It is testimony to the impression that these uncertain times made on Walter Somery that he chose a chance conversation, recalled at a distance of twenty years, rather than the more usual litany of broken bones and accident-prone horses that witnesses tended to recite on these occasions, to authenticate his testimony.[3]

This essay is about the changing reputation of Richard II during the seventy years or so after his death. I have started with Walter Somery's testimony because it serves as a reminder that personal memory and oral testimony would inevitably have played a large part in shaping that reputation. Bernard Guenée has suggested that the recollection of past events remained, for a span of about sixty to seventy years, clear and precise,[4] and there were, throughout much of the Lancastrian period, still influential people alive who could remember the deposed king well. Sir Simon Felbrigg, his former standard-bearer, made provision for masses to be said for Richard's soul (and pointedly omitted any similar provision for his successors) in 1442, for example,[5] while John Shirley, who had been secretary to Richard Beauchamp, earl of Warwick, and died at the age of 80 in 1456, had his own distinctive views on Richard's fate.[6] The testimony of these eye-witnesses had a demonstrable influence on the historical record: Robert Irliffe, clerk of the green cloth in Richard's household, provided John Hardyng with the report of its extravagance that found its way into the second ('Yorkist') recension of Hardyng's chronicle around 1460,[7] and such oral traditions were, in all probability, very influential in forming the Lancastrian images of Richard II. They are, though, only partially recoverable: we can rarely hear the alleged tavern-talk of men like John Freston, tailor, who, at Easter 1403, spoke slightingly of the young earl of Arundel and then launched into a tendentious but precise account of his father's downfall.[8] It is, in consequence, not with individual memories that I shall principally be concerned here but with the *social* memory of Richard's reign.

The concepts of 'memory' and, more especially, 'social memory' have reached that unenviable stage of historiographical development, shared with 'gender', the 'body', and several other perfectly valid topics of historical enquiry, in which they are commonly used to add a little life to otherwise predictable discussions of well-established topics; and if I use them in that sense, I hereby apologise in advance. Nevertheless, there seems to me to remain some value in investigating the memories of Richard II preserved during the Lancastrian era. In general, writers such as Mary Carruthers have argued for the central importance of *memoria*, the art of remembering, in medieval culture: that it was not simply the accurate recall of events in a sequential ordering, but one of the major modalities of medieval culture, enabling certain types of thought and behaviour and privileging some forms of behaviour over others.[9] To think about Richard II in memorial terms is, therefore, to get closer to how contemporaries thought about him. It is important, though, to see this process of remembering as something more than the sum of numerous individual acts of cognitive recall; it is, rather, an active process of construction, creating an agreed version of the past from the disparate influences of language, education and shared experience. The significance of this for the historian is that social memory is not simply about remembering, but also about the organisation of knowledge and the creation of what has been called a 'formative' past. These agreed versions of the past, emerging from the heterogeneity of collective memory, reveal much about the ways in which the groups that constructed them define and project themselves. One purpose of this essay will be to ask what the judgments passed on Richard II during the Lancastrian era reveal about the political culture that generated them.

Among medievalists, studies of the evolution of social memory have tended to concentrate on the earlier Middle Ages, when oral traditions were predominant.[10] By the fifteenth century, however, we are well within the 'era of artificial memory', as defined by Michael Clanchy, the point at which facts began to be established principally by documentary evidence, rather than by recourse to the unaided powers of human recollection.[11] The reconstruction of contemporary memory primarily through the analysis of textual evidence raises, of course, additional problems. One issue this essay considers is the way in which historical memories can be structured by the characteristic narrative lines of different literary genres; another is how far the changing predilections for particular narrative conventions can be related to the social and cultural contexts that produced them. Some distinction (the distinction I have tried to draw in my title) is also required between the *production* of historical narratives and their reception, between 'authoring', which belongs in the domain of the individual's memory, and 'authorising', which is a social and communal activity. As several historians have stressed, social memory involves a process of active restructuring, whereby the component elements of a story are constantly augmented, reordered or suppressed.[12] What was forgotten or omitted in accounts of Richard's reign was, as we shall see, often as interesting and significant as what was remembered.

This emphasis on the textual should not, finally, obscure the extent to which, even in the fifteenth century, social memory continued to draw upon a body of material wider than the formal historical record. Some authorities have argued for the dominance of a largely topographical structure to contemporary senses of the past, 'focussed less on time than on space, less on dates than places'.[13] In Richard's case, such a topographical structure seems largely absent; it may be that his memorial investment was concentrated so heavily at Westminster, the seat of government, that no autonomous *lieu de memoire* proved capable of establishing itself. Nevertheless, the persistent recurrence of certain beliefs about the king's reign which hardly feature in the formal historical record – for example, that it was a time of great plenty – attests to the influence of an independent sense of a 'common voice'; a consensus over what was generally agreed, compounded of textual, oral and material witnesses.

In view of these complexities, it is easiest, in studying the evolving social memory of Richard II, to start at the end – or, at least, from the point at which Richard's volatile reputation finally achieved some stability. Writing some years ago about attitudes towards Richard's reign in the Tudor period, Margaret Aston concluded that the verdict of history had, by then, become all but unanimous. In English Renaissance historiography, Richard appears chiefly as a 'constructed type', with certain features of his rule and character emphasised at the expense of others: 'his was the stock image of the weak, over-influenced minor, who failed in council, in religion and in war, whose inability to rise above the deficiencies of his youth were the overriding reason for his downfall'.[14] All the constituent elements of the Tudor image were already present in the historiography of the Lancastrian period, but they had yet to be fixed in relation to one another and had, in addition, to compete with rival evaluations that were both less precise and more favourable. David Lawton has argued that, in the political circumstances of fifteenth-century England, kingship was itself 'a text, to be explained, fixed and glossed'.[15] Contemporary accounts of Richard's reign were, in this respect, no different from the more abstract discussions of royal virtues produced by poets like Gower, Lydgate and Ashby, or by the various translators of the *Secreta Secretorum*. They remained open texts, constantly liable to revision and modification, as both their authors and their readers strove to confer upon them a stable meaning.

In the immediate aftermath of Richard's deposition, of course, certain sharply defined interpretations of the recent past established themselves. The most influential of these was the view of Richard encapsulated in the deposition articles, as a sovereign wielding both too much and too little authority, as guilty of both tyranny and insufficiency.[16] Although this was a reading of Richard's reign shaped by the exigencies of a precarious political situation, it continued to exert some influence throughout the Lancastrian period. In part, this was because the nature and contents of the deposition articles themselves proved of enduring interest to an intensely precedent-minded culture. Apart from the initial government-sponsored effort to circulate copies, private recensions continued to be made throughout the century; one version of the English *Brut*, compiled in 1484–5, is followed by a full set of the proceedings in Henry IV's first parliament.[17] Equally, the influence of Thomas Walsingham's *Chronica Majora*, completed in about 1408, which constructed a narrative of the reign largely around the interpretation of the king's character portrayed in the deposition articles,[18] was preserved and disseminated by his later epitomators, such as Thomas Otterbourne and John Capgrave,[19] as well as in shorter and less ambitious compilations based upon his work. Other adverse accounts contemporary with the king, such as the *Vita Ricardi Secundi*, which was translated into English at some point between about 1432 and 1450, also remained influential.[20] There were, of course, dissentient voices, still prepared to champion Richard's virtues in the face of Lancastrian disapproval. The defiant royalism of the *Dieulacres Chronicle*, which told of the king as a Christ-like innocent, betrayed by the unholy alliance of Herod and Pilate, was one,[21] while the annals compiled at Lough Ree (Co. Longford) maintained that 'there were few men in his time as estimable as he'.[22]

Historically legitimate though these polarised interpretations were, they were not wholly satisfactory in memorial terms. The search for a usable past demanded significance as well as accuracy and consequently sought a familiar explanatory framework within which to situate the king's rise and fall. This strain of thought was strongest within the lower reaches of political society where, for a few years at least, hopes were entertained of Richard as a once and future king, a powerful and unsettling presence who would soon return to claim his lost inheritance.[23] Within the learned textual community, too, the same search for significance was under way. Among the several explanatory discourses invoked, there were three that proved especially resonant: the scriptural, the providentialist and the prophetic.

The search for scriptural parallels to contemporary events was, of course, an impulse deeply embedded within later medieval culture. The Lancastrian revolution had already thrown up one powerful legitimating analogy, between Henry of Lancaster and Judas Maccabeus: the text of the sermon Thomas Arundel, archbishop of Canterbury, delivered before parliament on 6 October 1399 was taken from 1 Maccabeus – 'It behoves us to ordain for the kingdom' – and, ten days later, when issuing a mandate for prayers for Henry's prosperity, the archbishop had described him as acting 'as though another

Maccabees'.[24] For those seeking an explanation of Richard's tyranny, however, the irresistible *exemplum* was that of Rehoboam, king of Judah. Rehoboam was the biblical archetype of a tyrant, just as David and Solomon were types for the ideal Christian prince. His double dereliction, despising the counsels of the wise and heeding too much the advice of the young, rendered him a favourite recourse for medieval advice-givers. The author of the *Vita Edwardi Secundi* invoked his example at several points in his account of Edward's reign,[25] while Archbishop Stratford threatened the headstrong Edward III with his fate in 1341 – 'and what happened to him for that cause you, sire, know well'.[26] It was, though, the details of Rehoboam's conduct that offered such an alluring set of parallels for Lancastrian commentators: refusing the advice of his elderly counsellors that he should be a servant unto his people, Rehoboam had threatened them instead, saying that while his father had chastised them with whips, he would chastise them with scorpions; the severity of his taxation – a constant refrain in the presentation of the Lancastrian case against Richard – had provoked the Israelites to rebellion and led them to choose a new king.[27] Crucially, therefore, Rehoboam's case provided a scriptural justification for the setting-aside of a legitimate king by rebellion on the grounds of misrule. It was, in consequence, frequently invoked: the preacher Thomas Wimbledon had alluded to Rehoboam's fate as early as 1388,[28] and, in the aftermath of Richard's fall, Adam of Usk, together with the Kirkstall and Louth Park chroniclers, all fashioned their judgments on the late king in the light of its message.[29] The intellectual force of this demonstration derived, in turn, from contemporary understanding of the force of the biblical *exemplum*, which rendered the story of Rehoboam as not simply a record of previous political blunders, but as a normative type, constantly present throughout recorded history, defining a pattern of behaviour repeated down the ages. Remembering Richard in the context of the biblical past prefigured the future, and located contemporary events within the economy of salvation.

Appeal to such scriptural typologies was, perhaps, most characteristic of the years immediately succeeding Richard's deposition. Within a few years – perhaps as early as 1406 – it had become clear to all but the most purblind of Ricardian loyalists that the new Lancastrian regime had to be conceded, at least, the legitimacy of prescription. As the tasks of condemnation and justification became less urgent, a new emphasis was laid upon the need to address and answer those awkward questions that Richard's fall still posed: how, for example, could an anointed king forfeit the special favour and status in the sight of God that the rite of unction was taken to imply? In the interpretative space opened up by such persistent questions, the topic of mutability came to assume an increasingly significant position. The appeal of blind Fortune and her wheel sprang in part, of course, from the particular circumstances of Richard's fall. The sudden *περεπτεια*, from the height of his prosperity as conqueror of Ireland to a friendless fugitive among the hills of Wales within a month, offered an obvious topic for rhetorical elaboration. Adam of Usk reported leaving Richard, after observing his demeanour in the

Tower, 'much moved at heart, reflecting to myself on the glories of his former state and the fickle fortune of this world',[30] and similar, though generally less artful, reflections occur in the narratives of Creton, Froissart and Gower.[31] There was more to the popularity of Fortune as an organising device for the memory of Richard than familiarity and convenience, however. It expressed what seems to have been a more general sense of destabilisation, a feeling that Richard's fall had brought others crashing in its wake. In his *Regiment of Princes* (*c.* 1412), Thomas Hoccleve talks of the 'storm of descendyng' that has shaken the whole body politic:

> Me fyl to mynde how that noght long agoo
> Fortunes strouke doun threst estat real
> Into meschef, and I tok heede also
> Of many another lord that hadde a fal.
> In mene estat eke sykernesse at al
> Ne saw I non . . .[32]

The anonymous author of some verses on Richard's fall similarly remarks that the former king's death 'hath been dear bought',[33] while it was around 1410 that John Walton, working under the patronage of Thomas, Lord Berkeley, completed his translation into English of Boethius's *Of the Consolation of Philosophy*.[34]

For those who sought to memorialise Richard within the discourse of mutability, the topos possessed two particular advantages. Already the subject of a substantial body of literary and academic discussion, it was conveniently flexible, acting as a vehicle of debate as well as of explanation. Some commentators could draw from it a message of quietism. The author of the *Vita Ricardi Secundi*, reflecting on the fate of the Ricardian earls in January 1400, concluded: 'For Wisdom says – "who stands still, does not hasten to his fall".'[35] Others, like William Ferriby, the (alleged) author of the long reflection on mutability preserved in *Giles' Chronicle*, could use the topic to express a continuing sympathy with the deposed king, arguing (with copious examples) that God chastises those whom he loves, and finding in Richard's misfortunes a sign of continuing election: the grain must be threshed before it is gathered into the barn. Secondly, it shifted the focus of discussion away from Richard and his shortcomings by opening up a longer historical perspective – that of the 'sudden fall of princes' – in which the king himself appeared less personally culpable.[36]

This was a view of the recent past advanced, with his usual understated professionalism, by John Lydgate – most clearly so in one of his occasional poems, perhaps dating from the early 1430s, 'Of the Sudden Fall of certain Princes of France and England, now late in our day'. Here, through a brief consideration of a series of recent political unfortunates (Edward II, Richard II, Charles VI, Louis, duke of Orleans, Thomas, duke of Gloucester, John, duke of Burgundy, Robert de Vere, duke of Ireland), Lydgate deftly establishes *both* that Richard's reign had been a generalised 'time of troubles', threatening to the whole nation's safety and analogous to the disorder currently engulfing the French, *and*, by implication, that the Lancastrian accession had been necessary, in order to save England from a similar disorder.[37] Lydgate, though, was didactic as well as justificatory in his intentions, seeking to inculcate a view of Fortune as both random and purposeful. Mutability could be mitigated in its effects by the pursuit of wisdom and the avoidance of folly – the latter identified, in Richard's case, as the susceptibility to evil counsel that led him to mistreat the 'lords of his monarchy' – but there remained an irreducible element of chance in all human affairs, to which the former king had fallen victim. How far this line of thought could be used to rehabilitate Richard's memory appears best in the additions made by John Shirley, the earl of Warwick's secretary, to a copy of the *Brut*, where he comes close to suggesting that the king's fall was simply an unavoidable consequence of his former prosperity: 'the which Richard, of his nobility and providence had firm peace and love with all the Christian princes; how rich he was, how noble, how loved and how dread through all the realm and provinces; and how that fame and fortune by their cruel war subverted all his royal estate into misery, to the lamentation and piteous complaint of every gentle heart'.[38] Although Fortune had proved for Richard, as Polydore Vergil remarked, a savage stepmother, not a kindly mother,[39] the discourse of mutability increasingly allowed his reign to be memorialised in terms that did much to dissipate the sharpness of the original Lancastrian critique.

The treatment of Richard's memory within the discourse of prophecy had broadly the same effect. This was, in some respects, a surprising development, for, during his own lifetime, Richard seems to have made little impact on the corpus of prophetic literature: a manuscript owned by Bishop Despenser, which sought to present the king as the conquering and crusading world-emperor, represents a de luxe exception to the rule.[40] After his death, however, prophecy became one of the favoured recourses of the Ricardian loyalists, who sought to prove 'by prophecy' that the king was still alive, and 'by chronicle and prophecy' that he would enjoy his kingdom once more. The most popular of the surviving prophecies in which Richard obscurely appears is the 'Six Kings to follow John', a text incorporated, in English translation, into many manuscripts of the vernacular *Brut*. Here, each of the kings after John is represented by an animal – the dragon, goat, boar and so on; Richard is the ass, with feet of lead and head of steel, whose voice shall be heard in every land. Richard's reign is represented in a favourable light, as a time of plenty, when the ass ruled his land in peace.[41] There is, in addition, some suggestion of Ricardian influence upon the textual tradition, with the circulation of a revised version during the early fifteenth century describing the return of the ass to his throne, following the overthrow of his adversary and supplanter, the hideous moldwarp:

Sithen to the asse shall fall that lond
And he shall it yeme wele in his owne hond

This land of good playsir shal it be
Graciosly in his tyme yemed shal it be
His fomen in to frends turne thei will all
And sorow shal pas and joy thei wil have all.[42]

Over time, therefore, Richard became a figure of eschatology as well as history, attracting to himself discrete elements of the prophetic corpus. One late fifteenth-century manuscript, for example, apparently connected with the household of Henry Percy, fourth earl of Northumberland, has Richard confronted, while dining, by a talking hare. Richard asks the hare who will reign after him: 'after you a devil will reign', the animal replies, 'and after the devil a saint; after the saint a sword; after the sword a fool; and after the fool, nothing'.[43] This was not the first appearance of this prediction, which was reported, some thirty years earlier, in Walter Bower's *Scotichronicon*, as the speech of the White Hermit to Henry IV.[44] What effect the development of this prophetic *persona* for the deposed king had on memories of his reign is, given the nature of the material, hard to define. There was, however, a general tendency within prophetic discourse to shift responsibility away from the individual and to present the events of the recent past as the necessary fulfilment of an inevitable destiny. This seems to have worked to Richard's advantage, for the view of the former king in the prophetic literature circulating during the Lancastrian period was certainly not consistently hostile. It exercised some influence, too, upon the assessment of the king within the formal historical tradition; the shared emphasis in both sets of sources on the prosperity and plenty of Richard's reign is the most obvious example of this.

As the century progressed, this tendency to displace or moderate the hegemonic official narrative of Richard's tyranny and voluntary resignation began to achieve more unified and coherent expression. The earliest datable instance of this development is perhaps Lydgate's 'Kings of England since William the Conqueror', a skeletal verse chronicle, reciting the descent of the English crown from Alfred to Henry VI, written in about 1426, which memorialises Richard in these terms:

Son of Prynce Edward, Richard the Secound
In whos tyme was pes and gret plente,
Weddid Queen Anne of Bewme, as it is found,
Isabell aftir of Fraunce, who list see.
Xxii yeer he regned heer, parde:
At Langley buried first, so stood the cas,
Aftir to Westmynster his body caried was.[45]

Given Lydgate's laureate status, it is tempting to see some prompting behind this blandly eirenic account, in line with the insistence among the biographers of Henry V, all close to the Lancastrian court, on the close bond between their hero and the man [their] – sic – his father had deposed. In this case, however, the tone seems to have been set by the expectations of the audience, rather than by the preferences of a patron. Lydgate's verses were demonstrably popular, surviving in at least twenty-six manuscript copies; their appeal seems to have been to the growing market of literate lay consumers, with little formal academic training, but possessed of a strong historical curiosity and anxious for instruction. A second, anonymous, verse chronicle of a similar type, written about a decade later, shares the stance of Lydgate's verse, providing a slightly longer but still determinedly neutral account of Richard's reign.[46]

These verse chronicles were closely related in message and appeal to an established genre of historical production: genealogical chronicles, usually produced in roll form, with simple circle-and-line schemata and brief explanatory texts in Latin, French or English, that traced the descent of the kings of England back through Brutus to a biblical patriarch, usually either Adam or Noah. The origin of these chronicles seems to lie with the brief illustrated genealogies that Matthew Paris prefixed to his historical writings, although their production was given a further impetus by the interest in the 'British history' aroused by Edward I's claim to sovereignty over Scotland.[47] By the mid-fifteenth century it is possible to identify several different texts and formats in circulation, each apparently produced on a commercial basis, though whether by itinerant scribes or from a single, London-based workshop is less easy to determine. The earliest of them – an idiosyncratic text with a marked interest in Welsh and marcher affairs, that nevertheless achieved quite wide circulation about 1430 – dealt with the problems of presentation raised by Richard's reign by a simple act of suppression: a narrative that ran into the ground early in Edward III's reign was revived with a paragraph about the revolt of Owain Glyn Dŵr and its aftermath, with no notice given to the intervening years.[48] The text ascribed to the Carmelite friar, Roger of St. Albans, which achieved considerable popularity during the 1450s, was more forthcoming, though scarcely less evasive, in its judgment on Richard:

> Richard II that was son to prince Edward was crowned king after Edward III. This was a peaceable man and loved God and Holy Church. And in the two and twentieth year of his reign he renounced his crown and the governance of the realm in the Tower of London, and was put in keeping in the castle of Pontefract. And there he died and was buried at Langley. And afterwards King Henry V took up his bones from there and buried them at Westminster.[49]

Although the content of these chronicle rolls is itself largely banal, their reappearance and proliferation in the mid-fifteenth century is significant because their layout and decoration imposed the formal structures of academic memory-training upon the multiple impressions of popular memory, imparting coherence to the previously inchoate by reducing the regnal blocks of English history to a single, defined set of qualities to be permanently retained in the 'treasure bag' of memory. They were produced in response to a commercial imperative – the thirst for instruction among a rapidly expanding group of lay literates – but there was much in their message that suited the political situation of the time as well. For the Lancastrian monarchy and its supporters, the Yorkist claim to the throne could be conveniently relegated to the physical margins of the text; noble families like the Talbots and Butlers could commission bespoke versions, both advertising their own illustrious lineages and expressing their political preferences; as political divisions became more acute in the 1450s, partisan material could easily be intruded – one such roll has *occisus apud Sanctum Albanum* inscribed in the roundels for Edmund, duke of Somerset, and Henry, earl of Northumberland.[50] The real appeal of these rolls sprang, though, as much from their structure as their content. The genealogical form in which these chronicles were cast itself provided an assurance of continuity and stability that was greatly valued, as they traced the descent of Henry VI back through Brutus, 'the first king in this said land', to Japhet the son of Noah, assimilating the past and the present in a continuous stream of tradition. Rulers valued this assurance as a form of legitimation and took pains to have it publicised, but the consumers of historical literature in the Lancastrian age had, too, their own investment in the durability and sense of political identity that such a representation of past history provided. By concentrating on the formalities of legitimate succession in their accounts of Richard's reign, these brief chronicles delivered their own judgment on his kingship. Purged of its controversial content, Richard's rule took its place within a narrative of political continuity and national solidarity that was felt by most political actors to transcend the claims of dynastic partisanship on his memory.

Naturally, the accession of Edward IV challenged this emerging consensus. The Lancastrian 'Record and Process' had offered one coherent explanatory narrative for the events of Richard's reign: that of a kingdom suffering the consequences of its ruler's manifest inadequacy, until the longed-for advent of a providential deliverer.[51] Now Edward IV's declaration of his title to the throne, made in parliament in 1461, offered another, almost diametrically opposed in its reading of the nation's recent past. In this account, Richard had exercised his legitimate right to rule the kingdom 'in rest and quiet, without interruption or molestation' until the unjust and tyrannical usurpation of Henry of Lancaster, with the consequence that England 'in ancient times among all Christian realms laudably reported of great honour, worship and nobility, dread of all outward lands, then being the laureate of honour, prowess and worthiness . . .', had 'fallen from that renown into misery, wretchedness, desolation, shameful and sorrowful decline'.[52] Enthusiasm for this new narrative is not hard to identify within the historical tradition. John Capgrave, who had adopted a highly critical tone towards Richard in his *Liber de Illustribus Henricis*, a work composed for presentation to Henry VI in 1446,[53] took a very different stance in his *Abbreviation of Chronicles*, completed in about 1463–4 and addressed to Edward IV, seeing in Richard a Christ-like figure.[54] John Hardyng hastened to add a series of partisan prose notes to the second version of his *Chronicle*, presented to Edward IV at Leicester in 1463, recounting in detail the full extent of Richard's deception and Henry of Lancaster's perjury.[55] In the text of roll-chronicles produced in the aftermath of the Yorkist triumph, the studious avoidance of politically sensitive issues was replaced by a new plain-speaking: Henry of Lancaster had imprisoned and deposed Richard 'true king and heir of England and France . . . and he and his said heirs usurped the said crown, and occupied it unjustly, and possessed the same in bad faith'.[56] Throughout the Yorkist era, indeed, efforts were made to link the undeniable legitimacy of Richard II with the claims and fortunes of the house of York. As he entered Coventry in 1474, Edward, prince of Wales was greeted by a figure of Richard II exclaiming 'We all must bless the time of your Nativity / The right line of the royal blood is now as it should be',[57] while some late additions to copies of the *Brut* attempted to manufacture a connection between the former king and the symbolic resources of the house of York.

These revisions, necessarily hasty, also remained superficial, however: Capgrave was too tied to the text of his source, Thomas Walsingham, to extend his revisionism much beyond the confines of his prologue, while Hardyng's 'Yorkist' marginalia cannot disguise the fact that his interpretation of Richard's reign remained unchanged between the first and second recensions of his chronicle: that Richard had been an able and effective king 'reigning well in worship and honour/Far passing all Kings or Emperor . . . So free he was of heart and high noblesse', whose reign had spun startlingly out of control, impelled by greed and concupiscence.[58] Equally, the memorial tradition about Richard proved resistant to the simple substitution of one hegemonic narrative for another, and tenacious, instead, of an established, and more hostile, set of attributes. His reign continued to be remembered as a time of distress and disruption – 'the world being thus at the mercy of a malignant whirlwind of direful perturbations, which spread throughout nearly the whole of England', according to the second continuation of the Crowland Chronicle – while the character of the king himself was frequently rendered in the traditional terms of the Lancastrian critique.[59] John Rous described Richard in his *Historia Regum Anglie* as 'senseless and greatly unfortunate . . . as timid as a hare, much readier to flee from his enemies than to put them to flight',[60] while the northern rebels of 1469 revived, in their proclamations, the image of Richard as a king who – like Edward II – placed insupportable burdens upon his subjects through ill-counsel.[61]

The conclusions we have reached at the end of this survey may, therefore, seem rather unexciting ones: they are that, for much of the fifteenth century, the memory of Richard II within contemporary political culture was certainly less definite and, in certain respects, substantially less hostile than it was to be throughout the Tudor period, and that this memory was only marginally affected, whether positively or negatively, by the dynastic upheavals at mid-century. But these conclusions point, perhaps, to two more general points about the political culture that generated them. One is that the unremarkable, traditional and often deliberately uncontroversial nature of many of the judgments passed on Richard during the Lancastrian period needs to be seen in the context of David Lawton's comments about the 'dullness' of much fifteenth-century literature: that its commonplace and platitudinous character is not a sign of simple intellectual impoverishment, but is deliberate, a willed attempt to create continuity and unity where, in the actual centre of power, there was only instability and division.[62] The preference displayed in the text of the roll-chronicles for the display and exposition of dynastic continuity, beyond a record of the details of partisan conflict, seems to speak to the same desire. The second is prompted by some remarks of Jean-Philippe Genet, writing of the development of historical writing in fifteenth-century Europe. Genet concluded his survey with the observation that vernacular history, in particular, was still constrained by an imprecise vocabulary, which did not transcend the clichés of the *Mirror for Princes* literature: 'the disparate quality of the techniques, genres and languages leaves an impression of chaos'.[63] What Genet calls chaos can perhaps be more fruitfully seen as a move away from a single (learned) canon of interpretation and towards a plurality of competing viewpoints that proved, for contemporaries, both intellectually appealing and socially useful. It was also the result of the fruitful, and increasingly frequent, exchange between conventional historical narrative and the more versatile representations of social memory that occurred in the Lancastrian era.

Notes

1 This paper expands on themes explored in 'Richard II's reputation', in Gwilym Dodd (ed.), *The Reign of Richard II* (Stroud 2000), 119–28; 152–4.
2 *Calendar of Inquisitions Post Mortem* (HMSO, 1992), no. 655.
3 J. Bedell, 'Memory and proof of age in England, 1272–1327', *Past & Present*, 162 (1999), 3–27, esp. pp. 14, 17.
4 Bernard Guenée, 'Temps de l'Histoire et Temps de la Memoire au Moyen Age', *Bulletin de la societe de l'histoire de France annees 1976–1977*, 27–35, at p. 31.
5 J. D. Milner, 'Sir Simon Felbrigg, K. G.: The Lancastrian Revolution and Personal Fortune', *Norfolk Archaeology*, 37 (pt. 1, 1978), 84–91, esp. p. 89, referring to Felbrigg's monumental brass and will (The National Archives, PROB 11/1, f. 113v: Prerogative Court of Canterbury wills, 14 Rous).
6 It has not been possible to trace this reference. The best introduction to Shirley's manuscripts is in Jeremy Griffiths and Derek Pearsall (eds), *Book Production and Publishing in Britain, 1375–1475* (Cambridge, 1989), 284–8; and for Shirley himself see Jeremy Griffiths, 'Shirley, John (*c.* 1366–1456)', *Oxford Dictionary of National Biography* (Oxford University Press, 2004) [http://www.oxforddnb.com/view/article/25428, accessed 11 March 2005]
7 *The Chronicle of John Hardyng*, ed. Henry Ellis (London, 1812, reprinted 1974), p. 346; C. L. Kingsford, 'The first version of Hardyng's Chronicle', *English Historical Review* 27 (1912), 462–82; A. S. G. Edwards, 'The manuscripts and texts of the second version of John Hardyng's Chronicle', in Daniel Williams (ed.), *England in the Fifteenth Century: Proceedings of the 1986 Harlaxton Symposium* (Woodbridge, 1987), 75–84; Felicity Riddy, 'John Hardyng's Chronicle and the Wars of the Roses', in J. P. Carley and F. Riddy (eds), *Arthurian Literature XII* (Cambridge, 1993), 91–108. Changes in the versions of Hardyng's chronicle are discussed in Walker, 'Richard II's reputation', at pp. 124–5, and notes 23–28.
8 The National Archives, KB27/593, rex rot. 18.
9 Mary J. Carruthers, *The Book of Memory: A Study of Memory in Medieval Culture* (Cambridge, 1990), pp. 8, 189, 193, 250–1, 260.

10 For example, Matthew Innes, 'Memory, orality and literacy in an early medieval society', *Past & Present*, 158 (1998), 3–36; Paul Brand, ' "Time out of mind", the knowledge and use of the eleventh- and twelfth-century past in thirteenth-century litigation', *Anglo-Norman Studies*, 16 (1993), 37–54; Janet Coleman, *Ancient and Medieval Memories: Studies in the Reconstruction of the Past* (Cambridge, 1992), pp. 461–537.

11 M. T. Clanchy, *From Memory to Written Record: England 1066–1307* (Oxford, 1993), pp. 152–4, 177.

12 For this topic, see James Fentress and Christopher Wickham, *Social Memory* (Oxford, 1992).

13 D. R. Woolf, 'The "common voice": History, folklore and oral tradition in early modern England', *Past & Present*, 120 (1988), 26–52, quotation at p. 31.

14 Margaret Aston, 'Richard II and the Wars of the Roses', in *eadem*, *Lollards and Reformers: Images and Literacy in Late Medieval Religion* (London, 1984), 273–311, quotation at p. 309.

15 David Lawton, 'Dullness and the fifteenth century', *English Literary History*, 54 (1987), 761–99, quotation at p. 789.

16 *Rotuli Parliamentorum* (London 1783), iii. 416–32.

17 It has not been possible to identify the version referred to. There are some 170 mss of The Brut surviving. It may be Bodleian MS Digby 185. It is not *The Brut or The Chronicles of England*, ed. F. W. D. Brie, 2 vols, *Early English Text Society*, 131, 136 (1906, 1908), ii. 335–60. See L. M. Matheson, 'The Middle English Prose Brut: A location list of the manuscripts and early printed editions', *Analytical and Enumerative Bibliography*, iii (1979), 254–66.

18 *The St. Albans Chronicle. The 'Chronica Majora' of Thomas Walsingham*, vol. I, *1376–1394*, ed. and trans. John Taylor, Wendy R. Childs and Leslie Watkiss (Oxford, 2003). The basic sequence of Walsingham's compositions was established by V. H. Galbraith, 'Thomas Walsingham and the St. Albans Chronicle', *English Historical Review*, 47 (1932), 12–30, and revised by G. B. Stow, 'Richard II in Thomas Walsingham's Chronicle', *Speculum*, 59 (1984), 68–102.

19 For Thomas Otterbourne's chronicle: *Duo Rerum Anglicarum Scriptores Veteres, viz. Thomas Otterbourne and Johnnes Whethamstede*, ed. Thomas Hearne (2 vols., Oxford, 1732). Capgrave is discussed in Walker, 'Richard II's reputation', pp. 123–4. See also *Joannis Capgrave Liber de Illustribis Henricis*, ed. F. C. Hingeston (Rolls Series, 1858), 98–102, 108; *John Capgrave's Abbreviaçcion of Cronicles*, ed. P. J. Lucas, *Early English Text Society*, 285 (1983).

20 *Historia Vitae et Regni Ricardi Secundi*, ed. G. B. Stow, Haney Foundation Series, University of Philadelphia, 21 (1977).

21 M. V. Clarke and V. H. Galbraith, 'The deposition of Richard II', *Bulletin of the John Rylands Library*, 14 (1930), 164–81, at p. 174.

22 Bodleian Library, Rawlinson MS, B. 488.

23 See ch. 7.

24 *Rotuli Parliamentorum*, iii. 415; *Wykeham's Register*, ed. T. F. Kirby, *Hampshire Record Society*, 2 vols (1896–9), ii. 491–2.

25 *Vita Edwardi Secundii*, ed. and trans. Noël Denholm-Young, *Nelson's Medieval Texts* (1957), pp. 18, 36.

26 A. R. Myers (ed.), *English Historical Documents, IV, 1327–1485* (London, 1969), p. 72.

27 1 *Kings*, chapter 12, verses 6–14.

28 Nancy H. Owen, 'Thomas Wimbledon's Sermon: "Racionem Villicacionis Tue" ', *Mediaeval Studies, Pontifical Institute of Mediaeval Studies*, 28 (Toronto, 1966), 176–97, at pp. 183–4.
29 *The Chronicle of Adam Usk, 1377–1421*, ed. and trans, Christopher Given-Wilson, *Oxford Medieval Texts* (1997), pp. 76–7; *The Kirkstall Abbey Chronicles*, ed. and trans. John Taylor, *Thoresby Society*, 42 (1952), pp. 124–5; *Chronicon Abbatiae de Parco Ludae: The Chronicle of Louth Park Abbey, Lincolnshire Record Society*, ed. Edmund Venables with a translation by A. R. Maddison (Horncastle 1891), p. 41.
30 *Chronicle of Adam Usk*, pp. 62–5.
31 Jean Creton, *Histoire du Roy d'Angleterre Richard*, ed. J. A. C. Buchon, Collection des Chroniques Nationales Francaise, 24 (Paris 1826), 321–466; John Gower, *Cronica Tripertita* in *The Complete Works of John Gower*, ed. G. C. Macaulay (Oxford, 4 vols, 1899–1902), iv. 314–43; G. B. Stow, 'Richard II in Jean Froissart's Chroniques', *Journal of Medieval History*, 11 (1985), 333–45.
32 M. C. Seymour (ed.), *Selections from Hoccleve* (Oxford, 1981), p. 31; Derek Pearsall, 'Hoccleve's Regement of Princes: The Poetics of Royal Self-Representation', *Speculum*, 69 (1994), 390–1.
33 R. H. Bowers, 'A Middle English Wheel of Fortune Poem', *English Studies*, 41 (1960), 196–8.
34 *Boethius: De Consolatione Philisophiae*, ed. Mark Science, trans. John Walton, *Early English Text Society*, 170 (1927).
35 *Historia Vitae et Regni Ricardi Secundi*, p. 166.
36 *Incerti Scriptoris Chronicon Angliae de Regnis Trium Regum Lancastrensium Henrici IV, Henrici V, et Henrici VI*, ed. J. A. Giles (1848), 11–18, esp. 13, 14.
37 *The Minor Poems of John Lydgate*, II: *Secular Poems*, ed. H. M. McCracken, *Early English Text Society*, 192 (1934), pp. 660–1.
38 It has not been possible to identify which version of the Brut is referred to. See above, n 17.
39 British Library, MS Royal 18C VIII, ff. 203v–218.
40 British Library MS, Cotton Claudius E VIII, discussed by L. A. Coote, *Prophecy and Public Affairs in Late Medieval England* (Woodbridge, York Medieval Press, 2000), pp. 151–3.
41 British Library, MS Cotton Galba E IX, ff. 49–50v, printed in *The Poems of Laurence Minot*, ed. Joseph Hall (Oxford, 1914), 103–11.
42 It has not been possible to identify the source for this 'revised version'.
43 British Library, MS Cotton Vespasian E VII, f. 119v.
44 Walter Bower, *Scotichronicon*, 9 vols, ed. D. E. R. Watt (Aberdeen, 1987–98), VIII, p. 29.
45 *The Minor Poems of John Lydgate*, II: *Secular Poems*, pp. 710–16.
46 L. R. Mooney, 'Lydgate's "Kings of England" and another verse chronicle of the Kings', *Viator*, 20 (1989), 256–89, at pp. 283–4.
47 Genealogical chronicles are discussed in Walker, 'Richard II's reputation', pp. 126–7, and in notes pp. 153–4, esp. n. 34.
48 It has not been possible to identify this chronicle.
49 Bodleian Library, MS, e Musaeo 42, f. 31v.
50 British Library, Royal BVIII.
51 *Rotuli Parliamentorum*, iii, pp. 416–32.
52 *Rotuli Parliamentorum*, v, pp. 375–7, 463–7; S. B. Chrimes, *English Constitutional Ideas in the Fifteenth Century* (Cambridge, 1936), 26–32.

53 *Joannis Capgrave Liber de Illustribus Henricis*, pp. 98–102, 108.

54 *John Capgrave's Abbreviacion of Cronicles*, p. 9; P. J. Lucas, 'The growth and development of English literary patronage in the later middle ages and early renaissance', *The Library*, sixth series, 4 (1979), 226–30 contextualises the apparent volte-face.

55 British Library, Lansdowne 204, ff. 198–9 (with marginal note possibly in Hardyng's hand); *The Chronicle of John Hardyng*, pp. 340–1.

56 National Library of Wales, Brogyntyn Roll II, 52.

57 *The Coventry Leet Book*, ed. M. D. Harris, *Early English Text Society*, 134, 135, 138, 146 (1907–13), II, p. 391.

58 Walker, 'Richard II's reputation', pp. 124–5.

59 *Ingulph's Chronicle of the Abbey of Croyland, With the Continuations by Peter of Blois and Anonymous Writers*, trans. H. T. Riley (London, 1854), p. 355.

60 *Joannis Rossi Antiquarii Warwicensis Historia Regum Angliae*, ed. Thomas Hearne (Oxford, 1745), p. 205.

61 M. L. Kekewich, Colin Richmond, A. F. Sutton, Livia Visser-Fuchs and J. L. Watts (eds), *The Politics of Fifteenth-Century England: John Vale's Book* (Stroud, 1995), pp. 212–15.

62 Lawton, 'Dullness and the fifteenth century'.

63 These ideas are developed by Jean-Philippe Genet in 'Histoire et Système de communication' in *L'Histoire et les Nouveaux Publics dans l'Europe Médiévale (XIIIe–XVe siècles), Actes du Colloque International Organisé par la Fondation Européenne de la Science à la Casa de Velasquez, Madrid* (Paris, 1997), pp. 11–29; Genet, 'New politics or new language? The words of politics in Yorkist and early Tudor England', in J. L. Watts (ed.), *The End of the Middle Ages* (Stroud, 1998), 23–64.

9

Political saints in later medieval England

At one period two distinct tombs containing Esmiss Esmoor's remains were reported: one by the tannery, the other up near the goods station. Mr. McBryde visited them both and saw signs of the beginning of a cult – earthenware saucers and so on. Being an experienced official, he did nothing to irritate it, and after a week or so, the rash died down. 'There's propaganda behind all this,' he said . . .[1]

This paper is an investigation of the nature of political society in later medieval England, though the angle from which it approaches the question will be notably oblique. Its starting point is an attempt to investigate the nature and significance of the religious sanction enjoyed by the political order through an examination of the changes in the definitions of sanctity that occurred within this period. Such definitions provide an important collective representation, less of reality than of an imagined and widely approved ideal of private and public life; properly understood, they can help to make an important point about the nature of the later medieval polity. That ideals of sanctity were in a state of flux during this period, at both the officially approved level of papal canonisations and at the level of unsanctioned local cults, is common ground to most of the historians who have examined the issue.[2] In thirteenth-century England, there existed a general agreement over the qualities desirable and necessary in a saint. Taking example and inspiration from the martyrdom and subsequent canonisation of Thomas Becket, a number of conscientious diocesan bishops, several of them distinguished by their defence of the liberties of the English church against lay encroachment, were recognised as saints by the Holy See: Hugh, bishop of Lincoln (1220), Edmund of Abingdon, archbishop of Canterbury (1246), Richard Wych, bishop of Chichester (1262), and Thomas Cantilupe, bishop of Hereford (1320). In addition, several other bishops who conformed more or less closely to the 'Becket model' were the subjects of local veneration and ultimately unsuccessful petitions to the Curia on their behalf: Robert Grosseteste, bishop of Lincoln (died 1254), William de March (died 1302); Robert Winchelsey, archbishop of Canterbury (died 1313), and John Dalderby, bishop of Lincoln (died 1320).[3] From the middle of the fourteenth century, however, there is, if not a breakdown in the previous consensus over the qualities necessary for sanctity, then an interiorisation of the criteria for Christian perfection that made sanctity less straightforward to define, with the result that it is possible to identify a number of divergent, and occasionally competing, ideals of sanctity in later medieval England.

The episcopal model of sanctity was not abandoned entirely. Two bishops of Exeter, James Berkley and Edmund Lacy, enjoyed a local cult, while at Norwich cathedral the tombs of bishops Suffield and Salmon were both objects of devotion.[4] In none of these cases was the cult widespread, however, and the rapid decline of offerings to Suffield and Salmon, to be replaced by a remarkable pluralism of altars and shrines within the cathedral by the end of the century,[5] suggests that the English episcopate did not in general escape the crisis of definition and purpose that affected the western Church as a whole. Richard Fitzralph, archbishop of Armagh, was the only contemporary bishop to attract a persistent cult,[6] while the long-delayed canonisation in 1457 of Osmund, the first bishop of Salisbury (died 1102), was as much a recognition of the institutional influence and distinction of the Salisbury chapter as it was a promotion of an ideal of episcopal sanctity. Saints drawn from the religious orders, a particular feature of the era of Avignonese papacy across Western Europe as a whole, were only patchily represented in England. Besides the successful canonisation of John, prior of the house of Augustinian canons at Bridlington (1403),[7] the local cults of the religious do not suggest a consistent pattern to their appeal. Thomas Hale, a monk of the Benedictine priory at Dover, killed by French raiders in 1295; John Went, provincial minister of the Franciscans in England (died 1348); and Thomas Gresham, abbot of Thornton: each was reported to have performed miracles and to be the object of veneration, but there is little in common between their cults.[8] Equally, a third model of sanctity, the 'mystical invasion' of the calendar that is so notable a feature of European religious life after *c.* 1370, was represented in England only by the solitary figure of Richard Rolle of Hampole.[9] More numerous were the parish priests whose qualities of life and ministry earned them a localised veneration; indeed, there is a sense in which they seem to have replaced the conscientious diocesan bishop as the favoured type of clerical sanctity among the laity. They include Philip Ingleberd, rector of Kaylingham (Yorks.), and Richard Caister, vicar of St Stephen's, Norwich, besides the better-known figure of John Shorne, rector of North Marston (Bucks.).[10] In addition, later medieval England was unusually rich in one further group of candidates for sanctity, the 'political' saints; men whose claim to sanctity rested initially, and more or less exclusively, on their violent deaths in the course of a political conflict. The principal representatives of this group, who will receive more detailed attention in this paper, are well known: Simon de Montfort (died 1265), Thomas of Lancaster (died 1322), Edward II (died 1327), Richard Scrope, archbishop of York (died 1405), Henry VI (died 1471). It should not be forgotten, however, that there are other figures who fall into the same category. Simon de Montfort's companions, killed with him at Evesham, were sometimes associated with him in popular veneration, while a cult of Edward of Windsor, the only son of

Henry VI, was maintained at Tewkesbury; even Richard II's favourite, Robert de Vere, earl of Oxford, was thought a worthy object of devotion.[11]

This veneration of laymen as 'political' saints had precedent in England; its greater frequency in the later Middle Ages represents a change of emphasis rather than a wholesale shift in the paradigms of sanctity. The considerable devotion that grew up around the figure of Waltheof, earl of Northumbria, at Thorney in the early twelfth century finds an echo in the miracles reported at the tombs of Henry, the Young King, and William Fitzosbert, leader of the London opposition to the rule of Hubert Walter.[12] Nevertheless, there are two important respects in which the uniqueness of these political cults from the twelfth century onwards should be emphasised. Firstly, the degree to which their appearance marks a decisive break with the pre-Conquest past, in which sanctity was especially closely allied to the ruling dynasties of Anglo-Saxon England.[13] Secondly, they represent an especially English phenomenon, for in no other country was the connection between involvement in secular politics and a claim to sanctity as tightly drawn. There were several Scandinavian bishop saints – Eystein of Nidaros (died 1188); Byrnolf of Skara (died 1317) and Nicholas of Linköping (died 1387) – whose claims to sanctity were held to include an element of resistance to tyrannical royal and noble authority, although this was presented as only one element in the full ensemble of episcopal virtues to be expected in a bishop of the 'Becket model'.[14] Otherwise, political saints of the type relatively common in England, venerated wholly or in part for their involvement with, and death in, the course of secular political affairs, appear only rarely in the rest of Europe. Pietro Parenzo, the papal *podestà* of Orvieto, who eventually became the patron saint of the city after his death at the hands of the Ghibellines; Cabrit and Bassa, two obscure Majorcan patriots martyred for their resistance to the troops of Alfonso III of Aragon; and Charles of Blois, duke of Brittany, whose cult undoubtedly owed something (but not everything) to his death in battle against the English-backed Montfortist claimant of the duchy:[15] these provide the only important European counterparts to the well-established tradition of political saints in England. The contrast poses again the questions with which this discussion began. What was it about the English polity that encouraged the emergence of such cults? And what was their place and purpose within English political life?

Several historians have addressed themselves to these questions, though their answers have generally assumed one of two forms. The first is that no explanation is, in fact, required, since the existence of these cults is itself unremarkable, evidence only of 'the tendency of ignorant people to look for . . . a hero in any prominent figure who met a sudden and violent death', for once a cult had started 'simple-minded devotion would ensure its continuance'.[16] While this approach has the merit of emphasising the considerable value that continued to be placed upon violent death – 'the certain agony of martyrdom'[17] – as a sign of sanctity in popular religion, it remains an unsatisfactorily partial explanation, for murdered princes or politicians, however well known, could not automatically expect to be venerated as saints after their death. No cult of

Piers Gaveston grew up, despite Edward II's attempts to encourage one,[18] and neither Thomas of Woodstock nor Humphrey of Gloucester attracted any veneration, despite their relative popularity in life. Equally, 'simple-minded' devotion was not, of itself, enough to ensure a cult's continuance. The tomb of Richard, earl of Arundel, condemned to death as a traitor by Richard II in 1397, was the object of a veneration substantial enough to cause the king disquiet, but this enthusiasm proved short-lived; the last reference to Arundel's merits or miracles dates to *c.* 1404.[19] The second, and most widely accepted, explanation advanced concentrates upon the undoubted elements of political manipulation to be found in the promotion of these cults and takes that part of the answer for the whole. The motive behind the devotion to these political saints is, therefore, to be explained in primarily political terms, since such cults represented 'an easy and almost unpunishable way of showing hostility to the king'.[20] A more sophisticated version of the same argument connects the concentration of these 'political' cults in the fourteenth and fifteenth centuries with the contemporary expansion of the political nation; 'with the growing necessity of securing the affections of the commonalty, a new age of political leaders sought to channel and control this enthusiasm' by the skilled manipulation of popular religiosity.[21] This explanation has, at least, a certain empirical value. The alleged activities of Sir Reginald de Montfort and the mayor of Bristol in encouraging the cult of two of Thomas of Lancaster's followers executed there indicates that there were always interest groups quick to recognise the capital to be made from such cults.[22] Nevertheless, the suggested model of political promotion and manipulation, with its implicit assumption that the political and intellectual élite could write at will on the *tabula rasa* of popular devotion, seems at best only a partial explanation. It fails to account for the initial impulse of veneration, which preceded the annexation and 'construction' of these cults by particular interest groups, and was often tenaciously maintained in the face of considerable official discouragement. Nor does it adequately explain the survival and development of some cults and the swift disappearance of others. The fully worked out martyrdom scene, complete with accompanying miracles, offered by Thomas Walsingham in his description of the death of Archbishop Sudbury in 1381, like the report of miracles occurring at the tomb of the Carmelite friar tortured to death by a group of household knights in 1385,[23] provide instances where the initial movement of sympathy and veneration for the clerical victims of violent death was not – despite, in the case of Sudbury, some powerful backing – transformed into an effective cause. In this sense, the canonical tag *non poena sed causa* contains an important sociological truth; since all saints were saints 'for other people', their lives and reputations remodelled to correspond to collective mental representations of the holy,[24] there had to be something in the actions of the victim of violence, or in the circumstances of his death, that appealed to a substantial number of worshippers if his cult was to develop effectively. In order to establish the nature and effectiveness of the appeal exercised by the English political saints, it will be necessary to examine briefly the origins and principal manifestations of their cults, before going on to seek a more satisfactory explanation for their success.

The cult of Simon de Montfort, earl of Leicester, rapidly established itself following his death in battle against the royalist forces at Evesham in August 1265. The Dictum of Kenilworth, promulgated a little over a year later, already speaks of his reputation as a saint and of his reported miracles.[25] Chronicles from every part of the country confirm the widespread belief in his sanctity, frequently adding that reports of many more miracles worked by the new saint had been suppressed for fear of the king.[26] The surviving evidence of this veneration consists of a liturgical office in de Montfort's honour, a collection of his *miracula* produced at Evesham Abbey, and a number of motets and poems in both Latin and Anglo-Norman, celebrating his deeds and his martyrdom.[27] The 196 miracles ascribed to the earl's intercession suggest that devotion to his cause was spread widely across the southern Midlands, with outlying pockets of enthusiasm in Kent and London, and reveal a notably well-connected group of suppliants; de Montfort's miracles were performed on behalf of the countess of Gloucester and the baronial families of Roos, Cantilupe and Peverel, besides several knightly sufferers.[28] Yet although this evidence suggests de Montfort's cult gained rapid and widespread support, enthusiasm for his cause appears to have been short-lived. The last datable cure in his *miracula* took place in August 1279, while the latest of the manuscripts containing material in de Montfort's honour are from the early fourteenth century.[29] When Edward II had 'songs of Simon de Montfort' sung to him at Whorlton Castle in August 1323, it seems more likely that the songs commemorated his life and the justice of his cause than that they saluted him as a saint.[30]

Thomas of Lancaster's cult, though very similar in its origins to de Montfort's, shows some significant differences in its development. Following the earl of Lancaster's execution as a traitor, after a summary trial at Pontefract in July 1322, miracles were soon reported to be occuring at his tomb and the authorities unsuccessfully sought to repress the popular devotion which followed.[31] Within a decade of his death a hagiographic *vita* had been produced, probably at Pontefract,[32] and as in the case of de Montfort, the surviving evidence suggests a widespread and initially popular cult – a liturgical office in Lancaster's honour, and surviving fragments of a second;[33] chronicle reports of his miracles;[34] depictions and *memoriae* of his martyrdom in several mid-fourteenth century psalters and books of hours,[35] as well as evidence for the rapid institutionalisation of the Pontefract pilgrimage.[36] In contrast to the cult of Simon de Montfort, however, devotion to Thomas of Lancaster became a permanent feature of English spiritual life in the later Middle Ages, lasting in a more or less attenuated form until the Reformation. While the initial burst of enthusiasm for the cult may have begun to subside *c.* 1350, the patronage of two powerful noble families, the houses of Bohun and Lancaster, provided sufficient publicity and resources to maintain the shrine as a place of pilgrimage until the end of the fourteenth century, to the extent that in 1390 it was believed, erroneously, that Lancaster had been officially canonised.[37] The advent of the Lancastrian dynasty, determined to promote devotion to their own *Adelsheilige*, inevitably reinvigorated the cult; Henry IV presented vestments depicting the *historia* of Lancaster's martyrdom to St George's chapel, Windsor, in 1401, for example.[38] As a result, there is considerable evidence for Lancaster's continuing popularity as a saint in the fifteenth century: there are references to the existence of a guild of St Thomas at Pontefract itself; new polyphonic settings were written for the existing motets in his honour; his relics continued to be venerated and miracles at his tomb to attract public attention; the anniversary of his death was entered in some English liturgical calendars until well into the sixteenth century.[39]

Different from either of these cults was the fitful veneration that began to gather around the tomb of the murdered Edward II at Gloucester. It is especially difficult to gauge the appeal and success of this cult because, apart from the account of a Gloucester annalist writing at the end of the fourteenth century,[40] the evidence for Edward's veneration is very thin. Two points stand out from that account, however. In contrast to the other 'political' cults, the inception of Edward's cult did not follow immediately on his interment; the prayers and offerings are said to have begun in the time of Abbot Wigmore, who was elected in 1329. As a consequence, the 'oppositional' element in Edward's veneration – the degree to which it can be interpreted as a covert criticism of the regime of Isabella and Mortimer – can only have been slight, since Edward III began his personal rule within eighteen months. Indeed, what distinguishes Edward II's cult from those of either Simon de Montfort or Thomas of Lancaster is the degree to which it was dependent on royal encouragement, whether in the form of the substantial gifts made by Edward III and his family at the shrine in 1343 or in the determined campaign for his great-grandfather's canonisation launched by Richard II *c.* 1385.[41] Apart from these royal initiatives, the evidence for Edward's veneration is slight; no liturgical commemorations are known to survive while the scattered iconographical evidence, such as the depiction of the king, labelled *sanctus Edwardus*, in a Tewkesbury roll-chronicle compiled *c.* 1420, suggests a cult largely confined to the west of England.[42] It seems safest to conclude that the continuing popular debate over Edward's sanctity, to which Ranulf Higden alluded *c.* 1340,[43] had been generally settled to the king's disadvantage some years before Richard II vainly sought to revive enthusiasm for his veneration. It is noticeable that even the Gloucester annalist, writing in the shadow of Richard's campaign for Edward's canonisation, does not accord him the title of saint when describing the offerings at his tomb.

The cult of Richard Scrope, archbishop of York, executed in June 1405 for his rebellion against Henry IV presents no such problems of evidence, though it raises questions of interpretation to which it will be necessary to return. The popular veneration at Scrope's tomb was immediate and, initially, carried on in the face of royal prohibition.[44] The archbishop's subsequent miracles were widely reported and the offerings at his shrine were soon yielding very substantial sums.[45] Fittingly for a clerical martyr, Scrope's death generated a large body of literary material: two separate prose accounts of his trial and execution survive;[46] a Latin poem and a liturgical office in the archbishop's honour were composed soon after his death, and a number of further antiphons and *memoriae* for Scrope survive in contemporary calendars and books of hours.[47] In addition, the inventories of *ex voto* offerings at Scrope's tomb drawn up in 1500 and 1509 make it clear that his cult continued to attract popular devotion.[48] That it did so was certainly due to the continuing regard in which the 'martyr of York' was held, but it also came to owe something to the encouragement of the Yorkist kings, who saw in the archbishop's execution one of the chief demonstrations of the injustice and illegitimacy of Lancastrian rule.[49] It was accordingly at Edward IV's prompting (*regio impulso*) that the dean and chapter of York began to consider the possibility of Scrope's formal canonisation in 1462.[50] The archbishop had always had his enthusiastic devotees among the Minster clergy[51] but it seems likely that, by this date, his cult had begun to surrender some of its earlier prominence. Although there are no precise figures available for oblations at his tomb after 1421, the general level of offerings in the Minster, which had risen with the growth of Scrope's cult (from £31 6*s* 2*d* in 1405 to £56 12*s* 0½*d* in 1416 and £54 5*s* 9½*d* in 1419) had fallen back sharply by mid-century, with annual oblations running at about £25 *per annum* during the 1440s and £17 10*s* 0*d* during the following decade.[52] The corporate endeavour of the dean and chapter was consequently aimed at establishing the archbishop's cult securely among the many active devotions of the archdiocese[53] rather than according it the special prominence that Edward IV evidently desired. As in the case of Thomas of Lancaster, therefore, a cult that had its origins in a protest against the actions of royal government came to owe a degree of its continued popularity to direct royal sponsorship.

Similar considerations apply, with even greater force, to the cult of Henry VI. Following his death in the Tower and hasty burial at Chertsey Abbey, Henry's tomb soon became a place of pilgrimage, despite the alleged indifference of the monks of Chertsey, who were said to fear the disapproval of Edward IV.[54] Offerings were also being reported before an image of the king in York Minster as early as 1475.[55] It is difficult to assess the true dimensions of Henry's cult before the translation of his body from Chertsey to Windsor in 1484 – at which point it certainly becomes a devotion encouraged by the ruling dynasty – but there are several contemporary sources which ascribe some of Henry's reported miracles to the Chertsey period and the fame of his tomb was already enough to attract pilgrims from as far away as Norwich.[56] Following the 1484 translation, however, there is no doubt about the popularity of Henry's cult, which attracted very considerable numbers of pilgrims, generated a carefully edited collection of 174 miracles performed by the former king, and is commemorated in a considerable body of surviving devotional and liturgical material.[57] There seems good reason to believe that devotion to Henry VI, fuelled by his growing reputation as an effective protector against outbreaks of plague and sweating-sickness, replaced Thomas Becket as the most popular of English cults before the Reformation.[58]

This brief survey raises, at once, one of the principal points to be made about the cults of these political saints; that there is only a limited sense in which their veneration can be said to constitute a 'canonisation of opposition to the Crown'. That there was an element, more or less central, of political protest and defiance in the genesis of these cults seems, with the possible exception of Edward II, to be undeniable. But in four out of the five cases considered above, this oppositional statement came to be overlaid, and largely neutralised, by a degree of royal protection and encouragement that sought to harness the devotion these saints aroused in the interests of the crown. In the case of Thomas of Lancaster, this royal intervention was swift: Edward III began to press for his canonisation as early as 1327.[59] Though in Henry VI's case this royal initiative took a little longer (1471–84) to manifest itself, and in Scrope's the lapse of time was over half a century, it was only in the case of de Montfort's cause that the attitude of the royal authorities remained consistently hostile; Edward I would not allow the office in his honour composed by the Franciscans to be performed in his own lifetime.[60] As a result, to confine discussion of the phenomenon of 'political' saints in later medieval England to the extent to which they represented and encouraged a spirit of resistance to the claims of the crown is to ignore half the question that needs to be answered; which is, the degree to which these same saints contributed to the simultaneous, and generally more successful, enhancement of the spiritual status and claims of the English monarchy. It is in this context that it seems worthwhile to pursue the suggestion that political saints should best be interpreted as an inversion of the *mentalité* of holy monarchy, the claim to a special sacral status advanced with increasing insistence by kings in both England and France. As one of several contemporary but competing representations of the political order, the cult of political saints might be seen as a reaction against the sacral claims of kings which nevertheless continued to depend on the actions and reputation of the monarchy for its appeal and, in the long run, served only to reinforce the ideology it challenged.[61] Though admittedly speculative, this appears a useful hypothesis to pursue for it has, at least, the merit of calling attention to one of the most striking developments in the ideology of the English monarchy in the later Middle Ages; the growing conviction that kings stood in an especially close relationship to God, that they possessed certain distinct spiritual qualities by virtue of their exercise of secular office.

This was not, of course, a phenomenon confined solely to the later Middle Ages. Touching for scrofula, the royal miracle of healing, was performed as far back as Henry II's reign and, if Richard II believed that unique spiritual qualities had been conferred on him by the rite of unction performed at his coronation, Henry III's enthusiasm for the sacral aspects of monarchy 150 years earlier had moved Robert Grosseteste to remind him of the fate of Ozias, king of Judah, who was struck with leprosy for usurping the priestly office.[62] Even the matter-of-fact Edward III had ascribed to him magical powers while his eldest son could, on more than one occasion, be compared to the Son of God.[63] Nevertheless, the late fourteenth and fifteenth centuries appear to mark a new anxiety to emphasise the spiritual claims and powers of the English monarchy, epitomised in the adoption of the title 'most Christian king' and justified by Thomas Polton's argument at the Council of Constance that the English dynasty had the longest association with Christianity of any European ruling house.[64] This emphasis owed a good deal to the anxiety of the Lancastrian dynasty to consolidate their right to the crown, which led them to lay stress upon the divine sanction and approval conferred by their royal ancestry; 'twelve kings of the English successions, martyrs and confessors . . . and the emblems of their sanctity plain for all to see' greeted Henry V on his triumphal entry into London after Agincourt and offered him the sacramental elements of bread and wine, while Henry VI sought the canonisation of Alfred, the first ruler of a united English kingdom.[65] The development of these claims was, however, also testimony to a deeper-seated shift in the public perception of the function and necessity of monarchy fostered by the growing association of heresy with sedition. The Oldcastle rising, the Kentish scare of 1428 and the Perkins rebellion in 1431, as well as the ominous object lesson of contemporary Bohemia, all pointed to the same conclusion; that heresy led inevitably to sedition.[66] By the same token, sedition came increasingly to encompass, and be identified with, heresy. The connection was already immanent in the statute against unauthorised preaching passed, on the initiative of Henry, prince of Wales, in the Long Parliament, which included both Lollard evangelists and Ricardian loyalists within its prohibitions.[67] It was cemented into place by the allegation that Richard, earl of Cambridge, sought the aid of the Lollards for his plot to assassinate the king in 1415.[68] The defence of the Catholic orthodoxy, it was increasingly clear, depended upon the king successfully discharging his duties to maintain the social hierarchy and the public peace; to attack the king was, inevitably, to attack the Christian faith.

In the wake of heresy came a further, and closely related, threat to ecclesiastical and royal authority: sorcery. The association of magical activity – prophecy, divination, necromancy – with the enemies and opponents of the king seems a particular feature of the disturbed political scene between 1397 and 1406, when there was a sudden rash of accusations and counter-charges of reliance on prophecy and magic; as one French observer commented disapprovingly, the English 'very thoroughly believe in prophecies, phantoms and witchcraft, and employ them right willingly'.[69] Once established, the association grew closer throughout the fifteenth century. In 1419 Henry V announced himself to be the intended victim of a magician's plot and required the prayers of his diocesans in order to combat it, while Bishop Stafford of Bath and Wells warned his flock in 1431 that the glorious kingdom of England had twice lost the crown of glory through belief in magic and spells; the startling success of Joan of Arc, unambiguously seen in English sources as a sorceress, provided vivid confirmation of the power of magic to harm the English cause.[70] Accusations of involvement in sorcery and divination became the currency of domestic politics; Henry VI's government sought to win the propaganda war against the Cade rebels in 1450 by presenting their leader as a dabbler in sorcery and consorter with the devil; Jacquetta, duchess of Bedford, had to clear herself of accusations that she had sought the death of the king and his wife by witchcraft in 1470, while similar charges of witchcraft were preferred against the Woodville family by Richard III.[71] This connection between sorcery and treason was most clearly defined in two famous 'show trials', when Eleanor Cobham, duchess of Gloucester, was found guilty of imagining the king's death in 1441 on the grounds that she had sought to know when he would die by astrological means, and Dr Stacey, Thomas Blake and Thomas Burdet were condemned as traitors for calculating the nativities of the king and the prince of Wales in 1477.[72]

There are two points of relevance to the analysis of the phenomenon of political saints in these much-discussed cases. The first is that those involved were in both cases adjudged guilty of treason. This is in contrast to the outcome of earlier cases of a similar type. When the powerful Adam de Stratton, chamberlain of the Exchequer, was tried for corruption in 1289, the common talk of his sorcery found no place in the charges against him, while when Walter Langton, Edward I's treasurer, was accused of sorcery in 1303, the king continued to accord him his full support. Equally, when the prior of Coventry's servants were charged with plotting the death of Edward II and the Despensers by magical means in 1324, the crime was classified as a felony, not a treason.[73] Secondly, the grounds of the charge of treason in the two fifteenth-century cases was that the plotters had sought to 'destroy the cordial love' that should always regulate the relations of a king and his subjects.[74] This is an unusually clear statement of the implicit assumption behind much ecclesiastical and secular thinking on the nature of contemporary politics: that the public peace depended, in the final analysis, upon the maintenance of an ideal of charity between individuals. The political amity this ideal was intended to effect was, for instance, proclaimed as a principle of his government on more than one occasion by Henry IV; in 1400 he pardoned some of the rebels taken in arms against him in order to 'foster the faith and love of our subjects towards us', while in 1409 he explained his grant of a general pardon as a means of creating 'the mutual love without which all else is in vain' in order that 'our said lieges may lift up their hearts with greater joy to remain more truly in faith and love towards us and our heirs'.[75] How such an ideal of charity should operate in a properly constituted political society was explained with some precision by the commons in the 1401 parliament, when they sought to compare a session of parliament to the sacrifice of the Mass. The point of this elaborate conceit was that, just as the Mass was envisaged as offering a 'social miracle' to the devout and contrite, bringing harmony out of discord, so parliament, properly conducted, was the 'political miracle', reconciling the unreconciled and creating anew the body politic, 'by the grace of God all in one faithfully bound together' by the 'good and entire hearts' they bore towards one another. Within this process, it was the king who performed the priestly function, making 'the sacrifice to be offered to God by all Christians' through his preservation and protection of his lay and ecclesiastical subjects.[76] On this view, a king was as crucial to the political salvation of his subjects as a priest to the spiritual salvation of his flock. This was a vision of political relations, idealised but potent, that retained its currency throughout the fifteenth century. Edward IV, whose progress through England in 1471 was accompanied by miracles of divine approbation, justified his tenure of the Crown in the millenial terms of a conflict with, and victory over, 'our great adversary'; Richard III, said by John Rous to reign like Antichrist, was described by Henry VII as 'our adversary, *enemy of nature* and of all public weal'. The disturbance of the political order created by a usurping king was envisaged as a disturbance of the divinely sanctioned natural order as well.[77]

It is within the context of this set of beliefs – that the king was a priest-like figure whose task was to bring about a state of social amity on which the peace and wholeness of the body politic ultimately depended – that the cult of political saints in later medieval England can best be understood. Devotion to such saints was undoubtedly born in an atmosphere of political disorder and their cults contained within themselves, during the early stages of their development, a certain element of protest against the triumph of the unrighteous. Yet if such cults were to survive and prosper, they had to grow beyond their origins and answer the aspirations and concerns articulated in the set of beliefs that grew up around the powers of the monarch in the later Middle Ages, satisfying the desire for reconciliation and re-integration expressed, positively, in the ideal of 'cordial love' and, negatively, in the heavy penalties prescribed for those who destroyed that love. Their success or failure as cults depended, in general terms, on the success or failure with which they did so; if social amity enjoyed 'an intimate relationship with the process of salvation',[78] a saint who could not bring about that social amity could not, in turn, be regarded as a reliable source of salvation. The power of the saints, and their value in political life, was not in preventing disorder or rebellion, for this they manifestly could not do. It was in helping to restore a measure of harmony after the strife was over and in making reconciliation, even on unfavourable terms, easier for the losers by offering a higher, and more objective, constraint to which all could submit without dishonour. As Southern has remarked of the cult of Waltheof, the Anglo-Saxon hero whose tomb was attracting Anglo-Norman devotees by the reign of Henry I, 'the miracles were a common ground on which all men could meet'.[79] The cult of Archbishop Scrope, far from being straightforwardly 'anti-Lancastrian', prospered in precisely the same way; the offerings at his shrine covered the political spectrum, including both the livery badge of Richard II – 'a hart of gold, enamelled with white and green' – and the Lancastrian collar of SS, given by no less a figure than Archbishop Bowet's nephew.[80]

The characteristic development of a political cult along these lines is already foreshadowed in the most famous of them, that of Thomas Becket. The initial reaction of the Canterbury clergy to his murder, preserved in the lections for the anniversary of his martyrdom in the Sarum Breviary, was to emphasise the violence of the act and the political division that it bred – 'the powers of heaven were so disturbed that, as if in vengeance for the spilling of innocent blood, people rose up against people and kingdom against kingdom; even the realm was divided against itself'.[81] Becket's blood called out for vengeance 'more than the blood of the just man Abel, killed at the beginning of the world'.[82] Yet by the time of Becket's translation in 1220 the emphasis of the office written for the occasion – possibly by Stephen Langton[83] – was very different. It avoided the opportunity of restating the divisive claims to ecclesiastical immunity that lay at the root of Becket's martyrdom, concentrating instead on the Levitican idea of a jubilee as a time of repentance and remission and presenting the feast as a time of grace and reconciliation.[84] The author of the office was doing no more than reflect the favoured presentation of Becket's cult at Canterbury. 'What is so remarkable about a saint loving those who love him?' asked Benedict of Peterborough. 'Even the pagans and publicans do that. It is a narrow charity that admits friends and excludes enemies'.[85] It was a cardinal point in Becket's reputation for sanctity that his grace was known to extend to his former enemies, such as Gilbert Foliot and his servants, or the brother of his murderer, Robert de Broc. It was with the archbishop's help that Henry II's forces captured William the Lion in 1174 and that the king was subsequently able to establish 'so great and perfect a peace' throughout his kingdom.[86] The historical Becket had already given way to the emblematic episcopal martyr, dying for the good of the church but, at the same time, extending his patronage and favour to the whole English people.

Among the political saints discussed in this paper, there is too little evidence for the cult of Edward II to come to any firm conclusions as to how his devotees perceived him, and the case of Simon de Montfort presents some special features, best left to the end of the discussion. For the other three saints, however, it is possible to illustrate in some detail the way their cults developed beyond their immediate origins in an act of political defiance in order to exercise an appeal for a number of different audiences. In the case of Thomas of Lancaster, for instance, several constituents of his sanctity, several claims on the devotion of their audience, are held in tension by the surviving literary and liturgical evidence for his cult. The circumstances of, and reasons for, Lancaster's execution are never ignored; he is presented as a lover of truth and constant fighter for justice, more fearful of offending the divine majesty than its human representative.[87] In the Pontefract *vita*, these claims are given an extended exposition in terms that echo his own propaganda, emphasising the powers and responsibilities of his position as steward of England.[88] But this was only one element in the construction of Lancaster's cult. Besides the carefully crafted reminiscences of the Passion that appear in the *The Brut*'s account of his trial and execution, the most consistent emphasis is laid upon Lancaster's royal birth and knightly virtues. As a royal vessel, born of a royal bed, he will bring about the cure of the kingdom – a claim that seeks an association with, rather than an appropriation of, the thaumaturgic powers of the monarchy.[89] As the flower and gem of knighthood, the knight of the English church, who never held the poor in contempt, Lancaster is portrayed as an emblematic reminder to the nobility of their duty of protection towards the poor and orthodox.[90] Equally, when Lancaster is presented as the secular counterpart of Thomas Becket, it is the Becket of Langton's Translation office, offering salvation and reconciliation to the whole nation, on whom he is modelled; it is for 'the peace and tranquillity of the inhabitants of England' that Earl Thomas 'the champion of plentiful charity' is said to have died.[91] This transformation from partisan figure to national saint, a powerful patron at the court of heaven for the whole English people, was a swift one. As early as 1327 the commons were petitioning for the initiation of his canonisation process 'for the enhancing of the estate of the kingdom', while Edward III's letter to the pope on the same issue describes Thomas's holy blood, fertile and life-giving, flowing through all parts of England like the river of paradise.[92] These were the terms in which his cult continued to be envisaged. One of the fifteenth-century motets in his honour salutes him as the guardian of England (*tutor Angliae*), a peace-maker who brings grace to the hard hearts of sinners and creates concord out of discord.[93]

The evidence for the development of Archbishop Scrope's cult illustrates the same point: that a successful devotion soon grew beyond the circumstances of its origin. The Lancastrian government seems never, in fact, to have ascribed much significance to its potential as a rallying point for dissent. Though John of Lancaster was initially anxious to prevent any concourse of pilgrims at Scrope's tomb, by December 1405 Archbishop Arundel was already taking a more conciliatory line with the Minster clergy, insisting only that they refrain from inducing oblations and devotion on the grounds that these should await the judgement of God and the determination of the Church.[94] When the cult persisted, Henry IV and his advisers accepted it with good grace; the temporary prohibition on offerings at Scrope's tomb had been lifted, in practice, by 1409 and was formally revoked by Henry V early in his reign, while enthusiastic supporters of the dynasty, such as the Kenilworth chronicler John Strecche, nevertheless reported Scrope's miracles and the crowds of pilgrims at York.[95] This was not because the liturgical and devotional material in the archbishop's honour glossed over the circumstances of his death or refrained from passing judgement upon them. Most accounts of his martyrdom emphasise the injustice of his execution without due process of law, while to describe Scrope as a 'new Abel' clearly casts Henry IV in the role of a new Cain, shedding the blood of the righteous man.[96] Yet this aspect of his cult was balanced by several of the other claims for his sanctity advanced by Scrope's advocates, which served to generalise the appeal of his cause beyond the purely political. These included an emphasis on the excellence of Scrope's priestly virtues, as an *exemplum castitatis* whose first recorded miracle was to encourage a sinner to go to confession, and a closely allied association between his cult and the developing devotion of the Five Wounds, fostered by the manner of his death.[97] Comparison with the proto-martyr Stephen, encouraged by Scrope's burial in the chapel of St Stephen in the Minster, provided a narrative model of his death which necessarily involved the archbishop in calling on God to forgive his enemies;

Thomas Gascoigne's account of the martyrdom duly has Scrope praying that God will not revenge his death on the king or his servants.[98] When Richard Scrope was further compared to Thomas Becket, therefore, it was the familiar Becket of the liturgy, offering reconciliation to the whole English people, not the Becket of history, to whom reference was made; the convergence of royal and ecclesiastical interests in the intervening centuries had rendered a re-dramatisation of the issues originally in dispute between Henry II and his archbishop increasingly otiose.[99]

The successful transition from a claim to veneration born of a moment of political conflict to an established cult was effected in Scrope's case, as in Thomas of Lancaster's, precisely because devotion to the archbishop was held to offer a means of deliverance from such struggles. The office that salutes Scrope as a new Abel also calls upon the archbishop to dissolve the chains of conflict and re-create the compact of peace, going on to elaborate a parallel between Christ, who died outside the gates of Jerusalem, and Scrope, who died outside the gates of York; it is the task of the archbishop to turn York into a new Sion, an 'abode of peace'.[100] It was for this reason that Edward IV's attempts to re-interpret the Scrope cult in a more partisan and political light met with indifference and, ultimately, failure at York. The dean and chapter gave prolonged consideration to the king's intention to seek the archbishop's canonisation and ended by resolving, instead, to raise the celebration of the Minster's dedication to a double feast and to improve the existing celebrations on the feast of St William.[101] There is significance, as well as prevarication, in their decision. Scrope was valued as a local patron, the 'glory of York', accessible to all who invoked his aid, and faced with seeing him appropriated to act as the supernatural champion of a political faction, the dean and chapter responded by seeking to anchor his cult still more firmly within the spiritual and physical context of the Minster as the mother-church of the archdiocese.

As Edward IV sought, in this way, to exploit the reputation of one political saint for the advantage of his own dynasty, it was natural that he and his advisers should be wary of the growing popular devotion to the last Lancastrian king during the 1470s and should seek to restrain it.[102] Yet Henry VI's claims to sanctity were expressed, from the first, in terms that largely removed them from the arena of political debate. The continuator of the Crowland Chronicle accounted Henry a saint 'by reason of his innocence of life, his love of God and the Church and his patience in adversity'. Writing *c.* 1484, John Blacman produced a more detailed treatment of the king's virtues, portraying him as a saint of the *devotio moderna*, a contemplative and ascetic imitator of Christ, another Job in his sufferings.[103] Above all, Henry appears as the subject of a startling but benign *perepteia*, as the man who lost an earthly kingdom but gained a heavenly one. With the important addition of an emphasis upon the king's powers of healing, these were the terms in which the growing body of liturgical and devotional material in Henry's honour portrayed him as well. The 'prayer of Sixtus IV' uses Henry's life as an *exemplum* of patience and humility in prosperity and adversity, while the emphasis put on the same virtues by Bernard André, Henry VII's chaplain, suggests that this portrayal of Henry as the 'suffering Lamb' was the aspect of his reputation to enjoy the most enthusiastic official sanction.[104] As devotion to the king developed, however, two further elements in the powers and virtues ascribed to him, largely absent from the earlier material in his honour, began to emerge. The first, present also in the cults of Thomas of Lancaster and Richard Scrope, was the store set on Henry's actions as a peacemaker. 'Let there be peace on earth and not war' asks the popular invocation *Rex Henricus, sis amicus,* while one of the English prayers in his honour calls on Henry to 'set this realm in rest'.[105] The same idea was worked out, at greater length and in a secular context, in Petrus Carmelianus' poem on the birth of prince Arthur, in which the task of bringing peace to England's dynastic strife is delegated to Henry by the company of saints.[106] One of the king's early miracles illustrates how his intercession could bring such peace about; the parishioners of Ashby St Leger 'all bound by one chain of charity' at the bidding of their priest, successfully stilled the ravings of a woman possessed by the devil who threatened to disrupt the Mass by their prayers to the king. Besides this image of communities united in charity by the action of the saint,[107] a second and less predictable emphasis was upon Henry's power, upon the assertion of an authority in death that had been denied him in life. 'Those who disparaged you now come before you and adore your footprints' runs the versicle of the office in Henry's honour; an early woodcut of the king as a saint, towering massively above his suppliant subjects, vividly conveys the same idea.[108] Both words and image are reminiscent of the terms in which the *Anglo-Saxon Chronicle* celebrated the emergent cult of Edward the Martyr – 'those who would not bow to his living body now bend humbly before his dead body' – and the perception behind the celebration was very similar.[109] Henry's cult is seen as representing a reassertion of right order in the world, the peaceful triumph of divinely approved monarchical authority over the forces of discord that have temporarily threatened it.

Simon de Montfort's cult provides a significant exception, in several respects, from those examined above. The literary and liturgical material justifies his veneration in appropriately general terms, as a soldier of Christ, fighting for justice and the maintenance of the faith, a 'wall of Israel' for the people and clergy of England. Comparison with Becket's cause and martyrdom is particularly frequent; Thomas is the 'titan of the east', Simon the 'star of the west'.[110] Two features of the songs and prayers in his honour stand out as exceptional, however. One is that many of them were clearly produced very soon after the earl's death at Evesham, since they make reference to the contemporary political scene: de Montfort's office finishes by deploring the faithlessness and lawbreaking that continues throughout the country and calls upon the martyr to confound those who commit such crimes; the poem *Ubi fuit mons est vallis* ends with a similar lament for the destruction done by the *raptores in patria*; the song *Chaunter m'estoit* calls upon God to take care of those of Montfort's followers who are still in prison.[111] This helps to locate the context in which such material was produced, dating it to the period of violent social and tenurial disruption between Evesham and the Dictum of Kenilworth, when Henry III's government was seeking to implement a policy of absolute forfeiture against the Montfortians.[112] As a consequence, de Montfort's cult was valued by his devotees chiefly as a weapon in a continuing struggle, rather than as a means of reconciliation once the struggle was over, and the devotional material it generated preserved and perpetuated the divisions of the earl's secular career instead of seeking to transcend them. His office includes, for instance, two verses recording and celebrating the punishment of an 'ignoble esquire' who derided the nascent cult; one of his miracles describes a monk of Peterborough, doubtful of his status as a saint, confronted by the earl in a dream and faced with the choice of death or eating a raw piglet. The saint's reply to Margaret Maunsell, who enquired what would become of those who were his enemies during his lifetime, indicates the unconditional nature of the capitulation he demanded from his former opponents: 'some have repented, some will repent, and some have died a bad death without penitence'.[113]

There is significance in the contrast between the ordeal-miracle reported in de Montfort's *miracula* and the several deliverance miracles of Henry VI. A Derbyshire nobleman, giving a feast for his neighbours, encounters two persistent detractors of the earl; calling on Christ to prove that de Montfort had died for 'truth and justice in the land', he thrusts his hand into a cauldron of boiling water and it remains unharmed.[114] The miracle is used as a means of coercing agreement, of distinguishing unequivocally between right and wrong. In delivering a prisoner from gaol, and saving two others from the gallows, Henry VI acts, on the other hand, in conformity to an Augustinian tradition of indifference to the facts of guilt or innocence that provides a deliverance, not only from gaol, but from the divisive necessity of making a final judgement at all.[115] His action is typical of the ability of a successful cult to develop a more than factional appeal by offering the powers of its saint as protector, healer and intercessor to all those who invoked him. De Montfort's cult, alone of those examined in this paper, failed to reach this stage of development and remained enmeshed in the political circumstances of its inception. In consequence, once the immediate political and personal needs the cult had satisfied began to disappear, as the reconciliation of the majority of the Disinherited with Edward I took gradual effect,[116] so too did the belief in his sanctity. After 1280, evidence for de Montfort's veneration as a saint is hard to find, though his commemoration as a virtuous political leader remained common well into the fourteenth century.[117]

Political saints were, then, no different from the other saints venerated in later medieval England in being valued 'not primarily as exemplars or soulfriends, but as powerful helpers and healers in time of need'.[118] For their devotees, the virtues and vicissitudes of their earthly careers were of secondary importance when compared to the promise of assistance held out by their miracles. What set them apart from other saints was that their helping and healing characteristically extended beyond the individual to the community, seeking to effect the recreation of concord in a disordered body politic by the reintegration of the defeated and marginalised. Though fissile and disordered, later medieval English society was also rich in the resources of compromise and conciliation, not the least of which was this power of the saints. In reaching this conclusion there is always a danger of mistaking rhetoric for reality. In certain circumstances, the proclamation of harmony could become the assertion of a still-disputed hegemony, which only served to remove the conflict from one arena to another. The clerical promoters of the cult of Henry VI were quick to point out, for instance, that the sacral powers of a dead but legitimate king were greater than those of a living usurper.[119] Yet even in such cases, the existence of the rhetoric was itself of importance; it affirmed an ideal of political conduct to which all parties were anxious to appear to subscribe. If the conflicting claims embodied in the death of a political saint continued to be fought out in symbolic fashion, the subsequent cult nevertheless canalised and contained the most immediately destructive effects of the struggle. And once established, no cult could be maintained by pious aspiration alone; if the terms in which Thomas of Lancaster, Richard Scrope or Henry VI were presented had appeared irrelevant to their devotees, their cults would have lasted no longer than Simon de Montfort's. This continued popular support for the cults of political saints – in origin, cults of martyrs venerated at the place of their death, the oldest and most traditional type of devotion – was recognised by contemporaries to be significant, for it provided a means by which the popular and clerical conceptions of sanctity, in general increasingly divergent by the later Middle Ages, could be reconciled and the norms of canonical expectation internalised within the world of popular piety. It was for this reason that successive kings and their advisers concluded that such cults were better tolerated than suppressed. Far from being a threat to royal authority, they provided an important point of contact with a diverse popular audience, a potentially significant resource in the constant dialogue of rulers and ruled by which a polity as varied and sophisticated as later medieval England had necessarily to be governed.

Notes

1 E. M. Forster, *A Passage to India* (Harmondsworth, 1970), pp. 249–50.

2 A. Vauchez, *La sainteté en Occident aux dernières siècles du Moyen Age* (Bibliothèque des Écoles Françaises d'Athènes et de Rome, CCXLI, 1988), pp. 71–98, 449–89; A. M. Kleinberg, 'Proving Sanctity: Selection and Authentication of Saints in the Later Middle Ages', *Viator*, XX (1989), pp. 183–205.

3 E. W. Kemp, *Canonization and Authority in the Western Church* (Oxford, 1948), pp. 116–22, 176–7.

4 N. Orme, 'Two Saint-Bishops of Exeter. James Berkley and Edmund Lacy', *Analecta Bollandiana*, CIV (1986), pp. 403–18; N. Tanner, *The Church in Late Medieval Norwich* (P.I.M.S. Studies and Texts, LXVI, 1984), pp. 89–90.

5 J. R. Shinners, 'The Veneration of Saints at Norwich Cathedral in the Fourteenth Century' *Norfolk Archaeology*, XL (1988), pp. 137–9.

6 K. Walsh, *Richard Fitzralph in Oxford, Avignon and Armagh* (Oxford, 1981), pp. 455–61.

7 J. Hughes, *Pastors and Visionaries. Religion and Secular Life in Late Medieval Yorkshire* (Woodbridge, 1988), pp. 302–5.

8 P. Grosjean, 'Thomas de la Hale. Moine et martyr à Douvres en 1295', *Analecta Bollandiana*, LXII (1954), pp. 167–91; A. G. Little, *The Grey Friars in Oxford* (Oxford Historical Society, XX, 1892), p. 174; L. Boyle, *A Survey of the Vatican Archives and its Medieval Holdings* (P.I.M.S. Subsidia Medievalia, I, 1972), pp. 143–4. For the text of Richard II's petition for Thomas de la Hale's canonisation, *c.* 1380, see C.U.L. Ms Dd 53 f. 38.

9 R. M. Wooley, *The Officium and Miracula of Richard Rolle of Hampole* (1919).

10 *Chronica Monasterii de Melsa*, E. A. Bond (ed.) (3 vols, R.S., 1866–8), III, pp. 194–5; Tanner, *Church in Norwich*, pp. 221–3; W. Sparrow Simpson, 'Master John Schorne', *Records of Buckinghamshire*, III (1870), pp. 354–69.

11 *Historiae Rhythmicae: Liturgisches Reimoffizien des Mittelalters*, G. M. Dreves (ed.), II (Analecta Hymnica Medii Aevii, 13, Leipzig, 1892), p. 7; 'Miracula Simonis de Montfort', *The Chronicle of William de Rishanger*, J. O. Halliwell (ed.) (Camden Society, 1st series XV, 1840), p. 104; N. Rogers, 'The Cult of Prince Edward at Tewkesbury', *Transactions of the Bristol and Gloucester Archaeological Society*, CI (1983), pp. 187–9; M. R. James, *A Descriptive Catalogue of Manuscripts in the Fitzwilliam Museum, Cambridge* (Cambridge 1895), p. 121.

12 *The Ecclesiastical History of Orderic Vitalis*, M. Chibnall (ed.) (6 vols, Oxford, 1969–80), II, pp. 346–51; B. J. Levy, 'Waltheof, "Earl" de Huntingdon et de Northampton: la naissance d'un héros anglo-normand', *Cahiers de civilisation médiévale* XVII (1975), pp. 183–96; 'De Morte et Sepultura Henrici Regis Junioris', *Radulphi de Coggeshall Chronicon Anglicanum*, J. Stevenson (ed.) (R.S., 1875), pp. 265–73; *Chronicles of the Reigns of Stephen, Henry II, and Richard I*, R. Howlett (ed.) (4 vols, R.S., 1884–9), II, pp. 471–3.

13 S. J. Ridyard, *The Royal Saints of Anglo-Saxon England* (Cambridge, 1989), pp. 234–52; D. W. Rollason, *Saints and Relics in Anglo-Saxon England* (Oxford, 1989), pp. 115–29, 133–44.

14 Vauchez, *La sainteté en Occident*, pp. 202–3.

15 V. Natalini, *S. Pietro Parenzo* (Rome, 1936), pp. 76–133; *Bibliotheca Hagiographica Latina Antiquae et Mediae Aetatis* (Brussels, 1898–9), p. 234; A. Vauchez, 'Canonisation et politique au XIVe siècle', *Religion et société dans l'Occident mediévale* (Turin, 1980), pp. 237–60.

16 J. Sumption, *Pilgrimage. An Image of Medieval Religion* (1975), p. 282; J. R. Maddicott, *Thomas of Lancaster* (Oxford, 1970), p. 329.

17 Gregory of Tours, *Life of the Fathers*, E. James (ed.) (Liverpool, 1985), p. 60.

18 *Proceedings of the Commissioners for the Public Records of the Kingdom*, June 1832–August 1833, I (1833), p. 502; H. M. Colvin, R. Allen Brown and A. J. Taylor, and others, *The History of the King's Works*, (6 vols, 1963), I, p. 258.

19 John de Trokelowe and anonymous, 'Annales Ricardi Secundi et Henrici Quarti', in *Chronica et Annales*, H. T. Riley (ed.) (R.S., 1866), pp. 216–19; *Chronicon Adae de Usk*, E. M. Thompson (ed.) (2nd edn, 1904), p. 15; J. M. Theilmann, 'Political Canonization and Political Symbolism in Medieval England', *Journal of British Studies* XXIX (1990), pp. 261–3.

20 J. C. Russell, 'The Canonization of Opposition to the Crown in Angevin England', *Haskins Anniversary Essays*, C. H. Taylor (ed.) (New York, 1929), pp. 279–90

(quotation at p. 286). Russell's pioneering discussion has remained influential in many more recent analyses: e.g., Vauchez, *La sainteté*, p. 200; *Saints and their Cults*, S. Wilson (ed.) (Cambridge, 1983), pp. 34–5; J. R. Bray, 'Concepts of Sainthood in Fourteenth-Century England', *B.J.R.L.* LXVI (1983), p. 68; R. N. Swanson, *Church and Society in Late Medieval England* (Oxford, 1989), pp. 99–101, 288.

21 J. W. McKenna, 'Popular Canonization as Political Propaganda: the Cult of Archbishop Scrope', *Speculum*, XLV (1970), pp. 608–23 (quotation at p. 609); idem, 'Piety and Propaganda: the Cult of Henry VI', *Chaucer and Middle English Studies in Honour of Rossell Hope Robbins*, B. Rowland (ed.) (1974), pp. 72–88.

22 N. M. Fryde, *The Tyranny and Fall of Edward II* (Cambridge, 1979), pp. 152–3.

23 *Thomas Walsingham Historia Anglicana*, H. T. Riley (ed.) (2 vols, R.S., 1863–4), I, pp. 459–62; II, p. 114; *The Westminster Chronicle 1381–1394*, L. C. Hector and B. F. Harvey (eds.) (Oxford, 1982), p. 80. For further consideration of 'shrines that failed', B. Ward, *Miracles and the Medieval Mind* (1982), pp. 127–31.

24 P. Delooz, 'Pour une étude sociologique de la sainteté canonisée dans l'Eglise catholique', *Archives de sociologie des religions*, XIII (1962), pp. 22–3.

25 W. Stubbs, *Select Charters and other Illustrations of English Constitutional History* (9th edn, 1913), p. 409.

26 *The Chronicle of Bury St. Edmunds*, 1212–1301, A. Gransden (ed.) (1964), p. 33; 'Continuatio Willelmi de Newburgh', *Chronicles of Stephen, Henry II and Richard I*, II, p. 548; *Chronica Monasterii de Melsa*, II, p. 131; *The Historical Works of Gervase of Canterbury*, W. Stubbs (ed.) (2 vols, R.S., 1879–80), II, p. 243. For further evidence of de Montfort's reputation at Canterbury, Historical Manuscripts Commission, *Fifth Report* (1876), pp. 454–5.

27 G. W. Prothero, *The Life of Simon de Montfort* (1877), pp. 388–91; *Chronicle of William de Rishanger*, pp. 67–110; *Historiae Rhythmicae*, II, p. 7; P. M. Lefferts, 'Two English Motets on Simon de Montfort', *Early Music History*, I (1981), pp. 203–25; F. W. Maitland, 'A Song on the Death of Simon de Montfort', *E.H.R.* XI (1896), pp. 314–18; *Anglo-Norman Political Songs*, I. S. T. Aspin (ed.) (Anglo-Norman Text Society, XI, 1953), pp. 12–35.

28 R. Finucane, *Miracles and Pilgrims: Popular Beliefs in Medieval England* (1977), pp. 135, 169–70.

29 *Chronicle of William de Rishanger*, p. 108; *Anglo-Norman Political Songs*, pp. 24–5; H. Shields, 'The Lament for Simon de Montfort: an Unnoticed Text of the French Poem', *Medium Aevum*, XLI (1972), pp. 202–7.

30 P. R. O. Exchequer, Accounts Various, E 101/379/17 f. 1^v.

31 *Calendar of Inquisitions Miscellaneous* (7 vols, H.M.S.O., 1916–68), II, no. 2103, pp. 528–9; *Historical Papers and Letters from the Northern Registers*, J. Raine (ed.) (R.S., 1873), pp. 323–6.

32 *Anecdota ex Codicibus Hagiographicis Johannis Gielemans* (Société des Bollandistes, Brussels, 1895), pp. 92–100.

33 *The Political Songs of England, from the Reign of John to that of Edward II*, T. Wright (ed.) (Camden Society, old series VI, 1840), pp. 268–72; C. Page, 'The Rhymed Office for St. Thomas of Lancaster: Poetry, Politics and Liturgy in Fourteenth-Century England', *Leeds Studies in English*, XIV (1983), pp. 135–6.

34 *Flores Historiarum*, H. R. Luard (ed.) (3 vols, R.S., 1890), III, p. 314; *Polychronicon Ranulphi Higden*, C. Babington and J. R. Lumby (eds.) (9 vols, R.S., 1865–6), VIII, p. 314; *Croniques de London*, G. J. Aungier (ed.) (Camden Society, old series XXVIII, 1844), p. 46; *The Brut*, F. W. D. Brie (ed.), (2 vols, E.E.T.S. original series CXXXI,

CXXXVI, 1906–8), I, pp. 228–31; V. H. Galbraith, 'Extracts from the Historia Aurea and a French Brut', *E.H.R.* XLIII (1928), pp. 215–16; *The Anonimalle Chronicle*, 1307 to 1334, W. R. Childs and J. Taylor (eds.) (Yorkshire Archaeological Society, CXLVII, 1987), pp. 112–14.

35 Bodl. L. Ms Douce 231 f. 1; N. R. Ker, *Medieval Manuscripts in British Libraries*, III (Oxford, 1983), p. 518; E. G. Millar, *The Luttrell Psalter* (1932), p. 28; M. R. James, *Catalogue of Manuscripts in the Library of Clare College, Cambridge* (Cambridge, 1905), pp. 11–13; J. T. Micklethwaite, 'Antiquities and Works of Art Exhibited', *Archaeological Journal*, XXXVI (1879), pp. 103–4.

36 *C.I.P.M.* 1352–1361, p. 178; H. Tait, 'Pilgrim-Signs and Thomas, Earl of Lancaster', *British Museum Quarterly*, XX (1955–6), pp. 39–47.

37 *Letters from Northern Registers*, p. 385; *Calendar of Papal Registers, Petitions 1342–1419*, pp. 271–2; *John of Gaunt's Register 1372–1376*, S. Armitage-Smith (ed.) (Camden Soc., 3rd series XX, XXI, 1911), nos. 297, 949; *Testamenta Vetusta*, N. H. Nicholas (ed.) (1826), p. 68; Walsingham, *Historia Anglicana*, II, p. 191. For further evidence of Bohun patronage of Lancaster's cult, J. Edwards, 'The Cult of "St." Thomas of Lancaster and its Iconography', *Yorkshire Archaeological Journal*, LXIV (1992), pp. 112–13; A. Gransden, *Historical Writing in England* (2 vols, 1982), II, p. 74.

38 M. E. Bond, *The Inventories of St. George's Chapel 1384–1667* (Windsor, 1947), pp. 44–5.

39 *Testamenta Eboracensia*, J. Raine (ed.) (6 vols, Surtees Society, 1836–1902), I, p. 281; Borthwick I.H.R., Probate Register 2 f. 537; *Fifteenth Century Liturgical Music*, Andrew Hughes (ed.) (Early English Church Music, VIII, 1964), pp. 10–11; A. F. Johnston and M. Rogerson, *Records of Early English Drama: York* (2 vols, Toronto and Manchester, 1979), II, pp. 637, 858–9; *Abbreviata Chronica*, J. J. Smith (ed.) (Cambridge Antiquarian Society Publications, I, 1840–6), p. 10; Ker, *Medieval Manuscripts in British Libraries*, II, pp. 5, 10; M. R. James, *Catalogue of Manuscripts in the Library of King's College, Cambridge* (Cambridge, 1895), p. 50; M. L. Colker, *Trinity College Library, Dublin. Descriptive Catalogue of the Medieval and Renaissance Latin Manuscripts* (Aldershot, 1991), p. 958; *William Worcester Itineraries*, J. H. Harvey (ed.) (Oxford, 1969), p. 81.

40 *Historia et Cartularium Monasterii Sancti Petri Gloucestriae*, W. H. Hart (ed.) (3 vols, R.S., 1863–7), I, pp. 44–6.

41 Ibid., pp. 47–8; *Westminster Chronicle*, pp. 158, 436–9; *The Diplomatic Correspondence of Richard II*, E. Perroy (ed.) (Camden Society, 3rd series XLVIII, 1933), p. 210. Note that the record evidence suggests that Edward III's offering was originally made at the high altar, and then transferred to the shrine of Edward II by the monks; W. M. Ormrod, 'The Personal Piety of Edward III', *Speculum*, LXIV (1989), pp. 860, 870–1.

42 Bodl. L. Ms Lat. Misc. b 2 (R); J. Evans, *English Art, 1307–1461* (Oxford, 1949), pp. 164–5; F. E. Hutchinson, *The Medieval Stained Glass of All Souls College* (1949), pp. 47–8.

43 *Polychronicon Ranulphi Higden*, VIII, p. 326. For the likely date of the composition of this passage, J. Taylor, 'The Development of the Polychronicon Continuation', *E.H.R.* LXXVI (1961), pp. 22–3. The comments to the same effect in *Chronicles of the Reigns of Edward I and Edward II*, W. Stubbs (ed.) (2 vols, R.S., 1882–3), II, p. 290, *Annales Monastici*, H. R. Luard (ed.) (5 vols, R.S., 1864–9), IV, p. 348 and *Chronica Monasterii de Melsa*, II, p. 355 are all directly derived from Higden.

44 *The Fabric Rolls of York Minster*, J. Raine (ed.) (Surtees Society, XXXV, 1859), p. 196; *York Memorandum Book*, M. Sellers (ed.) (2 vols, Surtees Society, 1912–15), I, pp. 236–8.

45 *Eulogium Historiarum sive Temporis*, F. S. Haydon (ed.) (3 vols, R.S., 1858), III, pp. 405, 421; C. L. Kingsford, *English Historical Literature in the Fifteenth Century* (Oxford, 1913), pp. 282, 314; Trokelowe and anonymous, 'Annales', p. 410; *Chronicon Adae de Usk*, p. 99; Raine, *Fabric Rolls*, pp. 32, 37.

46 *The Historians of the Church of York and its Archbishops*, J. Raine (ed.) (3 vols, R.S., 1879–94), II, pp. 306–11; III, pp. 288–91. For the authorship and relationship of these accounts, W. A. Pronger, 'Thomas Gascoigne', *E.H.R.* LIII (1938), pp. 607–10, which remains preferable to the conjecture of S. K. Wright, 'The Provenance and Manuscript Tradition of the Martyrium Ricardi Archiepiscopi', *Manuscripta*, XXVIII (1984), pp. 92–102.

47 Bodl. L. Ms Lat. Liturg. F2, ff. 146^{v}–147; Y.M.L. Ms XVI K. 6 f. 27^{v}, Add. Ms 2 ff. 100^{v}–101^{r}, Add. Ms 54, p. 3, Add. Ms 67 ff. 102^{r-v}; *Political Poems and Songs relating to English History*, T. Wright (ed.) (2 vols, R.S., 1859–61), II, pp. 114–18; *Historiae Rhythmicae*, VII, p. 317; M. R. James, *A Descriptive Catalogue of Manuscripts in the Library of St. John's College, Cambridge* (Cambridge, 1913), pp. 162–5; *idem*, *A Descriptive Catalogue of Manuscripts in the Library of Sidney Sussex College, Cambridge* (Cambridge, 1895), pp. 44–5; *Hymns to the Virgin and Christ*, F. J. Furnival (ed.) (E.E.T.S., original series XXIV, 1867), p. 128.

48 Raine, *Fabric Rolls*, pp. 225–7.

49 *Political Poems and Songs*, II, p. 267; *C.C.R. 1468–71*, II, 188–90.

50 Y.M.L. M2/1 (f), ff. 70–72^{v}.

51 E.g., the request of Thomas Rothwell, chaplain, that his executors have made a wax image 'in the likeness of a canon', worth 4 marks, to be offered to the blessed Richard Scrope: Y.M.L. L2/4 f. 332^{v}.

52 Y.M.L. E 3/6–8, 12–23.

53 E.g., the practice of requiring penitents to make offerings at a circuit of shrines, which included the tombs of Scrope and St William at York, St Wilfrid at Ripon and St John at Beverley: Borthwick I.H.R. D/C, A.B. 1 ff. 118^{v}, 193.

54 *Henrici VI Angliae Regis Miracula Postuma*, P. Grosjean (ed.) (Société des Bollandistes, Subsidia Hagiographica, XXII, 1935), pp. 182*, 112.

55 Raine, *Fabric Rolls*, p. 82 (though this roll is best dated 1475–6, not 1473). Note, too, the sudden rise in offerings in the Minster which takes place between 1473 (£10 4*s.* 10*d.*) and 1475/6 (£49 16*s.* 6*d.*): Y.M.L. E 3/26–7.

56 R. Lovatt, 'A Collector of Apocryphal Anecdotes: John Blacman Revisited', in *Property and Politics: Essays in Later Medieval English History*, A. J. Pollard (ed.) (Gloucester, 1984), pp. 177–9.

57 *Henrici VI Angliae Regis Miracula*; W. Maskell, *Monumenta Ritualia Ecclesiae Anglicanae* (2nd edn, 3 vols, Oxford, 1882), III, pp. 367–71; *Trevelyan Papers*, J. P. Collier and others (eds.) (3 vols, Camden Soc., old series LXVII, LXXXIV, CV, 1857–72), I, pp. 53–60; *Henry the Sixth: A Reprint of John Blacman's Memoir*, M. R. James (ed.) (Cambridge, 1919), pp. 12–14, 50–1; F. A. Gasquet, *The Religious Life of Henry VI* (1923), pp. 128–9; *The Miracles of Henry VI*, R. Knox and S. Leslie (eds.) (Cambridge, 1923), pp. 5, 11; James, *A Descriptive Catalogue of Manuscripts in the Fitzwilliam Museum*, pp. 138–9; *idem*, *A Descriptive Catalogue of the Manuscripts in the Library of Lambeth Palace. The Medieval Manuscripts* (Cambridge, 1932), pp. 747–50.

58 B. Spencer, 'King Henry of Windsor and the London Pilgrim', *Collectanea Londiniensia: Studies in London Archaeology and History presented to Ralph Merrifield*, J. Bird, H. Clapman and J. Clark (eds.) (London and Middlesex Archaeological Society, Special Papers, II, 1978), pp. 283–9. Note, too, the steep decline in the offerings made at the tomb of St Thomas after *c.* 1420: C. E. Woodruff, 'The financial aspect of the cult of St. Thomas of Canterbury, as recorded by a study of the monastic records', *Archaeologia Cantiana*, XLIV (1932), pp. 22–4.

59 *Foedera, Conventiones, Litterae*, T. Rymer (ed.) (new edn, 4 vols in 7, Record Commission, 1816–69), II (ii), p. 695.

60 *Chronica de Mailros (The Melrose Chronicle)*, J. Stevenson (ed.) (Edinburgh, 1835), p. 212.

61 G. Duby, 'Ideologies in Social History', *Constructing the Past*, J. Le Goff and P. Nora (eds.) (Cambridge, 1985), pp. 152–6.

62 M. Bloch, *The Royal Touch: Sacred Monarchy and Scrofula in England and France* (1973), pp. 21–7; H. G. Wright, 'The Protestation of Richard II in the Tower in September, 1399', *B.J.R.L.* XXIII (1939), pp. 157–9; M. T. Clanchy, 'Did Henry III have a Policy?', *History*, LIII (1968), p. 213.

63 *Adami Murimuthensis Chronica sui Temporis*, T. Hog (ed.), (English Historical Society, VIII, 1846), p. 226; R. Barber, *Edward, Prince of Wales and Aquitaine* (Woodbridge, 1978), pp. 213–14; *Political Poems and Songs*, I, p. 97.

64 J. W. McKenna, 'How God became an Englishman', *Tudor Rule and Revolution*, D. J. Guth and J. W. McKenna (eds.) (Cambridge, 1982), pp. 25–43; G. M. D. Crowder, *Unity, Heresy and Reform, 1378–1460* (1977), pp. 118–20. For the prior claim of the French monarchy to be the 'most Christian Kings', C. Beaune, *The Birth of an Ideology. Myths and Symbols of Nation in Late-Medieval France* (Berkeley, 1991), pp. 172–93.

65 *Gesta Henrici Quinti: The Deeds of Henry the Fifth*, F. Taylor and J. S. Roskell (eds.) (Oxford, 1975), pp. 106–8; *Memorials of the Reign of Henry VI: Official Correspondence of Thomas Bekynton, Secretary to Henry VI, and Bishop of Bath and Wells*, G. Williams (ed.) (2 vols, R.S., LVI, 1872), I, pp. 118–19.

66 M. Aston, *Lollards and Reformers: Images and Literacy in Late Medieval Religion* (1984), pp. 1–47.

67 *R.P.* III, pp. 583–4.

68 T. B. Pugh, *Henry V and the Southampton Plot* (Southampton Records Series, XXX, 1988), p. 169.

69 J. Creton, *Histoire du Roy d'Angleterre Richard*, J. T. Webb (ed. and trans.), *Archaeologia*, XX (1824), p. 170.

70 *The Register of Henry Chichele, Archbishop of Canterbury, 1414–1443*, E. F. Jacob (ed.) (4 vols, Canterbury and York Society, XLII, XLV–XLVII, 1937–47), IV, pp. 206–7; *The Register of John Stafford, Bishop of Bath and Wells, 1425–1443*, T. S. Holmes (ed.) (2 vols, Somerset Record Society, XXXI, XXXII, 1915–16), I, pp. 104–8; W. T. Waugh, 'Joan of Arc in English Sources of the Fifteenth Century', in *Historical Essays in Honour of James Tait*, J. G. Edwards, V. H. Galbraith, E. F. Jacob (eds.) (Manchester, 1933), pp. 388–91.

71 Historical Manuscripts Commission, *Fifth Report* (1876), p. 455; *R.P.* VI, pp. 232, 240–2.

72 R. A. Griffiths, 'The Trial of Eleanor Cobham: An Episode in the Fall of Duke Humphrey of Gloucester', *B.J.R.L.* LI (1968–9), pp. 381–99; M. Hicks, *False, Fleeting, Perjur'd Clarence* (revised edn, Bangor, 1992), pp. 119–22.

73 Bartholomew de Cotton, *Historia Anglicana*, H. R. Luard (ed.) (R.S., XVI, 1859), pp. 171–2, 180; *Calendar of Papal Registers, Papal Letters* (15 vols, H.M.S.O., 1893–1960), I, p. 607; A. Beardwood, 'The Trial of Walter Langton, Bishop of Lichfield, 1307–12', *Transactions of the American Philosophical Society*, LIV, iii (1964), pp. 7–8; *Select Cases in the Court of King's Bench*, G. O. Sayles (ed.) (7 vols, Selden Society, 1936–71), IV, pp. 154–7.
74 J. G. Bellamy, *The Law of Treason in England in the Later Middle Ages* (Cambridge, 1970), pp. 127–8.
75 P. R. O. Exchequer, Pleas of the Hall, E 37/28 m. 1; Sayles, *Select Cases in the Court of King's Bench*, VII, pp. 174–5.
76 R.P. III, p. 466. For the 'social miracle' of the Mass, J. Bossy, 'The Mass as a Social Institution, 1200–1700', *P.P.* C (1983), pp. 29–61 and, for subsequent discussion and elaboration, M. Rubin, *Corpus Christi. The Eucharist in Late Medieval Culture* (Cambridge, 1991), pp. 2, 265–7 and E. Duffy, *The Stripping of the Altars. Traditional Religion in England, c. 1400–c. 1580* (New Haven, 1992), pp. 91–130.
77 *Historie of the Arrivall of Edward IV in England and the Finall Recoverie of his Kingdomes from Henry VI, A.D. 1471*, J. Bruce (ed.) (Camden Society, old series I, 1838), pp. 13–14; Rymer, *Foedera*, XI, pp. 709–11; *Joannis Rossi Antiquarii Warwicensis Historia Regum Angliae*, T. Hearne (ed.) (Oxford, 1716), p. 218; *York Civic Records*, A. Raine and others (eds.) (9 vols, Yorkshire Archaeological Society, XCVIII, 1939–78), I, p. 25.
78 J. Bossy, 'Some Elementary Forms of Durkheim', *P.P.* XCIX (1982), p. 12.
79 R. W. Southern, *Medieval Humanism and other Studies* (Oxford, 1970), p. 137.
80 Raine, *Fabric Rolls*, pp. 226, 235.
81 *Breviarium ad Usum Insignis Ecclesiae Sarum*, F. Proctor and C. Wordsworth (eds.) (3 vols, Cambridge, 1879–86), I, cols. ccxlvii–cclxi.
82 *Materials for the History of Thomas Becket, Archbishop of Canterbury*, J. C. Robertson and J. B. Sheppard (eds.) (7 vols, R.S., LXVII, 1875–85), II, p. 29.
83 A. Duggan, 'The Cult of St. Thomas Becket in the Thirteenth Century', in *St. Thomas Cantilupe, Bishop of Hereford. Essays in His Honour*, M. Jancey (ed.) (Hereford, 1982), pp. 37–41.
84 *Breviarium ad Usum Insignis Ecclesiae Sarum*, III, pp. 445–51.
85 *Materials for the History of Thomas Becket*, II, p. 128.
86 Ibid., I, pp. 251–2; II, pp. 149–50; III, pp. 546–8.
87 All Souls College, MS 182 ff. 73–4.
88 *Anecdota . . . Johannis Gielemans*, p. 96; L. W. Vernon Harcourt, *His Grace the Steward and Trial by Peers* (1907), pp. 138–69.
89 *The Brut*, I, pp. 221–4; *The Political Songs of England*, p. 269.
90 *The Political Songs of England*, p. 270; *Historiae Rhythmicae*, II, p. 7; Micklethwaite, *Arch. J.* XXXVI (1879), p. 104.
91 *Political Songs of England*, pp. 268, 272; Edwards, *Yorks. Arch. J.* LXIV, pp. 118–21. For the close association of the cults of Becket and Lancaster in the fifteenth century, R. Foreville, *Le Jubilé de Saint Thomas Becket: du XIIIe au XVe siècles (1220–1470)* (Paris, 1958), pp. 111, 129.
92 *R.P.* II, p. 7; *Foedera*, II, ii, p. 695.
93 *Historiae Rhythmicae*, VII, p. 321.
94 Raine, *Fabric Rolls*, pp. 193–5.
95 Ibid., pp. 198–200 (which conflates a number of separate decisions of the chapter;

Y.M.L. H2/1 ff. 19ᵛ, 25ᵛ, 58ᵛ); *The Chronicle of John Hardyng*, H. Ellis (ed.) (1812), p. 372; B.L. Add. Ms 35295, f. 265.

96 Bodl. L. MS Lat. Liturg. F2, f. 147.

97 Y.M.L. Add. Ms 54, p. 3; Raine, *Historians of the Church of York*, II, p. 309; T. Gascoigne, *Loci e Libro Veritatum*, J. E. T. Rogers (ed.) (Oxford, 1881), p. 227; *Hymns to the Virgin and Christ*, p. 128; R. W. Pfaff, *New Liturgical Feasts in Later Medieval England* (Oxford, 1970), p. 86.

98 *Political Poems and Songs*, II, p. 115; Raine, *Historians of the Church of York*, II, p. 307.

99 Y.M.L. Add. Ms 2 f. 101ʳ; Add. Ms 54, p. 3; *Political Poems and Songs*, II, p. 116; R. W. Southern, *Western Society and the Church in the Middle Ages* (1970), pp. 51–2.

100 Bodl. L. Ms Lat. Liturg. F2, f. 147.

101 Y.M.L. M2/1 (f), ff. 70–72ʳ.

102 *The Records of the Northern Convocation*, G. W. Kitchin (ed.) (Surtees Soc., CXIII, 1907), pp. 349–51; *Acts of the Court of the Mercer's Company 1453–1527*, L. Lyell and F. D. Watney (eds.) (Cambridge, 1936), p. 139.

103 *The Crowland Chronicle Continuations 1459–1486*, N. Pronay and J. Cox (eds.) (1986), pp. 128–30; James, *Henry the Sixth*, pp. 4, 6, 8–22; R. Lovatt, 'John Blacman: Biographer of Henry VI', in *The Writing of History in the Middle Ages: Essays presented to R. W. Southern*, R. H. C. Davis and J. M. Wallace-Hadrill (eds.) (Oxford, 1981), pp. 440–5.

104 Maskell, *Monumenta Ritualia*, p. 370; Collier, *Trevelyan Papers*, p. 58; Bodl. L. Ms Gough Liturg. 19 f. 32ᵛ; *Historia Regis Henrici Septimi a Bernardo Andrea Tholosate Conscripta*, J. Gairdner (ed.) (R.S., X. 1858), pp. 21–3.

105 Bodl. L. Ms Jones 46 ff. 117ᵛ–18; Ms Gough Liturg. 7 f. 119; James, *Henry VI*, p. 50.

106 B. L. Add. Mss 33736 ff. 4–6.

107 *Henrici VI Regis Angliae Miracula*, pp. 19–21; note also pp. 141–3, 176–8.

108 Maskell, *Monumenta Ritualia*, p. 371; G. Dodgson, 'English Devotional Woodcuts of the Late Fifteenth Century', *Walpole Society*, XVII (1928–9), pp. 104–8 and plate XXXVII.

109 *English Historical Documents, c. 500–1042*, D. Whitelock (ed.) (2nd edn, 1979), pp. 230–1.

110 Lefferts, *Early Music History*, I, pp. 222–3; Prothero, *Simon de Montfort*, p. 389; Maitland, *E.H.R.* XI, p. 317.

111 Prothero, *Simon de Montfort*, pp. 390–1; Maitland, *E.H.R.* XI, p. 318; *Anglo-Norman Political Songs*, p. 32.

112 C. H. Knowles, 'The Resettlement of England after the Barons' War, 1264–67', *T.R.H.S.* 5th series XXXII (1982), pp. 25–7.

113 Prothero, *Simon de Montfort*, p. 390; *Chronicle of William de Rishanger*, pp. 81–2, 99–100.

114 *Chronicle of William de Rishanger*, p. 85.

115 *Henrici VI Regis Angliae Miracula*, pp. 41–4, 106–12, 185–90; E. James, '*Beati pacifici*: Bishops and the Law in Sixth-Century Gaul', *Disputes and Settlements. Law and Human Relations in the West*, J. Bossy (ed.) (Cambridge, 1983), pp. 33–5.

116 Knowles, *T.R.H.S.* 5th series XXXII, pp. 37–41.

117 E.g., *Vita Edwardi Secundi*, N. Denholm-Young (ed.) (1957), p. 18, where de Montfort is described as having died for the cause of justice but is only 'the

noble man'. Note, too, the use of de Montfort's struggle as a piece of anti-English polemic in Scotland. An early sixteenth-century Scottish source preserves the story that two horsemen appeared before the sacrist of Glastonbury on the eve of Bannockburn, saying that they were on their way to deal vengeance for the unjust death of Simon de Montfort; Ker, *Medieval Manuscripts in British Libraries*, II, p. 523.

118 Duffy, *The Stripping of the Altars*, p. 178.

119 *Henrici VI Regis Angliae Miracula*, pp. 122–3.

10

The Yorkshire risings of 1405: texts and contexts

Early in May 1405 Henry Percy, earl of Northumberland, attempted to ambush his great rival for pre-eminence in the north of England, Ralph Neville, earl of Westmorland, as he dined with Sir Ralph Eure. Westmorland was forewarned of the plot and managed to make good his escape to the safety of Durham Castle but the incident was, as Thomas Walsingham justly remarked, 'the beginning of great evil'.[1] Within a fortnight, sporadic disturbances throughout the North and East Ridings had gathered sufficient momentum to attract the leadership of some prominent local gentry. A substantial force was assembled in Cleveland and began advancing south through the North Riding towards York, until it was dispersed at Topcliffe, apparently after a brief armed encounter, by Westmorland and John of Lancaster, the king's son. Although the areas most directly affected by these disturbances are conventionally identified as Cleveland, Allertonshire and the area around Topcliffe itself, it is clear that the disruption associated with this movement spread over a much wider area. Malton and the vale of Pickering saw considerable disturbances, as did the liberties of Ripon and Beverley; the keepers of the town of Beverley were still concerned enough at the situation on 5 June, when most of the trouble was over, to order the sparring of the town gates.[2] In York, meanwhile, the discontent that the citizens and local clergy felt at the heavy financial burdens placed upon them by the new Lancastrian regime found articulate expression in the preaching of the archbishop, Richard Scrope. Alarmed at the disorder he saw around him and especially concerned, it seems, by the evidence of dissension among the great magnates of his archdiocese – Percy, Neville and Mowbray – Scrope allied himself with Thomas Mowbray, the earl marshal, and led a mixed body of York citizens and clergy, afforced by the household men of the two captains, out to Shipton Moor. There they remained for three days, demanding the public redress of their grievances that the parliamentary process seemed no longer to offer, until, on 29 May, the assurances of the earl of Westmorland that their complaints would be addressed persuaded them to disband. It proved a fatal error: Scrope and Mowbray were immediately detained to await the king's pleasure and, some ten days later, both were executed as traitors. Within a month, Henry IV could write with satisfaction to his councillors, reporting the final reduction of the Percy strongholds in Northumberland to royal obedience.[3]

These events are well attested and their significance for the reign of Henry IV is obvious: the king's suppression of the Yorkshire risings and his successful reassertion of royal authority on the northern march proved to be vital turning-points that allowed a crisis-ridden regime to assume, at last, some appearance of permanence. The motives and ambitions of the insurgents have proved more debatable. Polydore Vergil's change of heart, which led him to cast Sir William Plumpton, rather than Archbishop Scrope, as the ring-leader of the Yorkshire rising in the second and subsequent editions of his *Anglica Historia*, is only one instance of the explanatory dilemma the episode has posed, both to contemporaries and to later commentators.[4] Among current professional historians, however, a considerable degree of consensus about the nature and causes of the rising has emerged, largely fashioned around the valuable reconsideration of the evidence undertaken, some thirty years ago, by Peter McNiven.[5] His argument, in summary, was that the 'clerical prejudice' of the chroniclers had led to an undue emphasis upon the agency of the archbishop in the Yorkshire risings when it was, in fact, the earl of Northumberland who was 'the active leader of a single, greater conspiracy'. Northumberland's ambush of his rival was to be the opening move in a carefully concerted plan; with the Lancastrian regime's chief partisan in the region safely in his grasp, Northumberland would move down from the far North, systematically consolidating the troops that his allies and retainers had collected into a single great army. Archbishop Scrope was not, therefore, acting on his own initiative but was brought into the conspiracy as a subordinate, whose principal role was 'to lend a spurious air of religious mission to the earl's rebellion'. Even in this respect, his performance was not judged to be impressive: his 'activities' on Shipton Moor – the repeated preaching to his followers, the celebration of mass – were 'futile and dangerous time-wasting', while the programme of reform he set out was 'naive nonsense', suggesting only the defective political sensibilities of his audience.[6]

It should be emphasized that, in many respects, McNiven's article retains its value; but I shall argue in this study that it is mistaken in most of its principal conclusions. If Scrope was 'betrayed', it was not by Northumberland; the archbishop was an independent political actor, whose demands were informed and politically astute. Conversely, the earl of Northumberland had little direct association with the disturbances in Yorkshire; there was, indeed, no 'great conspiracy', organized by the Percies or anybody else, but rather a series of loosely connected and largely spontaneous risings, united in a common idiom of protest. The events of May 1405 are best treated as three separate, and perhaps sequential, episodes: Northumberland's failed *coup de main*, which sent him in rapid retreat towards Berwick; an armed demonstration among some of the North Riding gentry and their tenants, inspired both by their sympathy with the Percies and by apprehension at the broader consequences of Northumberland's failure; and a movement of protest at the disorder prevalent in the region, led by the archbishop, which sought to articulate the grievances of the citizens and clergy of York in politically acceptable terms. In order to demonstrate this, I shall first look at the narrative sources for the risings and seek to show that a close and informed reading of them, which pays due attention to their rhetorical structure and polemical purpose, can support such an interpretation of events. In the second half of the essay, I shall assess the plausibility of this analysis by examining in more detail the contexts in which such a widespread act of political defiance, one that united significant elements of the shire's nobility, gentry, clergy and townsmen into a single movement, came to be regarded as both possible and justified.

Texts

The narrative sources for a study of the Yorkshire risings fall into four principal categories: judicial proceedings against the rebels; chronicle accounts of the risings; hagiographical accounts of the archbishop's martyrdom; and reports of the rebels' manifestos. I shall examine them in turn.

Judicial proceedings

Two strong commissions of *oyer et terminer* to punish participants in the rising were issued early in June 1405 but, if the commissioners ever acted under their powers, no record of their sessions has survived. It may well be that the general pardon issued a week later rendered their work otiose.[7] The evidence for any common-law proceedings against the rebels is, in fact, very sparse. The only incident associated with the Yorkshire risings to appear in the records of King's Bench, the killing of Sir Thomas Colville in the forest of Galtres by George Darell of Sessay and others, was brought there on a writ of error as late as April 1409.[8] This is because the main work of judicial retribution was done in the Court of Chivalry, where judgement was rendered upon the king's record.[9] Fortunately, the most important of these proceedings is preserved in the 'record and process' of Northumberland and Bardolf's attainder recited during the Long Parliament.[10] This recalls how the temporal Lords, assembled before the king on 19 June, had been asked by Prince Henry the previous week to render judgment against Henry Percy *et autres de sa covyne*, in the light of the process formerly begun against them in the Court of Chivalry, according to the laws and usages of arms.

This is an important document for our understanding of the Yorkshire risings, supplying a better chronology and a more detailed account of its course than any other source, but its nature and contents need to be studied quite carefully for their full significance to become apparent. The record starts by reciting how Sir John Fauconberg, Sir Ralph Hastings, Sir John Fitzrandolf and Sir John Colville assembled a force of 7,000–8,000 men at Topcliffe, Allerton and Cleveland, falsely declaring that the intent of their insurrection was to address certain mischiefs and defaults in the kingdom, and to punish certain malefactors around the person of the king and his council, without informing the king either of the alleged mischiefs or of the names of the malefactors, as the custom of the realm required (articles 2–3), Fauconberg, Hastings and the others subsequently assembled their forces together at Topcliffe, until John of Lancaster, with Westmorland and Lord Fitzhugh, dispersed them (*fesoit voider le champ*) and captured them in their flight (article 4). Afterwards (*Item puis apres*), Richard Scrope, archbishop of York, Thomas Mowbray, earl marshal, Sir William Plumpton, Sir Robert Lamplugh and Sir Robert Persay assembled forces in several places within the county, falsely declaring that their intent was to amend and redress certain grievances within the realm and to punish certain evil-doers who were of the king's council. Assembling together on Shipton Moor, with a force of 8,000–9,000 men, Scrope and Mowbray continued in their traitorous purpose, until they were taken on the moor on 29 May (article 5).

It is at this point that the judicial record turns to the culpability of the earl of Northumberland, reciting and, in some cases, documenting a whole string of potentially treasonable actions: the detention of the king's messenger, Robert Waterton; seditious correspondence with the Scots and French; the capture and sack of Berwick; the defiance of the Northumbrian castellans; Northumberland's subsequent residence in Scotland and his continued contact with the rebels in Wales (articles 6–12). The transition from one set of alleged treasons to the other is effected by the statement that Northumberland conspired with and counselled (*estoit conspirant, conjectant et conseillant*) Scrope and Mowbray, as well as with Fauconberg, Hastings and their accomplices. This is, of all the sources we shall examine, the strongest statement of direct Percy involvement in either the North Riding gentry risings or in Scrope's York-centred protest. Yet it is clearly an assertion of a very different order from the other charges against the earl, lacking either the detailed substantiation provided for his treasonable correspondence or the public notoriety of his capture of Berwick and detention of Waterton. In assessing it, a degree of scepticism is in order; the clear purpose of the narrative that supports it is to reformulate several distinct acts of resistance as a single, and unquestionably treasonable, conspiracy to rebel, disguising the unsubstantiable nature of its pivotal assertion of complicity by a carefully detailed rehearsal of times, names and places. An alternative reading would suggest that the Yorkshire rebels were pursuing an agenda quite distinct from Northumberland's declared purpose. Northumberland is very clear, in his letter to the duke of Orleans (article 9), that his struggle is a dynastic one: his intention and firm purpose is to sustain the rightful quarrel of King Richard, if he is still alive, and to avenge his death if he is not, for which reason he has moved war against Henry of Lancaster, currently regent of England. This is consistent with the strain of legitimist defiance evident in most of the other Percy manifestos issued in and after 1403 but quite at odds with the consistently reformist nature of the demands made by the Yorkshire rebels, as reported by the chroniclers and tacitly acknowledged, in the 'Record and Process' itself, by reference to the 'falsely' moderate nature of the insurgents' demands. Questions about the Lancastrian authority to rule were easier to resist and marginalize when they were couched in terms of self-interested loyalty to an absent and unpopular predecessor than when they were expressed as a series of widespread protests at the excessive demands and inadequate responses of a new and fragile dynasty. In conflating the two idioms, the 'Record and Process' was performing one of the characteristic rhetorical manoeuvres of the nascent Lancastrian regime, exaggerating the threat posed by a real but manageable danger in order to justify a disproportionately rigorous response.[11]

The principal judicial record relating to the Yorkshire rising provides important evidence, then, for the actions and demands of the insurgents, but its assertion of Percy complicity needs to be treated with caution, for it serves a clear polemical purpose, and it is supported, as we shall see, only very equivocally in the other narrative sources for the rising. In this respect, it should be noted that, although the official version of events won credence over time,[12] the government's tendentious narrative of the risings had still to gain full conviction in 1406, when significant sections of the political nation showed themselves anxious to preserve some distinction between the actions and intentions of Northumberland and his immediate associates, on the one hand, and the rest of the Yorkshire rebels, on the other. Asked for their verdict on the process initiated in the Court of Chivalry, the peers replied that certain actions of the earl of Northumberland were treasons and that Thomas, Lord Bardolf, was of his counsel and alliance; they were therefore to be summoned to appear before the king and, if they failed to respond, were to be held convicted and attainted of the aforesaid treasons. Asked the same question with regard to Scrope and Mowbray, the peers temporized: according to the information given to them by the Constable, it seemed to them that the case was treasonable; nevertheless, they wished for further deliberation before giving their answer to the king. There was no scope for an immediate response, for parliament adjourned for the harvest on the same day; and when it reassembled in the autumn, the question of Scrope and Mowbray's alleged treason had disappeared from view. It was the Commons who raised the issue once again, on 30 November, when they asked the king if they could know what had been done touching the late rebellions, at Shrewsbury and elsewhere; the answer was to finalize the attainder of Northumberland and Bardolf alone, with no further reference made to the guilt of the earl marshal and the archbishop.[13]

Chronicle accounts

The disturbances in the North, and particularly Archbishop Scrope's part in them, attracted considerable attention from contemporary chroniclers. The events they recounted were clearly important in themselves but they were also dramatic and invited reformulation within certain clearly recognizable narrative conventions: the stratagem by which Scrope and his allies were allegedly persuaded to disband their forces belonged to the world of *fabliaux* and folk-tales, while the execution of the archbishop was readily rendered as a martyrdom. There is a great deal to be gained from a close reading of these accounts, not least a series of explanations for the rebels' actions largely at odds with the official account, though their understandable concentration on the person of the archbishop tends to simplify a more complex picture. The accounts that particularly concern us are those either written close in time to the events they describe or given a particular authority by their northern provenance: the various recensions of Thomas Walsingham's chronicle; the Franciscan continuation of the *Eulogium Historiarum*; John Strecche's Kenilworth chronicle; the narrative preserved in the compilation known as *Giles' Chronicle*; and the divergent accounts of the rising given by John Hardyng.

The most circumstantial of these, and the account that agrees most closely with the official narrative of the 'Record and Process', is Thomas Walsingham's. For Walsingham, the Yorkshire risings presented particular difficulties of organization and interpretation, for they brought two of the guiding principles of his historical writing, loyalty to the Catholic Church and support for the Lancastrian dynasty, into direct conflict. A rebellion led by an archbishop could not easily be reduced to his favourite narrative formula, 'the objectification of opponents in a sufficiently vivid form to permit a reciprocal stabilisation of the Lancastrian king as the guarantor of civil order and ecclesiastical orthodoxy'.[14] For this reason Walsingham seems to have devoted considerable care to his account of the 1405 rebellion. At least three versions survive: the long narrative of the *Chronica Majora*, most probably composed within a couple of years of the events it describes, and two shorter versions for his *Chronica Minora*, one – the earlier? – substantially longer than the other.[15] This extended process of composition creates, in certain respects, an 'open text', constantly subject to revision. For some particularly sensitive issues, such as whether the king played any direct part in the archbishop's condemnation, Walsingham provides three different answers. Whereas the *Chronica Majora* version specifically states that Henry refused to see Scrope, one recension of the *Chronica Minora* describes an interview between them, during which the archbishop's staff is snatched from his hand; the shorter text of the *Chronica Minora*, perhaps Walsingham's final version of events, avoids committing itself on the issue entirely and seeks to distance the king as far as possible from the execution.[16]

It is within this context of indeterminacy that Walsingham's assertion of collusion between Scrope and Northumberland – one of the mainstays of McNiven's argument – should be viewed. For Walsingham, the explanatory considerations were finely balanced: associating Scrope's initiative with the activities of a proven traitor like Northumberland was discreditable to the archbishop, but provided a stronger justification for the king's harsh action. The earlier account of the *Chronica Majora* appears to concur in the accusation of conspiracy made by the 'Record and Process': far away in Wales, the king hears how the archbishop of York and the earl marshal, on the one hand, and the earl of Northumberland and Lord Bardolf, on the other, have gathered together *an* army. As the Lancastrian kings secured themselves more firmly on the throne, Walsingham's growing confidence that they enjoyed the mandate of heaven allowed him to shift the burden of culpability a little and take a more questioning stance towards the issue of treasonable collusion. The later *Chronica Minora* account is substantially less dogmatic: the earl and the archbishop have, *it is said*, received comfort from Northumberland; the rest of the narrative treats Percy resistance to Henry's authority in the far North as a parallel but entirely separate set of developments.

The well-informed account in the continuation of the *Eulogium Historiarum*, one apparently composed in a Franciscan house, in all likelihood before the end of Henry IV's reign, takes this interpretation of events one step further, by treating the Yorkshire rising quite separately from its account of the king's campaign to return the Northumbrian castles to royal hands.[17] It is supported in this respect by the Whalley Abbey continuation of the *Polychronicon*, a text that displays a particular and knowledgeable interest in the deeds of the Percy family between 1400 and 1408, but makes no connection between the Yorkshire risings and its tale of the relentless royal pursuit of Northumberland.[18] John Strecche's chronicle, too, treats the rebellions of Scrope and the earl of Northumberland as two entirely separate movements, linking Scrope's protest, instead, to the forthright criticism of Henry's government voiced in previous parliaments.[19] Finally, the compilation known as *Giles' Chronicle* casts doubt upon Henry Percy's complicity from another angle. Notable both for its strong connections to York and its access to official documents, the account in *Giles* is especially sympathetic to Scrope, whom it clearly treats as a saint undergoing martyrdom, and suggests the king's treatment of Thomas Mowbray, earl marshal, as the original cause of the rising. 'Ancient hatred' between Mowbray and certain other lords had led Henry to deprive the earl marshal of his hereditary offices and persuaded Scrope, taking into account as well many other grievances, to exhort the people to fight for justice.[20]

The last, and in some ways most problematic, of the chronicle accounts that need to be considered are those of John Hardyng. Hardyng is in some ways a prime witness: a Northumbrian by birth, he had spent many years in the household of Henry Percy, the earl of Northumberland's eldest son. Although he had left Percy employment by 1405, it was only to take service with Sir Robert Umfraville, one of the earl of Westmorland's most reliable lieutenants, and a man who played a significant part in the suppression of the Yorkshire rising itself. Hardyng was, however, writing with the benefit of half a century of hindsight, and successive recensions of his chronicle present significantly different versions of events. His second recension, completed in 1463 and intended for presentation to Edward IV, is the only unequivocal witness for the view that the Yorkshire risings involved a deliberate collaboration between Scrope and Northumberland. Hardyng explains that the rising was part of a broader conspiracy among the lords to regain royal favour for the earl and describes how the army Scrope and Mowbray assemble on Shipton Moor is made up:

Of their owne and their frendes also,
Of therles menne of Northumberland that were
To the nombre of twenty thousand tho,
Afore the daye assigned that was so
By therle then of Northumberland,
That there cheften with theim should have stand.[21]

He then emphasizes the Percy connection further by describing the gentry leaders of the North Riding insurgents as 'knightes . . . full manly / To therle of Northumberland openly'. Such an interpretation of the rising is, however, wholly absent from his first recension. Completed in 1457 and intended for presentation to the Lancastrian royal family, this presents a substantially different account, which disclaims all knowledge of Scrope and Mowbray's motivation – 'for what cause or encheson / I know no thynge what so was their reson' – although it does imply that their agenda was a reformist rather than a dynastic or legitimist one. The earl and archbishop are persuaded to disband their forces:

Supposyng than in parlement of Recorde
All shulde bene wele and putte in gode accorde
Reformed hole as most to gode myght plese
For thair worship and for the comon ese.

At one point, Hardyng describes how John of Lancaster and the earl of Westmorland were at Durham when they first heard news of the Yorkshire rising and asserts that they initially intended to stay there and garrison the castle in strength 'for dread then of the earl of Northumberland', but this refers to the existing disruption in the far North created by Percy's castellans rather than to any preconcerted plan on Northumberland's part to join with the Yorkshire insurgents. No connection is alleged between the earl and the rising's gentry captains.[22]

There are, of course, no clear criteria by which one version of Hardyng's narrative can be privileged over another but, in assessing the strong assertion of Percy involvement in the Yorkshire risings that he makes in the second recension of his chronicle, it is important to consider the context in which it was made. At his accession, Edward IV made some effort to encourage the cult of Archbishop Scrope, representing his execution as one of the chief demonstrations of the injustice and illegitimacy of Lancastrian rule. Hardyng was alert to this current of opinion and did his best to conform to it, adding to the second recension of his chronicle the claim that Henry Hotspur had rebelled in 1403 'by the good advice of Master Richard Scope'.[23] His emphasis on the further collaboration of Scrope and Percy in 1405 had the effect of uniting the two most substantial acts of resistance to Henry IV's rule into a single movement and conferring the authority of the saintly archbishop upon the Percies' legitimist protests, couched in terms that directly anticipated the Yorkist claim to the crown.

In considering the various chronicle accounts of the Yorkshire risings, I have sought to show that our sense of scepticism about the motives imputed to the rebels in the official version of events, and specifically the claim that the insurgents acted in collusion with the earl of Northumberland, can be both sharpened and informed by the stories they have to tell. The chronicles provide very little support for the claim of Percy involvement, preferring to treat Scrope's rising and Northumberland's continued defiance as two separate episodes. They do, however, direct our attention to some alternative lines of inquiry, suggesting that the grievances of the earl marshal played a significant part in bringing the archbishop's own sense of disillusion with the Lancastrian dynasty to the point of action and associating his protests with the criticisms of royal government voiced by the Commons in parliament.

Hagiographical narratives

Richard Scrope was the first English archbishop to be executed after condemnation before a secular court and, even in an era of notably close collaboration between the secular and ecclesiastical authorities, his death was bound to attract attention. A cult of the martyred archbishop was soon in evidence at York, and several hagiographical accounts were composed to encourage and confirm this devotion.[24] With one exception, they have little to say about the rising that preceded the archbishop's death, preferring to dwell upon the signs of sanctity the victim displayed and the miracles that followed his execution. The exception is the theologian Thomas Gascoigne's account of Scrope's death, which was subsequently worked up by the Bridgettine monk, Clement Maidstone, into the *Historia de martyrio Ricardi archiepiscopi*.[25] Gascoigne had kinsmen among the rebels and was the great-nephew of William Gascoigne, chief justice of King's Bench, who was said to have refused the king's order to pass judgment upon the archbishop. His sources of information were unusually good, therefore, and, while his rendering of Scrope's address to his followers on Shipton Moor may be too fluent to carry full conviction, it provides some insight into what informed gentry opinion considered the rising to be about.[26] In it, Scrope protests against the financial oppression of the clergy but calls God to witness that he intends no harm against the king; he has gathered his followers together because he needs their support in his endeavour to mediate in the many quarrels of the magnates, most especially that between the Neville family and Thomas Mowbray – 'quia jam quis dominus poterit equitare sine multitudine?'[27] The profession of loyalty is to be expected, but the emphasis on the archbishop's desire to be a peacemaker between the lords is an interesting amplification of the statement in *Giles' Chronicle* that it was the hostility between Mowbray and certain other lords that first lured Scrope into rebellion.

Manifestos

There are three sets of articles traditionally associated with the Yorkshire rising, though only one of them can plausibly be dated to 1405. These are the 'York articles', included by Walsingham in his *Chronica Majora* and said to be a literal translation of the original English manifesto affixed by the archbishop and his supporters to the doors of the churches of York. There seems little reason to doubt that this is what they are; the digest of Scrope's demands given in several other chronicles is close enough to Walsingham's text to suggest that the chroniclers had the same document in front of them.[28] In these articles, Scrope calls for a freely elected parliament to be held in London, at which several issues for reform will be addressed: alleviating the insupportable burdens being placed upon the clergy; finding a remedy for the subjection and annihilation to which the lords of the land have been subject; ordaining a remedy for the excessive taxation imposed on all the estates of the realm and punishment for those who have put the wealth of the commons to their private use. On several of these demands, the account in the continuation of the *Eulogium Historiarum* provides a further gloss, complaining particularly of the Lancastrian regime's dependence on loans and frequent recourse to household purveyance, while identifying as the principal target of the insurgents the 'avaricious and greedy counsellors around the king, gorging themselves on the wealth ordained for the common good (*ad commune subsidium ordinata*)'. If all this is done, Scrope's manifesto continues, better resistance can be made to the country's enemies and, in particular, to those rebelling in Wales, who have promised they will return to their former obedience if these reforms are implemented.

Of the other manifestos associated with Scrope, one clearly dates from before the rising and one from after his execution. A list of ten Latin articles, issued by the 'proctors and defenders of the republic', was erroneously ascribed to Scrope's authorship during the Yorkist era.[29] The articles rehearse at length Henry of Lancaster's perjury and treachery in 1399, and detail the many deaths for which he has subsequently been responsible, ending with the recent (*novissime vero*) death of Henry Hotspur. They pay particular attention to Henry's oppressions of the church, including among these the Lancastrian regime's continued use of the Statute of Provisors, which is said to be especially destructive of the well-being of the universities. Apparently the work of a group of clerical Ricardian loyalists, they can be dated on internal grounds to the period between July 1403 and May 1405. Although a verbose and academic production, the articles have some value in demonstrating the degree of hostility that existed towards the new dynasty among some sections of the clergy.[30] It is worth noting that the proctors finally state as their intentions, besides the restoration of the right heir to the English throne, the creation of peace with the Welsh and other enemies of the kingdom and an end to all unjust fiscal exactions: two promises that also appear in Scrope's York articles. Finally, there is a list of reasons for Scrope's execution, said by Thomas Gascoigne, plausibly enough, to have been circulated by the earl of Northumberland and his allies in 1406. It faithfully rehearses most of the demands made in the York articles but adds to them a strain of legitimist criticism that is notably absent from Scrope's own manifesto; the archbishop is said to have been executed because he wished the crown of England to be restored to the right line of blood, and counselled the king to do penance for the perjury he committed in forcing the late king Richard to resign.[31]

In assessing the motives of the Yorkshire insurgents, then, it is the York articles that are of most direct concern. They display several striking features. One of the most obvious is their strict adherence to the hierarchical ideology of the three orders; the grievances of each order – clergy, nobility and commons – are dealt with in successive articles. Equally noticeable is the estate rhetoric that the manifesto employs, presenting the three separate orders of society as united in their concern for the commonwealth: the articles are issued 'by the assent of the commons'; reforms are demanded to redress the injuries and harms done to the 'estates, both temporal and spiritual'; if accomplished they will be for the salvation of the kingdom and the 'redress of the estate of the faithful commons'.[32] Such an idiom of protest seems to place the Yorkshire risings of 1405 squarely within the 'rising of the commons' tradition – risings that sought to defend a traditionally articulated social hierarchy from the damage inflicted upon it by a ruling regime seemingly unmindful of its own responsibilities. Such protests, stretching from the rebellion of 1381 to the Pilgrimage of Grace, possess a series of common features that the 1405 rising also displays: an articulate and politicized agenda, objecting to particular royal policies while continuing to profess loyalty to the person of the king; a broad social composition, expressing the confluence of disparate grievances; and a clear plan of campaign, in which a centre of regional or national government becomes the goal and muster-point of the insurgent forces. They were, in general, attempts to express dissent within a context of obedience, both to legitimate political authority and to the demands of the existing social order.[33] Within Yorkshire, elements of this tradition are already apparent in the disturbances around Doncaster and Beverley in 1392, and are more fully articulated in the 'Robin of Redesdale' agitation in 1469 and the 1489 rising, in which the fourth earl of Northumberland lost his life.[34]

Considered as a whole, therefore, the narrative evidence suggests that the part played by the earl of Northumberland and his ambitions in the Yorkshire risings was not a dominant one. It points, instead, to the independence of the disturbances in the county and emphasizes the significance of the earl marshal's grievances in prompting Archbishop Scrope to take up the cause of reform. An examination of the rebels' demands suggests that their movement had as its object much the same set of concerns as animated the parliamentary Commons: the complaint about purveyance and the attack on the malign influence of Henry's intimates had both, for example, been anticipated in Sir Arnold Savage's frank exchange with the king in the parliament of Hilary 1404.[35] In the second section of this essay, I shall examine in more detail the composition of the insurgents, in order to specify more precisely the nature of their grievances against the rule of Henry of Lancaster.

Contexts

The feature of the Yorkshire risings that most struck contemporaries was the considerable degree of clerical involvement.[36] Comparison with the Great Revolt of 1381 suggests that it was less the sheer number of clerical insurgents that set the 1405 rebellion apart than their higher social status. Scrope was supported in his protest by members of his own household, including his nephew, Geoffrey Scrope; his chancellor, Richard Conyngston, archdeacon of York; and Robert Wolveden, one of his vicars-general.[37] Several other members of the York chapter also feared for their position in the aftermath of the revolt, while five vicars-choral and a chaplain in the Minster were pardoned for their part in the rising.[38] If this was the core of Scrope's clerical following, the support of the secular clergy of York, such as John Whitwell, the rector of All Saints', North Street, was significant in giving additional impetus to the rising in the city. The part played by one chaplain in particular, William Forster, in rousing the citizens was acknowledged by the display of his head on Ouse Bridge.[39] Beyond York, the evidence for clerical participation is more difficult to determine. Very few mendicants sought pardons, although the continuator of the *Eulogium Historiarum* claimed that all four orders were involved in the rising and included a graphic account of the humiliation of a group of eighteen Franciscans among Scrope's forces.[40] Among the rest of the religious, the impoverished house of Austin canons at Warter supplied the archbishop with some adherents, and a former prior of the Gilbertine house at Malton also appears among the list of those who sought pardons.[41] The pattern of participation appears slightly different among the secular clergy, where those beneficed priests identifiable among the rebels tended to come from parishes dominated by one of the gentry insurgents.[42]

Naturally, a whole variety of grievances exercised this disparate gathering of the clergy. As a substantial local landowner, the York chapter cultivated good relations with the neighbouring gentry and shared many of the concerns that animated landed society. The vicars-choral depended on an overwhelmingly urban portfolio of rents for their prosperity and had interests as well as grievances in common with the citizens of York, while among the mendicants doubts as to the legitimacy of Henry IV's title to rule remained particularly strong.[43] The issue of most general and immediate concern to the clergy of the diocese was, however, the unaccustomed weight of royal taxation. Discontent at the king's demands had been growing for some time throughout the northern province. A combination of administrative confusion and Lancastrian insolvency meant that, between Henry IV's accession and the outbreak of the Yorkshire rising, the northern clergy had already been called upon to pay four clerical tenths and were committed to finding the resources for a further tenth within the next twelve months.[44] The most recent of these grants had, in addition, been extended to apply to benefices customarily exempted on the grounds of poverty: in June 1404 the contribution threshold had been lowered from £10 to 10 marks, and in the following December it was, for this grant only, removed altogether. The imposition of unaccustomed fiscal burdens upon the poorest members of the clerical estate inevitably evoked protests from an already recalcitrant Convocation. This fact was most forcibly expressed in June 1404, when a grant was made with the attached condition that inquisitions and distraints carried out by royal commissioners 'against the liberty of the Church and ancient custom of the Church in England' should cease.[45] Although this stipulation may have been no more than an expression of the general sense of secular oppression prevalent among the clergy in the early fifteenth century, it is significant that it also articulated a specific grievance of the archbishop himself, over the crown's evident disinclination to recognize the full immunities enjoyed by the see of York. Conflict had centred on the liberty of Beverley: the archbishop's claim to deliver his own gaols there and at Ripon had been overridden, apparently for the first time in more than a century, as recently as 1403, while in August 1404 Scrope had found it necessary to procure an additional royal grant, preventing the steward and marshal of the household from exercising their jurisdiction within the liberty of Beverley.[46] In choosing, in his manifesto, to demand remedies for the insupportable burdens placed upon the clerical estate and for the injuries done to the liberties of Holy Church, Scrope was addressing issues of immediate concern to himself and his *familia* but calculated also to create a broad platform of support among the clergy of his province.

A second distinctive feature of the Yorkshire risings was the whole-hearted participation of the townsmen of York, who, as nearly all the chronicle accounts emphasize, formed a major part of Scrope's host. Walsingham describes 'almost all the citizens of York who could bear arms' as joining the archbishop, while the king's reported anger towards the city, which he threatened to raze to the ground, and the dramatic abasement of the citizens, 'lying on the earth as though it was another Judgment Day' as they sought the king's pardon, substantially confirms this analysis.[47] The individual pardons issued by chancery supply very few names of York townsmen involved in the rising, most of whom sought protection under the terms of the general pardon the city purchased, at a cost of 500 marks, in early August.[48] The context within which they chose to embark upon such an unprecedented act of defiance can, however, be suggested. One element must be the appreciable downturn in the volume of wool and cloth exports through the city's outport at Hull in the years immediately after 1400, although York's status as a regional market centre, and its consequently diversified economic structure, indicate that this was unlikely to have been a decisive consideration.[49] A more immediate grievance was the heavy fiscal demands made upon the city by the new Lancastrian regime. York had provided vital assistance to Henry of Lancaster with a loan of 500 marks, 'delivered to him in his necessity before he undertook the government of the realm', and continued to prove a reliable lender: in the six years between Henry's return to England and the outbreak of the 1405 rising, the city's loans to the crown averaged £265 per annum.[50] York's governors clearly entertained hopes of swift repayment, agreeing to allow the mayor a small commission on any sums he recovered, but there is little sign that their efforts met with success. The string of murages and pontages that the city secured in these years had to serve as inadequate recompense.[51]

Allied to the heavy national taxation of these years, and the regular commitment of the fee farm, this was a substantial financial burden for the city to bear, made all the more galling by the knowledge that some of York's subsidy payments were being put to meet the costs of an unpopular royal household.[52] The natural resentment that many civic corporations felt at the level of crown demands upon their resources was accentuated, in York's case, by the revival of dissension within the city's governing groups and given a particular focus by growing discontent at the predominance enjoyed by the mayor, William Frost, throughout the early years of Henry IV's reign. In December 1399 a panel of twelve influential arbitrators had been appointed to consider the grievances set out in a bill exhibited by Thomas Santon, one of the city's chamberlains. Santon's bill was sufficiently controversial for the arbitrators to be unable to agree among themselves, and he was required, instead, to enter into a recognizance that he would not again transgress against the peace 'either by insurrections, confederations, illegal congregations, or by treacherous threats'. A month later, an 'ordinance' of the commons of the city, criticizing the aldermanic policy on admission to the freedom and asking that the crafts be given sufficient time to consult before responding to any request for taxation, 'without being rebuked or compelled against their will to grant any such tax', was repealed (or, perhaps more likely, rejected).[53]

William Frost, the mayor who quashed the commonalty's initiative, was a controversial figure in early Lancastrian York. Drawn from a local gentry family, and with little direct involvement in overseas trade, his proven ability to mediate successfully between York and Westminster must have made him an obvious choice to guide the city through the uncertain years of a new dynasty.[54] Frost proved highly adept at this task but his services did not come cheap: for his first year in office (February 1400–1), the customary mayor's fee of £50 was augmented with an additional remuneration of £20 and two pipes of wine. In the following year, the city agreed to meet the expenses of the man-at-arms Frost had sent on the king's Scottish expedition, and by the time of his fifth successive election as mayor in February 1404, his additional remuneration had climbed to £50. Frost's vice-regal conception of the mayoralty was not only expensive; it also ran counter to a more collegial approach to the office, embodied in a neglected ordinance of 1393, that limited both the mayor's emoluments and his length of tenure. By February 1405, when Frost was unexpectedly replaced as mayor, his activities had clearly provoked a reaction in the city. His successor, Adam del Bank, was no radical: a wealthy dyer, he had long since run through the *cursus honorum* of civic office. He was, however, prepared to adopt a less lavish approach towards the mayor's office, accepting the 'customary' mayor's fee of £50 and immediately effecting further economies within the mayor's household.[55] The implication of these changes seems clear. Within the city of York, an internal power-struggle preceded the outbreak of rebellion. Discontent with the burdensome and authoritarian regime of William Frost served to crystallize a more general sense of dissatisfaction with the new Lancastrian dynasty and created a climate of opinion in which the citizens were willing to give voice to their grievances. In choosing to complain of the impoverishment of the merchants' estate through the insistent royal demand for loans, as well as by the raising of excessive tolls and customs, Scrope had read the anxieties of his urban followers well.

Analysis of the gentry insurgents, the majority of them engaged in the North Riding rising, throws up a different set of issues. The names of many of the major figures are easily recovered, but identifying a common context for their decision to rebel remains problematic. While it is clear that some of the Percy affinity in Yorkshire was directly involved in the rising, privileging the agency of the earl of Northumberland and his followers does not provide a sufficient explanation for the composition and concerns of the rebels. One reason for this lies in the actions of the earl himself; the earlier version of Hardyng's chronicle makes it clear that, after the failed ambush at Sir Ralph Eure's residence, Northumberland withdrew rapidly northwards, taking a number of his most prominent Yorkshire retainers with him.[56] This meant that, although a number of Percy adherents and well-wishers were implicated in the rising, including two of the captains of the North Riding insurgents, Sir John Colville and Sir John Fauconberg, their influence upon the rebels' actions and demands was never a decisive one.[57] Another of the leaders of the North Riding rising, Sir John Fitzrandolf, took a fee from the earl of Westmorland, for example, while several of the insurgents enjoyed some form of royal patronage: Sir John Colville was a king's knight, as well as a Percy retainer; Sir Robert Lamplugh, a royal annuitant; Sir Robert Persay was forester of the duchy of Lancaster forest of Pickering.[58] Indeed, one striking characteristic common to some of the gentry insurgents was the strength of their family connection to the duchy of Lancaster. Sir Ralph Hastings, executed for his part in the rising, was the son of one of John of Gaunt's most favoured retainers; another ringleader, Sir William Plumpton, was the son of a duchy annuitant; Sir Alexander Metham, his brother Thomas and Gerard Usflete the younger, all subsequently pardoned, were also the sons of Lancastrian servants.[59] There were, in addition, strong ties of association among some of the participants, quite independent of the claims of lordship. A significant nucleus among them were active local administrators within the North Riding: Persay, Colville, Fitzrandolf and John Percy of Kydale were all frequently commissioned to collect the parliamentary subsidy and to administer the various fiscal experiments attempted by the new Lancastrian regime; Persay and George Darell of Sessay had also acted as coroners within the riding.[60]

Such men make unlikely revolutionaries. It suited the Lancastrian regime to represent their armed protest as a real threat to the maintenance of social and dynastic order, forcing the king to resist the restless demands of the multitude lest the whole kingdom perish, but the violence of the rebels was restrained and relatively discriminating.[61] At the heart of their concerns was the sharp readjustment in the traditional alignments of county society precipitated by the Neville family's permanent acquisition of the honour of Richmond in 1399 and confirmed by Ralph Neville, earl of Westmorland's, emergence as Henry IV's chosen lieutenant in the North.[62] Some of the insurgents had already suffered in the cause of the Nevilles advance: as early as 1372, Sir John Fauconberg's father, the unstable Thomas, Lord Fauconberg, had been persuaded to surrender two East Riding manors to John, Lord Neville.[63] Among their companions, resentment towards the beneficiaries of this emergent new order was strong. The chief – and perhaps the only – victim of the rebels was Sir Thomas Colville, who embodied in his own person the coalescence of the Neville and Lancastrian affinities that defined it, while lesser servants of the Nevilles also suffered: John Norton complained that, although he had purchased the office of warrener of Ripon from Archbishop Scrope for 20 marks, he had subsequently been ousted from his post, at the suit of Sir John Scrope and Sir William Plumpton, 'because he was of the livery, and in the service, of the earl of Westmorland'.[64] Royal lands and servants were also targeted: the king's tenants at Kilburn reportedly sustained great losses at the hands of the insurgents, while a royal esquire, John Haukswell, had his haystacks and granges plundered.[65]

Yorkshire had suffered considerable disruption in the aftermath of Hotspur's defeat at Shewsbury, with the continued show of strength made by Percy partisans around Beverley and York considered threatening enough to require the king's presence in the shire. The consequent disorder had been called to Henry's attention by the parliamentary Commons at Hilary 1404, when they requested the king to charge the earls of Northumberland and Westmorland, on their return to their countries, to impose upon their servants, tenants and familiars the same unity and concord that they had themselves sworn to observe. 'Lying rumours' were, nevertheless, still reported to be stirring the county to strife and discord.[66] It was against this background of regional disorder that the crown was proving powerless to control that the Yorkshire gentry insurgents chose to make their protest. In their eyes, it was Henry IV's partisan deployment of his considerable influence within the shire that, by fuelling the fire of magnate rivalries, had created the disorder that plagued the region. Their solution was to reassert a threatened local solidarity, taking direct action against the most prominent agents of the new order while demanding a return to a more familiar pattern of lordship – 'that the heirs of noblemen be wholly restored to their honours and inheritances, according to the condition of their birth'.[67]

It was consequently his status as the most prominent casualty of Neville aggrandizement that conferred upon Thomas Mowbray, earl marshal, the significance in the outbreak of the Yorkshire rising that most of the chroniclers acknowledge. Although he held substantial estates around Epworth and the Isle of Axholme, on the southeastern borders of the county, Mowbray could not be counted as a major regional magnate: his Yorkshire estates yielded approximately £160 per annum in 1399 and delivered a lump sum of only

£80 to his coffers in 1403–4.[68] On the evidence of those pardoned, he had few clients among the shire gentry but relied, principally, upon the resources of his household and estate administration to provide his forces.[69] It was rather the nature of his grievances that placed the young earl marshal at the centre of the 1405 rising. The Mowbrays were hereditary marshals of England but, since Thomas Mowbray had been too young to exercise the office at Henry IV's coronation in 1399, it had been granted, instead, to Ralph Neville, earl of Westmorland, for life.[70] Mowbray was permitted the style earl marshal but not the substance of the marshal's authority. The subordination of the young Mowbray's rights and claims to the consolidation of a new Neville ascendancy was further underlined by the commitment of Mowbray manors in Yorkshire to the keeping of Westmorland during his minority.[71] Although he was granted early livery of his inheritance in November 1403, Thomas Mowbray's continuing disaffection had rendered him a known malcontent by February 1405, when he admitted concealing his knowledge of the duke of York's intention to abduct the heirs of Roger Mortimer from the court. His animosity towards the Lancastrian regime intensified when his claim for precedence in parliament over Richard Beauchamp, earl of Warwick, was rejected by the council.[72] Mowbray's complaints against the government of Henry IV were particular and personal but they attracted considerable support in the region, where they replicated the concerns of the coalition of interests opposed to the rise of the Nevilles and their clients that imparted to the Yorkshire rising some sense of common purpose.

What remains to be explained is why the earl marshal's grievances evoked so strong a response from Scrope himself, prompting the archbishop to preach against the evils that afflicted the kingdom, both in his own cathedral and in the surrounding churches, and then to issue his manifesto, calling on every man to lay out his strength for justice and to be strong in zeal for reform.[73] One element in Scrope's actions was clearly his concern for ecclesiastical liberties. He had associated himself with Archbishop Arundel's blunt defence of the Church against the threat of disendowment, made at the Coventry Parliament in October 1404.[74] The king's subsequent proposal, that stipendiary chaplains, and others customarily exempt from the subsidies granted by Convocation, should now be called upon to contribute to the defence of the realm, can only have increased his anxieties; it was perhaps to discuss the implementation of this demand that Scrope was summoned to meet with the king at Worcester in late April 1405.[75] But while there was an established tradition of clerical advice and admonition on the ills of the kingdom, exemplified in the open letter addressed by Philip Repingdon to Henry IV in 1401, it offered no sanction for Scrope's decision to seek popular support for his chosen remedies.[76]

There is, as we have seen, little contemporary evidence that Scrope was encouraged to do so by the earl of Northumberland, and there is no sign, in the York articles, of sympathy with the legitimist arguments that formed an important part of the Percies' platform: Scrope's ecclesiastical advancement had owed more to papal patronage, and his own considerable abilities, than to the favour of Richard II, while he had played an active part in securing the late king's resignation.[77] The narrative accounts seem, rather, to indicate that Scrope's intention was to offer himself as a mediator, initially between the feuding northern magnates, and then between the king and his critics. As the son of a Yorkshire nobleman, Henry, first Lord Scrope of Masham, the archbishop's lineage allowed him to contemplate the first part of this plan; his nephew, Henry, third Lord Scrope of Masham, was to display a similarly misplaced confidence in his ability to manage and resolve a major political crisis in 1415.[78] The language of his manifesto might also suggest that, in aspiring to extend the scope of his mediation to the kingdom as a whole, Scrope was responding, as primate of England, to an imperative that was as much pastoral as political. Impelled by an active and ascetic piety, he had already sought to reform the public worship of his province; now he turned to the spiritual health of the nation, calling upon his people to follow the path of truth and justice, to be 'helpers (*adjutores*) in your salvation, and in ours'.[79] His hopes proved vain but he managed, by imposing structure and purpose upon the unresolved grievances thrown up by six years of Lancastrian rule, briefly to rally around himself a regional coalition of protest as broadly based as any in fifteenth-century England.

Notes

1 'Annales', p. 400. The date conventionally assigned to the outbreak of the revolt in official records, 1 May, may also represent the actual date of Northumberland's attempted ambush: *CIPM*, 1399–1405, nos. 451, 1152.

2 Beverley, Humberside Record Office, BC II/6/4, Expense communis pecunie.

3 *POPC*, I, 275–6.

4 D. Hay, *Polydore Vergil, Renaissance Historian and Man of Letters* (Oxford, 1952), p. 193; his account is most readily accessible in *Plumpton Correspondence*, ed. T. Stapleton, Camden Society old s. 4 (London, 1839), p. xxiv. Compare with J. H. Ramsay, *Lancaster and York: A Century of English History, 1399–1485*, 2 vols. (Oxford, 1892), I, 88: 'What Scrope hoped to effect it is not easy to divine . . .'.

5 P. McNiven, 'The Betrayal of Archbishop Scrope', *BJRL* 54 (1971), 173–213. P. McNiven, *Heresy and Politics in the Reign of Henry IV: The Burning of John Badby* (Manchester, 1987), pp. 123–5 offers a similar interpretation. General accounts of the period that clearly base their account of the rising upon McNiven's include M. H. Keen, *England in the Later Middle Ages* (London, 1973), pp. 311–13; A. Tuck, *Crown and Nobility 1272–1461* (London, 1985), pp. 230–2; P. Heath, *Church and Realm 1272–1461* (London, 1988), pp. 240–3; A. J. Pollard, *Late Medieval England, 1399–1509* (London, 2000), pp. 49–51. J. A. F. Thomson, *The Transformation of Medieval England, 1370–1529* (London, 1983), p. 168 offers a more neutral formulation, while A. Goodman, *A History of England from Edward II to James II* (London, 1977), p. 207, provides an analysis that preserves the independence of the Yorkshire risings.

6 McNiven, 'Betrayal', pp. 186, 192, 209 and 185.

7 *CPR, 1405–8*, pp. 65, 40; *CCR, 1402–5*, p. 517.

8 KB 27/592 Rex, m. 14; KB 27/594 Rex, m. 2.

9 BL MS Additional 9021, fols. 8–9 (Sir Henry Boynton); *Rot. Parl.*, III, 633 (Sir Ralph Hastings).

10 *Rot. Parl.*, III, 604–7; M. H. Keen, 'Treason Trials under the Law of Arms', *TRHS* 5th s. 12 (1962), 85–103, and J. G. Bellamy, *The Law of Treason in England in the Later Middle Ages* (Cambridge, 1970), pp. 159, 180 and 182–3, deal with some of the legal issues the document raises, while A. L. Brown, 'The Commons and the Council in the Reign of Henry IV', *EHR* 79 (1964), 1–30 situates the process it reports within the chronology of the Long Parliament (pp. 12–25).

11 P. Strohm, *England's Empty Throne: Usurpation and the Language of Legitimation, 1399–1422* (London, 1998), pp. 34–6 and passim.

12 'John Benet's Chronicle for the Years 1400 to 1462', ed. G. L. Harriss and M. A. Harriss, *Camden Miscellany XXIV*, Camden Society 4th s. 9 (London, 1972), pp. 175–6.

13 The unexpected nature of the Commons' intervention is clear in the original enrolment, where it required the hasty addition of another membrane: C 65/69, m. 2.

14 Strohm, *England's Empty Throne*, pp. 81–2; R. G. Davies, 'After the Execution of Archbishop Scrope: Henry IV, the Papacy and the English Episcopate, 1405–8', *BJRL* 59 (1976–7), 40–74 examines in detail the ecclesiastical difficulties created by Scrope's execution.

15 'Annales', pp. 402–12; *Historia Anglicana*, II, 268–71, 422–3. The account in *Ypodigma Neustriae, a Thoma Walsingham, quondam monacho monasterii S. Albani, conscriptum*, ed. H. T. Riley (London, 1876), pp. 412–15, follows the shorter *Chronica Minora* version. For the relationship and dating of these accounts, see *The St Albans Chronicle, 1406–1420*, ed. V. H. Galbraith (Oxford, 1937), pp. liii–lxvi.

16 Note also that Scrope's rebellion was one of the episodes where Walsingham's readers felt most free to criticize his conclusions. Compare the outraged exclamations at the earl of Westmorland's deception in Oxford, Bodleian Library, MS Bodley 462, fol. 278v (*falsum est*) with Thomas Otterbourne's careful exculpation of Ralph Neville's actions: *Duo Rerum Anglicarum Scriptores Veteres*, ed. T. Hearne (Oxford, 1732), p. 256.

17 *Eulogium Historiarum*, III, 405–8; this is the basis for the vernacular account of the rising in *An English Chronicle of the reigns of Richard II, Henry IV, Henry V and Henry VI written before 1471*, ed. J. S. Davies, Camden Society old s. 64 (London, 1856), pp. 31–4.

18 C. L. Kingsford, *English Historical Literature in the Fifteenth Century* (Oxford, 1913), pp. 279–91 (p. 282). Note the similar interpretation of events in BL MS Additional 29504, a northern roll chronicle that pays close attention to the doings of the Percies but makes no connection between their rebellions and Scrope's rising.

19 BL MS Additional 35295, fols. 263v–264; for the date of this passage (*c.* 1417–22), see 'Chronicle of John Strecche for the reign of Henry V (1414–1422)', ed. F. Taylor, *BJRL* 16 (1932), 137–87 (pp. 139–40).

20 *Incerti Scriptoris Chronicon de regnis . . . Henrici IV, Henrici V, et Henrici VI*, ed. J. A. Giles (London, 1848), pp. 43–8; M. V. Clarke, *Fourteenth Century Studies* (Oxford, 1937), pp. 82–6.

21 *Hardyng*, pp. 362–4 (quotation at p. 362); the relationship between Hardyng's career and his writings is further discussed in C. L. Kingsford, 'The First Version of Hardyng's Chronicle', *EHR* 27 (1912), 462–82 and F. Riddy, 'John Hardyng's

Chronicle and the Wars of the Roses', in *Arthurian Literature XII*, ed. J. P. Carley and F. Riddy (Cambridge, 1993), pp. 91–108.

22 BL MS Lansdowne 204, fols. 206v–207.

23 *Hardyng*, p. 351; S. Walker, 'Political Saints in Later Medieval England', in *The McFarlane Legacy: Studies in Late Medieval Politics and Society*, ed. R. H. Britnell and A. J. Pollard (Stroud, 1995), pp. 77–106 (pp. 84–5). One consideration exercising Hardyng in the composition of his second recension was a desire to promote the case for the restoration of Percy influence in the North: A. J. Pollard, *North-Eastern England during the Wars of the Roses* (Oxford, 1990), pp. 285–300.

24 *The Historians of the Church of York and its Archbishops*, ed. J. Raine, 3 vols. (London, 1879–94), II, 429–32; *Political Poems and Songs relating to English History*, ed. T. Wright, 2 vols. (London, 1859–61), II, 114–18; J. W. McKenna, 'Popular Canonisation as Political Propaganda: The Cult of Archbishop Scrope', *Speculum* 45 (1970), 608–23; J. Hughes, *Pastors and Visionaries: Religion and Secular Life in Late Medieval Yorkshire* (Woodbridge, 1988), pp. 305–15.

25 *Historians of the Church of York*, ed. Raine, III, 288–91; Thomas Gascoigne, *Loci e libro veritatum*, ed. J. E. Thorold Rogers (Oxford, 1881), pp. 225–9 (Gascoigne's account); *Anglia Sacra*, ed. H. Wharton, 2 vols. (London, 1691), II, 369–72 (Maidstone's). The relationship between these accounts is discussed in S. K. Wright, 'The Provenance and Manuscript Tradition of the *Martyrium Ricardi Archiepiscopi*', *Manuscripta* 28 (1984), 92–102, though none of the conjectures offered is entirely convincing.

26 W. A. Pronger, 'Thomas Gascoigne', *EHR* 53 (1938), 606–26 (pp. 607–10).

27 *Historians of the Church of York*, ed. Raine, III, 288.

28 'Annales', pp. 403–5; *Eulogium Historiarum*, III, 405–6; *Incerti Scriptoris Chronicon*, ed. Giles, p. 44.

29 E 163/6/16 is the earliest extant version, but cannot be the text on which later copies, printed in *Anglia Sacra*, ed. Wharton, II, 362–8 and *Historians of the Church of York*, ed. Raine, II, 292–304 are based. The ascription to Scrope appears to have originated with the compiler of BL MS Cotton Vespasian E VII (at fols. 96v–103v). L. A. Coote, *Prophecy and Public Affairs in Later Medieval England* (York, 2000), pp. 225–6, emphasizes the Percy connections of this manuscript.

30 Compare the denunciation of Henry's usurpation and exhortation to the English to rise against his rule preserved in Oxford, Bodleian Library, MS Ashmole Rolls 26 and MS Bodley 623, fols. 96–7.

31 *Historians of the Church of York*, ed. Raine, II, 304–5; Gascoigne, *Loci e libro veritatum*, pp. 229–31. The heading, 'Articuli Nobilium' is an editorial insertion; Oxford, Bodleian Library, MS Auctar. 4. 5, fols. 102–3.

32 'Annales', pp. 403–4.

33 M. James, *Society, Politics and Culture: Studies in Early Modern England* (Cambridge, 1986), pp. 4–5, 259–69; M. Bush, 'The Risings of the Commons in England, 1381–1549', in *Orders and Hierarchies in Late Medieval and Renaissance Europe*, ed. J. Denton (Basingstoke, 1999), pp. 109–25, 187–9.

34 *Select Cases in Court of King's Bench under Richard II, Henry IV and Henry V*, ed. G. O. Sayles, Selden Society 88 (London, 1971), pp. 83–7; C. Ross, *Edward IV* (London, 1974), pp. 126–7, 439–40; M. Hicks, *Richard III and his Rivals: Magnates and their Motives in the Wars of the Roses* (London, 1991), pp. 395–418.

35 C. M. Fraser, 'Some Durham Documents relating to the Hilary Parliament of 1404', *BIHR* 34 (1961), 192–9 (p. 198).

36 *Eulogium Historiarum*, III, 406: 'Et collecto exercitus de burgensibus, villanis, presbyteris, et religiosis . . .'; *The Register of Philip Repingdon, 1405–1419: Memoranda, 1405–1411*, ed. M. Archer, Lincoln Record Society 57 (Lincoln, 1963), p. 136: '. . . nonnullos potentes et proceres dicti regni ac eciam alios inferioris status necnon viros ecclesiasticos seculares et regulares . . .'.

37 *CPR, 1405–8*, p. 19; *A Calendar of the Register of Richard Scrope, Archbishop of York, 1398–1405*, ed. R. N. Swanson, 2 vols., Borthwick Texts and Calendars: Records of the Northern Province 8 and 11 (York, 1981–5), I, 38 (Scrope); *Register of Richard Scrope*, ed. Swanson, I, 15, 47 and 334 (Conyngston); *Register of Richard Scrope*, ed. Swanson, II, 956, 963 (Wolveden); *Fasti Ecclesiae Anglicanae, 1300–1541: Northern Province*, ed. B. Jones (London, 1963), p. 18.

38 R. L. Storey, 'Clergy and Common Law in the Reign of Henry IV', in *Medieval Legal Records*, ed. R. F. Hunnisett and J. B. Post (London, 1978), pp. 342–408 (pp. 394–5); *CPR, 1405–8*, pp. 71–2.

39 *CPR, 1405–8*, pp. 79, 69; *Register of Richard Scrope*, ed. Swanson, II, 966 (Whitwell). John de Burton, rector of St Helen on the Walls, was also implicated in the rising: *CPR, 1405–8*, p. 44, *Register of Richard Scrope*, ed. Swanson, II, 766.

40 *Eulogium Historiarum*, III, 407. The participation of the mendicants is also especially emphasized in the 'Waltham annals': BL MS Cotton Titus D XV, fol. 51. Fr John Tokhost and Fr William Thorpe are the only mendicants whose pardons are enrolled: *CPR, 1405–8*, pp. 76, 193.

41 *CPR, 1405–8*, pp. 55, 287; *Register of Richard Scrope*, ed. Swanson, II, 708, 726 for Warter's poverty.

42 *CPR, 1405–8*, pp. 34, 196 (Thomas Anlaby, rector of Spofforth); *CPR, 1405–8*, pp. 1, 14, 49; *Register of Richard Scrope*, ed. Swanson, I, 391 (Simon Wentislaw, rector of Cowlam); E 28/22/27 (William Gibson, rector of Slingsby).

43 York, York Minster Library, E 1/38 shows the chapter paying fees to several local lawyers and administrators for Easter term 1405; *Charters of the Vicars Choral of York Minster: City of York and its suburbs to 1546*, ed, N. J. Tringham, Yorkshire Archaeological Society Record Series 148 (Leeds, 1993), pp. xxiii–xxxix; D. W. Whitfield, 'Conflicts of Personality and Principle: The Crisis in the English Franciscan Province, 1400–1409', *Franciscan Studies* 17 (1957), 321–62.

44 I. R. Abbot, 'Taxation of Personal Property and of Clerical Incomes, 1399 to 1402', *Speculum* 17 (1942), 471–98 (pp. 489–98); A. Rogers, 'Clerical Taxation under Henry IV', *BIHR* 46 (1973), 123–44 (pp. 127–33).

45 *Register of Richard Scrope*, ed. Swanson, II, 767, 773.

46 JUST 3/82/1–3; *CPR, 1401–5*, p. 95; R. B. Pugh, *Imprisonment in Medieval England* (London, 1968), pp. 297–8; E. G. Kimball, 'Commissions of the Peace for Urban Jurisdictions in England, 1327–1485', *Transactions of the American Philosophical Society*, 121 (1977), 448–74 (pp. 466–7).

47 'Annales', pp. 405, 408; *Incerti Scriptoris Chronicon*, ed. Giles, p. 44; *Chronicle of Adam Usk*, p. 202.

48 *CPR, 1405–8*, p. 40; E. Miller, 'Medieval York', in *VCH Yorkshire: The City of York*, ed. P. M. Tillot (Oxford, 1961), pp. 25–116 (p. 58).

49 J. Kermode, *Medieval Merchants: York, Beverley and Hull in the Later Middle Ages* (Cambridge, 1998), pp. 167–72; P. J. P. Goldberg, *Women, Work and Life Cycle in a Medieval Economy. Women in York and Yorkshire c. 1300–1520* (Oxford, 1992), pp. 23–6.

50 *CPR, 1399–1401*, p. 354; *CPR, 1401–5*, pp. 251, 403, tabulated in L. Attreed,

The King's Towns: Identity and Survival in Late Medieval English Boroughs (New York, 2000), p. 159. This is a minimum figure, as the city received further requests, to which the response is unclear.

51 [York,] Y[ork] C[ity] A[rchives] MS D 1, fol. 10; *CPR, 1399–1401*, p. 224; *CPR, 1401–5*, pp. 166, 333 and 352.

52 E 101/512/23.

53 YCA MS D 1, fols. 349v, 348; *House of Commons*, IV, 304–5; S. Rees Jones, 'York's Civic Administration, 1354–1464', in *The Government of Medieval York. Essays in Commemoration of the 1396 Royal Charter*, ed. S. Rees Jones, Borthwick Studies in History 3 (York, 1997), pp. 108–40 (pp. 121–2).

54 *House of Commons*, III, 138–41; R. B. Dobson, 'The Crown, the Charter and the City, 1396–1461', in *The Government of Medieval York*, ed. Rees Jones, pp. 34–56 (pp. 41–4).

55 YCA MS D 1, fols. 10r–10v; J. Kermode, 'The Merchants of York, Beverley and Hull in the Fourteenth and Fifteenth Centuries' (unpublished Ph. D. dissertation, University of Sheffield, 1990), Appendix 1; R. B. Dobson, *Church and Society in the Medieval North of England* (London, 1996), pp. 267–84 (pp. 278–9).

56 BL MS Lansdowne 204, fol. 206v; these included Sir Henry Boynton, Sir Gerard Salvayn, John Aske and Randolph del See: *Rot. Parl.*, III, 605; *CPR, 1405–8*, pp. 24, 67 and 69.

57 *CPR, 1401–5*, p. 297 (Colville); *CPR, 1388–92*, p. 513; *CPR, 1399–1401*, p. 24; *CCR, 1399–1402*, p. 366; G. E. Cokayne, *The Complete Peerage*, 13 vols. in 12 (London, 1910–57), V, 276–81 (Fauconberg). Other members of the Percy affinity involved in the rising included Richard Fairfax, John Percy of Kydale and Nicholas Tempest: *CPR, 1401–5*, p. 297; *CPR, 1405–8*, p. 79 (Fairfax); *CIM, 1399–1422*, no. 451 (Tempest); *CPR, 1401–5*, p. 297; *CPR, 1405–8*, p. 48 (Percy). Robert Vavasour of Rudstan had more distant links with the Percies: *CIPM, 1405–13*, no. 341.

58 *CCR, 1405–8*, p. 194 (Fitzrandolf); *CPR, 1401–5*, p. 42 (Colville); *CPR, 1399–1401*, p. 135; *CFR, 1399–1405*, p. 162 (Lamplugh); *CPR, 1405–8*, p. 57; *CCR, 1409–13*, p. 10 (Persay).

59 *CPR, 1405–8*, pp. 69, 478 (Hastings); *CPR, 1405–8*, p. 63; *CCR, 1402–5*, p. 469 (Plumpton); *CPR, 1405–8*, pp. 78, 79 (Metham); *CPR, 1405–8*, p. 71 (Usflete). For their duchy connections, S. Walker, *The Lancastrian Affinity, 1361–1399* (Oxford, 1990), pp. 271, 275, 278 and 283; DL 29/738/12096, m. 4.

60 *CFR, 1383–91*, pp. 70, 159 and 265; *CFR, 1391–9*, pp. 27, 141 and 264; *CFR, 1399–1405*, pp. 115, 148, 190, 256, 286 and 291; *CCR, 1396–9*, p. 262 (Persay); *CCR, 1402–5*, p. 439 (Darell). For Persay and his fellows acting under these commissions, *Inquisitions and Assessments relating to Feudal Aids*, 6 vols. (London, 1899–1920), VI, 261–2; E 359/19, rots. 2, 4, 6; E 179/211/41, 43.

61 *Register of Philip Repingdon, 1405–19*, ed. Archer, pp. 136–8.

62 *CPR, 1399–1401*, p. 24; C. D. Ross, 'The Yorkshire Baronage, 1399–1435' (unpublished D. Phil. dissertation, University of Oxford, 1950), pp. 10–14; R. L. Storey, 'The North of England', in *Fifteenth-century England, 1399–1509*, ed. S. B. Chrimes, C. D. Ross and R. A. Griffiths (Manchester, 1972), pp. 129–44 (pp. 134–7).

63 *CFR, 1399–1405*, pp. 112–13; *CIPM, 1399–1405*, no. 427. Thomas, Lord Fauconberg, may himself have been involved in the rising: *CPR, 1405–8*, pp. 123, 282.

64 *House of Commons*, II, 638–9 (Colville); E 28/22/19 (Norton).

65 *CPR, 1405–8*, pp. 43, 55 and 56.

66 *POPC*, I, 209–10; *Rot. Parl.*, III, 525; *CCR, 1402–5*, p. 515.

67 *Eulogium Historiarum*, III, 406.

68 SC 6/1087/14; BL Additional Charter 16556, m. 9.

69 Mowbray followers implicated in the rising include his cousin, Ivo, son of John, Lord Welles; Sir Robert Lamplugh; Sir Nicholas Colfox; John Burgh, receiver of his Yorkshire lands; William Fencotes, steward of Thirsk; William Bachelor, his cook; Robert Botvelayn; John Haldeburgh; Nicholas Hall; John Holbourne; and 'Yeven'. *CPR, 1405–8*, pp. 38, 99; *Complete Peerage*, XII, ii, 443 (Welles); *CPR, 1405–8*, p. 73; BL Add. Ch. 16556, m. 12 (Lamplugh); *CPR, 1405–8*, p. 80; *Anglo-Norman Letters and Petitions*, ed. M. D. Legge, Anglo-Norman Text Society 3 (Oxford, 1941), no. 386 (Colfox); *CPR, 1405–8*, pp. 73, 110; BL Add. Ch. 16556, m. 9 (Burgh); *CPR, 1405–8*, p. 70; SC 6/1087/14 (Fencotes); *CPR, 1405–8*, pp. 38, 73; BL Add. Ch. 16556, m. 22 (Bachelor); *CPR, 1405–8*, pp. 68, 80; *CPR, 1401–5*, p. 335 (Botvelayn); *CPR, 1405–8*, p. 32; BL Add. Ch. 16556, m. 8 (Haldeburgh); *CPR, 1405–8*, p. 41; BL Add. Ch. 16556, m. 4 (Hall); *CPR, 1405–8*, p. 41; *CPR, 1401–5*, p. 335 (Holbourne); BL Add. Ch. 16556, m. 16 (Yeven).

70 *CPR, 1399–1401*, p. 9; R. E. Archer, 'Parliamentary Restoration: John Mowbray and the Dukedom of Norfolk in 1425', in *Rulers and Ruled in Late Medieval England*, ed. R. E. Archer and S. Walker (London, 1995), pp. 99–116 (pp. 104–5).

71 *Anglo-Norman Letters and Petitions*, ed. Legge, nos. 383, 386; *CPR, 1401–5*, p. 322; *CCR, 1402–5*, pp. 68, 225 and 250; *CFR, 1399–1405*, p. 29.

72 'Annales', pp. 398–9; *POPC*, II, 104–5. Mowbray may have feared that defeat on the precedence issue would also jeopardise his tenure of the lordship of Gower, where his family had been in dispute with the Beauchamps for half a century: J. B. Smith and T. B. Pugh, 'The Lordship of Gower and Kilvey in the Middle Ages', in *Glamorgan County History*, ed. G. Williams, 6 vols. (Cardiff, 1936–80), III, 205–65 (pp. 249–56).

73 *Incerti Scriptoris Chronicon*, ed. Giles, p. 44.

74 'Annales', p. 392.

75 *POPC*, II, 100–1; *Signet Letters*, no. 328; *Register of Richard Scrope*, ed. Swanson, II, 993. Henry was acting against the advice of several of his councillors in seeking this additional grant: *POPC*, II, 101–3.

76 *Chronicle of Adam Usk*, pp. 136–42, discussed in F. Grady, 'The Lancastrian Gower and the Limits of Exemplarity', *Speculum* 70 (1995), 552–75 (pp. 552–5).

77 M. Harvey, *The English in Rome, 1362–1420* (Cambridge, 1999), p. 138; R. G. Davies, 'Richard II and the Church in the Years of "Tyranny" ', *Journal of Medieval History* 1 (1975), 329–62 (pp. 345–9); *Chrons. Rev.*, pp. 163–6, 169, 171–2. The fullest recent account of Scrope's career is in B. Vale, 'The Scropes of Bolton and Masham, *c.* 1300–1450: A Study of a Northern Noble Family', 2 vols. (unpublished D. Phil. dissertation, University of York, 1987), I, 143–90.

78 T. B. Pugh, *Henry V and the Southampton Plot of 1415*, Southampton Record Series 30 (Southampton, 1988), pp. 109–21.

79 *Index Britanniae Scriptorum. John Bale's Index of British and Other Writers*, ed. R. L. Poole and M. Bateson (Oxford, 1902), p. 358; *Catalogue of the Library of Syon Monastery, Isleworth*, ed. M. Bateson (Cambridge, 1898), p. 76; Hughes, *Pastors and Visionaries*, pp. 73, 203 and 267; 'Annales', pp. 403, 405.

11

Civil war and rebellion, 1200–1500

Writing a little before 1470, Sir Thomas Malory drew a clear lesson for his own time from the tale of the civil war between King Arthur and Sir Mordred that destroyed the fellowship of the Round Table:

> Lo! you, all Englishmen. See you not what a mischief here was? For he that was the most King and noblest Knight of the world and most loved the fellowship of noble knights and by him they were all upholden, and yet might not these Englishmen hold them content with him. Lo! thus was the old custom and usages of this land, and men say that we of this land have not yet lost that custom. Alas! this is a great default of us Englishmen, for there may us nothing please no term.[1]

Malory was not alone in condemning the restless and violent search for novelty he saw as characteristic of his countrymen. The Cornish clerk John Trevisa compared the English to the Romans, who could only be overcome in their own land, while the harassed Milanese ambassador in Paris, seeking to explain the latest twist of English dynastic fortunes to his paymasters in 1471, wished that 'the people and their country were plunged deep into the sea, because of their lack of stability'.[2] When Philippe de Commynes attributed the troubles of Henry VI's reign to an excess of natural aggression on the part of his subjects, he was only the most articulate in a long line of French commentators on the violence and uncertainty of English political life. What most impressed them was the unfortunate fate of so many English kings. The Chancellor of France informed the Estates-General in 1484 that the English had suffered twenty-six changes of dynasty since the foundation of their monarchy,[3] and there were sufficient recent examples – Edward II, Richard II, Henry VI and Edward V, all done to death by their captors – to lend plausibility to his estimate.

Contemporary commentators, at home and abroad, had no doubts that civil war and rebellion were among the defining features of English political life in the later Middle Ages. This is an analysis that historians have generally accepted, seeking to draw from the study of these periodic breakdowns in political co-operation more general conclusions about the nature of the English monarchy in this period. Richard Kaeuper has argued, for example, that a distinction should be drawn between the political troubles of the thirteenth century, which were the result of a temporary disequilibrium in the balance between the costs and benefits of royal government, and the rebellions of the fourteenth and fifteenth centuries, which were brought about by a more corrosive disillusion with the ability of the monarchy to perform the tasks expected of it. E. B. Fryde has made a similar point more bluntly in explaining the popular rebellions of the period as a result of 'the worst deterioration in the quality of internal government that England had experienced since the civil wars of the thirteenth century'.[4] As these quotations make clear, the frequent incidence of civil war and rebellion in the later Middle Ages stands at the centre of a debate about the nature of English society: was the disruption they embodied pathological, the result of structural weaknesses in the English state that rendered political violence inevitable, or was it accidental, a sign of short-lived disturbance within a generally peaceful and effective political system? In order to reach a conclusion, a series of related questions needs first to be answered. Were there any recurrent situations or grievances that provoked political violence in England? Was there an increasing disposition over time to resolve political differences by a resort to arms? Were the civil wars of late medieval England more frequent, or more destructive, than in the other monarchies of Western Europe during the same period?

As a starting-point, some distinctions should be drawn between the motivations and objectives of the various rebellions and insurrections. Four principal types of disturbance can be identified. First, 'reformist' rebellions, intended to correct what were perceived to be abuses in the king's government and to remove from his presence those advisers considered responsible for the abuses. Such movements characteristically generated a set of formal demands, to which the king was requested, or compelled, to acquiesce, such as those embodied in Magna Carta (1215), the Provisions of Oxford (1258) and the Ordinances (1311). Each of these documents proved to be the occasion for an outbreak of civil war, though violence was not the inevitable result of such reformist proposals. There were similar sets of demands, such as the so-called Paper Constitution (1244) or the Remonstrances, a list of grievances circulated following a meeting of many of the higher nobility at Montgomery in June 1297, presented to the king in an atmosphere of great political tension, whose explosive potential was nevertheless successfully defused. What distinguished these more peaceful protests was less the content of the demands made on the king than the degree of flexibility that both sides were prepared to show in negotiating around them. Henry III refused to accept the reform proposals in 1244, but dropped the demand for an aid from the baronage that had initially provoked them, while the crisis of 1297 ended with the issue of the *Confirmatio Cartarum*, a concession by the king's council that embodied a number of the demands of the Remonstrances.

Such accommodations were as frequent as the breakdowns of consensus that issued in violence, and they were facilitated, in the later part of this period, by a shift in the focus of reformist ambition away from the attempt to manipulate the institutional details of royal government that characterised the thirteenth-century reform movements, towards a concentration on the task of removing from the king's presence those of his advisers who were held responsible for the misgovernment. 'Evil counsellors' had always been one of the targets for reform – Magna Carta called for the exile of Gerard d'Athée and his numerous kindred, while Henry III's most unpopular advisers, Guy and Geoffrey de Lusignan, together with William and Aymer de Valence, were forced to leave the kingdom in 1258 – but concentration on purging the personnel of royal government became the central characteristic of reformist rebellions in the later fourteenth and fifteenth centuries. The actions of the Appellants against Richard II had their origins in a widespread anger at the king's failure to implement a programme of administrative reform proposed in Parliament in October 1385, yet the bulk of their lengthy indictment of Richard's rule concentrated on itemising the misdeeds of the five named counsellors whom they held responsible for the king's derelictions. Richard duke of York's protests against Henry VI's conduct of government in the 1450s were expressed in similarly personal terms, ascribing its shortcomings to the dominance that his great rival, the duke of Somerset, enjoyed in the king's counsels. It was this growing concentration on the personalities rather than the principles of royal government that led William Stubbs to characterise the political struggles of the later Middle Ages as 'contests of personal and family factions, not of great causes'.[5] In reality, the change was more one of tactics than of substance. It sprang from a realistic recognition, born of experience, that however ingenious the administrative constraints laid upon the monarchy, an adult king in his right mind could only be effectively prevented from doing what he wanted by force. Removing a ruler's favourite advisers was, in the final analysis, less drastic than imposing a permanent restraint upon his prerogative powers, and correspondingly less likely to lead to the violence all parties wished to avoid.

Reformist movements could nevertheless be transformed, in the appropriate circumstances, into the second major category of rebellions to be considered: dynastic risings, whose declared intent stretched beyond the criticism of royal policies to an attempt to remove the king held responsible for them from power. Richard duke of York's relations with the Lancastrian government provide the clearest instance of this transformation, for they progressed from protestations of injured loyalty in 1450, through an armed demonstration of dissatisfaction in 1452, to the defeat in open battle of the king's party in 1455 and finally to his claim to the throne of England in 1460. Between the 'Epiphany rising' of 1400, an attempt by a group of his former intimates to restore the deposed Richard II, and the final defeat of Perkin Warbeck, the self-styled duke of York, in 1499, such dynastic rebellions were largely a fifteenth-century phenomenon, given sanction and plausibility by the successful Lancastrian deposition of Richard II in 1399. The loyalty of the English to the Plantagenet dynasty was not absolute; nearly three-quarters of the baronage were prepared to support the claim of Louis, son of Philip Augustus of France, in preference to that of the young prince Henry in 1216; on the grounds that they had previously renounced their allegiance to Henry's father, John. With that one exception, however, dynastic rebellions were animated by the belief that the ruler of the kingdom was king 'in fact, but not by right' and sought to replace the usurper with a claimant more directly descended from the true blood of the Plantagenets.

Richard duke of York made his claim on the grounds that, as the great-grandson of Lionel of Antwerp, duke of Clarence, he was descended from Edward III by a line of blood senior to that of the reigning Lancastrian dynasty. The justification for doing so, clearly articulated in the declaration of the Yorkist title in Edward IV's first Parliament, was that this would itself effect a reform of the kingdom's government, putting an end to the 'unrest, inward war and trouble, unrighteousness, shedding and effusion of innocent blood' and other evils that were the inevitable result of a disturbance in the divinely-ordained succession.[6] Only in 1212, when Eustace de Vesci and others allegedly plotted to assassinate John and replace him with the elder Simon de Montfort, and again in 1327, when Roger Mortimer threatened Edward II with a successor who was not of the royal line if he did not abdicate in favour of his son, was there ever a suggestion that the accepted rules of inheritance, to which every landowner looked to guarantee the secure transfer of his own property to his children, should be set aside in the case of the Crown.

The third major group of rebellions consists of the popular risings: pre-eminently the 'English rising' of 1381 and Cade's rebellion in 1450, both insurrections by the peasantry of south-eastern England which succeeded in gaining temporary control of the capital, though there were also significant disturbances among the commons of Yorkshire between 1469 and 1471 and again in 1489, while the south-western rebellion in 1497 was serious enough to put Henry VII's control of the kingdom in question, at least for a moment. Though these popular risings were concentrated in the later part of the period, this does not mean that the common people had previously been politically passive. Many peasants were involved in the civil wars of 1264–65, and their actions were, at least on occasion, informed by an understanding and support for the cause of baronial reform such as that displayed by the villagers of Peatling Magna (Leicestershire), who accused one royalist captain of acting 'against the welfare of the community of the realm and against the barons'.[7] It was principally the changed economic conditions after 1350, notably the relative abundance of land and the high daily wages created by the fall in population, that gave the later medieval peasantry the confidence and resources to co-ordinate the independent expression of their grievances at a regional, even national, level. None of the risings in this group was, in fact, exclusively a revolt of the peasantry; the participation of the Londoners was a significant element in 1381, while Cade's rebellion enjoyed a significant measure of support from the lesser Kentish gentry, and the 'Robin of Redesdale' rising in 1469 included many gentry partisans of the earl of Warwick among the participants. They were, nevertheless, 'popular' risings in the sense that, in contrast to the two previous types of rebellion, which were invariably led by members of the aristocracy, the most prominent rebels were drawn from social levels below the nobility and gentry – Wat Tyler and John Ball in 1381, the pseudonymous Jack Cade in 1450, Ralph Flammanck in 1497. As a consequence, there was in all these revolts a substantial element of social and economic grievance against the operation of a lordship, whether seigneurial or royal, that was perceived as unjust and oppressive. In 1381 the rebels sought to abate this lordship by demanding the abolition of villeinage and a fixed rent of 4*d* an acre for tenanted land, while the high rents and entry fines exacted by landlords, together with their continued enforcement of labour services, remained a grievance for many of the Cade rebels in 1450. In general, however, the peasant rebellions sought to moderate the oppressions of lordship by claiming for their participants a place within the existing political process, not by seeking to create a new one, and their demands followed the same agenda as those of their social superiors, concentrating on the reform of particular abuses in the king's government and the removal of those royal advisers held responsible for them – 'John of Gaunt, duke of Lancaster, together with the great officers of state in 1381, the 'false progeny and affinity' of the duke of Suffolk in 1450.

It was left to the last group of rebellions, the religious risings, to articulate a more radical set of social and political demands. Both the rebellion of Sir John Oldcastle in 1414 and the rising at Abingdon in 1431, led by the weaver William Perkins, sought a complete overthrow of the existing secular and ecclesiastical hierarchies and an inauguration of the rule of the godly – in this case, the adherents of the body of heretical doctrine associated with the teachings of John Wyclif, who sought to cleanse the Church of its corruption by a forcible disendowment of its temporalities. Oldcastle's alleged intention was to kill the king and his magnates, force the clergy into secular occupations and distribute the wealth of the churches among his followers. Though the project appears a far-fetched one, the contemporary success of the Hussite rebels in Bohemia in implementing a programme of clerical disendowment directly inspired by Wyclif's teachings meant that the threat of religious rebellion was always taken seriously by the ecclesiastical authorities – the archbishop of Canterbury's vigilance was thought to have prevented a further rising in 1428 – and exercised an influence on their actions far greater than the rebels' real prospect of success ever warranted.

Similar considerations affected the conduct of secular affairs, for the prospect of a further rising by the common people was, in the aftermath of 1381, an ever-present element in the calculations of the king's advisers. It was only the rumour of such a rising among the commons of Kent that finally allowed the Appellants to overcome Richard II's stubborn resistance to the execution of his favourite, Sir Simon Burley, in 1388. Frequent though rebellions were in later medieval England, therefore, the record of their actual incidence is only a partial guide to their political importance and influence. Fear of rebellion was, itself, a significant factor in the formulation of state policy. Behind the legislative and administrative reforms of Edward I's early years lay the anticipation of a renewal of Montfortian resistance in the Midlands, while the principal brake on Edward III's financial demands between 1336 and 1340 was his ministers' fears that any further taxation would provoke a general rising of the people. There was a further concern that a rebellion, once begun, would release the generalised social tensions that underlay medieval society, creating a downward spiral of widespread violence. The chronicler Adam Usk viewed the death of the rebellious lord Despenser at the hands of the townsmen of Bristol in 1400 with foreboding, fearing 'that they will make this an excuse to wield the sword against their lords more often in future'.[8] Such fears were at their height during Edward II's reign, when the king's general failure to maintain an acceptable standard of public order meant that the frequent armed demonstrations against his actions made by Thomas earl of Lancaster and his allies could not be contained within the bounds of the political process. Indiscriminate violence accompanied the harrying of the Despensers' estates in the March of Wales during 1321–22, while a series of local risings broke out in Bristol, Bury St Edmunds and St Albans, Hampshire, south Lancashire and Glamorgan, adding a further element of local grievances and jealousies to the general disorder of the reign and its aftermath.

It was to guard against such dangers that, however frequently practice failed to live up to theory, the political ideal subscribed to by all sides in later medieval England – including the peasant rebels of 1381 – was one of monarchical authority, limited only by certain customary expectations. These expectations are well exemplified in the opening clauses of the Dictum of Kenilworth, drawn up in October 1266 as an instrument of pacification following the Monfortian civil war: the king was to rule freely and without the impediment or contradiction of anyone, provided always that he observed the liberties of the Church and the provisions of Magna Carta and the charter of the Forest (in the reissues of 1225); he also undertook to appoint worthy men to 'strengthen the throne and royal majesty with justice' by administering the realm according to its praiseworthy laws and customs.[9] Justice was, indeed, the quality most valued in a king, and contemporary understanding of the term encompassed both the unhindered operation of the due process of law and a broader sense of an expectation of equitable, and hence predictable, treatment. Robert Grosseteste, bishop of Lincoln, succinctly expressed this ideal – in a tract known to Simon de Montfort – when he wrote that 'all things connected with rule should be directed by reason, the guardian of justice and equity'.[10] Denial of justice, whether it was the kind of favouritism alleged against Henry III in cases affecting the Lusignans, when 'he who should have been a propitious judge . . . became a terrible enemy',[11] or the more generalised abuse of legal procedure for the private advantage of Henry VI's household men complained of by the Cade rebels, or the setting aside of the fundamental customs of inheritance that drove the Marcher barons to arms in 1321–22, was the course of action most calculated to provoke a violent response from the king's subjects. Closely related to the denial of justice, and scarcely less fatal, was the misdirection of royal resources in the king's gift, since this inevitably implied a failure to act equitably by rewarding the deserving as well as punishing the unworthy. The emergence of a favourite, towards whom a disproportionate amount of royal patronage was directed, was a certain source of political tension. This was the case with William de Valence at Henry III's court, Piers Gaveston and Hugh Despenser in Edward II's reign, Robert de Vere in Richard II's, and William de la Pole under Henry VI. Each aroused the apprehension and hostility of the aristocracy and each was forcibly removed from his favoured prominence. With the possible exception of Piers Gaveston, it was not the position and actions of the favourite alone that created the conditions for rebellion. Rather, it was the existence of a single, and apparently easily remediable, grievance shared by a wide body of opinion that provided a focus for otherwise disparate discontents and alienated the king from his natural body of supporters. In 1258, for example, dissatisfaction with Henry III's government ranged over a variety of issues: the financial burdens of the general eyre then in progress; the actions of the royal sheriffs and, more generally, the oppressive policy of the Exchequer that lay behind their misdeeds; the king's inability to resist the encroachments of Llywelyn in the March of Wales; and the anticipated fiscal and military burden created by Henry's undertaking to enforce papal overlordship in Sicily. Yet it was the widespread dislike of the Lusignans, and the fear that the young prince Edward was about to fall under their control, that led to the sworn confederation of April 1258 and the confrontation with the king that followed.

What was at stake in these cases was not simply the resources favourites were able to gather to themselves, though this was always a significant consideration. Neither the Despensers' ability to triple the value of their estates in the decade after 1317 nor the Woodvilles' startling success in the marriage-market after 1464 went unnoticed by their enemies. Equally important was the more general denial of access to the king that a favourite's position supposed; a particular charge against the Despensers was that they would not allow anyone to approach Edward II unless one or other of them were present. Complaints about the distribution of patronage were, in this respect, more a symptom of discontent than a cause of rebellions, for what was distinctive about the king's distribution of his favour was that it was the principal attribute of his kingship still to depend – in a way that, after John's reign, the doing of justice could not – on the exercise of his unfettered will. In order to harness and domesticate this disturbing liberty the monarch was expected to be accessible and receptive to the advice of his greater subjects; in contemporary terms, to take good counsel. Failure to take counsel was the third great dereliction of which English kings could be guilty and it features frequently in the complaints preferred against them. Usually the failure was blamed upon 'evil counsellors', such as those Richard earl of Cornwall rose against in 1238 and the lords Ordainer sought to expel from the realm in 1311, estranging the king from his natural, noble, companions, though this convenient fiction did not free every ruler from a share of the blame; the Lancastrian deposition articles complained in 1399 that Richard II would not accept advice in Council, sharply censuring those who attempted to give it. Questions of counsel and patronage were, of course, intimately related, for kings tended to reward most generously those whose advice they valued most highly, but the issue of counsel was especially important to the king's opponents for the public dimension it possessed, introducing questions of national interest – decisions over taxation and foreign policy – into the essentially private dialogue between the king and his greatest tenants. The imposition of a named and approved body of councillors, sworn to maintain the common good and charged with the control of appointments and overall supervision of the administration, was the favourite remedy for rebels faced with the practical problem of reforming royal government. It was an expedient attempted in 1258, 1311, 1385–88 and advocated, in a vaguer fashion, by the Cade rebels in 1450 when they called upon Henry VI to gather round himself 'the true Lords of his royal blood of this his realm'.[12]

The ability to do justice, a disposition to act equitably and a ready accessibility to his greater subjects were, then, the three qualities most valued in a king. If he could provide them, it was likely that the common advantages to be derived from maintaining the political concord and social harmony that guaranteed the privileged position of both Crown and nobility would outweigh whatever grievances might be entertained against him. For every baronial rebellion in later medieval England, there was another armed demonstration that failed to attract sufficient support to present a serious threat to the kingdom's rulers, such as Henry earl of Lancaster's protest against the rule of Isabella and Mortimer in 1328–29 or Richard duke of York's march on the court in 1452. Yet when rebellion and civil war did break out, this was not solely the fault of incompetent kings. Aristocratic restraint was as important as royal sensitivity in maintaining the peace and it, too, was sometimes lacking. Political circumstance and private interest could combine to create as great an intransigence on the part of the king's opponents as Edward II or Richard II ever displayed. The shifting demands of the northerners, growing in scope and ambition as John's position weakened between 1212 and 1215, did as much to create the conditions for a civil war as the king's fiscal and administrative excesses. Purely factional disturbances, designed to further the concerns of their protagonists alone and conducted without reference to a wider political vocabulary, were rare, largely because their chances of success were slim. The rising of William de Forz in 1221 and Fawkes de Bréauté's attempt to preserve his position as 'more than a king in England'[13] four years later were two such incidents, but on both occasions the collective discipline of the English nobility proved durable enough to withstand their challenges.

Some magnates were, nevertheless, violent and self-seeking by nature and their single-minded pursuit of their own ambitions in a highly-charged political context could act as a catalyst for violence, as the careers of Robert Ferrers, earl of Derby, during the period of baronial reform, and of Henry Holland, duke of Exeter, in Henry VI's reign, demonstrate. If they were the exceptions to a general rule of responsible acceptance of royal lordship, even the most inflexible opponents of royal tyranny sometimes aroused the suspicion that adherence to constitutional principle could come close to the protection of private interest. Simon de Montfort incurred criticism for the generosity with which he rewarded his family and servants, while Thomas of Lancaster used his years of dominance in government to pursue a family quarrel with the earl Warenne. Even within the wider political struggle, the pursuit of personal advantage and the settling of old scores remained a priority; William de Ferrers and Brian de Lisle sought to use each turn of events in the civil war of 1216–17 to assert their control over the disputed castle of the Peak, while Roger Mortimer's summary execution of the Despensers in 1326 was a further violent episode in a feud between the two families stretching back at least two generations. Such struggles were the common currency of landed society and, given a degree of responsibility on the part of the protagonists, could usually be resolved through the traditional channels of royal and magnate lordship. Yet there can be little doubt that unchecked local disputes, such as the struggle for dominance in the south-west between William lord Bonville and Thomas Courtenay, earl of Devon, during Henry VI's reign, or the feud between the Stanley and Harrington families in Lancashire under Edward IV, served to undermine traditional loyalties and contributed to the polarisation of the political community. Similar considerations of self-interest lay at the root of a further source of conflict – the reluctance of loyal magnates, elevated to a position of unusual eminence by the support they had lent their king in a crisis, to surrender any of the political and financial advantages they gained in consequence as normal circumstances returned. This was the common characteristic shared by the revolts of the Percys in 1403, of the earl of Warwick in 1469 and of the duke of Buckingham in 1483.

Relations between kings and their nobles therefore continued to be vulnerable to occasional failures of political management by both sides, though the frequent rebellions against the rule of the Anglo-Norman kings and the prolonged instability of Stephen's reign make it seem unlikely that there was any general deterioration in the ability of the political nation to withstand and absorb these frictions over time. Yet there were two additional circumstances of political life, specific to the later Middle Ages, which contributed to its volatility. One was the dynastic uncertainty created by the deposition of Richard II in 1399. Under the canon law, deposition was a legitimate recourse for a king's subjects, provided that he could be shown to be insufficient to the task of ruling, incorrigible in his faults, and guilty of great crimes. The ceremonies removing Edward II and Richard II were careful to advertise the ways in which both kings satisfied these criteria. Edward II's abdication was, however, less of a threat to political stability than Henry of Lancaster's deposition of Richard II, which involved a break in the accepted line of succession to the throne. The difficulties this could entail had already been foreshadowed in

December 1387 when the victorious Appellants, having apparently resolved to renounce their allegiance to the king, were forced to restore Richard to the throne because they could not agree among themselves on his rightful successor. The disruptive effect of the Lancastrian usurpation on fifteenth-century political life was felt in several ways. At times when the king had no son – which was, in practice, for just over half the century – it created an uncertainty and debate over the succession which was, in itself, unsettling. Richard duke of York's belief that he should be publicly recognised as Henry VI's heir-apparent served to sharpen the political differences between himself and his rivals for that recognition, the Holland and Beaufort families. As an almost inevitable corollary, the existence of alternative candidates with a claim to the Crown undermined the basis of mutual trust that should ideally have existed between a ruler and his greatest subjects, creating suspicion on the part of the king and unease among the suspected nobles. Even Archbishop Arundel, Henry IV's closest ally, was accused of supporting the Mortimer claim to the throne during Henry IV's early years, while the fate of Edward earl of Warwick, the great-nephew of Edward IV, held in captivity for fourteen years by Henry VII and finally executed on fabricated charges in 1499, was a striking illustration of the dangerous distinction royal blood conferred. Less directly, the dynastic instability of the century increasingly created among the nobility and gentry a wary reluctance to commit themselves irrevocably to any single claimant to the throne which, in turn, made the task of satisfying the political nation's appetite for firm rule all the harder. Richard duke of Gloucester sought to justify the pre-emptive deposition of his nephew, the young Edward V, on the grounds that he alone could maintain the precarious stability the Yorkist dynasty had achieved, and lost his throne when he failed to deliver the peace he had promised.

The second, and more important, development specific to the later Middle Ages was the increasing demand made by the English monarchy upon the resources of its subjects. Before 1215, baronial rebellions in medieval England had either arisen as adjuncts to a dispute over the succession to the throne, such as those that occurred immediately after the accession of both Henry I and Stephen, or as the result of the exclusion of too powerful an individual or too numerous a group from the king's favour – a state of affairs that prompted the risings of Odo of Bayeux (1088), Robert of Mowbray (1095) and Henry the Young King (in both 1173 and 1182). Though these two motives were, at times, scarcely distinguishable, the rebellions they fuelled were essentially disputes over the extent and destination of what the king had to give, rather than protests against the burden of what he was taking. It was not until the reign of John that, in response to the king's determined efforts to raise sufficient capital to recover his lost duchy of Normandy, the fiscal and administrative exactions of royal government were first placed at the centre of the demands of the king's opponents. Thereafter, the cost of defending the continental possessions of the English Crown by military and diplomatic means escalated rapidly, and the financial burden that the Crown's subjects were required to bear increased commensurately. Henry III spent some £80,000 on his campaign to regain Poitou in 1242, whereas Edward I had to set aside approximately £750,000 for his military commitments between 1294 and 1298 and Edward III spent a similar sum on his campaigns against the French between 1337 and 1341. Henry III had initially sought to meet these costly commitments by a more rigorous exploitation of the traditional fiscal prerogatives of the Crown; the failure of this policy underlay many of the grievances – such as the abuses of Forest law, the exactions of the justices in eyre and the excessive farms imposed on the shires – expressed in the Petition of the Barons. It soon became clear that such high levels of expenditure could only be met by the creation of a national system of regular direct and indirect taxation, which England possessed in all its essentials by 1300. The effect of this was to endow the Crown, even in peacetime, with unprecedented resources. Edward I had approximately £40,000 p.a. at his disposal before the onset of the military crisis of 1294–97, but his response to that crisis nearly doubled the sums available to him annually for the remainder of his reign and created a set of financial precedents that his son and grandson successfully exploited. Direct and indirect taxation, which had produced no more than 15 per cent of the Crown's income in the early twelfth century, was accounting for 80 to 90 per cent of all Exchequer receipts by the reign of Henry IV.

The search for such sums was itself bound to cause hardship and create resentment – the barons were complaining to Henry III, as early as 1244, that all in the kingdom were so oppressed by amercements and aids that they had little left to give. Resistance to the Crown's financial demands was, in consequence, an element common to many rebellions in the late Middle Ages. This element of fiscal protest is clearest in the risings of the commons; resentment at the heavy and inequitable incidence of the three 'poll taxes' imposed since 1377 was the catalyst for the great rebellion of 1381, while the regional risings of 1489 and 1497 were both protests against attempts to collect Parliamentary subsidies. Nor were high levels of taxation the only burden that the Crown's military ambitions laid upon its subjects. The feudal obligation of service in the king's army remained a contentious one, whose scope the king's opponents consistently sought to limit. The considerable resistance John encountered over the issue in 1213–14 was repeated when Edward I demanded service from his tenants-in-chief in Flanders, while the lords Ordainer went one step further in 1311 by seeking to deny altogether the king's ability to make war or to leave the country without the consent of the baronage in Parliament. Equally, the king's acknowledged right to purvey goods for the sustenance of his household was extended, under the pressure of war financing, into a quasi-national levy for victualling the royal armies. As a consequence, purveyance became another familiar target for the king's opponents. The Petition of the Barons complained that purveyors were taking two or three times as much as the needs of his household required, and similar complaints were echoed in the Remonstrances, the Ordinances, the manifesto issued by Archbishop Scrope in 1405 and the petitions of the Cade rebels.

It was not, however, simply the burden of royal demands that created the conditions for rebellion and civil war, though the heavy incidence of such demands was the justification most commonly cited by the rebels themselves. The social group most prominent in seeking to restrain the claims of the English state upon its subjects, the higher nobility, was itself only marginally affected by the fiscal aspect of the Crown's commitment to overseas warfare; Roger Bigod, earl of Norfolk, who led the resistance to Edward I's demands in 1297, paid less than 5 per cent of his estate revenue in taxation during the crisis years of 1294–97. More important was the gradually altered relationship between the king and the political community created by the era of intensive warfare that followed the loss of Normandy. The threat of attack and invasion by a common enemy – whether Scots, Welsh or French – conferred on the Crown's defensive measures a representative authority to speak and act on behalf of the English nation as a whole that it had not previously possessed. This had several significant consequences. It served to accentuate the traditional expectation that individual kings would discharge their duty of defence successfully and to intensify the penalties of failure. 'The road from Bouvines to Runnymede was direct, short and unavoidable';[14] the loss of Gascony and Scotland through 'bad counsel and bad custody' was one of the justifications cited for the deposition of Edward II;[15] the fear of a French invasion of the south coast and the widespread perception that the natural defenders of the national interest were failing in their duty were important elements in the risings of 1381 and 1450. At the same time, the growth of direct taxation sanctioned by a representative assembly enlarged the circle of those who could claim a legitimate voice in how that duty of defence should be fulfilled. Against the enormous new resources conferred on the Crown by the growth of national taxation was balanced a novel justification for resistance to its demands, appeal to the interests of the 'community of the realm'. Concern for the provision of an effective national defence inevitably expanded from an initial preoccupation with the raising and funding of suitable forces to debate over the strategic priorities that underlay the Crown's demands. Disagreement over the direction of foreign policy, first openly manifested in the unanimous baronial opposition to Henry III's commitment to the conquest of the Sicilian kingdom, became an increasingly dangerous fault-line in English politics; readily comprehensible, highly emotive and capable of uniting disparate groups of the disaffected into an effective political alliance, as Richard II in 1387 and Henry VI in the 1450s both discovered to their cost.

Finally, the prominence of warfare in the Crown's calculations gave the king's opponents a new ability to make their misgivings effective. This arose from changes in the Crown's methods of military recruitment during the fourteenth century. Once the English kings ceased to depend upon the obligations of feudal tenure for a substantial part of their forces and chose, instead, to rely upon a contract army, in which the principal captains were paid at fixed rates for the troops they brought with them, the Crown was rendered technically indebted, often for quite substantial sums, to its principal subjects. Indebtedness had previously been one of the means by which successive kings, especially John and Edward I, had sought to discipline their recalcitrant magnates. Now it became a source of political leverage for the magnates, even, on occasion, a reason for rebellion; the Percys cited the £120,000 allegedly owed them by Henry IV as a justification for their rising in 1403. More significant, though, was the personal stake in the issue of Crown solvency this system of war financing gave the nobility and the additional incentive it provided to concern themselves with the details of royal income and expenditure – details that inevitably raised the issues of patronage, counsel and prerogative that formed the staple of debate between the king and his subjects. The debts Edmund Mortimer, earl of March, contracted in financing his campaigns abroad fuelled his support for the impeachment of Edward III's courtiers in the Good Parliament (1376), while the £26,000 owed Richard duke of York by 1446 for the costs of his lieutenancy in France only increased his determination to secure a more influential place in Henry VI's counsels.

In certain circumstances, therefore, the development of a 'war state' in later medieval England, highly taxed and intensively governed, does seem to have generated additional political tensions, and these sometimes spilled over into armed resistance to the demands of the Crown. Yet there were opportunities as well as dangers in this turn of events. Defeat abroad was perennially damaging, but victory was now doubly beneficial, not only enhancing the prestige of the individual ruler, but also confirming the representative legitimacy of the monarchy. It is no accident that the longest periods of domestic peace later medieval England experienced – from 1327 to 1381 and 1415 to 1450 – were ushered in by the spectacular victories of Edward III and Henry V in France. How the balance of advantage between opportunity and danger is to be struck largely depends upon an estimate of the seriousness of the civil wars and rebellions considered in this chapter. It can be argued that, for all the strictures of contemporary commentators, the civil disturbances England experienced in this period were a relatively small price to pay for the development of the financial and administrative capacities of the state that the enterprise of war necessitated and for the sense of common political purpose it fostered.

When the record of English rebellions is set against the experience of other Western monarchies, there is little to suggest that English politics were uniquely violent or unusually prone to civil strife. The dynastic disruption so remarked upon by French observers was equally evident elsewhere: most notably in the German kingdom, which suffered a long interregnum between 1254 and 1273, followed by depositions in 1298 and 1400 and the murder of a third king in 1308; but also in Castile, where revolts of the nobility saw the actual deposition of one king in 1366 and the attempted deposition of another in 1465, and in Scotland, where James I was assassinated in 1437 and James III killed in battle against his nobles in 1488. Although France was unusual in escaping a change of dynasty, its political life suffered at least as much from court factions, noble feuds and royal incapacity as England's. Princely resistance to the regency of Blanche of Castile between 1226 and 1234; the provincial leagues of 1314–15; the Navarrese crisis (1356–58); the highly damaging struggle between Armagnac and Burgundian factions for control of Charles VI's court; the 'war of the public weal' (1465) and the *Guerre Folle* (1488): these were only the most spectacular instances of the French monarchy's failure to reach a lasting accommodation with an exceptionally powerful and independent noble caste, while the popular insurrections that disturbed the kingdom, such as the *Pastoureaux* movements in 1251 and 1320, or the *Jacquerie* (1356), were notably more destructive than their English equivalents.

Measured against these standards, the level of destruction that inevitably accompanies civil war seems to have been contained within generally acceptable bounds in England. Though the forces involved were sometimes considerable, as were the casualties at battles like Evesham and Towton, campaigns were usually short, and deliberate destruction of the countryside, a standard tactic of the English armies in France, was rare – Henry of Lancaster's punitive ravaging of Cheshire in 1399 and the depredations of Margaret of Anjou's army in 1460–61 are, in this respect, exceptional. Towns were occasionally sacked and looted, as happened at Winchester in 1265 and Stamford in 1461, but prolonged siege warfare, a staple of continental civil strife, was infrequent, as a result of the unprepared condition of most urban defences. In the treatment of defeated enemies, the rigours of the laws of war were often mitigated; John's decision to spare the defenders of Rochester in 1216 was more typical than Edward II's execution of the garrison of Leeds castle in 1321. When reprisals were unavoidable, prudent commanders, aware that popular support for their cause was a considerable political asset, sought to spare the commoners caught up in the quarrels of their masters.

In the light of these European comparisons, three features of English rebellions in the later Middle Ages stand out as distinctive: that there were no exclusively urban risings; that every rebellion became, however it began, a matter of national concern, defining its aims and demands by reference to the debates of national politics rather than simply seeking a remedy for regional grievances; and that this was as true of popular insurrections as of noble revolts. The internal politics of English town life was often contested and occasionally explosive, resulting in such spectacular demonstrations of defiance as occurred at Bristol (1312–16) and Norwich (1443), yet the matters under dispute were usually so specific that it was only at times of national political disturbance, notably in 1263–65 and 1381, that urban unrest took on a general significance. Equally, certain regions proved, by reason of their tenurial geography or the reserves of military manpower they possessed, particularly fertile breeding-grounds for rebellion. One such area was the March of Wales, where Richard Marshall was able to oppose Henry III with impunity in 1233, the baronial opponents of Edward I met to discuss their grievances in 1297 and a coalition of local barons first defeated Hugh Despenser in 1321. Yet though the March provided the setting for a show of defiance, the object of each of these protests was to effect a significant change in the course of national politics, not to resolve a local difficulty. Even a rising as localised and eccentric as the disturbances in Oxfordshire at Easter 1398 possessed a wider political dimension, for its leader, Thomas Gildesowe of Witney, claimed to be the young earl of Arundel'[16] – the son of a popular magnate unjustly executed by Richard II six months earlier.

This was partly a matter of geography, partly a matter of history. England was a small country, its extreme nothern border less than a week's hard ride away from London. Even a remote regional rising posed a potential threat to the execution of government, which the authorities had to treat correspondingly seriously; it took the south-western rebels less than a month to march from Taunton to Blackheath in 1497. Conversely, it was what happened at the political and administrative centre that was decisive in determining the outcome of many revolts. The keys to the kingdom lay in control of London, the capital city and the only commercial metropolis the country possessed, and it was the point towards which every rebel force sought to gravitate. It was the alliance between London and his opponents that finally forced John to concede Magna Carta and the Londoners' consistent support for reform that saved Simon de Montfort in 1263 and forced a compromise with the Disinherited on Henry III in 1267. The rising of the Londoners in October 1326 paralysed the attempts of the Despenser regime to organise any resistance to Queen Isabella's invasion, while the refusal of the London oligarchs to support him condemned Richard II to defeat in December 1387. Wise kings sought to purchase the capital's approval and support; Richard III's promise to bring Southwark within the jurisdiction of the City was only the most generous of many royal favours. Popular rebellions were no different in this respect from noble risings, seeking to gain control of the capital as a means of enforcing their demands; the willingness of the Londoners to admit the rebel forces in 1381 and 1450 ensured their short-term success, just as their refusal to open the gates to Thomas Fauconberg led to the dissolution of his forces in 1471.

Yet although England was a small, highly centralised state, in which control of the country was largely dependent upon control of a single city, there was no core of professional administrators – similar to the *baillis* and *intendants* of the Valois kings, or the *pesquisdores* and *corregidores* of the Castilian monarchy – to manage the machinery of government. In their absence, the Crown had to rely upon a broad group of greater and lesser landowners to staff the local administration of the shires and to develop, through the county courts and quarter sessions, regular channels of communication between centre and locality. This inevitably bred a responsive political culture, in which a relatively extensive ruling class possessed a vested interest in the political health and fiscal credit of the Crown, and the political leverage to make their views effective. Political awareness was widely disseminated and the issues at stake between the king and his opponents well understood; petitions and complaints to the king and council made frequent and generally accurate reference to the great reforming measures of 1215, 1258 and 1311. The inevitable result of this was that any substantial failure of political management – whether at the king's court, in Parliament, or in dealing with the individual communities of city and county – generated widespread friction, of a kind that successive kings, dependent for much of their effective authority on the co-operation of the political classes and vulnerable to any withdrawal of goodwill, were ill-prepared to resist. This balance of power created conditions conducive to frequent civil strife, but it was only on rare occasions, and for brief periods (1264–65, 1321–22, 1459–61), that the protagonists in such conflicts abandoned the disposition to negotiate and compromise bred into them by the experience of self-government at the king's command. Rebellion and civil war in later medieval England should not, therefore, be regarded as evidence of a serious deterioration in the quality of government, but as the price to be paid for the development of a cohesive and generally successful political culture. They were a vindication of the belief in the identity of interest between successive kings and their subjects, expressed with vigour by a group of Kentish sailors in 1450, that 'the crown of England . . . was the community of the said realm, and that the community of the realm was the crown of the realm'.[17]

Notes

1 *The Works of Sir Thomas Malory*, edited by E. Vinaver (Oxford, 1947), iii, 1,229.
2 *Polychronicon Ranulphi Higden*, edited by C. Babington and J. R. Lumby (Rolls Series, 1865–66), ii, 169; *Calendar of State Papers and Manuscripts existing in the archives and collections of Milan* (London, 1912), p. 154.
3 P. S. Lewis, 'Two pieces of fifteenth-century political iconography', *Journal of the Warburg and Courtauld Institute*, xvii (1964), 319.
4 R. W. Kaeuper, *War, Justice and Public Order: England and France in the Later Middle Ages* (Oxford, 1988); E. B. Fryde and N. Fryde, 'Peasant rebellion and peasant discontents', in *The Agrarian History of England and Wales, 1348–1500*, edited by E. Miller (Cambridge, 1991), p. 744.
5 W. Stubbs, *The Constitutional History of England* 4th edn (Oxford, 1906), ii, 319.
6 *Rotuli Parliamentorum* (London, 1783), v, 464.
7 *Select Cases of Procedure without Writ under Henry III*, edited by H. G. Richardson and G. O. Sayles, Selden Society, lx (1941), 43; D. A. Carpenter, 'English peasants in Politics 1258–1267', *Past and Present*, cxxxvi (1992), 3–42.
8 *Chronicon Adae de Usk*, edited by E. M. Thompson (London, 1904), p. 203.
9 W. Stubbs, *Select Charters and other illustrations of English Constitutional History* 9th edn (Oxford, 1913), pp. 407–8.
10 D. A. Carpenter, 'Simon de Montfort: the first leader of a political movement in English history', *History*, lxxvi (1991), 20.
11 *Annales Monastici*, edited by H. R. Luard (Rolls Series, 1864–69), i, 459.
12 *The Peasants' Revolt of 1381*, edited by R. B. Dobson (London, 1983), p. 342.
13 *Annales Monastici*, i, 64.
14 J. C. Holt, *The Northerners: a Study in the Reign of King John* (Oxford, 1961), p. 100.
15 M. V. Clarke, *Medieval Representation and Consent* (London, 1936), p. 183.

16 *Oxfordshire Sessions of the Peace in the Reign of Richard II*, edited by E. G. Kimball, Oxfordshire Record Society, liii (1983) 85.

17 R. Virgoe, 'The death of William de la Pole, duke of Suffolk', *Bulletin of the John Rylands Library*, xlvii (1964–65), 501.

A bibliography of the published writings of Dr Simon Walker

Compiled by Edmund King

1983

'Lancaster v. Dallingridge: a franchisal dispute in fourteenth-century Sussex', *Sussex Archaeological Collections*, 111, 87–94.

1985

'Profit and loss in the Hundred Years War: the subcontracts of Sir John Strowther, 1374', *Bulletin of the Institute of Historical Research*, 58, 100–6.

1986

'John of Gaunt and his "affinity": a prosopographical approach to bastard feudalism', in Françoise Autrand (ed.), *Prosopographie et histoire de l'état*, (Paris), pp. 209–22.

1988

'Geoffrey Chaucer and his family' and 'The Lollards', in Edmund King, *Medieval England* (Oxford), pp. 222–3, 242–3.

Review: Joan Greatrex, *Account Rolls of the Obedientiaries of Peterborough* (Northamptonshire Rec. Soc. 33, 1984), in *English Historical Review*, 103, 186–7.

1989

'Law and lordship in the palatinate of Lancaster, 1370–1400', *Journal of British Studies*, 28, 325–48.

'Autorité des magnats et pouvoir de la "gentry" en Angleterre à la fin du moyen âge', in Philippe Contamine (ed.), *L'état et les aristocraties, XIIIe–XVIIe siècles* (Paris), pp. 189–211.

'British History, 1200–1500', *International Review of Periodical Literature*, I, pp. 23–37.

Review: Nigel Saul, *Scenes from Provincial Life: Knightly Families in Sussex, 1280–1400* (Oxford, 1986), in *English Historical Review*, 104, 721–2.

1990

The Lancastrian Affinity, 1361–1399 (Oxford Historical Monographs: Oxford; reprinted 1996), xii + 350 pp.

'Sir Richard Abberbury and his Kinsmen: the rise and fall of a gentry family', *Nottingham Medieval Studies*, 34, 113–40.

Review: Ralph A. Griffiths and James Sherborne (eds), *Kings and Nobles in the Later Middle Ages* (Gloucester, 1986), in *English Historical Review*, 105, 168–9.

1991

'Letters to the dukes of Lancaster in 1381 and 1399', *English Historical Review*, 106, 68–79.

1992

'A context for Brunanburh?', in Timothy Reuter (ed.), *Warriors and Churchmen in the High Middle Ages: Essays Presented to Karl Leyser* (London), pp. 21–39.

Review: S. J. Payling, *Political Society in Lancastrian England: The Greater Gentry of Nottinghamshire* (Oxford, 1991), *History*, 77, 292.

Review: W. M. Ormrod, *The Reign of Edward III: Crown and Political Society in England, 1327–1377* (New Haven/London, 1991); Scott L. Waugh, *England in the Reign of Edward III* (Cambridge, 1991), in *English Historical Review*, 107, 384–6.

Review: Michael K. Jones and Malcolm G. Underwood, *The King's Mother: Lady Margaret Beaufort, Countess of Richmond and Derby* (Cambridge, 1992), *Times Literary Supplement*, 10 April 1992, 22.

Review: Christine Carpenter, *Locality and Polity: A Study of Warwickshire Landed Society, 1401–1499* (Cambridge, 1992); Joel T. Rosenthal, *Patriarchy and Families of Privilege in Fifteenth-Century England* (Philadelphia, 1995), *Times Literary Supplement*, 31 July 1992, 22.

1993

'Yorkshire justices of the peace, 1389–1413', *English Historical Review*, 108, 281–313.

'Home thoughts from abroad: Rome to York in 1452', *Journal of Ecclesiastical History*, 44, 679–88.

Review: Anthony Goodman, *John of Gaunt: The Exercise of Princely Power in Fourteenth-Century England* (London, 1992); C. Allmand, *Henry V* (London, 1992), *Nottingham Medieval Studies*, 27, 136–41.

Review: Michael Hicks, *Richard III and his Rivals: Magnates and Their Motives in the Wars of the Roses* (London, 1991), *History*, 78, 92–3.

Review: Michael Hicks (ed.), *Profit, Piety and the Professions in Later Medieval England* (Gloucester, 1990), *English Historical Review*, 108, 1009.

1994

Ed., with Michael Jones, 'Private indentures for service in peace and war,

1278–1476', *Camden Miscellany XXXII* (Camden Society 5th series, volume 3), pp. 1–190.

Review: J. S. Roskell, L. Clarke and C. Rawcliffe (eds), *The history of Parliament: The House of Commons 1386–1421* (Stroud, 1993), *Nottingham Medieval Studies*, 38, 172–7.

Review: J. L. Catto and A. R. Evans (eds), *The History of the University of Oxford, II: Late Medieval Oxford* (Oxford, 1992), in *Medium Ævum*, 63, 170–1.

1995

Ed., with Rowena E. Archer, *Rulers and Ruled in Late Medieval England: Essays Presented to Gerald Harriss* (London), xxvii + 270 pp.

'Richard II's views on kingship', ibid., pp. 49–63.

'Political saints in later medieval England', in R. H. Britnell and A. J. Pollard (eds), *The McFarlane Legacy: Studies in Late Medieval Politics and Society* (Stroud), pp. 77–106.

Review: Anthony Goodman and Anthony Tuck (eds), *War and Border Societies in the Middle Ages* (London, 1992), in *English Historical Review*, 110, 987–8.

1996

'Civil war and rebellion', in Christopher Given-Wilson (ed.), *An Illustrated History of Late Medieval England* (Manchester), pp. 229–47.

'The college and the late medieval church: the career of Richard Andrew', in J. McConica (ed.), *Unarmed Soldiery: Studies in the Early History of All Souls College* (Oxford: All Souls College), pp. 14–32.

Review: Andrew Ayrton, *Knights and Warhorses: Military Service and the English Aristocracy Under Edward III* (Woodbridge, 1994), in *History*, 86, 252.

Review: John Watts, *Henry VI and the Politics of Kingship* (Cambridge, 1996), *Times Literary Supplement*, 11 November 1996, 28.

Review: Michael Hicks, *Bastard Feudalism* (London, 1995), in *Southern History*, 18, 159–60.

1997

Review: Nigel Saul, *Richard II* (New Haven/London, 1997), in *London Review of Books*, 4 September 1997, 16–17.

Review: S. H. Rigby, *English Society in the Later Middle Ages: Class, Status and Gender* (London, 1995), in *English Historical Review*, 112, 968–9.

Review: J. L. Kirby (ed.), *The Hungerford Cartulary* (Wiltshire Rec. Soc., 49, 1994), in *History*, 82, 307–8.

1998

Review: Charles R. Young, *The Making of the Neville Family in England, 1166–1400* (Woodbridge, 1996), in *English Historical Review*, 113, 702–3.

Review: Anthony Gross, *The Dissolution of the Lancastrian Kingship: Sir John Fortescue and the Crisis of Monarchy in Fifteenth-Century England* (Stamford, 1996), in *English Historical Review*, 113, 718–19.

1999

'Janico Dartasso: chivalry, nationality and the man-at-arms', *History*, 84, 31–51.

'Between church and crown: master Richard Andrew, king's clerk', *Speculum*, 74, 956–91.

Review: Paul Strohm, *England's Empty Throne: Usurpation and the Language of Legitimation, 1399–1422* (New Haven/London, 1998), in *London Review of Books*, 10 June 1999, 27–8.

Review: Andrew G. Watson, *A Descriptive Catalogue of the Medieval Manuscripts of All Souls College, Oxford* (Oxford, 1997), in *English Historical Review*, 114, 701–2.

Review: Richard Britnell, *The Closing of the Middle Ages? England, 1471–1529* (Oxford, 1997), in *English Historical Review*, 114, 966–7.

2000

'Rumour, sedition and popular protest in the reign of Henry IV', *Past & Present*, 166, 31–65.

'Richard II's reputation', in Gwilym Dodd (ed.), *The reign of Richard II* (Stroud), pp. 119–28, 152–4.

Review: Carolyn C. Fenwick (ed.), *The Poll Taxes of 1377, 1379 and 1381. Part I: Bedfordshire-Leicestershire* (Oxford, 1998), in *English Historical Review*, 115, 701–2.

Review: Michael Hicks, *Richard III* (Stroud, 2000), *Times Literary Supplement*, 20 October 2000, 30.

2001

Review: Helen Castor, *The King, the Crown, and the Duchy of Lancaster: Public Authority and Private Power* (Oxford, 2000), *Times Literary Supplement*, 26 January 2001, 32.

Review: Colin Richmond, *The Paston Family in the Fifteenth Century: Endings* (Manchester, 2000), *Times Literary Supplement*, 3 August 2001, 25.

2003

'The Yorkshire risings of 1405: texts and contexts', in Gwilym Dodd and Douglass Briggs (eds), *Henry IV: The Establishment of the Regime* (York), pp. 161–84.

'Remembering Richard: history and memory in Lancastrian England', in Christine Carpenter and Linda Clark (eds), *Political Culture in Late Medieval England* (The Fifteenth Century, IV, Woodbridge), 21–31.

Review: Jonathan Hughes, *Arthurian Myths and Alchemy: The Kingship of Edward IV* (Stroud, 2002), in *London Review of Books*, 10 July 2003, 25–7.

Review: Ann Wroe, *Perkin: A Story of Deception* (London, 2003), *Times Literary Supplement*, 11 April 2003, 28.

2004

14 articles in *Oxford Dictionary of National Biography*:

Abberbury family (*per. c.* 1270–*c.* 1475), 1:6–7

Dartasso, Janico (*d.* 1426), 15:171–2

Erpingham, Sir Thomas (*c.* 1355–1428), 18:512–14

Farrington, Sir William (*c.* 1348–1416/17), 19:130–1

Grey, John, third Baron Grey of Codnor (1305´×11?–1392), 23:861–2

Hastings family (*per. c.* 1300–*c.* 1450), 25:730–1

Ive, William (*d.* 1486), 29:445–6

John, duke of Aquitaine and duke of Lancaster, styled king of Castile and León (1340–1399), 30:174–83

Katherine, duchess of Lancaster (1350?–1403), 30:888–90

Lovell, John, fifth Baron Lovell (*c.* 1342–1408), 34:524–5

Maidstone, Clement (*c.* 1389–1456), 36:163

Percy, Sir Henry (1364–1403), 43:702–4

Pole, Michael de la, second earl of Suffolk (1367/7–1415), 44:713–14

Sudbury, Simon (*c.* 1316–1381), 53:271–4

2006

'Order and law', in Rosemary Horrox and Mark Ormrod (eds), *A Social History of England, 1200–1500* (Cambridge, 2006), pp. 91–112.

Forthcoming

Ed., *The Building Accounts of All Souls College, 1438–1443* (Oxford Historical Society, n.s. 31).

'Les deux procès de Richard Scrope, archevêque de York, 1405–1406', in Brigitte Marin (ed.), *Les procès politiques (XIVe–XVIIe siècles)* (Collection de l'École Française de Rome).

Index